THE ROMANTIC MOVEMENT

GARLAND REFERENCE LIBRARY
OF THE HUMANITIES
(VOL. 217)

THE ROMANTIC MOVEMENT
A Selective and Critical Bibliography for 1982

Edited by
David V. Erdman

with the assistance of
Brian J. Dendle
Robert R. Mollenauer
Augustus Pallotta
James S. Patty

GARLAND PUBLISHING, INC. • NEW YORK & LONDON
1983

Library of Congress Cataloging in Publication Data
Main entry under title:

The Romantic movement.

(Garland reference library of the humanities ; v. 217)
1. Romanticism—Bibliography. I. Erdman, David V.
II. Title. III. Series.
Z6514.R6R645 1983 [PN603] 016.809'9145 83-16354
ISBN 0-8240-9507-3

PN
603
R57

1982, cop. 2

Printed on acid-free, 250-year-life paper
Manufactured in the United States of America

This bibliography is compiled by a joint bibliography committee of the Modern Language Association representing groups General Topics II (now Comparative Studies in Romanticism and the Nineteenth Century), English 9 (English Romantic Period), French 6 (Nineteenth-Century French Literature), German 4 (Nineteenth- and Early Twentieth-Century German Literature), Italian 2 (Italian Literature, Seventeenth Century to the Present), and Spanish 4 (Eighteenth- and Nineteenth-Century Spanish Literature). It is designed to cover a "movement" rather than a period; though the English section, for example, is largely limited to the years 1789–1837, other sections extend over different spans of years.

It is our intent to include, with descriptive and, at times, critical annotation, all books and articles of substantial interest to scholars of English and Continental Romanticism. Studies of American Romanticism that relate to this interest are selectively included. We also make note of items of minor but scholarly interest, except those which may be expected to appear in the annual *MLA International Bibliography*. Major and controversial works are given what is intended to be judicious if necessarily brief review.

The approximate size of a book is indicated by report of the number of pages. Book prices are noted when available.

We continue the practice of including available current (1983) reviews of listed books.

The editorial committee gratefully acknowledges the help of its collaborators, whose names are given at the heads of the respective sections.

To ensure notice in the next issue of the bibliography, authors and publishers are invited to send review copies of relevant books or monographs and offprints of articles to: David V. Erdman, 58 Crane Neck Road, Setauket, N.Y. 11733.

CONTENTS

JOURNALS SEARCHED

All journals regularly searched are listed here. The editor welcomes notice of omissions, to be made good in the next annual.

ABC	*American Book Collector* (new series)
ABI	*Accademie e Bibliotheche d'Italia*
	Académie d'Angers. Mémoires
AConf	*Les Annales, Conferencia*
ActaG	*Acta Germanica (Capetown)*
	Acta Musicologicae
ActaN	*Acta Neophilologica*
	Adam: International Review
ADPh	*Arbeiten zur deutschen Philologie*
	Aevum: Rassegna di Scienze Storiche, Linguistiche, Filologiche
AFLSHA	*Annales de la Faculté des Lettres et Sciences Humaines d'Aix*
AG	*Anglica Germanica*
AHR	*American Historical Review*
AHRF	*Annales Historiques de la Revolution Française*
AI	*American Imago*
AION-SG	*Annali Instituto Universitario Orientale, Napoli, Sezione Germanica*
AJ	*Art Journal*
AJES	*Aligarh Journal of English Studies*
AJFS	*Australian Journal of French Studies*
AKG	*Archiv für Kulturgeschichte*
	Akzente: Zeitschrift für Literatur
AL	*American Literature*
	Albion
ALett	*L'Approdo Letterario*
ALittASH	*Acta Litterarica Academiae Scientiarum Hungaricae. Magyar Tudomanyos Akademia. Budapest*
	Allegorica
ALM	*Archives des Lettres Modernes*
	American Art Journal
	American Art Review
	American Journal of Sociology
	American Political Science Review
AmG	*L'Amitié Guérinienne*

AN&Q   *American Notes & Queries*
AnBret   *Annales de Bretagne*
            Anglia
            Annales de Bourgogne
            Annales de l'Academie de Mâcon
            Annales de l'Est
            Annales de l'Université de Dakar
            Annales de l'Université de Toulouse-le Mirail
            Annales du Centre Universitaires Méditerranéen
            Annales du Midi
            Annales Universitaires (Avignon)
            Annales: Economies, Sociétés, Civilisations
            Annali della Facoltà di Lingne e Letterature
              Straniere (Bari)
            L'Année Balzacienne
AnS   *Annals of Science*
            Antaeus
Anzeiger   *Anzeiger, Oesterreichische Akademie der Wissen-*
              schaften, philosophisch-historische Klasse
APh   *Archives Philosophiques*
APhilos   *Archives de Philosophie*
            Apollo
AQ   *American Quarterly*
AR   *Antioch Review*
            Arbor: Revista General de Investigación y Cultura
            L'Arc: Cahiers Méditerranéens (Aix-en-Provence)
            Arcadia: Zeitschrift für vergleichenden Literatur-
              wissenschaft
Arch   *Archivum*
Archiv   *Archiv für das Studium der Neueren Sprachen und*
              Literaturen
ArH   *Archivo Hispalense*
ArielE   *Ariel: A Review of International English Liter-*
              ature
ArM   *Archiv für Musikwissenschaft*
ArQ   *Arizona Quarterly*
ArtB   *Art Bulletin*
            Art History
ArtQ   *Art Quarterly*
            Arts Magazine
ASch   *American Scholar*
ASLHM   *American Society Legion of Honor Magazine*
            Association des Amis d'Alfred de Vigny. Bulletin
ASSR   *Archives de Sciences Sociales des Réligions*
AUB   *Analele Universitatü, Bucuresti*
AUMLA   *Journal of the Australasian Universities Language*
              and Literature Association
Aurora   *Aurora: Eichendorff-Almanach*
AWR   *Anglo-Welsh Review*

xi

BAAD	Bulletin de l'Association des Amis d'Alexandre Dumas
BAGB	Bulletin de l'Association Guillaume Budé
BAWS	Bayerische Akademie der Wissenschaften. Philosophischhistorisch Klasse, Sitzungsberichte
B&BM	Books & Bookmen
BB	Bulletin of Bibliography
BBaud	Bulletin Baudelairien
BBMP	Boletin de la Biblioteca Menéndez Pelayo
BC	Book Collector
BCLF	Bulletin Critique du Livre Français
BduB	Bulletin du Bibliophile
	Belfagor: Rassegna di varia Umanità
	Bennington Review
	Berkshire Review (Williams College)
BF	Book Forum
BFE	Boletín de Filología Española
BGDSL	Beiträge zur Geschichte der deutschen Sprache und Literatur
BH	Bulletin Hispanique
BHR	Bibliothèque d'Humanisme et Renaissance
BHS	Bulletin of Hispanic Studies
	Bibliothèque de l'Ecole des Chartres
BIHR	Bulletin of the Institute of Historical Research (London)
BioC	Biologia Culturale
BIQ	Blake: An Illustrated Quarterly
BJA	British Journal of Aesthetics
BJHS	British Journal for the History of Science
BJRL	Bulletin of the John Ryland Library
BL	Beiträge zur Literaturkunde
	Blackwood's Magazine
BLAM	Bulletin de la Librairie Ancienne et Moderne
BLR	The Bodleian Library Record
BM	The Burlington Magazine
BMMLA	Bulletin of the Midwest MLA
	Boletin de la Academía argentina de Letras
	Les Bonnes Feuilles
	Boundary
BPhilos	Bibliography of Philosophy
BRAE	Boletín de la Real Academia Española
BRAH	Boletín de la Real Academia de la Historia
BRH	Bulletin of Research in the Humanities
	The British Library Journal
BRP	Beiträge zur romanischen Philologie (Berlin)
BS	Blake Studies
BSAP	Bulletin de la Société des Amis de Marcel Proust et des Amis de Combray
BSUF	Ball State University Forum
BUJ	Boston University Journal

Bulletin de l'Académie royale de Langue et de Littérature Françaises (Brussels)
Bulletin de l'Association des Amis d'Alain
Bulletin de l'Association des Amis de J.-J. Rousseau
Bulletin de l'Association des Amis de Rabelais et de La Devinière
Bulletin de l'Association J.-K. Huysmans
Bulletin de la Bibliothèque Nationale
Bulletin de la Société Belge des Professeurs de Français
Bulletin de la Société d'Histoire du Protestantisme Français
Bulletin de la Société Jules Vernes
Bulletin des Amis d'André Gide
Bulletin des Amis de Flaubert
Bulletin des Amis de Jules Romains
Bulletin of the Faculty of Literature (Kyushu University)
Byron Journal

BYUS   *Brigham Young University Studies*
CA   *Cuadernos americanos*
CACP   *Cahiers de l'Amitié Charles Peguy*
           Cahiers Canadien Claudel
CahiersC   *Cahiers Césairiens*
           Cahiers d'Analyse Textuelle
           Cahiers d'Histoire
           Cahiers de l'Ecole Supérieure des Lettres de Beyrouth
           Cahiers des Amis de Valery Larbaud
           Cahiers Diderotiens
           Cahiers François Mauriac
           Cahiers Internationaux du Symbolisme
           Les Cahiers Naturalistes
CahiersS   *Cahiers Staëliens*
CAIEF   *Cahiers de l'Association Internationale des Etudes Françaises*
CalSS   *California Slavic Studies*
CamR   *Cambridge Review*
           Canadian Journal of Research in Semiotics
CB   *Cuadernos bibliográficos*
CE   *College English*
CentR   *Centennial Review*
CeS   *Cultura e Scuola*
CG   *Colloquia Germanica*
CH   *Church History*
CHA   *Cuadernos Hispanoamericanos (Madrid)*
ChLB   *Charles Lamb Bulletin*
CHR   *Catholic Historical Review*

ELWIU	*Essays in Literature (Western Illinois University*
EM	*English Miscellany*
	Encounter
	English
EnlE	*Enlightenment Essays*
EP	*Etudes philosophiques*
ES	*English Studies*
ESA	*English Studies in Africa (Johannesburg)*
ESC	*English Studies in Canada*
	Esprit
ESQ	*Emerson Society Quarterly*
ESR	*European Studies Review*
	Essays in French Literature
EstF	*Estudios Filosóficos*
ETJ	*Educational Theater Journal*
ETR	*Etudes Théologiques et Réligieuses*
	Etudes Bernanosiennes
	Etudes Françaises
	Etudes Gobiniennes
	Euphorion: Zeitschrift für Literaturgeschichte
	Europe
	Explicator
Fabula	*Fabula: Zeitschrift für Ersählforschung*
FemS	*Feminist Studies*
FHS	*French Historical Studies*
FilM	*Filologia Moderna*
FL	*Le Figaro Littéraire*
	Le Flambeau (Haiti)
FLe	*Fiera Letteraria*
FM	*Le Français Moderne*
FMLS	*Forum for Modern Language Studies*
	Foi et Vie
	Folklore
	Fontes Artis Musicae
	Forum Italicum
FR	*The French Review*
	Francia
	French Forum
	French Monographs (Macquarie University)
	French News
	The French-American Review
FS	*French Studies*
FSSA	*French Studies in Southern Africa*
FurmS	*Furman Studies*
GaR	*Georgia Review*
GBA	*Gazette des Beaux-Arts*
	Genre
	Germanistik

Interpretations (Memphis State University)
IPQ *International Philosophical Quarterly*
IQ *Italian Quarterly*
IS *Italian Studies*
Italica
Italianistica
IUB *Indiana University Bookman*
JAAC *Journal of Aesthetics and Art Criticism*
JAF *Journal of American Folklore*
JBS *Journal of British Studies*
JDH *Jahresverzeichnis der deutschen Hochschulschriften*
JDSG *Jahrbuch der deutschen Schiller-Gesellschaft*
JEGP *Journal of English and Germanic Philology*
JEH *Journal of Ecclesiastical History*
JES *The Journal of European Studies*
JFDH *Jahrbuch des Freien deutschen Hochstifts (Tübingen)*
JFI *Journal of the Folklore Institute*
JfV *Jahrbuch für Volksliedforschung*
JHA *Journal of the History of Astronomy*
JHI *Journal of the History of Ideas*
JHK *Jahrbuch der Hamburger Kunstammlungen*
JHP *Journal of the History of Philosophy*
JIG *Jahrbuch für internationale Germanistik*
JIH *Journal of Interdisciplinary History*
JJPG *Jahrbuch der Jean-Paul-Gesellschaft*
JLS *Journal of Literary Semantics*
JMH *Journal of Modern History*
JML *Journal of Modern Literature*
JMRS *Journal of Medieval and Renaissance Studies*
JNH *Journal of Negro History*
JNL *Johnsonian News Letter*
JNT *Journal of Narrative Technique*
Journal of Library History
Journal of Religious History
Journal of Women's Studies in Literature
JPC *Journal of Popular Culture*
JR *Journal of Religion*
JRG *Jahrbuch der Raabe-Gesellschaft*
JS *Journal des Savants*
JSH *Journal of Social History*
JSUB *Jahrbuch der schlesischen Friedrich-Wilhelms-*
Universität zu Breslau
JWCI *Journal of the Warburg and Courtauld Institutes*
JWGV *Jahrbuch des Wiener Goethe-Vereins*
KantS *Kant-Studien*
Kenyon Review
KFLQ *Kentucky Foreign Language Quarterly*
Konsthistorisk Tidskrift
KRQ *Kentucky Romance Quarterly*

KSJ Keats-Shelley Journal
KSMB Keats-Shelley Memorial Bulletin
KuL Kunst und Literatur
     Das Kunstwerk
Kurbiskern Kurbiskern: Literatur und Kritik
L&H Literature and History
     Langages
Lang&L Language & Literature
     Language and Style
LanM Les Langues modernes
L&P Literature and Psychology
     Lavoro critico
LC Library Chronicle (University of Pennsylvania)
LCUT Library Chronicle of the University of Texas
LE&W Literature East and West
LenauA Lenau-Almanach (Wien)
LenauF Lenau-Forum. Vierteljahresschrift für vergleich-
     ende Literaturforschung (Wien)
LetN Lettres Nouvelles
     Letras
LHR Lock Haven Review (Lock Haven State College, Pa.)
LI Lettere Italiane
     Library
     The Library Quarterly
     La Licorne (Faculté des Lettres et des Langues
     de l'Université de Poitiers)
LiLi Zeitschrift für Literaturwissenschaft und
     Linguistik
     Lingua et Stile
     Literature and Ideology
LitR Literary Review
     Littérature
     Littératures
LJ Library Journal
LJGG Literaturwissenschaftliches Jahrbuch. Im Auftrage
     der Littérature Gorres-Gesellschaft. N.F.
LMFA Literature, Music and Fine Arts
LNL Linguistics in Literature
LR Les Lettres Romanes
LSoc Language in Society
LuK Literatur und Kritik
     Lumière et Vie
LWU Literatur in Wissenschaft und Unterricht
LY Lessing Yearbook
MA Le Moyen Age
M&L Music and Letters (London)
     Marche Romane

NDQ	*North Dakota Quarterly*
	Neohelicon
Neophil	*Neophilologus (Groningen)*
NEQ	*New England Quarterly*
	New Left Review
	New Statesman
	New York Times Book Review
NFS	*Nottingham French Studies*
NGC	*New German Criticism*
NGS	*New German Studies*
NL	*Nouvelles littéraires*
NLB	*The Newberry Library Bulletin*
NLH	*New Literary History*
NM	*Neuphilologische Mitteilungen*
	Novel: A Forum on Fiction
NR	*New Republic*
NRev	*The New Review (London)*
NRF	*Nouvelle Revue française*
NRFH	*Nueva Revista de Filologia Hispánica*
NRRS	*Notes and Records of the Royal Society of London*
NRs	*Neue Rundschau*
NS	*Die Neueren Sprachen*
NUQ	*New Universities Quarterly*
NY	*New Yorker*
NYRB	*New York Review of Books*
O&C	*OEuvres et Critiques*
	L'OEil
ÖGL	*Österreich in Geschichte und Literatur*
OGS	*Oxford German Studies*
OHis	*Ottawa Hispanica*
OL	*Orbis Litterarum*
OLR	*Oxford Literary Review*
ON	*Otto-Novecento*
	Opera
	Opera News
OPL	*Osservatore Politico Letterario*
OUR	*Ohio University Review*
P&L	*Philosophy and Literature*
	Pantheon
P&P	*Past and Present*
PAPS	*Proceedings of the American Philosophical Society*
P&R	*Philosophy and Rhetoric*
	Paragone: Rivista Mensile di Arte Figuritiva e Letteratura
PBSA	*Papers of the Bibliography Society of America*
PCL	*Perspectives on Contemporary Literature*
PEGS	*Publications of the English Goethe Society*
	Pensiero Politico
Person	*The Personalist*

PFSCL   *Papers on French Seventeenth Century Literature*
         Philobiblon
         Philologica Pragensia
PhJ   *The Philosophical Journal*
PhJb   *Philosophisches Jahrbuch*
         *Pisa: Annali della Scuola Normale Superiore di
         Pisa*
PL   *Philosophischer Literaturanzeiger*
PLL   *Papers on Language and Literature*
PMHB   *Pennsylvania Magazine of History and Biography*
PMLA   *Publications of the Modern Language Association
         of America*
         Poesie
         Poetica (Tokyo)
         *Poetica: Zeitschrift für Sprach- und Literatur-
         wissenschaft*
         *Poetics: International Review for the Theory of
         Literature*
         *Poétique: Revue des Théories et d'Analyse Litté-
         raire*
Polit   *Polit: A Journal for Literature and Politics*
PQ   *Philological Quarterly*
PR   *Partisan Review*
PRAN   *Proust Research Association Newsletter*
Prépub   *Pré(publications)*
         Preuves
ProceedingsICLA *Proceedings of the Congress of the International
                 Comparative Literature Association (Actes du
                 congrès de l'Association Internationale de
                 Littérature Comparée)*
PS   *Prose Studies*
PSA   *Papeles de Son Armadans*
PSch   *Prairie Schooner*
         Psychoanalytic Review
PTL   *PTL: A Journal for Descriptive Poetics and Theory*
         Publications de l'Institut de France, Paris
         Publications of the Center for Baudelaire Studies
PULC   *Princeton University Library Chronicle*
QJS   *Quarterly Journal of Speech*
QL   *La Quinzaine Littéraire*
QQ   *Queen's Quarterly*
         Quaderni Francesi
RA   *Revue d'Allemagne*
RABM   *Revista de Archivos, Bibliotecas y Museos*
         Rapports
RBPH   *Revue Belge de Philologie et d'Histoire*
RCEH   *Revista Canadiense de Estudios Hispánicos*
RCSF   *Rivista Critica della Storia della Filosofia*
RDM   *Revue des Deux Mondes*
RdS   *Revue de Synthèse*
RE   *Revue d'Esthétique*

RMus   Revue de Musicologie
RNL   Review of National Literatures
RO   Revista de Occidente
          Romania
          Romanica Wratislaviensia
          Romanistische Zeitschrift für Literaturgeschichte/
            Cahiers d'Histoire des Littératures Romanes
          · Romantisme
RomN   Romance Notes (University of North Carolina)
RP&P   Romanticism Past and Present
RPFE   Revue Philosophique de la France et de l'Etranger
RPh   Romance Philology
RPL   Revue Philosophique de Louvain
RPP   Revue Politique et Parlementaire
RR   Romanic Review
RS   Research Studies (Washington State University)
RSC   Royal Society of Canada
RSH   Revue des Sciences Humaines
RSPT   Revue des Sciences Philosophiques et Théologiques
RUO   Revue de l'Université d'Ottawa
RUS   Rice University Studies
RusL   Russian Literature
S   Spectator
Saeculum   Saeculum: Jahrbuch für Universalgeschichte
Saggi   Saggi e Ricerche di Letteratura Francese
          Salmagundi
          San Jose Studies
SAQ   South Atlantic Quarterly
S&S   Science and Society
SAR   South Atlantic Review
SatR   Saturday Review
SB   Studies in Bibliography
SC   Stendhal Club
SCB   South Central Bulletin
Scheidewege   Scheidewege: Vierteljahresschrift für skeptisches
            Denken
SchM   Schweitzer Monatshefte für Politik, Wirtschaft,
            Kultur
ScHR   Scottish Historical Review
SCR   South Carolina Review
SCr   Strumenti Critici
SECC   Studies in Eighteenth-Century Culture (Univ. of Wisconsin)
SEEJ   Slavic and East European Journal
SEL   Studies in English Literature, 1500-1900 (Rice
            University)
          Seminar: A Journal of Germanic Studies
          Semiolus
          Semiotext
          Semiotica: Revue Publiée par l'Association Inter-
            nationale de Sémiotique

SFI   *Studi di Filologia Italiana*
SFR   *Stanford French Review*
SFr   *Studi Francesi*
SGr   *Studi Germanici*
ShawR   *The Shaw Review*
        Shenandoah
SHPS   *Studies in the History and Philosophy of Science*
SHR   *Southern Humanities Review*
ShS   *Shakespeare Survey*
        Signs
SiR   *Studies in Romanticism (Boston University)*
SJP   *Southern Journal of Philosophy*
SJW   *Shakespeare Jahrbuch (Weimar)*
SlavR   *Slavic Review*
SLIm   *Studies in the Literary Imagination*
SLJ   *Scottish Literary Journal*
SN   *Studia Neophilologica*
SNNTS   *Studies in the Novel (North Texas University)*
SÖAW   *Sitzungsberichte der Österreichischen Akademie*
          der Wissenschaften im Wien, Philosophisch-
          historisch Klasse
        Société Chateaubriand, Bulletin
        Société de Linguistique de Paris. Bulletin
        Société des Amis de Montaigne. Bulletin
        Société Paul Claudel. Bulletin
SoR   *Southern Review (Louisiana State University)*
SoRA   *Southern Review (Adelaide, Australia)*
        Soundings: A Journal of Interdisciplinary Studies
        Soviet Studies in Literature
SovL   *Soviet Literature*
SP   *Studies in Philology*
SPCT   *Studi e Problemi de Critica Testuale*
        Sprachkunst
SQ   *Southern Quarterly*
SR   *Sewanee Review*
SSEL   *Salzburg Studies in English Literature*
SSF   *Studies in Short Fiction*
SSL   *Studies in Scottish Literature (University of*
          South Carolina)
StF   *Studia Filozoficzne*
        Storia dell'Arte
        Structuralist Review
        Studi de Letteratura Francese
        Studi Piemontesi
        Studies in Browning
        Studies in the Humanities
        Style

STTH *Science/Technology and the Humanities*
STZ *Sprache im technischen Zeitalter*
    Sub-stance: A Review of Theory and Literary Criticism
SuF *Sinn und Form*
    Sur
SVEC *Studies in Voltaire and the Eighteenth Century*
SWJP *Southwestern Journal of Philosophy*
SWR *Southwest Review*
    Symposium
SZ *Stimmen der Zeit: Monatsschrift der Gegenwart*
TAH *The American Hispanist*
TCBS *Transactions of the Cambridge Bibliographical Society*
TDR *The Drama Review*
    Tel Quel
    Theater Heute
    Theatre Quarterly
    Thought: A Review of Culture and Idea
ThR *Theatre Research*
ThS *Theatre Survey*
TLL *Travaux de Linguistique et de Littérature (U. of Strasbourg)*
TLS *Times Literary Supplement (London)*
TM *Les Temps Modernes*
TN *Theatre Notebook*
    Topic: A Journal of the Liberal Arts (Washington, Pa.)
TR *Table Ronde*
    Travail Théâtral
TRI *Theatre Research International*
    Tropos
TSE *Tulane Studies in English*
TSL *Tennessee Studies in Literature*
TSLL *Texas Studies in Literature and Language*
TuK *Text und Kritik*
TWC *The Wordsworth Circle*
UKPHS *University of Kansas Humanistic Studies*
UMSE *University of Mississippi Studies in English*
Unisa *Unisa English Studies*
Univ *Universitas: Zeitschrift für Wissenschaft, Kunst und Literatur*
UQ *Universities Quarterly*
UR *University Review (Kansas City, Missouri)*
UTQ *University of Toronto Quarterly*
UWR *University of Windsor Review*
    Vestnik, Seria 10, Filologia (U. of Moscow)
    Viertelsjahrhefte für Zeitgeschichte

VLang	Visible Language
VN	Victorian Newsletter
VP	Victorian Poetry
VQR	Virginia Quarterly Review
VS	Victorian Studies
W&L	Women and Literature
WasacanaR	Wasacana Review (University of Regina, Canada)
WB	Weimarer Beiträge
WCR	West Coast Review
	Westerly: A Quarterly Review
	Westermanns Monatshefte
WHR	Western Humanities Review
WLT	World Literature Today
WMQ	William and Mary Quarterly
	The World of Music
WS	Women's Studies
WuW	Welt und Wort
WVUPP	West Virginia University Philological Papers
WW	Wirkendes Wort
WZPHP	Wissenschaftliche Zeitschrift der Pädagogischen Hochschule Potsdam
WZUB	Wissenschaftliche Zeitschrift der Humbolt-Universität zu Berlin
WZUH	Wissenschaftliche Zeitschrift der Martin-Luther-Universität Halle-Wittenberg
WZUJ	Wissenschaftliche Zeitschrift der Friedrich-Schiller Universität Jena
WZUL	Wissenschaftliche Zeitschrift der Karl-Marx-Universität Leipzig
YCGL	Yearbook of Comparative and General Literature
YES	Yearbook of English Studies
YFS	Yale French Studies
YIS	Yale Italian Studies
YR	Yale Review
YULG	Yale University Library Gazette
YWMLS	Year's Work in Modern Language Studies
ZAA	Zeitschrift für Anglistik und Amerkanistik
ZDA	Zeitschrift für deutsches Altertum und deutsche Literatur
ZDP	Zeitschrift für deutsche Philologie
	Zeitschrift des deutschen Vereins für Kunstwissenschaft
	Zeitschrift für Ästhetik und allgemeine Kunstwissenschaft
	Zeitschrift für Kirchengeschichte
	Zeitschrift für Kunstgeschichte
ZFSL	Zeitschrift für französische Sprache und Literatur

ZG(Korea)	Zeitschrift für Germanistik (Korea)
ZG(Leipzig)	Zeitschrift für Germanistik (Leipzig)
ZPhF	Zeitschrift für Philosophische Forschung
ZRG	Zeitschrift für Religions- und Geistegeschichte
ZRL	Zagadnienia Rodzajów literackich
ZRP	Zeitschrift für Romanische Philologie (Halle)
ZS	Zeitschrift für Slawistik
ZV	Zeitschrit für Volkskunde

THE ROMANTIC MOVEMENT

GENERAL

(Compiled by David V. Erdman with the assistance of
Thomas L. Ashton, Irene H. Chayes, Robert A. Hartley,
Bishop C. Hunt, Robert Mollenauer, Augustus Pallotta,
James S. Patty, Jeffrey C. Robinson, Robert Michael
Ryan, and Mark T. Smith)

1. BIBLIOGRAPHY

See the respective "Bibliography" and "General" sections for
each language, below. *The Romantic Movement Bibliography* has
been published in its present form beginning with the *Bibliography* for 1979, in 1980. For previous years, see the "Bibliography of the Romantic Movement" in *English Language Notes*
(*ELN*), September supplements, 1965-79. In 1973 a cumulative
reprint since 1936 was published in seven volumes by the
Pierian Press and R.R. Bowker, New York. For the most extensive general listing, in all languages, without commentary,
see the annual *MLA International Bibliography*, Volumes I and
II.

Borck, Jim Springer, ed. *The Eighteenth Century: A Current
Bibliography*. New York: AMS Press. (Abbrev. ECCB)

The volumes for 1977 and 1978, ed. Robert R. Allen, and
the volume for 1979, ed. Paul Korshin, have been published.
The 1980 volume, ed. Borck, appeared in 1983.

Harris, Laurie Lanzen, ed. *Nineteenth-Century Literature
Criticism: Excerpts from Criticism of the Works of Novelists,
Poets, Playwrights, Short Story Writers, and Other Creative
Writers Who Lived between 1800 and 1900*. Vol. 3. Detroit:
Gale Research, 1982. Pp. 600; cumulative index. $64.00.

Kiell, Norman, ed. *Psychoanalysis, Psychology, and Literature:
A Bibliography*. 2nd edition. 2 vols. Metuchen, N.J.: Scare-
crow Press, 1982. Pp. xii+1269. $65.00.

Pingree, Elizabeth E., ed. *Humanities Index*, Vol. 9. June 1982
to March 1983. New York: H.W. Wilson Co., 1982-83.

   Continuing and cumulative.

Winans, Robert B. *A Descriptive Checklist of Book Catalogues
Separately Printed in America, 1693-1800.* Worcester: American
Antiquarian Society, 1981. Pp. xxxi+207. $35.00.

   Rev. by Peter Drummery in *NEQ* 55 (1982): 311-13.

Wolf, Edwin, and Marie Elena Korey. *Quarter of a Millennium:
The Library Company of Philadelphia 1731-1981, a Selection.*
Philadelphia: Library Company of Philadelphia, 1981. Pp.
viii+355. $25.00.

   Rev. by Marcus A. McCorison in *PMHB* 106 (1981): 585-86.
   The Wolf memorial exhibit catalogue exposes much of American literary taste in the eighteenth and early nineteenth
centuries. (T.L.A.)

Wortman, William A. *A Guide to Serial Bibliographies for
Modern Literatures.* New York: Modern Language Association,
1982. Pp. xvi+125. $16.50; $8.75 paper.

   A guide to current bibliographies in all literatures as
well as in nonliterary fields important to literary scholars.

See also Hester ("German 1. Bibliography") on database searching.

Review of book previously listed:

   HARRIS, Wendell V., *British Short Fiction in the Nineteenth
   Century: A Literary and Bibliographic Guide* (see *RMB* for
   1979, p. 30), rev. by Nicola Bradbury in *RES* 33 (1982):
   347-49.

2. ENVIRONMENT: ART, PHILOSOPHY
POLITICS, RELIGION, SOCIETY

Anninger, Anne. "Costumes of the Convention: Art as Agent
of Social Change in Revolutionary France." *HLB* 30 (1982):
179-203.

   In 1794, the Committee of Public Safety commissioned
David "to submit his ideas and sketches on ways of improv-
ing the national costume to make it more appropriate to the

mores of the Republic." The results were engraved by Denon
and proposed a national costume at once "simple, frugal,
and easily alterable, so as to designate age and different
public functions without undermining the sacred precept of
equality." Very few people seem to have accepted David's
proposal. As a contemporary remarked, "people only smiled
at these eccentricities." (R.A.B.)

Baker, Keith Michael. "A Script for a French Revolution: The
Political Consciousness of the Abbé Mably." *E-CStudies* 14
(1981): 235-63.

In 1772 Mably was writing a political script in the
language of classical republicanism which, fifteen years
later, Frenchmen found themselves enacting.

Bergeron, Louis. *France under Napoleon*. Trans. R.R. Palmer.
Princeton University Press, 1981. Pp. xiv+230. $18.75;
$7.95 paper.

Rev. and praised by Owen Connelly in *AHR* 87 (1982): 1105.

Bier, Jesse. "Benjamin Franklin: Guilt and Transformation."
PMHB 106 (1982): 89-97.

Carter, E.C., J.C. Van Horne, and L.W. Formwalt, eds. *The
Papers of Benjamin Henry Latrobe. Journals*. Vol. III: 1799-
1820. Yale University Press, 1981. Pp. xxxiv+351. $65.00.

Rev. by Michael McMahon in *PMHB* 106 (1982): 133-34.

Castan, Nicole. *Les Criminels de Languedoc: Les Exigences
d'ordre et les voies du ressentiment dans une société pre-
revolutionnaire (1750-1790)*. University of Toulouse, 1980.
Pp. x+362.

Rev. by Colin Lucas in *JMH* 54 (1982): 790-92.
A major work. (T.L.A.)

Cochran, Thomas C. "Philadelphia: The American Industrial
Center, 1750-1850." *PMHB* 106 (1982): 323-40.

By the dean of American business historians. (T.L.A.)

Coleman, Francis X.J. "John Jay on War." *JHI* 43 (1982): 145-
51.

Countryman, Edward. *A People in Revolution: The American
Revolution and Political Society in New York, 1760-1790*.
Johns Hopkins University Press, 1981. Pp. 388. $24.50.

Rev. by Douglas Greenberg in *PMHB* 106 (1982): 297-99.
Countryman brings "social, economic, intellectual, and
political history ... to bear upon one another in systemic
fashion." The result "is simply one of the best books ever
written about the American Revolution."

Darnton, Robert. *The Literary Underground of the Old Regime.*
Harvard University Press, 1982. Pp. ix+258. $16.50.

Rev. by Norman Hampson in *NYRB*, Oct. 7, 1982, pp. 43-44;
by Robert Nisbet in *The New Criterion* 1 (Jan. 1983): 74-78.
Police ledgers and publishers' records supply a documentation in sharp detail of the French Grub Street before the
Revolution, the underworld of illicit printing and publishing that supplied the pre-revolutionary counterculture. A
"preliminary reconnoitering" of the economic and social
conditions in which the books were made which contributed
to "the first great revolution of modern times."
An important chapter details the career of Brissot as
"A Spy in Grub Street": "his spying deserves emphasis, not
in order to pass judgment on Brissot, but in order to understand him." (D.V.E.)

Deutsch, Sarah. "The Elusive Guineamen: Newport Slavers, 1735-
1774." *NEQ* 55 (1982): 229-53.

"The Newport merchant Guinea-trader has eluded historians
because, as such, he did not exist.... Except in moments of
desperation or periods of experimentation, the slave trade
never exceeded a purely incidental role" in the affairs of
Newport merchants. For ship captains, however, "the Guinea
trade held the lure of social as well as economic advancement.... The captains, not the merchants, consistently gained
in the slave trade."

Draper, Theodore. "Hume and Madison: The Secrets of Federalist
Paper No. 10." *Encounter* 58 (Feb. 1982): 34-47.

First secret: James Madison found his idea of the "extended republic" in Hume's *Idea of a Perfect Commonwealth.*
Second secret: Hume could just as easily have been quoted
as supporting the opposite side of the question. Other
less important secrets as well. (M.T.S.)

Eichner, Hans. "The Rise of Modern Science and the Genesis
of Romanticism." *PMLA* 97 (1982): 8-30.

Elliott, Marianne. *Partners in Revolution: The United Irishmen and France.* Yale University Press, 1982. Pp. 430. $30.00.

By far the most thoroughly "researched" study of the United
Irish movement yet presented, and particularly valuable for
the critical analysis (disputable, of course) that accompanies
the account. "At the outset" in 1791, the United Irishmen
"were republican in the manner of the classical republicanism
of the English 'country' or 'real Whigs,' the eighteenth-
century 'Commonwealthmen' or the writers of the Enlightenment.... Their transformation into a militantly anti-English,
anti-monarchical republican movement" is examined in the context of the wider reform movement--among the French, the
Dutch, the Belgians, the Savoyards, and the Poles--and its
complicated, shifting reactions to the general European
crisis of the 1790s. Its cosmopolitan intellectual and
political nature is given more attention than in most attempts
to comprehend the events of 1793-95. The English and Scottish
connection still suffers from neglect, though Elliott does
note the leaders' "ability to move with ease among England's
plebian democrats" (xiv).
A valuable work, perhaps especially for its emphasis on
the "peculiar character of each country" and of each crisis,
treating the example of Ireland as "a notable, if disturbing, reminder that the pattern of an 'Atlantic Revolution'
cannot be applied unmodified to every country caught up in
that crisis." (D.V.E.)

Ellis, Geoffrey. *Napoleon's Continental Blockade: The Case
of Alsace.* (Oxford Historical Monographs.) Oxford: Clarendon
Press, 1981. Pp. xvi+355. $49.95.

Rev. by James K. Kieswetter in *AHR* 87 (1982): 188-89.

Les Études Philosophiques, Jan. 1982.

Special Issue on "Ideologie," with articles on Destutt
de Tracy, Maine de Biran, La Mettrie, Cabanis, Bichat, and
John Hunter.

Fliegelman, Jay. *Prodigals and Pilgrims: The American Revolution against Patriarchal Authority, 1750-1800.* Cambridge
University Press, 1982. Pp. 328. £20.00.

Rev. by Robert A. Ferguson in *TLS*, Oct. 22, 1982, p. 1169,
as bringing vitality "to the age-old assumption that the
novel and America connect in a peculiar and intimate way."
Broadly concerns the intellectual and emotional revolution.

Forrest, Alan. *The French Revolution and the Poor.* New York:
St. Martin's Press, 1981. Pp. x+198. $25.00.

Rev. by Lynn Hunt in *JMH* 54 (1982): 793-94, as "balanced
in vantage point, and ... useful to anyone interested in a
general review of the social programs laid out during the
Revolution."

Forster, Robert. *Merchants, Landlords, Magistrates: The Depont
Family in Eighteenth-Century France*. Johns Hopkins University Press, 1980. Pp. xii+275. $22.50.

Rev. by J.F. Bosher in *JMH* 54 (1982): 369-71.
Burke addressed his *Reflections* to Charles-François Depont,
the friend of 1785 he liked to call "young Picky Pokey."
(T.L.A.)

Freedeman, Charles E. *Joint Stock Enterprise in France, 1807-
1867: From Privileged to Modern Corporation*. University of
North Carolina Press, 1979. Pp. xvi+234. $17.50.

Rev. by Noureddine Dougui in *JMH* 54 (1982): 586-88.

Gillispie, Charles Coulston. *Science and Polity in France at
the End of the Old Regime*. Princeton University Press, 1980.
Pp. xii+601. $40.00.

Rev. by Maurice Crosland in *JMH* 54 (1982): 580-82; by
Dora B. Weiner in *AHR* 87 (1982): 186-87 as a "treasure chest
of a book."
Chapters: "The State and Science," "Science and the State,"
"Science and Medicine," "Scientists and Charlatans" (with
a section on Mesmerism), "Trades and Agriculture," "Indus-
try and Invention," "Engineering, Civil and Military."
Treasure chest indeed. (R.A.H.)

Grayson, David, Robert J. Taylor, Marc Friedlander, and
Celeste Walker, eds. *Diary of John Quincy Adams*. 2 vols.
The Belknap Press of Harvard University, 1981. Pp. 415;
521. $60.00.

Rev. by Robert H. Ferrell in *NEQ* 55 (1982): 606-08.
The first two volumes of a multi-volume series. Adams
began his diary on Nov. 12, 1779. Volume two concludes in
Dec. 1788, by which time Adams had travelled in France,
the Netherlands, and Russia, attended Harvard, and begun
to study law.

Harris, John. *The Palladians*. London: Trefoil Books (in
association with R.I.B.A. Drawings Collection), 1981; New
York: Rizzoli, 1982. Pp. 132. £11.95; £5.95 paper.

Rev. by Timothy Connor in *BM* 124 (June 1982): 369.

Heartz, Daniel. "The Beginnings of the Operatic Romance: Rousseau, Sedaine, and Monsigny." *ECS* 15 (1981-82): 149-78; 9 illus.

Hendry, John. "Mayer, Herschel and Prévost on the Solar Motion." *AnS* 39 (1982): 61-75.

Higonnet, Patrice. *Class, Ideology, and the Rights of Nobles during the French Revolution.* Clarendon Press, Oxford University Press, 1981. Pp. xvii+358. $55.00.

> Rev. by Thomas D. Beck in *AHR* 87 (1982): 1298-99; by Colin Lucas in *TLS*, Dec. 17, 1982, p. 1388, rather obtusely.
> "The men of the French Revolution were caught up in a social drama whose true nature was very hard to grasp" (174)--either by the participants or by historians. Higonnet, closely watching the lively debate of modern historians to rethink and comprehend The Revolution, and returning again and again to the thoughts and acts of the participants themselves, and closer perhaps to the revisionists than to the Marxists--yet deriving his central argument from the early Marx himself (3)--brings considerable illumination to the revolutionary decade by focusing on the shifting politics of "anti-nobilism" (a neologism, coined as class-specific). Historians have been too long beguiled by the hypocritical language of politicians engaged in ideological scape-goat tactics in their determination to have "no enemies on the left."
> A "Thematic Index" will lead the knowing reader to "Bourgeois universalism," to "Historians" of various brands, and to other reconsidered matters. Familiarity with the events and persons is generally assumed, and the French quotations are not translated. (D.V.E.)

Hindman, Sandra, ed. *The Early Illustrated Book: Essays in Honor of Lessing J. Rosenwald.* Washington, D.C.: Library of Congress, 1982. Pp. xv+260; 174 figs.; 8 color plates.

> Four articles on "Fifteenth- and Sixteenth-century Dutch and Flemish Books"; four on "Landscape and the Early Illustrated Book"; three on "The Illustration of Vergil in Printed Books." Preceded by "An Appreciation" by William Matheson of Rosenwald and his collection, and the editor's introduction: "Probing the Roswenwald Collection." Rich fare. The color plates demonstrate that modern printers still *can* approach perfection. (D.V.E.)

Jacob, Margaret C. *The Radical Enlightenment: Pantheists, Freemasons and Republicans.* (Early Modern Europe Today.) London: Allen & Unwin, 1981. Pp. xvi+312.

Jacob demonstrates the politically conservative associations
of Newtonian science (thus vindicating Blake's view of Newton)
and explores the politically radical associations of Pantheism. Though a great deal more work needs to be done in
this area, Jacob's book is a helpful (though repetitious) introduction. The relationship between Jacob's subject and
Romanticism is a rich area for historical scholarship; it
has by no means been exhausted by McFarland's *Coleridge and
the Pantheistic Tradition*. Must reading for Romanticists.
(R.A.H.)

Johnson, Paul E. "The Modernization of Mayo Greenleaf Patch:
Land, Family, and Marginality in New England, 1766-1818."
NEQ 55 (1982): 488-516.

A valuable essay on the effects of the industrial revolution. Mayo Greenleaf Patch and Abigail McIntire Patch "were
among the first New Englanders to abandon farming and take
up factory labor. They did so because rural society had no
room for them, and their history is a tale of progressive
exclusion from an agrarian world governed by family, kinship,
and inherited land." (R.A.B.)

Katz, Jacob. *From Prejudice to Destruction: Anti-Semitism,
1700-1933*. Harvard University Press, 1980. Pp. viii+392.
$20.00.

Rev. by Richard S. Levy in *JMH* 54 (1982): 78-80. Katz
"must deal with many half-baked intellectuals and assorted
cranks; he does so with seriousness.... In dealing with the
'giants'--Voltaire, Kant, Herder, Hegel, Renan, Marx, and
Wagner--he does not simply interpret their isolated anti-
Jewish utterances ... [but] relates the anti-Jewish senti-
ments of these thinkers to their general intellectual outlook and work."

Kelley, Donald Brooks. "'A Tender Regard to the Whole Creation':
Anthony Benezet and the Emergence of an Eighteenth-Century
Quaker Ecology." *PMHB* 106 (1982): 69-88.

Anthony Benezet (1713-1784), a French Huguenot emigré,
lived first in London, then in Philadelphia. His ecological
perspective contrasts with the Puritan thinking that scholars
have typically assumed "dominated everything north of the
Chesapeake." Far from advocating the exploitation of nature,
Benezet shared with other Friends "a commitment to 'the
value and mystery of all living things.'" In *A First Book
for Children* (1778), he "warned his tiny 'scholars' against
the 'murder' of 'yonder harmless fly' simply on the contention

that 'tis good for nothing.' If superior beings might ar-
bitrarily destroy the life of an inferior, might not Almighty
God in justice blot out the life of an insubordinate child,
'good for nothing'?" (R.A.B.)

Kennedy, Michael L. *The Jacobin Clubs in the French Revolution:
The First Years*. Princeton University Press, 1982. Pp. xii+
381. $27.50.

The title is misleading, since the Jacobin Club of Paris
is not included except as the "mother society" of the "network" of some 921 provincial Clubs. But their story is fascinating indeed, both in its particulars and its sweep,
offering a very different feeling about revolutionary action
and idea in 1789-91 from that of the standard history focused
on Paris. For those of us interested in the view from London,
here is much about the "corresponding" of British and French
societies that will come as news. Let me cite two examples.
"Contacts between the clubs and the Revolution Society [of
London] commenced in November 1789, when the latter saluted
the National Assembly for vanquishing 'aristocracy and
despotism.' This act was one of the principal causes of the
foundation of the Paris Jacobins. It also led two recently
established provincial clubs to seek affiliation with the
London body" (234). Are we curious about the club in Blois,
where Wordsworth lived for many months in 1792? It was
founded Jan. 20, 1791, a year before he got there; it sub-
scribed to two newspapers: the popular *Annales patriotiques
et littéraires*, of Cara, and the *Courier des départements*,
of Gorsas, a name important to Wordsworth. Cornell Words-
worthians happen (?) to have a run of the Gorsas paper and
can see what news and views it made available during his
residence there. (D.V.E.)

Krahé, Peter. "Historie und Heldenverehrung: zur Rezeption
eines Zwischenfalls der Weltumsegelung des Francis Drake
in der Geschichtsschreibung des 19. Jahrhunderts." *Anglia*
100 (1982): 68-91.

Lambert, Barbara, ed. *Music in Public Places*. Volume 1. *Music
in Colonial Massachusetts: 1630-1820*. Boston: Colonial Society of Massachusetts, 1980. Pp. xlvi+404. $25.00.

Rev. by Nym Cooke in *NEQ* 55 (1982): 457-59.
Along with 240 illustrations and 73 melodies and texts,
the book contains essays on American country dances, military
music, Revolutionary-era songs, and colonial American broad-
sides and their music.

Le Goff, T.J.A. *Vannes and Its Region: A Study of Town and Country in Eighteenth-Century France.* Oxford University Press, 1981. Pp. xii+445. $74.00.

Rev. by Timothy Tackett in *JMH* 54 (1982): 371-73. "For many readers, the book's most fascinating insights will be those relating the origins of the counter-revolution of the 1790s."

Lehning, James R. *The Peasants of Marlhes: Economic Development and Family Organization in Nineteenth-Century France.* University of North Carolina Press, 1980. Pp. xiv+218. $19.50.

Rev. by Elizabeth Fox-Genovese in *AHR* 87 (1982): 189-90.

Levy, Darline Gay. *The Ideas and Careers of Simon-Nicolas-Henri Linguet: A Study in Eighteenth-Century French Politics.* University of Illinois Press, 1980. Pp. x+384. $30.00.

Rev. by Rolf Reichardt in *JMH* 54 (1982): 123-25. Levy "provides the most thorough biography yet written of the publicist, who may be said to have been as noted by his contemporaries as he has been neglected by modern historical research." The author of *Memoires de la Bastille* (1783), Linguet was at once seen as a champion of the poor and as a monarchist. "Levy's interpretations of Linguet's thinking ... throw new light on the central problem of transition from the *ancien régime* to the French Revolution."

Lopez, Claude-Anne. "The Man Who Frightened Franklin." *PMHB* 106 (1982): 515-26.

The man who frightened Franklin was Peter Allaire, an American who spied on Franklin in Paris for the British. (R.A.B.)

Maccubbin, Robert P., et al., eds. *Eighteenth-Century Life* 7,ii (Jan. 1982). "Science & Technology and Their Cultural Contexts." (Special Issue. Pp. 147.)

Eleven essays, mostly focusing on "changes"--in botany, in the calendar, in clocks, in self-concepts, in medicine, in fantasies of human flight. Enlightening.
Directly dealing with our period are Shelley M. Bennett, "Thomas Stothard's Adaptation to the Semi-Industrial Arts" (19-31, illus.); Samuel L. Macey, "Clocks and Chronology in the Novels from Defoe to Austen" (96-104); and Alexander M. Ospovat, "Romanticism and German Geology: Five Students of Abraham Gottlob Werner" (105-17).

MacKenzie, Norman. *The Escape from Elba: The Fall and Flight of Napoleon, 1814-1815.* Oxford University Press, 1982. Pp. 320. $14.95.

Madariaga, Isabel de. *Russia in the Age of Catherine the Great.* Yale University Press, 1981. Pp. xii+698.

Rev. by Marc Raeff in *JMH* 54 (1982): 635-38.

Malone, Dumas. *Jefferson and His Time.* Volume 6. *The Sage of Monticello.* Boston: Little, Brown & Co., 1981. Pp. xxiii+551.

Rev. by Jacob E. Cooke in *PMHB* 106 (1982): 135-36, who finds it "an appropriate finale to one of the great biographies of our time"; by Larry R. Gerlach in *NEQ* 55 (1982): 604-06.

Mansel, Philip. "Monarchy, Uniform and the Rise of the *Frac* 1760-1830." *P&P*, no. 96 (Aug. 1982): 103-32; illus.

The trend toward less formal dress was universal, and its political and social overtones have been exaggerated.

Mason, Haydn. *Voltaire: A Biography.* Johns Hopkins University Press, 1981. Pp. xvi+194. $14.95.

Rev. by Arnold Ages in *QQ* 89 (1982): 634-35; by Victor G. Wexler in *AHR* 87 (1982): 185-86.

Monnier, Raymonde. *Le faubourg Saint-Antoine: 1789-1815.* (Bibliothèque d'Histoire Revolutionnaire, Third Series, 21.) Paris: Société des Études Robespierristes, 1981. Pp. 367.

Rev. by Michael L. Kennedy in *AHR* 87 (1982): 1104-05 as, in the tradition of Soboul, Cobb, and Rudé, a study of the urban masses based on meticulous research.
Not seen.

Paul, Charles B. *Science and Immortality: The "Eloges" of the Paris Academy of Sciences (1699-1791).* University of California Press, 1980. Pp. xi+203.

Rev. by Michael T. Ryan in *JMH* 54 (1982): 373-75.

Paulson, Ronald. "John Trumbull and the Representation of the American Revolution." *SiR* 21 (1982): 341-56.

On two differing views of the Revolution reflected in contemporary imagery: the aggressive, Oedipal, and iconoclastic, a "fiery Orc" rampaging, held mainly by "hostile

or sympathetic" outsiders (Burke, Paine, Blake); and the
contractual or covenantal, the breaking and reestablishment
of a political compact, held by the Founding Fathers themselves. Trumbull's paintings in the Capitol Rotunda represent
the latter.

Petersen, Susanne. *Lebensmittel Frage und revolutionäre Politik
in Paris 1792-1793: Studien zum Verhältnis von revolutionärer
Bourgeoisie und Volksbewegung bei Herausbildung der Jakobin-
erdiktakur.* Munich and Vienna: R. Oldenbourg Verlag, 1979.
Pp. 305. DM 58.00.

Rev. by Geoffrey Ellis in *JMH* 54 (1982): 584-86. By concentrating "on the period of the Girondist Convention, from
September 1792 to June 1793," Petersen's "book amply achieves
its aim of filling a gap" between Braesch's work and Soboul's
study "of the popular movement in Paris during the French
Revolution."

Potts, Alex. "Winckelmann's Construction of History." *Art
History* 5 (1982): 377-407; 17 illus.

Primmer, Brian. "Unity and Ensemble: Contrasting Ideals in
Romantic Music." *NCM* 6,iii (1982): 97-140.

Reinalter, Helmut. *Aufgeklärter Absolutismus und Revolution:
Zur Geschichte des Jakobinertums und der Frühdemokratischen
Bestrebungen in der Habsburger monarchie.* Vienna: Hermann
Böhlaus, 1980. Pp. 560. DM 134.00.

Rev. by F.A.J. Szabo in *JMH* 54 (1982): 617-19.

Roberts, J.M. *The French Revolution.* Oxford University Press,
1978. Pp. ix+176. $6.95 paper.

Just received. A valuable modernization of historical and
recent documentation and interpretation. While "the French
Revolution" can no longer be understood as a cohesive whole
"even by specialists," it does have unity "in the eye of
the beholder," and each generation must look at the events
of the Revolution "in the light not only of fresh scholarship but of its own preoccupations." Roberts judiciously
and lucidly sorts out the continuities and discontinuities
of the Revolution, as history and as myth. (D.V.E.)

Rogerson, Kenneth F. "The Meaning of Universal Validity in
Kant's Aesthetics." *JAAC* 40 (1981-82): 301-08.

Rousseau, G.S., and Roy Porter, eds. *The Ferment of Knowledge: Studies in the Historiography of Eighteenth-Century Science.* Cambridge University Press, 1980. Pp. viii+500, index. $39.50.

Rev. by Roger A. Hambridge in *SAQ* 81 (1982): 235-37. A collection of essays by several authors. Not seen.

Runes, Dagobert D., and Harry G. Schrickel, eds. *Encyclopedia of the Arts.* Detroit: Gale Research Company, 1982. Pp. 1064. $68.00.

A reprint, unrevised, of a 1946 publication by some 150 collaborators. Mostly valuable for its definition of technical terms, conveniently grouped and cross-referenced. The general surveys, e.g., "AESTHETICS, recent trends in" (ending with the inauguration of *JAAC* in 1942), are perhaps of historical interest. A typical sequence: "high Gothic, Highland fling, high-level street, high relief, high tension porcelain, high warp." Another: "lintel, lion, lip read, Litany, LITERARY CRITICISM, litharge, lithography." (D.V.E.)

Ruud, Charles A. *Fighting Words: Imperial Censorship and the Russian Press, 1804-1906.* University of Toronto Press, 1982. Pp. viii+327. $30.00.

Rev. by Josef L. Altholz in *VPR* 15 (1982): 155-57.

Samuel, Raphael, and Gareth Stedman Jones, eds. *Culture, Ideology and Politics: Essays for Eric Hobsbawm.* (History Workshop Series.) Boston: Routledge & Kegan Paul, 1982. Pp. xi+368. $14.95 paper.

Seventeen essays ranging from early Christianity to "Hobsbawm and Jazz," with "a unifying preoccupation with the symbolic order and its relationship to political and religious belief" (ix). Some of the discussions are timeless, for example, Maurice Godelier's fine-spun deconstruction of the age-old debate between ideas and social realities, which he pretends to "caricature outrageously" ("The Ideal in the Real": 2-38). An essay which focuses on the 1790s is Gwin A. Williams' "Druids and Democrats: Organic Intellectuals and the First Welsh Radicalism" (246-76). Close to German Romanticism is "State Formation, Nationalism and Political Culture in Nineteenth-Century Germany" (277-301). A complex and edifying "workshop" assortment. (D.V.E.)

Schwartz, Stuart B. "Patterns of Slaveholding in the Americas: New Evidence from Brazil." *AHR* 87 (1982): 55-86.

   Demonstrates that the structures of slaveholding in the
southern U.S. and Brazil were similar.

Shaw, Peter. *American Patriots and the Rituals of Revolution*.
   Harvard University Press, 1981. Pp. 279. $17.50.

   Rev. by Joseph Conforti in *NEQ* 55 (1982): 125-28. The
   British were unable to understand the causes of revolution
   because they were "the victim of Oedipal forces.... Needless
   to say, such a Freudian view radically reduces the significance
   of ... political-constitutional issues" in favor of "coming-
   of-age rituals."

Shelton, Cynthia. "Labor and Capital in the Early Period of
   Manufacturing: The Failure of John Nicholson's Manufacturing
   Complex: 1793-1797." *PMHB* 106 (1982): 341-63.

   An interesting contribution to the study "of how the early
   industrial factory system changed" and "why it developed from
   the quite different form of urban handicraft production."
   (R.A.B.)

Staum, Martin S. *Cabanis: Enlightenment and Medical Philosophy
   in the French Revolution*. Princeton University Press, 1980.
   Pp. xii+430. $27.50.

   Rev. by Thomas E. Kaiser in *JMH* 54 (1982): 121-23, who
   finds that Staum has written a "finely-crafted monograph"
   on this "key figure in the Ideologue circle" who sought to
   preserve continuity between the heritage of the *philosophes*
   and the intellectual ferment of the French Revolution.

Stone, Bailey. *The Parlement of Paris, 1774-1789*. University
   of North Carolina Press, 1981. Pp. x+227. $19.00.

   Rev. by William Doyle in *JMH* 54 (1982): 375-76, as "a
   short, confused essay, prosaic and undistinguished in style,
   and methodologically misconceived."

Stych, F.S. "[J.C. Eustace:] An Anglo-Irish Traveller in
   Tuscany during the Napoleonic Wars." *RLMC* 34 (1981): 271-85.

Tackett, Timothy. "The West in France in 1789: The Religious
   Factor in the Origins of the Counter-revolution." *JMH* 54
   (1982): 715-45.

   Socio-economic issues were reinforced by religious attitudes
   in the area of France where rural opposition to the revolution began earliest and most violently. Ultimately this
   opposition led to the uprising to which the Revolutionary
   regime responded with the Reign of Terror. (R.A.B.)

Tomes, Nancy. "The Domesticated Madman: Changing Concepts of Insanity at the Pennsylvania Hospital, 1780-1830." *PMHB* 106 (1982): 271-86.

An introduction for and publication of excerpts from *Cases of Several Lunatics in The Pennsylvania Hospital, the Causes There Of in Many Cases,* a short memorandum book compiled by Samuel Coates, a lay manager of the hospital. "The character of madness in late eighteenth and early nineteenth century Philadelphia is nowhere better captured." (R.A.B.)

Tsigakon, Fami-Maria. *The Rediscovery of Greece: Travellers and Painters of the Romantic Era.* London and New York: Thames and Hudson, 1981.

On a show at the Fine Art Society.

Twohig, Dorothy, ed. *The Journal of the Proceedings of the President, 1793-1797.* In *The Papers of George Washington.* W.W. Abbot, ed. University of Virginia Press, 1981. Pp. xvii+ 393. $25.00.

Rev. by Kenneth R. Bowling in *PMHB* 106 (1982): 434-35.

Vaughan, William. *German Romanticism and English Art.* Yale University Press, 1982. $50.00; $16.95 paper.

First edition listed in *RMB* for 1979, pp. 46-47.

Walker, Geoffrey J. *Spanish Politics and Imperial Trade, 1700-1789.* Indiana University Press, 1979. Pp. xviii+297. $17.50.

Rev. by Michael Morineau in *JMH* 54 (1982): 606-09.

Weissbach, Lee Shai. "Artisanal Responses to Artistic Decline: The Cabinetmakers of Paris in the Era of Industrialization." *JSH* 16:ii (Winter 1982): 67-77.

"The skilled workers in cabinetmaking maintained an image of themselves as artists throughout the 19th century, and continued to be concerned with issues of artistry and fine craftsmanship even as they became increasingly involved with more practical and pressing proletarian issues."

Wessell, Leonard P. *Karl Marx, Romantic Irony, and the Proletariat: The Mythopoetic Origins of Marxism.* Louisiana State University Press, 1979. Pp. 267. $20.00.

Rev. by Hayden White in *SiR* 21:1 (Spring 1982): 105-07.

Whitcomb, Edward A. *Napoleon's Diplomatic Service*. Duke University Press, 1979. Pp. xiii+218. $16.25.

Rev. by Jeremy Black in *DuJ*, n.s. 44 (1982): 97-98.

Williams, C.I.M. "Lusieri's Surviving Works." *BM* 124 (Aug. 1982): 492-96; 7 illus.

Watercolors by an artist popular with English travellers in Italy and Greece before the Revolutionary and Napoleonic wars.

Wills, Antoinette. *Crime and Punishment in Revolutionary Paris*. (Contributions in Legal Studies, 15.) Westport, Ct.: Greenwood Press, 1981. Pp. xxi+227. $32.50.

Rev. by Colin Lucas in *JMH* 54 (1982): 790-92, as "a useful rapid summary for students"; by Julius R. Ruff in *AHR* 87 (1982): 188.

Wilson, Daniel J. *Arthur O. Lovejoy and the Quest for Intelligibility*. University of North Carolina Press, 1980. Pp. xviii+248. $18.00.

Rev. by James Gutman in *QQ* 89 (1982): 215-17.

See also Jones ("English 2. Environment"); Pieske ("English 4. Byron").

Reviews of books previously listed:

BILLINGTON, James H., *Fire in the Minds of Men: Origins of the Revolutionary Faith* (see *RMB* for 1981, p. 5), rev. by James A. Leith in *QQ* (1982): 439-42; CLAY, Jean, *Le Romantisme* (see *RMB* for 1981, p. 6), **rev. by** F. Huser in *L'Observateur*, Feb. 2, 1981; DIEFENDORF, Jeffrey M., *Businessmen and Politics in the Rhineland, 1789-1834* (see *RMB* for 1981, p. 261), rev. by David F. Crew in *JMH* 54 (1982): 159-61, finding an important understanding "of the turning point at which German history failed to turn"; DOYLE, William, *Origins of the French Revolution* (see *RMB* for 1981, p. 7), rev. by Paul H. Beik in *AHR* 87 (1982): 187-88; by J.F. Bosher in *JMH* 54 (1982): 582-84; FURET, François, *Interpreting the French Revolution* (see *RMB* for 1981, p. 8), rev. by Paul H. Beik in *AHR* 87 (1982): 1103-04; HARRISON, J.F.C., *The Second Coming: Popular Millenarianism 1780-1850* (see *RMB* for 1979, pp. 7-8), rev. by Stuart Mews in *JMH* 54 (1982): 350-53, as a "major contribution"; HASKELL, Francis, and Nicholas Penny, *Taste and the Antique: The Lure of Classical Sculpture, 1500-1900* (see *RMB* for 1981, p. 10), rev. by H.W. Janson in *NYRB*,

June 11, 1981, pp. 42-43; by Jennifer Montague ("Fallen
Idols") in *Art History* 5 (1982): 117-19; LASLETT, Peter,
et al., *Bastardy and Its Comparative History* (see *RMB* for
1981, p. 12), rev. by Paul Slack in *EHR* 97 (1982): 143-44;
RYKWERT, Joseph, *The First Moderns: The Architects of the
Eighteenth Century* (see *RMB* for 1981, p. 16), rev. by Adrian
Von Buttlar in *BM* 124 (Jan. 1982): 39-40; SCHMIDGALL, Gary,
Literature as Opera (see *ELN* 16, Supp., 24), rev. by John
Warrack in *M&L* 61 (1980): 186-88; SEWELL, William H., Jr.,
Work and Revolution in France (see *RMB* for 1981, p. 17),
rev. by Lynn Hollen Lees in *JIH* 13 (1982-83): 551-52; SWEET,
Paul R., *Wilhelm von Humboldt: A Biography*, vol. II (see
RMB for 1979, p. 13, for vol. I), rev. by Peter Hans Reill
in *JMH* 54 (1982): 157-59; TATAR, Maria M., *Spellbound: Studies
on Mesmerism and Literature* (see *ELN* 17, Supp., p. 25), rev.
by Volker Hoffmann in *Germanistik* 22 (1981): 360-61; by
Anthony J. Niesz in *Monatshefte* 74 (1982): 83; WICKWIRE,
Franklin and Mary, *Cornwallis: The Imperial Years* (see *RMB*
for 1981, p. 53), rev. by Sylvia R. Frey in *ECS* 16 (1982):
224-28, as "a full scholarly discussion," sometimes over-
sympathetic, but telling us "just about everything we would
want to know about Cornwallis"; WIEDMANN, August, *Romantic
Roots in Modern Art: Romanticism and Expressionism: A Study
in Comparative Aesthetics* (see *RMB* for 1980, p. 14), rev. by
Morse Peckham in *SiR* 21 (1982): 259-60, as "a fairly typical
example ... of contemporary mechanical scholarship, ...
humanistic technology."

Composite review:

Rosovsky, Nitza. "Pilgrims to the Holy Land." *NR*, Dec. 13,
1982, pp. 37-38.

Reviewing Neil Asher Silberman, *Digging for God and Country:
Exploration, Archeology, and the Secret Struggle for the Holy
Land, 1799-1917* (New York: Knopf, 1982; pp. 228; $16.95),
along with Louis Vaczek and Gail Buckland, *Travelers in
Ancient Lands: A Portrait of the Middle East, 1839-1919*
(Boston: New York Graphic Society, 1981; pp. 202; $35), and
Robert Blake, *Disraeli's Grand Tour: Benjamin Disraeli and
the Holy Land, 1830-31* (Oxford University Press, 1981; pp.
141; $14.95).

3. CRITICISM

Aarsleff, Hans. *From Locke to Saussure: Essays on the Study of Language and Intellectual History.* University of Minnesota Press, 1982. Pp. viii+422. $29.50; $12.95 paper.

A valuable shelf companion in these linguistic days. The fifteen great names in the fourteen historical essays gathered here have Wordsworth in the center, with Wilkins, Locke, Leibniz, and Condillac among the precursors and Balzac, Taine, and Saussure among the successors. (For our review of the Wordsworth essay, see *RMB* for 1980, p. 133.)
   Other frequent names (see the well-organized index) include: Adam, Bacon, Boehme, Breal, Chomsky, Coleridge (on ten pages), Cousin, Descartes, Destutt de Tracy, Diderot, Du Marsais, Herder, Humboldt, Maupertuis, Rousseau, Sprat, Stewart. (D.V.E.)

Alpers, Paul. "What Is Pastoral?" *CritI* 8 (1982): 437-60.

An interesting inquiry, making use of Kenneth Burke's concept of the "representative anecdote." One of the examples of non-classical pastoral cited is *The Prelude*, book 8, in which Wordsworth "rewrites" Spenser's May eclogue.

Andrew, Dudley. "Interpretation, the Spirit in the Body." *BMWMLA* 15 (1982): 57-70.

With general comments on Romanticism.

Armstrong, Nancy. "The Rise of Feminine Authority in the Novel." *Novel: A Forum on Fiction* 15 (1982): 127-45.

Bloom, Harold. *Agon: Towards a Theory of Revisionism.* Oxford University Press, 1982. Pp. xiv+336. $19.95.

Rev. by Harold Bloom himself in *YR* (see below); by William Freedman in *CP* 15,ii (1982): 89-93; by David O'Hara in *Criticism* 24 (1982): 297-300.
   There is no index; one has to read and misread straight through this "culmination" of Bloom's "highly personal" revisions. Or dip for riches: "If I were reading [Freud's] essay ... as I have learned to read Romantic poems, I would be on the watch for a blocking-agent in the poetic ego, a shadow that Blake called the Spectre and Shelley a daemon or Alastor.... But if we take Freud as Sublime poet rather than empirical reasoner, if we see him as the peer of Milton rather than of Hume ... then we can speculate rather precisely about the origins of the psychoanalytical drive ..." (114-15).

The jacket has a photograph by Jeanne Bloom of Harold pro-
jecting his introjection. (D.V.E.)

Bloom, Harold. *The Breaking of the Vessels*. (The Wellek Library
Lectures.) University of Chicago Press, 1982. Pp. xiii+107.
$10.00.

Rev. by Dan O'Hara in *JAAC* 41 (1982-83): 99-101, who wonders
if we can "really afford this silly vision of literary creation any longer." O'Hara's review also raises the question
whether we really need another silly response to Bloom's
demanding vision. (R.A.B.)

About wrestling and a wrestling bout, Harold Bloom's most recent book returns again to the scene of his instruction, where,
with characteristic energy and wit, he mounts another defense
of his well-known revisionary ratios. Bloom both supplies
the play-by-play for the great engagements of "wrestling
Waldo," "wrestling Sigmund," and wrestling Jacob and stages
his own ferocious struggles with renowned past champions.
The ostensible occasion of this brief collection of essays
was the inauguration of the series of Wellek Library Lectures
at the University of California at Irvine, but its real occasion is the peculiar celebrity of Harold Bloom, who, having
strenuously endeavored (and with estimable success) to invent
a tradition that would name him as its rightful heir, has
designed for himself the necessity of justifying his invention and his election in one death-defying grapple after
another. On this occasion we are treated to the familiar
themes, considerably distilled: temporality, the family
romance, power, sacrifice, and will. Bloom revises slightly
to foreground the themes and tropes of the pneuma, transference, and, preeminently, transumption. The arguments are made
as convincingly here as they have been made elsewhere. The
concluding reading of the image or trope of the blank in
its transumptive passage from Milton to Stevens under the
eye of Emerson is a fine demonstration of Bloom's method
and his gifts. (Jerome Christensen)

Bloom, Harold. "The Criticism of Our Climate." *YR* 72 (1982):
116-20.

Reviewing his own works, *Agon* and *The Breaking of the
Vessels* (see preceding items), Bloom exemplifies the normative apothegm with which he concludes: "It is not required
of you that you complete the work, but neither are you free
to desist from it."

Boly, John. "Auden as Literary Evolutionist: Wordsworth's Dream
and the Fate of Romanticism." *Diacritics* 12,i (Spring 1982):
65-74.

Boly recasts Auden's critique of Romanticism in *The Enchafed Flood* in structuralist terminology. He analyzes Auden's analysis of the "romantic lexicon," "metagrammar," and "code." Because the last two were in conflict (in Boly's view of Auden's view), Romanticism was destined to fail; however, it is redeemed because it knew it would, as Wordsworth's dream in *Prelude* V reveals. A difficult but not unrewarding essay, if only because it leads us to read or re-read Auden. (R.A.H.)

Bromwich, David. "Wordsworth, Frost, Stevens, and the Poetic Vocation." *SiR* 21 (1982): 87–100.

Compares "Resolution and Independence" with Frost's "Two Tramps in Mud Time" and Stevens's "The Course of a Particular." The difference between Wordsworth and his modern successors "lies not so much in 'the love of man' as in his simple copresence with another figure, radically unassimilable to himself, and the troubling possibilities that this brings." (M.T.S.)

Cardinal, Roger. *Figures of Reality: A Perspective on the Poetic Imagination.* New York: Barnes and Noble, 1981. Pp. 245. $23.50.

Rev. by Hazard Adams in *ELN* 20 (1982): 106–08; by Germaine Brée in *WHR* 36 (1982): 186–87.

Cayton, Mary K. "'Sympathy's Electric Chain' and the American Democracy: Emerson's First Vocational Crisis." *NEQ* 55 (1982): 3–24.

Centre du Romantisme anglais. *Romantisme anglais et Eros.* Préface de Ch. La Cassagnère. (Publications de la Faculté des Lettres de Clermont, II.) Clermont-Ferrand: Association des Publications des Lettres et Sciences Humaines de Clermont-Ferrand, 1982. Pp. 200. Fr. 80.00.

Not seen.

Droixhe, Daniel, ed. *Livres et lumières au pays de Liège (1730–1830).* Liège: Desoer, 1980. Pp. 401.

Rev. by Raymond Birn in *JMH* 54 (1982): 789–90. Walloon enlightenment.

Elliott, Emory. *Revolutionary Writers: Literature and Authority in the New Republic, 1725–1810.* Oxford University Press, 1982. Pp. x+324. $19.95.

Rev. by Ronald Bosco in *NEQ* 55 (1982): 622-25; by Michael Kammen in *PMHB* 106 (1982): 571-73.

Elliott, Robert C. *The Literary Persona*. University of Chicago Press, 1982. Pp. xiv+174. $17.00.

A small but very wise book on a large subject: writers' use of the first-person pronoun. Elliott examines the thinking of the interpreters of poetry "in our formally self-conscious age" who have found useful--or rejected--the term *persona* "as a way of coming to terms with the paradoxes" of relation between the poetic "I" and the empirical "I." The paradoxes remain, but even in physical science "such paradoxes afford their own kind of light." How *can* we know the dancer from the dance?

Even for those of us who have learned to accept the coexistence of our Spectres, that third of the book devoted to Swift's "I" and "Swift's Satire" affords a delightful course in critical insight, with Elliott pointing out--and noticing how Swift himself pointed out--"the rules of the game." Bob Elliott has died, young; his "I" shines eternally in these printed essays. (D.V.E.)

Fehrman, Carl. *Poetic Creation: Inspiration or Craft*. Trans. Karin Petherick. University of Minnesota Press, 1980. Pp. vii+229. $20.00.

Rev. by Don Callen in *JAAC* 40 (1981-82): 342-43.
Chapter 2 on the Italian *improvisatori* and later Romantic interest in them, and chapter 3 on Coleridge and *Kubla Khan*, add to the appeal of this valuable study. (T.L.A.)

Fischer, Michael. "Deconstruction: The Revolt against Gentility." *Democracy* 1 (Oct. 1981): 77-86.

A sober send-up of the liberationist rhetoric of Bloom, Hartman, and Derrida. (D.V.E.)

Gans, Eric. "The Victim as Subject: The Esthetico-Ethical System of Rousseau's *Rêveries*." *SiR* 21 (1982): 3-31.

Gans begins provocatively: Rousseau invented "the most successful mechanism for self-maintenance in the center of the human universe" since that of Jesus. Both exploited the central position of the victim, revising the Old Testament tradition of turning defeat into a sign of divine election. Gans opposes those denunciators and deconstructors, such as Derrida and De Man, who omit the anthropological perspective and thus undervalue the power of Rousseau's total system.

"Both absolutely passive ... and absolutely active,"
Rousseau became the "evangelist of his own martyrdom." In
an inimitable way, Rousseau combined "Greek esthetic with
Judaeo-Christian moral discourse" and thus ushered in Romanticism and modern history. After some close readings and
some brilliant insights, Gans defaces his monumental efforts
with a screeching anticlimax: acknowledging that Rousseau
and Jesus would probably not be pleased with his conclusion,
he asserts that our consumer society's "*a priori* egalitarian-
ism and *a posteriori* differentiation make it arguably the
most moral society man can produce." Gans does not argue
this allegedly arguable proposition, but does add a conclusion even more provocative than the opening: each individual
self in a consumer society compensates for its "victimary
role," as did Rousseau, by "its assumption of the active
centrality of the Subject of representation." (M.T.S.)

Gura, Philip. *The Wisdom of Words: Language, Theology, and
Literature in the New England Renaissance*. Middletown, Ct.:
Wesleyan University Press, 1981. Pp. x+201. $17.50.

    Rev. by Hilary Schor in *NEQ* 55 (1982): 132-34.

Halperin, David M. *Before Pastoral: Theocritus and the Ancient
Tradition of Bucolic Poetry*. Yale University Press, 1982.
Pp. 304. $26.00.

    Argues that the "pastoral genre" is a modern phenomenon,
    clearly distinct from the "bucolic poetry" of Theocritus.
    Correction of a long-standing error in historical criticism.

Hammond, Alexander. "On Poe Biography." *ESQ* 28 (1982): 197-211.

    Discussing the work of Mankowitz (1978), Miller (1977,
    1979), Quinn (1970), Symons (1978), Thomas (1978), and
    Thompson (1979).

Hassler, Donald M. *Comic Tones in Science Fiction: The Art
of Compromise with Nature*. Westport, Ct.: Greenwood Press,
1982. Pp. xiv+143. $25.00.

    Explores "a kinship between modern science fiction and the
    literature of the Enlightenment, a kinship derived from the
    common experience of living in a period of immense and
    frightening change."
    Hassler's critical acquaintance with the Romantics, espe-
    cially Wordsworth--and with Erasmus Darwin--helps a lot.
    (D.V.E.)

Hayashi, Tetsuro. *The Theory of English Lexicography 1530-1791.*
(Amsterdam Studies in the Theory and History of Linguistic
Science, Series III: Studies in the History of Linguistics,
18.) Amsterdam: John Benjamin B.V., 1978. Pp. xii+168.
Hfl. 45.00.

Rev. favorably by Doreen M.E. Gillam in *ES* 32 (1982):
165-67, and by Hans Kasemann in *Anglia* 100 (1982): 160-62.
Not seen.

Irwin, John T. *American Hieroglyphics: The Symbol of the
Egyptian Hieroglyphics in the American Renaissance.* Yale
University Press, 1980.

Irwin is aware of the Romantics' interest in hieroglyphics
and makes a number of references to Shelley, Coleridge, and
Wordsworth.

Knapp, Bettina L. *The Prometheus Syndrome.* Troy, N.Y.: Whitson,
1979. Pp. 286. $15.00.

Rev. by M. Byron Raizis in *MLJ* 66 (1982): 74-75.

Kuhns, Richard. "The Beautiful and the Sublime." *NLH* 13 (1982):
287-307.

Lemay, J.A. Leo, and Paul M. Zall, eds. *The Autobiography of
Benjamin Franklin: A Genetic Text.* University of Tennessee
Press, 1981. Pp. lxiv+288. $28.00.

Rev. by Peter Davison in *Library* 4 (1982): 200-01.

Le Tellier, Robert Ignatius. *Kindred Spirits: Interrelations
and Affinities between the Romantic Novels of England and
Germany (1790-1820).* (SSEL, Romantic Reassessment, 33:3.)
University of Salzburg, Austria, 1982. Pp. v+423. $12.50.

Subtitle: "with special reference to the work of Carl
Grosse (1768-1847) forgotten Gothic Novelist and Theorist
of the Sublime."
A heavily documented work, written in a somewhat deliberate
"dissertation" manner, with two declared purposes. Le Tellier
points to a series of affinities evident in the English
Gothic novel and German *Schauerroman*, under such general
headings as "character" and "setting," the level of his
commentary veering between intimations of "archetypal"
resemblance and a concern for detail which borders on plot-
telling. The book also attempts to revive the reputation of
Carl Grosse, whose *Der Genius* (1791-95)--re-named *Horrid
Mysteries* on its second appearance in English--Le Tellier

considers an important milestone, thematically and technically, in the development of the Romantic novel. Other individual authors treated are more predictable: Radcliffe,
M.G. Lewis, and Maturin as mainstream English Gothicists;
Tieck, Jean Paul, and Eichendorff as comparable Germans.
Le Tellier's more general observations--on the cataclysmic
shock of the French Revolution, its manifestation in the
lapsed and confusing world presented by the Gothic novelists,
and the increasing structural intricacy of the narratives
dealt with--are unlikely to startle specialists in the
field. Readers curious to know if Austen and Peacock were
drawn to anything other than the title of *Horrid Mysteries*
will remain curious. (P.D.G.)

Lokke, Kari Elise. "The Role of Sublimity in the Development
of Modern Aesthetics." *JAAC* 40 (1981-82): 421-29.

"There is ... a direct chain of influence from Burke's
treatise, by way of Kant and Schiller and the Schlegal
brothers, through Mme. de Stael to the French Symbolists."
By "tracing this chain," Lokke argues that "nineteenth-
century standards of poetic beauty are a transformation
of the late eighteenth-century concept of sublimity."
(R.A.B.)

McGann, Jerome J. "Romanticism and Its Ideologies." *SiR* 21
(1982): 573-99.

Culled from a forthcoming book, recants a previous one.
Attempting to "replace an Idealist and romantic [critical
method] with a materialist and historical one," McGann
deconstructs the idea of "poetic development" (along with
eternal truths and transcendental categories) as promulgated
by many critics, including McGann himself in *Fiery Dust*
("most to be deplored" there). Fine. One can certainly agree
that "the scholarship and criticism of romanticism and its
works are dominated by a Romantic Ideology, by an uncritical
absorption in romanticism's own self-representations," but
reading on, one finds that McGann simply sets up a rival
system of mystification. When he writes that "the literary
criticism of romantic works will justify itself, therefore,
when it is seen to have followed the example of the poetry
itself," what else is he doing but privileging his own
implicit greater Truth, after demolishing the very notion
of doing so? He means that the Romantic poets confronted
contradictions, unmasked illusions, and therefore teetered
on the "edge of defenselessness," and calls on critics to
take the same painful chances. One must admire him for
courage, but infinite regress of this sort (in which I am

now lamentably engaging) is the ratio which Blake (the only
one of the big six absent from this essay) warns us against.
The formula is too blatant in this new Ideology; much better
are McGann's specifics of the historical method applied to
Wordsworth and Byron. (M.T.S.)

Macpherson, Jay. *The Spirit of Solitude: Conventions and
Continuities in Late Romance.* Yale University Press, 1982.
Pp. xv+349. $24.50.

Mandelkow, Robert, and Klaus Heitman, eds. *Europäische
Romantik* I & II. 2 vols. (Neues Handbuch der Literaturwissenschaft, Band 14 & 15.) Wiesbaden: Athenaion, 1982.

Rev. by Alain Montandon in *Romantisme* 38 (1982): 155-56.

Miller, D.A. *Narrative and Its Discontents: Problems of Closure
in the Traditional Novel.* Princeton University Press, 1981.
Pp. xv+300. $20.00.

This is a sophisticated, modern treatment of the old
problem that something has to happen in a novel, but it
cannot happen too soon or there would not be any novel.
Miller begins by questioning Sartre's "Une chose commence
pour finir," and argues "not that novels do not 'build'
toward closure, but that they are never fully or finally
governed by it" (xiv). He supports this argument by detailed
and sensitive readings of Austen, George Eliot, and Stendhal,
using Freudian concepts of displacement and repression, and
a vocabulary of "narratability," "closural nomination,"
and "pseudoclosures." He sees Austen as welcoming a closure
of conversion because for her narratability is "the development of everything most unwelcome"--events that her moral
code believed really ought not to have happened; Eliot as
managing ambiguous compromises; Stendhal as resisting
closure by constant reopenings of narratability. This
survey Miller sees as a triangulation of the traditional
novel: corners which he calls "normal," "neurotic," and
"perverse" or "conservative," "liberal," and "libertarian."
The book profits from a readable, modest style--full of
questions, easy figures, and engaging recognition that to
make its points it may be overstating or speculating
dubiously--capped by an awareness that there is no certainty
"that a case for the constitutive unrest of narrative is
ultimately any less closural than the narrative closure it
deconstructs" (282). (J.E.J.)

Morris, Wesley. *Friday's Footprint: Structuralism and the
Articulated Text.* Ohio State University Press, 1979. Pp.
xix+253.

Rev. by Marshall Grossman in *Clio* 11 (1981–82): 91–93.
Not seen. Includes a reading of *Sartor Resartus*.

Pike, Burton. *The Image of the City in Modern Literature*.
Princeton University Press, 1981. Pp. xv+168. $15.00.

Rev. by Blanche Gelfant in *AL* 54:3 (Oct. 1982): 460–61.
(Includes Wordsworth.)

Pocock, Douglas C.D., ed. *Humanistic Geography and Literature:
Essays on the Experience of Place*. New York: Barnes &
Noble, 1981. Pp. 224. $27.00.

Rev. by A. Norman Jeffares in *WHR* 36 (1982): 176–78.
Contains Peter Newby's essay "Literature and the Fashion-
ing of Tourist Taste," which discusses Wordsworth.
Not seen.

Quinby, Lee. "Thomas Jefferson: The Virtue of Aesthetics and
the Aesthetics of Virtue." *AHR* 87 (1982): 337–56.

"Rather than a morality ruled by either reason or science,
Jefferson adumbrated what I call an aesthetics of virtue,
a fusion of art and morals, whereby reflective beings are
capable of discerning the path to virtue through aesthetic
experience."

Raizis, M. Byron. *From Caucasus to Pittsburgh: The Prometheus
Theme in British and American Poetry*. Athens: "Gnosis"
Publishing Co., [1982]. Pp. xvi+290.

Originally a 1966 Ph.D. thesis now rewritten and "aug-
mented by almost fifty per cent," this book with index,
bibliography, and summaries of 70 British and American poems
on Prometheus makes a useful reference tool. More descriptive than analytical, it initially distinguishes among the
Greek sources of the Prometheus myth (Hesiod, Aeschylus,
Apollonius, "Apollodorus," Lucian). Between the Greeks
and Byron and Shelley, the "Major Exponents" of the myth
(pp. 76–96: they were "the first English poets to fully
understand the dynamics and potentialities of the Promethean
legend"), Raizis briefly surveys Promethean references by
the Roman writers (pp. 24–31), the English philosophers
(pp. 32–35), and English poets, Chaucer to Thomas Medwin
(pp. 36–52), the latter's translation of *Prometheus Bound*
published in 1832. Another short chapter, on "The Comic
and Satiric Vein" (pp. 62–75), introduces us to the likes
of George Colman's "Fire; or the Sun-Poker" (1816), Joseph
Lloyd Brereton's *Prometheus Britannicus, or John Bull and
the rural police* (1840), and (my favorite) the American

William Pitt Palmer's poem *The Promethean Flame* (1868),
which was read at the annual dinner in New York City of
The National Board of Fire Underwriters. The Byron-Shelley
chapter offers nothing new but surveys some recent secondary
criticism and reminds us that little serious or extended
English poetry on Prometheus existed before the Romantic
age (the first Greek text of *Prometheus Bound* was not published in England until 1663; the first English translation,
by Thomas Morell, not until 1773). In subsequent chapters,
we encounter summaries of such poems as Horace Smith's "The
Shriek of Prometheus" (1825) and Hartley Coleridge's "Prometheus, a Fragment" (begun 1820). The remainder of the book
concerns Prometheus poems written by later English and by
American writers. The "Pittsburgh" of the book's title comes
from Lawrence Lee's three-act drama *Prometheus in Pittsburgh*
(1952). It should be added that with no or little reference
to the Prometheus legend in the other arts or even in prose
fiction (no *Frankenstein* here), this book does not pretend
to study the cultural or even the literary development of
the myth. (C.E.R.)

Renascence 34:4 (1982): 197-320. "The Aesthetic Theory of
Jacques Maritain."

Special issue.

Robinson, David M. "Margaret Fuller and the Transcendentalist
Ethos: *Woman in the Nineteenth Century*." *PMLA* 97 (1982):
83-98.

Rogers, Katherine M. *Feminism in Eighteenth-Century England*.
University of Illinois Press, 1982. Pp. 291. $18.95.

Begins by situating eighteenth-century women historically
and argues that radical changes toward marriage fostered
a new self-awareness. Using a wide range of literary texts
Rogers then illustrates how questioning and the application
of rationalist principles to the realities of women's lives
positively affected their sense of self. (Hilda L. Smith
investigates the relationship between rationalist ideas and
the lives of earlier women in *Reason's Disciples: Seventeenth-
Century English Feminists*. University of Illinois Press,
1982.) Rogers finds that sentimental fiction, with its
primacy on feeling, similarly generated an improved self-
image. She distinguishes between moderate feminists, who
viewed subordination as necessary to law and order and
turned demands for propriety-related virtues into sources
of pride, and radicals, who challenged discriminatory ideas

about sexual difference, approved of sexual passion, and
advocated social and legal change.

Rogers' examples from numerous major and minor eighteenth-
century women authors highlight what has been till now an
unjustly neglected part of literary history; her exposé
of the deleterious influence of pious conventions and concepts such as chastity should help re-visions of this
literature. It should, however, be noted that a woman's
right to autonomy had been argued for and established by
precedent long before John Locke.

A biographical appendix of 110 writers suggests the
literary range and richness of eighteenth-century female
authorship. (M.F.)

Sadowska-Guillon, Irène. "Mazeppa, héros romantique: le thème
dans les littératures anglais, française, polonaise, et
russe." *LR* 36 (1982): 125-47, 235-49, 317-41.

Babinsky's word was and is last. (T.L.A.)

Schneider, Richard J. "Humanizing Henry David Thoreau." *ESQ*
27 (1981): 57-71.

Shaffer, E.S. "Laocoön and the Languages of the Arts." Editor's
note, pp. xi-xxiii, in *Comparative Criticism: A Yearbook*,
vol. 4. Cambridge University Press, 1982.

Shusterman, Richard. "Aesthetic Blindness to Textual Visuality."
JAAC 41 (1982-83): 87-96.

Among the reasons for the neglect in modern aesthetics "of
the visual or graphic in the literary text," Shusterman cites
attacks by Shelley and Hegel "on literary visuality." For
Shelley and Hegel, literature's superiority "to other art
forms" is "based on the alleged invisible transparency and
spiritual puity of its medium, language, which is claimed to
relate to thought alone." When Shelley incorporates "sound
into the essence of poetry," however, he corrupts this pure
relationship. (R.A.B.)

Smith, Gayle L. "Style and Vision in Emerson's 'Experience.'"
ESQ 27 (1981): 85-95.

Sötér, István, and Irene Neupokoyeva, eds. *European Romanticism*.
Trans. E. Rona. Budapest: Akadémia Kiadó, 1977. Pp. 541.
$34.00.

Not seen. A review by Philip N. Gilbertson in *CRCL* 9 (1982):
282-83 calls the volume "significant," but does not indicate

if the translation only is current; see also *RMB* for 1981,
p. 270. (T.L.A.)

Steinbrink, Jeffrey. "The Past as 'Cheerful Apologue': Emerson
on the Proper Uses of History." *ESQ* 27 (1981): 207-21.

Thelander, Dorothy R. "Mother Goose and Her Goslings: The
France of Louis XIV as Seen through the Fairy Tale." *JMH*
54 (1982): 467-96.

An interesting catalogue. (T.L.A.)

Thomas, Brook. "*The House of Seven Gables*: Reading the Romance
of America." *PMLA* 97 (1982): 195-211.

Thomas, D.M. *The Bronze Horseman: Selected Poems of Alexander
Pushkin*. New York: Viking, 1982. Pp. 261. $15.95.

Review article by John Bayley in *NYRB*, Feb. 3, 1983, pp.
35-38, goes sensitively into the question of the transmuta-
tions of translations.

Toliver, Harold. *The Past the Poets Make*. Harvard University
Press, 1981.

Rev. favorably by Joseph Wittreich in *JEGP* 81 (1982):
429-51.

Townsend, Dabney. "Shaftesbury's Aesthetic Theory." *JAAC* 41
(1982): 205-13.

Vajda, György, ed. *Le Tournant du Siècle des Lumières 1760-
1820. Les genres en vers des Lumières au Romantisme*. (Histoire
comparée des Littératures de Langues européennes.) Budapest:
Akadémiai Kiadó, 1982. Pp. 684. $39.50.

Relevant contents: Henry H.H. Remak, "Avant-propos";
György Vajda, "Preface"; István Sötér, "Phénomènes poétiques
à la fin du XVIIIe et à l'aube du XIXe siècle"; Domokos
Kosáry, "Un demi-siècle d'histoire. Arrière-plan historique
de la poésie entre les Lumières et le Romantisme"; Miklós
J. Szenczi, "La vision du monde des poètes"; György Vajda,
"La dimension esthétique de la poésie"; László Sziklay, "Les
genres en vers dans les littératures de langues européennes
entre les Lumières et le Romantisme"; Lajos Csetri, "Théories
de la langue entre les Lumières et le Romantisme"; Robert
Auty, "Métrique"; Mihály Szegedy-Maszak, "La poésie anglaise";
László Ferenczi, "Poésie en France"; Mária Kajtár, "Poésie
de langue allemande"; Péter Sárközy, "Poésie italienne";

David Thatcher Gies, "Evolution/révolution dans la poésie espagnole"; György M. Vajda, "La découverte d'une époque"; "Index des noms"; "Index des titres."
Numerous articles deal with other literatures.

Van Anglen, Kevin P. "A Paradise Regained: Thoreau's *Wild Apples* and the Myth of the American Adam." *ESQ* 27 (1981): 28-39.

Waddington, Patrick. *Turgenev and England*. New York University Press, 1981. Pp. x+382.

> Rev. by Harold Orel in *CL* 34 (1982): 283-86.
> Carlyle figures prominently.

Watson, George. "'La Nouvelle Critique': Portrait of a Dinosaur." *SR* 90 (1982): 541-54.

> A notable attack--a self-styled funeral-oration welcoming the demise of French criticism of the 1960s and 1970s, as a sterile and ultimately trivial form of "word-spinning scholasticism." Reminds me of Henry James's comment on "the bottomless frivolity of the French." (B.C.H.)

Will, Frederic. "The Epigram or Lapidary Engravings." *AR* 40 (1982): 153-70.

> An interesting survey of the epigram as a form from classical times on, with plenty of quotations and some attention to the Romantics. (B.C.H.)

Woodward, Anthony. "Romanticism, Faust, and George Santayana." *ESA* 25 (1982): 1-10.

Ziff, Larzer. *The Declaration of Cultural Independence in America*. New York: Viking, 1981. Pp. xxv+333. $20.00.

> Rev. by M.E. Korey in *PMHB* 106 (1982): 143-45.

See also Swialecka ("English 4. Coleridge").

Reviews of books previously listed:

AGULHON, Maurice, *Marianne au combat: l'imagerie et la symbolique républicaine de 1789 à 1880* (see *RMB* for 1981, p. 21), rev. by Linda Nochlin in *Oxford Art Journal* 4 (1981): 62-64; BLOOM, Harold, *Poetry and Repression* (see *ELN* 15, Supp., 18), rev. by Richard Machin in *BJA* 22 (1982): 377-78; CULLER, Jonathan, *The Pursuit of Signs: Semiotics,*

Literature, Deconstruction (see *RMB* for 1981, p. 23), rev.
by Mas'd Zavarzadeh in *JAAC* 40 (1981-82): 329-33; ENGELL,
James, *The Creative Imagination: Enlightenment to Romanticism*
(see *RMB* for 1981, pp. 23-24), rev. in *NYRB*, Nov. 18, 1982,
pp. 71-73, with authority, by W. Jackson Bate, as an "important book ... concerned with an important subject, which it
handles with authority, learning, and originality"; by Robert
Beum in *SR* 90 (1982): xxxix-xli; by Ralph Cohen in *Criticism*
24 (1982): 174-80; by Denise Degrois in *EA* 35 (1982): 473-74;
by Lilian R. Furst, enthusiastically, in *JEGP* 81 (1982): 268-
70; by Carl B. Hausman (mixed) in *JAAC* 40 (1981-82): 437-39;
by Zachary Leader in *English* 31 (1982): 252-57; by Thomas
McFarland in *KSJ* 31 (1982): 198-202; by Alex Page in *TWC* 13
(1982): 150-51; by R. Quintana in *MLR* 77 (1982): 688-89;
by Frederick W. Shilstone in *SHR* 16 (1982): 362-63; by L.J.
Swingle (mixed) in *MLQ* 43 (1982): 89-97 (this latter really
an essay); by Hoyt Trowbridge in *MP* 80 (1982): 185-90, who
finds it unconvincing; FRYE, Northrop, *The Great Code: The
Bible and Literature* (see *RMB* for 1981, p. 24), rev. by
Michael Fixler in *Commentary* 74 (Aug. 1982): 76-80; by
Frank Kermode in *NYTimes Book Review*; by Francis Sparshott
in *P&L* 6 (1982): 180-89, with sharp questions about methodology; FURST, Lilian R., *The Contours of European Romanticism*
(see *RMB* for 1980, p. 19), rev. by R.A. Foakes in *RES* 33
(1982): 477-78; by Gerald Gillespie in *KRQ* 29 (1982): 218-
19; by John Jordan in *CLS* 19 (1982): 81-82; by Richard
Littlejohns in *MLR* 77 (1982): 156-57; FURST, Lilian R., ed.,
European Romanticism: Self-Definition (see *RMB* for 1980,
p. 19), rev. by R.A. Foakes in *RES* 33 (1982): 477-78;
HAGSTRUM, Jean H., *Sex and Sensibility: Ideal and Erotic
Love from Milton to Mozart* (see *RMB* for 1980, pp. 19-20),
rev. by Jeffrey C. Robinson in *ELN* 20 (1982): 63-66; by
Patricia Meyer Spacks in *ECS* 16 (1982): 177-78, emphasizing
its "power of large vision"; HARTMAN, Geoffrey, *Criticism
in the Wilderness: The Study of Literature Today* (see *RMB*
for 1980, p. 20), rev. by Sarah Lawall in *CL* 34 (1982):
177-81; LAWLER, Justus George, *Celestial Pantomime: Poetic
Structures of Transcendence* (see *RMB* for 1979, pp. 21-22),
rev. by J.E. Chamberlin in *JR* 62 (1982): 314-20; LOBB, Edward,
T.S. Eliot and the Romantic Critical Tradition (see *RMB* for
1981, pp. 26-27), rev. by Karl Kroeber, critically, in *AL*
54 (1982): 129-30; by Ruth Z. Temple in *MP* 80:3 (Feb. 1983):
329-33; RAJAN, Tilottama, *Dark Interpreter: The Discourse
of Romanticism* (see *RMB* for 1980, p. 24), rev. by Nancy M.
Goslee in *KSJ* 31 (1982): 204-06; SPENGEMANN, William, *The
Forms of Autobiography: Episodes in the History of a Literary
Genre* (see *RMB* for 1980, p. 27), rev. by Kathleen Ethel
Welch in *PQ* 61 (1982): 227-29.

Composite reviews:

Bruckmann, Patricia. "Am'rous Causes." *UTQ* 51 (1982): 298-303.

   Review of Jean H. Hagstrum, *Sex and Sensibility: Ideal and Erotic Love from Milton to Mozart*, and Robert Halsband, *The Rape of the Lock and Its Illustrations, 1714-1896* (see *RMB* for 1980, pp. 19-20 and 39).

Gunn, Janet Varner. "The *Bios* of Autobiography." *JR* 62 (1982): 192-200.

   Reviews James Olney, ed., *Autobiography: Essays Theoretical and Critical* and William C. Spengemann, *The Forms of Autobiography* (see *RMB* for 1980, p. 27).

Gura, Philip. *NEQ* 55 (1982): 448-54.

   Reviewing: Richard Bridgman, *Dark Thoreau* (University of Nebraska Press, 1982) and William Howarth, *The Book of Concord: Thoreau's Life as a Writer* (New York: Viking, 1982), Gura has much to say about Thoreau studies and Romanticism. (T.L.A.)

ENGLISH

(Compiled by Thomas L. Ashton, University of Massachusetts; Robert A. Brinkley, University of Maine at Orono; Irene H. Chayes, Kensington, Maryland; Moira Ferguson, University of Nebraska; Peter J. Garside, University College, Cardiff; Robert A. Hartley, Port Washington, New York; Bishop C. Hunt, College of Charleston; John E. Jordan, University of California, Berkeley; Charles E. Robinson, University of Delaware; Jeffrey C. Robinson, University of Colorado; Robert Michael Ryan, Rutgers University, Camden, New Jersey; Mark T. Smith, Southwest Missouri State University)

1. BIBLIOGRAPHY

Aitken, W.R., ed. *Scottish Literature in English and Scots. A Guide to Information Sources*. Detroit: Gale Research Co., 1982. Pp. xxiv+421. $40.00.

Gathers biographical information on Scottish literature in Scots and English, under the same chronological headings as the *New Cambridge Bibliography of English Literature*: Medieval-Renaissance, 1660–1800, 1800–1900, 1900–80. Also includes sections on (1) general studies of Scottish literature and (2) folk/popular literature. Romantics specialists will find entries (with brief introductions and occasional evaluations of critical items) on Hogg, Scott, Galt, Carlyle, and—an unusual national appropriation?—Byron. Articles mentioned only infrequently. Comprehensively indexed. (P.D.G.)

Engel, Wilson F., III. "Shakespeare in Edinburgh Playbills: The Theatre Royal, 1810–1851." *ThS* 20:2 (1979): 27–61.

Includes a dated list of all productions advertised in the playbills.

Harris, Laurie Lanzen, ed. *Nineteenth-Century Literature Criticism*. Excerpts from Criticism of the Works of Novelists,

Poets, Playwrights, Short Story Writers, and Other Creative
Writers Who Lived between 1800 and 1900, from the First
Published Critical Appraisals to Current Evaluations. Detroit:
Gale Research, 1981 (vol. 1), 1982 (vol. 2). Each ca. 600 pp.
$74.00 per vol.

Vol. I covers 29 authors, including 7 of "ours": Austen,
Brentano, Edgeworth, Galt, Hunt, Nerval, Sue. Vol. II has
28, including Byron, Darley, Flaubert, Hoffmann, Kleist,
Sand. Future volumes (number not given) will include about
56 of ours, from the Arnims, Balzac, Baudelaire, and Blake
to Tieck, Tommaseo, and Wordsworth.

Each author is allotted a brief biography and list of
principal works, followed by excerpts from known and little-
known critics up to the present. To take Byron for a sample
of the longer units (96 columns), after a page and a half
of life and works, with portrait, there are 24 excerpts from
criticism during his lifetime, then 29 up to 1979, plus a
list of 19 for suggested reading. Most of us will find strange
inclusions and omissions. W.H. Marshall has the longest excerpt, of 6 columns; L.A. Marchand one of the shortest, half
a page. The editor seems unaware of the Pforzheimer volumes.
G. Wilson Knight's maverick but valuable books are not mentioned; only his "Burning Oracle" essay is listed, without
excerpt.

These volumes will in some respects be useful supplements
to the encyclopedias, at least in aiding the preparation of
undergraduate papers. (D.V.E.)

Library 4 (1982).

Peter Davison gives up his editorship of *Library* with this
volume, having put countless scholars in his debt for the
most careful scholarship known. (T.L.A.)

Mack, D.S. "The Year's Work in Scottish Literary Studies 1980:
Early 19th Century." *SLJ* 9 (1982): supp. 17, pp. 40–41.

Mell, Donald C., Jr., ed. *English Poetry, 1660–1800: A Guide
to Information Sources.* (Vol. 40 in English Information
Guide Series, Literature.) Detroit: Gale Research, 1982.
Pp. xviii+501. $42.00.

Part I is a bibliography of "Reference Materials," "Background Resources," and "Literary Studies." Part 2 consists
of 31 individual author bibliographies, among them Blake
and Crabbe.

Pendleton, Gayle Trusdel. "Towards a Bibliography of the *Re-flections* and *Rights of Man* Controversy." *BRH* 85 (1982): 65-103; illus.

Until now the titular figures Burke and Paine have held most of the attention given to the pamphlet war that surged around their *Reflections* and *Rights*. Pendleton now analyzes and categorizes and tabulates the publication records of a host of other pamphleteers participating in the strife. Burke and Paine "remained remarkably popular," she observes, because the "logic of personalities" tended to rise above the "logics of events and ideas," as the combatants turned into "straw men" and partially replaced their own ideas as objects of debate. (D.V.E.)

Pitcher, E.W. "Henry Mackenzie and the Essays Signed 'Z' in the *Westminster Magazine* (1773-1785)." *Library* 4 (1982): 415-17.

Pitcher, E.W. "The Miscellaneous Publications of George Brewer (1766-1816?)." *Library* 4 (1982): 320-23.

Aside from serials in the *European* and the *Ladies Monthly Magazine*, the decidedly minor novelist and dramatist gave us a series of seven letters to the *Pic Nic*, which Pitcher thinks is a continuous story (29 Jan. 1803-2 April 1803)-- and over the signature "The Man in the Moon." It appeared in complete form in 1804. Any takers? (T.L.A.)

Pollin, Burton R., ed. *Word Index to Poe's Fiction*. New York: Gordian Press, 1982. Pp. 512. $25.00.

Reiman, Donald H., ed. "Some Recent Romantic Texts: Reviews." *SiR* 21 (1982): 477-546.

Concluding section of *Romantic Texts, Romantic Times* (see Eaves, "English 3. Criticism--Festschrift"). In his intro-ductory essay, Reiman surveys the history and problems of editing Romantic texts. Recently published editions of Wordsworth, Blake, Byron, Mary Shelley, Coleridge, and Keats are reviewed by Reiman and others. (On p. 486 Reiman mis-takenly attributes to Erdman the style sheet of the *Collected Coleridge*.)

Rose, E. Alan, comp. *A Checklist of British Methodist Periodi-cals*. Bognor Regis, West Sussex: World Methodist Historical Society, 1981. £0.75.

Rev. by Lionel Madden in *VPR* 15 (1982): 78-79.

Simpson, K.G. "The Year's Work in Scottish Literary Studies
  1980: 1650-1800." *SLJ* 9 (1982): supp. 17, pp. 25-37.

Wing, Donald, comp.; Timothy J. Crist, ed. *Short-Title Catalogue of Books Printed in England, Scotland, Ireland, Wales,
  and British America and of English Books Printed in Other
  Countries, 1641-1700.* Vol. II. New York: Modern Language
  Association, 1982. Pp. xvii+690. $300.00.

See also Gilson ("English 4. Austen"); Bentley, Essick, Johnson and Grant, Minnick and Dörrbecker, Natoli ("English 4.
  Blake").

Review of book previously listed:

REIMAN, Donald H., *English Romantic Poetry, 1800-1835: A
  Guide to Information Sources* (see *RMB* for 1979, p. 31),
  rev. by E.B. Murray in *RES* 33 (1982): 479-80.

2. ENVIRONMENT: ART, PHILOSOPHY, POLITICS, RELIGION, SOCIETY

Ardley, Gavin. *The Common Sense Philosophy of James Oswald.*
  Aberdeen University Press, 1980. Pp. x+102. £11.00.

  Rev. by Michael J. Cormack in *SLJ* 9 (1982): supp. 16,
  pp. 7-8.
  Apparently not as interesting as Oswald. (T.L.A.)

Atiyah, P.S. *The Rise and Fall of Freedom of Contract.* Oxford: Clarendon Press, 1979. Pp. 791. £30.00; $59.00.

  Rev. by Randall McGowan in *VS* 25 (1982): 386-88 as a
  work of profound importance, "essential" for "historians
  of nineteenth century England." Its central contention is
  that "freedom of contract was not simply a market mechanism.
  It was far more of an ethical commitment."
  Not seen.

Bain, Iain. *Thomas Bewick: An Illustrated Record of His Life
  and Work.* Newcastle: Tyne and West County Council Museums,
  1979. Pp. 112; illus. £2.40.

  Rev. in *BC* 31 (1982): 7-10, 13-14, 16-18.

Bain, Iain, ed. *The Watercolours and Drawings of Thomas
  Bewick and His Workshop Apprentices.* 2 vols. London: Gordon
  Fraser Gallery, 1982. 43 illus., 202 color plates. £125.00.

Rev. in *BC* 31 (1982): 7–10, 13–14, 16–18; by Alan Bell in *BM* 124 (Dec. 1982): 774–75; by David Bindman ("Great Truths of Creation") in *TLS*, Oct. 22, 1982, p. 1168, as excellent in its sensitive presentation and in its reproductions: "I shall treasure my copy"; by Jon Glynne in *Art History* 5 (1982): 353–58; by Graham Reynolds in *Apollo* 115 (1982): 415.

[Barker, Nicolas?]. "Geoffrey Keynes." *BC* 31:4 (Winter 1982): 411–26.

Personal reminiscence.

Beames, M.R. "The Ribbon Societies: Lower-Class Nationalism in Pre-Famine Ireland." *P&P*, no. 97 (Nov. 1982): 128–43.

Generally consistent with Garvin (below).

Beckett, J.V. *Coal and Tobacco: The Lowthers and the Economic Development of West Cumberland, 1660–1760.* Cambridge University Press, 1981. Pp. xiii+278. $47.50.

Rev. by Peter Roebuck in *AHR* 87 (1982): 171, who says that Beckett refutes the "romantic Wordsworthian notion (adopted by Macaulay and later accepted by Trevelyan) that this part of north-west England contained a static and poverty-stricken society until the nineteenth century."

Berridge, Virginia, and Griffith Edwards. *Opium and the People: Opiate Use in 19th-Century England.* New York: St. Martin's, 1982. Pp. 370. $25.00.

Rev. by Stephen Brook in *New Statesman*, April 30, 1982, p. 28, as "dry and colourless"; by David M. Fahey in *Albion* 14 (1982): 314–15, as "definitive" within limits.

Bicknell, Peter. *Beauty, Horror and Immensity.* Cambridge University Press, 1981. £18.50; £6.95 paper.

Rev. by Graham Reynolds in *Apollo* 115 (1982): 415.

Blondel, Madeleine. "Images de l'*Amelia* de Fielding des deux côtés de la manche, au XVIIIe siècle." *GBA* 99 (Feb. 1982): 55–62; 6 illus.

Comparison of illustrations by Brion de la Tour (1786) and D. Dodd (1780).

Bolt, Christine, and Seymour Drescher, eds. *Anti-Slavery, Religion, and Reform: Essays in Memory of Roger Anstey.* Hamden, Ct.: Archon, 1980. Pp. xii+377.

Rev. by Frank O'Gorman in *EHR* 97 (1982): 152-54.

Boyce, D. George. *Nationalism in Ireland*. Johns Hopkins
University Press, 1982. Pp. 441. $32.50.

Rev. by David W. Miller in *Albion* 14 (1982): 327-38, as
a thoughtful, useful description and analysis of Irish
nationalism from its beginnings.

Brown, Kenneth D. *The English Labour Movement, 1700-1951*.
London: Gill and Macmillan, 1982. Pp. 322. £20.00.

Rev. by Edward Royle in *HT* 32 (Sept. 1982): 53.
Not seen.

Brown, Laurence. *British Historical Medals 1760-1960*. London:
Seaby, 1980. £45.00.

Rev. by Geoffrey Wills in *Apollo* 116 (1982): 349.

Burgess, Renate. "A Portrait of Wright of Derby." *BM* 124
(Mar. 1982): 155-56; 3 illus.

Oil painting of Richard Wright, the artist's brother.

Burnett, John, ed. *Destiny Obscure: Autobiographies of Childhood, Education and Family from the 1820's to the 1920's*.
London: Allen Lane, 1982. £9.50.

Not seen. A collection of autobiographies of ordinary men
and women, intended as a source for social history. Extracts
published in *HT* 32 (Sept. 1982): 8-15.

Calhoun, Craig. *The Question of Class Struggle: Social Foundations of Popular Radicalism during the Industrial Revolution*. University of Chicago Press, 1982. Pp. xiv+321.
$25.00.

Rev. by Robert Glen in *AHR* 87 (1982): 1386-87, who finds
in it "perceptive analyses and criticisms" of E.P. Thompson's
The Making of the English Working Class.
Not seen.

Campbell, R.H., and Andrew Skinner, eds. *The Origins & Nature
of the Scottish Enlightenment*. Edinburgh: John Donald;
distrib. by Humanities Press, Atlantic Highlands, N.J.,
1982. Pp. 231. $31.50.

Rev. by T.H. Cook in *Albion* 14 (1982): 325-36, as a
compact and useful digest: "had it been printed 150 years
ago, the volume could almost have passed for a quarterly
issue of the *Edinburgh Review*."

Cave, Kathryn, ed. *The Diary of Joseph Farington, R.A., Volumes VII and VIII: January 1805 through December 1807.* Yale University Press, 1982. Pp. 313, 385. $90.00.

> Not seen.

Chase, Myrna. *Élie Halévy: An Intellectual Biography.* Columbia University Press, 1980. Pp. x+293. $17.50.

> Rev. by Rosemary Jann in *VS* 25 (1982): 381-82.
> Of interest to Victorian scholars, but also to Romanticists; Halévy's account of the growth of English Philosophical Radicalism is still the one to beat. (B.C.H.)

Chester, Norman. *The English Administrative System, 1780-1870.* Oxford: Clarendon Press, 1981. Pp. 398. $67.50.

> Rev. by Derek Fraser in *AHR* 87 (1982): 779-80.
> Not seen.

Christie, Ian R. *Wars and Revolutions: Britain 1760-1815.* Harvard University Press, 1982. Pp. 384. $22.50.

> Rev. in *ContR* 241 (Oct. 1982): 223.

Clarke, Michael. *The Tempting Prospect: A Social History of English Watercolours.* London: Colonnade Books, British Museum Publications, 1981. £14.95.

> Rev. by Graham Reynolds in *Apollo* 115 (1982): 415.
> Not seen.

Cookson, J.E. *The Friends of Peace: Anti-War Liberalism in England, 1793-1815.* Cambridge University Press, 1982. Pp. 330. $39.50.

> Rev. by W. Kent Hackmann in *Albion* 14 (1982): 312-13, as rescuing an important group from obscurity: "the definitive work on the newly identified friends of peace."

Cullen, Fintan. "Hugh Douglas Hamilton in Rome 1779-92." *Apollo* 115 (1982): 86-91.

Davis, J.C. *Utopia and the Ideal Society: A Study of English Utopian Writing, 1516-1700.* Cambridge University Press, 1981. Pp. x+427. $49.50.

> Rev. by Arthur Ferguson in *AHR* 87 (1982): 446-47, who calls it the "best as well as the most intensive treatment" of the subject; by William Lamont in *EHR* 97 (1982): 367-71.

Davis, R.W. "The Tories, the Whigs, and Catholic Emancipation, 1827–1829." *EHR* 97 (1982): 89–98.

   Concludes that Wellington's "old fashioned ideas" of constitutional behavior were responsible for allowing the issue of Catholic emancipation to break up the Tory party.

Dearden, James S. *Turner's Isle of Wight Sketchbook*. Hunnyhill Publications, 1980. £80.00.

   Rev. by Evelyn Joll in *Apollo* 115 (1982): 136.

Dinwiddy, J.R. "The Early Nineteenth-Century Campaign against Flogging in the Army." *EHR* 97 (1982): 308–31.

   The motives of the reformers were basically humanitarian, not political.

Doncaster, Susan. *Some Notes on Bewick's Trade Blocks*. Newcastle: Newcastle Imprint Club and History of the Book Trade in the North, 1980. Pp. vi+26.

   Rev. in *BC* 31 (1982): 7–10, 13–14, 16–18.
   Not seen.

Drabble, John E. "Mary's Protestant Martyrs and Elizabeth's Catholic Traitors in the Age of Catholic Emancipation." *CH* 51 (1982): 172–85.

   In the years before Catholic Emancipation "political tensions led Catholic, Anglican, and Whig historians to revive the many quarrels about the past. Of these disputes, the persecutions under Mary I and the alleged treason of Elizabethan Catholics seemed most relevant to the issue of Catholic freedom."

Duffy, Michael. "'The Noisie, Empty, Fluttring French': English Images of the French, 1689–1815." *HT* 32 (Sept. 1982): 21–26; illus.

   A brief but lively and informative account, with illustrations by Gillray and Cruikshank, among others. Using prints in the British Museum, Duffy plans to elaborate the theme in a forthcoming book, *The Englishman and the Foreigner*. (R.A.H.)

Endelman, Todd. *The Jews of Georgian England, 1714–1830: Tradition and Change in a Liberal Society*. Philadelphia: Jewish Publication Society of America, 1979. Pp. xiv+370. $14.50.

Rev. by Paula E. Hyman in "The History of European Jewry: Recent Trends in the Literature," a review article in *JMH* 54 (1982): 303–19, which finds Endelman's book to be a "fine and intelligent analysis."

Epstein, James. *The Lion of Freedom: Feargus O'Connor and the Chartist Movement, 1832–1842.* London: Croom Helm, 1982. Pp. 327. £14.95.

Rev. by David Jones in *TLS*, June 25, 1982, p. 686, as setting in motion "a major reappraisal" of the Movement.

Finley, Gerald. "*Ars Longa, Vita Brevis*: The *Watteau Study* and *Lord Percy* by J.M.W. Turner." *JWCI* 44 (1981): 241–47; 2 illus.

Ford, Trowbridge H. "Peterloo: The Legal Background." *DUJ*, n.s. 43 (1982): 211–25.

Argues that reactionary law-enforcement officials provoked the confrontation in an attempt to derail impending reforms in criminal justice procedures. The main focus is on Henry Brougham's efforts for reform.

Forgan, Sophie, ed. *Science and the Sons of Genius: Studies on Humphry Davy.* London: Science Reviews Ltd., 1980. Pp. xii+247. £7.50.

Rev. by H.E. LeGrand in *AnS* 39 (1982): 80–81. A collection of essays on the Romantic scientist, with a number of references to the poets.

Franklin, Jill. *The Gentlemen's Country House and Its Plan, 1835–1914.* Boston: Routledge and Kegan Paul, 1981. Pp. xvi+279. $40.00.

Rev. by Stefan Muthesius in *AHR* 87 (1982): 782–83. Not seen.

Frantz, Ray W. "The London Library Society: A Turning Point." *Library* 4 (1982): 418–22.

On Gloucester's first circulating library (1800).

Frew, J.M. "Gothic in English: John Carter and the Revival of the Gothic as England's National Style." *ArtB* 64 (1982): 315–19.

Frey, Sylvia R. *The British Soldier in America: A Social History of Military Life in the Revolutionary Period.* University of Texas Press, 1981. Pp. xii+211. $25.00.

    Rev. by Lawrence Delbert Cress in *PMHB* 106 (1982): 301–05.
    Despite the harshness of the life ("disease, not the ball
and bayonet, was responsible for eighty to ninety per cent
of military fatalities"), "the great majority of soldiers
remained loyal" because "the institutional totality of life ...
left soldiers dependent on the army for social, personal and
psychological satisfaction."

Fullerton, Peter. "Patronage and Pedagogy: The British Insti-
    tution in the Early Nineteenth Century." *Art History* 5 (1982):
    59–72.

    The background, history, and influence of the British
Institution for Promoting the Fine Arts in the United Kingdom
(1805–1867).

Garvin, Tom. "Defenders, Ribbonmen and Others: Underground
    Political Networks in Pre-Famine Ireland." *P&P*, no. 96
    (Aug. 1982): 133–55.

    Argues that the Ribbon societies of the early nineteenth
century, "usually described as a series of local and uncon-
nected groups, showed distinct signs of politicization and
articulation over long distances, although no really effective
central authority emerged...." See also Beames (above).

Gash, Norman. "The Tortoise and the Hare: Liverpool and
    Canning." *HT* 32 (Mar. 1982): 12–19; illus.

    Sir John Neale Lecture, University College, London, Dec.
7, 1981.

Gillen, Mollie. "The Botany Bay Decision, 1786: Convicts, Not
    Empire." *EHR* 97 (1982): 740–66.

Gossman, Lionel. *The Empire Unpossess'd: An Essay on Gibbon's
    "Decline and Fall."* Cambridge University Press, 1981. Pp.
    xvi+160.

    Rev. by Dominick LaCapra in *CL* 34 (1982): 78–83.

Greenberg, Dolores. "Reassessing the Power Patterns of the
    Industrial Revolution: An Anglo-American Comparison." *AHR*
    87 (1982): 1237–61.

    "Increased output, rather than increases in steam utiliza-
tion, is the benchmark of the Industrial Revolution until
1850."

Greggus, David. "The British Army and the Slave Revolt: Saint Domingue in the 1790's." *HT* 32 (July 1982): 35-39; illus.

   Toussaint l'Ouverture and yellow fever finally forced the British out in 1798.

Guillaud, Jacqueline and Maurice, eds. *Turner en France*. Paris: Centre Culturel du Marais, 1981. Pp. 637; 1136 illus. Approx. £15.00.

   Rev. by Cecilia Power in *Art History* 5 (1982): 254-55.

Gunther, A.E. *The Founders of Science at the British Museum 1753-1900*. Suffolk: Halesworth Press, 1981. Pp. ix+219; 32 illus. £9.90; $20.00.

   Rev. by P.J.P. Whitehead in *AnS* 39 (1982): 95-97.
   Not seen.

Hay, Douglas. "War, Dearth and Theft in the Eighteenth Century: The Record of the English Courts." *P&P*, no. 95 (May 1982): 117-60.

   "The evidence presented here suggests that the wholesale rejection of the eighteenth-century judicial statistics as guides to criminality may be premature." However, Hay emphasizes that the establishment's data must be interpreted in light of other forms of evidence.

Hayward, Helena, and Pat Kirkham. *William and John Linnell.* London: Studio Vista/Christies, 1980. £52.50.

   Rev. by Geoffrey Wills in *Apollo* 115 (1982): 131.

Heleniak, Kathryn Moore. "John Gibbons and William Mulready: The Relationship between a Patron and a Painter." *BM* 124 (Mar. 1982): 136-41; 7 illus.

Hempton, David N. "Thomas Allan and the Methodist Politics." *History* 67 (1982): 13-31.

Holcomb, Adele H. "John Constable as a Contributor to the 'Athenaeum.'" *BM* 124 (Oct. 1982): 628-29.

Hood, William. "Four Early Portraits by Wright of Derby." *BM* 124 (Mar. 1982): 156; 4 illus.

Hopkins, Eric. "Working Hours and Conditions during the Industrial Revolution." *EHR* 35 (1982): 52-66.

"... the belief that everywhere the majority of workers became the slaves of a new work discipline during the Industrial Revolution is of doubtful validity."

Horn, Pamela. *The Rural World, 1780-1850: Social Change in the English Countryside.* New York: St. Martin's Press, 1980. Pp. 331. $25.00.

Rev. by Travis L. Crosby in *AHR* 87 (1982): 172-73.

Horsman, Reginald. *Race and Manifest Destiny; The Origins of Racial Anglo-Saxonism.* Harvard University Press, 1981. Pp. 367. $22.50.

Rev. by Robert C. Bannister in *PMHB* 106 (1982): 309-10. As Horsman's early articles relating to the subject make clear, English Romanticism is not foreign to this important study. (T.L.A.)

Houston, Rab. "The Literacy Myth?: Illiteracy in Scotland 1630-1760." *P&P*, no. 96 (Aug. 1982): 81-102.

Houston concludes: Literacy in Scotland was only somewhat higher than in most of Europe, no higher than in northern England, and no higher among women and lower-class males; the higher literacy was not the product of a superior educational system; only after 1760 did the gap in literacy between Scotland and England widen in the former's favor.

James, F.G. "The Church of Ireland and the Patriot Movement in the Late Eighteenth Century." *Eire* 17,ii (1982): 46-55.

Jeremy, David J. *Transatlantic Industrial Revolution: The Diffusion of Textile Technologies between Britain and America, 1790-1830s.* MIT Press, 1981. Pp. xviii+384. $32.50.

Rev. by Mario Creet in *QQ* 89 (1982): 659-61; by Philip Scranton in *PMHB* 106 (1982): 111-21.

Jones, J.R. *Britain and the World 1649-1815.* Atlantic Highlands, N.J.: Humanities Press; Brighton, England: Harvester Press, 1980. Pp. 349. $31.50.

Rev. by Charles R. Ritcheson in *AHR* 87 (1982): 448-49.

Jouve, Michel. "L'Objet dans la peinture anglaise du XVIIIe siècle: quelques reflexions sur un problème de réprésentation." *GBA* 100 (Nov. 1982): 167-74; 4 illus.

Works by Wright of Derby, George Morland, and Gillray are cited as examples of the subordination of objects to man in English painting.

Kitteringham, Guy. "Science in Provincial Society: The Case of
Liverpool in the Early Nineteenth Century." *AnS* 39 (1982):
329-48.

The rich tended to see science as a form of recreation, but
some of the middle class saw that science's inductive methodology "held out the promise of technological, moral, and
social advance."

Koss, Stephen. *The Rise and Fall of the Political Press in
Britain*, Volume 1: *The Nineteenth Century*. North Carolina
University Press, 1981. Pp. viii+455; 12 illus. $29.00.

Rev. by Alfred Gollin in *VS* 25 (1982): 500-01; by Peter
Stansky in *VPR* 15 (1982): 74-78.

Kramnick, Isaac. "Republican Revisionism Revisited." *AHR* 87
(1982): 629-64.

Reasserts the centrality of Locke for the American revolu-
tionaries and English radicals from 1760 through the French
Revolution.

Laqueur, Thomas W. "The Queen Caroline Affair: Politics as Art
in the Reign of George IV." *JMH* 54 (1982): 417-66.

Laqueur has not only written an intriguing analysis of the
Queen Caroline Affair; his article also provides a brilliant
method for studying politics as a narrative art. What concerns
Laqueur is "the function of the trivial ... what it is about
certain political systems, considered both institutionally
and culturally, that allows them to mask the serious behind
the silly, to sustain level upon level of complicated but
innocuous stories, dramatic but ultimately trivial narratives,
which overwhelm potentially more dangerous discourse" (417-18).
When Caroline became "a radical cause," that cause was then
"rendered harmless by being transformed into melodrama, farce,
and romance." At the same time, the melodrama produced a
silence, for--as Hazlitt noted--because "England was mad
about the poor Queen," it took no notice of other injustices.
"The striking characteristic of the English political system
is how seldom the governors confronted the governed....
[T]he exercise of power and the limits of protest against
it were defined by its representations, its organizations,
and rituals.... [T]he Caroline agitations made manifest ... a
polity deeply grounded in civil society, one which in
Tocqueville's sense binds the social to the political through
layer upon layer of intermediate institutions. These in
turn determined the kinds of narratives the society produced

about itself. It was a monarchy, a parliament, a jury system,
and adversarial judicial procedures which, using a vast cultural reservoir, generated the stories in which the radical
representation of Caroline's plight became mired." (R.A.B.)

Lesourd, Jean-Alain. *Sociologie du catholicisme anglais, 1767-
1851.* (Publications Université Nancy II.) Université de Nancy,
1981. Pp. 212. F 113.00.

    Rev. by Clive D. Field in *AHR* 87 (1982): 779.
Not seen.

Levere, Trevor H. "Humphrey Davy and the Idea of Glory."
RSC, 4th series 18 (1980): 247-61.

    A survey of Davy's career as a "romantic chemist," includ-
ing his relationships with contemporary poets.

Lindsay, Jack. *Thomas Gainsborough, His Life and Art.* New
York: Universe Books; London: Granada, 1981. Pp. 244; 29
illus. £12.50.

    Rev. by John Hayes in *Apollo* 115 (1982): 509-10; by Ellis
Waterhouse in *BM* 124 (Mar. 1982): 170.

Lottes, Gunther. *Politisches Aufklärung und plebejisches
Publikum: Zur Theorie und Praxis des englischen Radikalismus
im späten 18. Jahrhundert.* Munich and Vienna: R. Oldenbourg
Verlag, 1979. Pp. x+411. DM 98.00.

    Rev. by Keith Tribe in *JMH* 54 (1982): 558-60, as a "care-
ful and inventive analysis." Rather than the traditional
presentation of English Jacobinism at the end of the eighteenth century in the context of the nineteenth century,
Lotte's book "seeks to change our perspective by" envision-
ing it "both as the product of an eighteenth-century radical
tradition and as part of the changing social structure of
late eighteenth-century Britain...." A careful and inventive analysis. (T.L.A.)

MacDougall, Elizabeth B., ed. *John Claudius Loudon and the
Early Nineteenth Century in Great Britain.* Washington:
Dumbarton Oaks, 1980. Pp. 133; 26 illus. $17.50.

    Rev. by William Howard Adams in *AJ* 42 (1982): 255-63; by
Kenneth Woodbridge in *Apollo* 115 (1982): 135.

Mahard, Martha R. "The Fortunes of a Penny Showman: The Career
of John Richardson." *HLB* 30 (1982): 204-38.

From 1798 to 1836 when Richardson died, his traveling theater spread popular drama throughout England. "Not since the 1720s and '30s ... had fairground theatricals enjoyed the popularity they were to enjoy under Richardson's management." (R.A.B.)

Marshall, J.D., and John K. Walton. *The Lake Counties from 1830 to the Mid-Twentieth Century: A Study of Regional Change.* Manchester University Press, 1981. Pp. xii+308. £13.50.

Rev. by Ian Keil in *AHR* 87 (1982): 783-84. Not seen.

McClure, Ruth K. *Coram's Children: The London Foundling Hospital in the Eighteenth Century.* Yale University Press, 1981. Pp. xiii+321. $27.50.

Rev. by R.S. Tompson in *AHR* 87 (1982): 1087-88, as a good account of the hospital but weak on the social context.

McKenzie, Lionel A. "The French Revolution and English Parliamentary Reform: James Mackintosh and the Vindiciae Gallicae." *ECS* 14 (1980-81): 264-82.

Examines the *Vindiciae* as exhibiting the "political languages" available to a British Commonwealth man--but blending them inconsistently; concludes "that Mackintosh's conversion by Burke was imminent in the *Vindiciae Gallicae* itself." The "war with France" is dismissed as simply a hastening factor.

Metcalfe, Alan. "Organized Sport in the Mining Communities in South Northumberland, 1800-1889." *VS* 25 (1982): 469-95.

Morrell, Jack, and Arnold Thackray. *Gentlemen of Science: Early Years of the British Association for the Advancement of Science.* Oxford University Press, 1981. Pp. xxiii+592. $49.95.

Rev. by Charles C. Gillispie in *AHR* 87 (1982): 1092-93, who says the authors "turn to Coleridge's assistance in generalizing their material and make a great play with the notion that the membership of the Association constituted a scientific clerisy."
Chapter 1 has two sections on Coleridge's concept of a clerisy or intelligentsia.

Munsche, P.B. *Gentlemen and Poachers: The English Game Laws, 1671-1831.* Cambridge University Press, 1981. Pp. ix+255. $37.50.

Rev. by J.S. Cockburn in *AHR* 87 (1982): 1385, as a
"balanced, compelling account that deserves to become the
classic treatment of this fascinating topic."

Murdoch, Alexander. *"The People Above": Politics and Administration in Mid-Eighteenth-Century Scotland*. Atlantic Highlands,
N.J.: Humanities Press, 1980. Pp. xii+199. $30.00.

Rev. by Arthur Marwick in *JMH* 54 (1982): 555-58, as
"splendid."
The title phrase is Adam Ferguson's of 1761 and means, as
Murdoch well knows, "The Power Elite." (T.L.A.)

Musson, A.E. "The British Industrial Revolution." *H* 67 (1982):
252-58.

Good redefinition.

Neale, R.S. *Bath 1680-1850: A Social History; or A Valley of
Pleasure, yet a Sink of Iniquity*. Boston: Routledge and
Kegan Paul, 1981. Pp. xiv+466. $45.00.

Rev. by Norma Landau in *AHR* 87 (1982): 777-78.

O'Day, Rosemary, and Felicity Heal, eds. *Princes and Paupers
in the English Church, 1500-1800*. Leicester University Press,
Pp. 283. £13.00.

Rev. by N.L. Jones in *HT* 32 (Sept. 1982): 55-56.
Not seen.

O'Neill, James W. "A Look at Captain Rock: Agrarian Rebellion
in Ireland, 1815-1845." *Eire* 17,iii (1982): 17-34.

Paradis, James, and Thomas Postlewaite, eds. *Victorian Science
and Values: Literary Perspectives*. (Annals of the New York
Academy of Sciences, 360.) The New York Academy of Sciences,
1981. Pp. xiii+362; 3 plates. $75.00.

Rev. by W.H. Brock in *AnS* 39 (1982): 422.
Not seen. A collection of essays, at least one of which
is about Romanticism.

Parris, Leslie. *The Tate Gallery Constable Collection*. London:
Tate Gallery Publications, 1981. £15.00.

Rev. by Graham Reynolds in *Apollo* 115 (1982): 415.

Paulson, Ronald. *Literary Landscape: Turner and Constable*.
Yale University Press, 1982. Pp. xii+274; 83 illus. $18.95.

Rev. (contentiously) by John Barrell ("Significant Terrain") in *TLS*, Jan. 7, 1983, p. 8, with reply by Paulson, Jan. 28, 1983, p. 85.

"Literary" has more than one meaning here: the earlier tradition of history painting and *ut pictura poesis*; Turner's and Constable's own inscriptions and legends on their paintings, as well as their own interpretations; the visual puns, metaphors, and symbols discernible in their landscapes; and Paulson's critical vocabulary, which applies literary terms ("georgic structure," *locus amoenus*) to his pictorial material. His ultimate model of the work of art, expounded in his Conclusion, is psychoanalytic, based on the Freudian "dream-work": an ambitious concept which accommodates the critic and the public together with the artist in a complex, ongoing process.

In this short study, which grew out of a series of lectures and journal essays, Paulson is at his best analyzing individual pictures. Unfortunately, he is not well served by the illustrations, all in black and white except on the jacket, whose small size and murky quality often obscure the details being discussed. (I.H.C.)

Payne, Christiana. "John Linnell and Samuel Palmer in the 1820s." *BM* 124 (Mar. 1982): 131-36; 9 illus.

On the "positive aspects" of their relationship, including the stylistic influence of Palmer on Linnell's early drawings.

Paz, D.G. *The Politics of Working-Class Education in Britain, 1830-50*. Manchester University Press, 1980. Pp. xi+203. $30.00.

Rev. by William J. Baker in *AHR* 87 (1982): 453. Not seen.

Peters, Marie. *Pitt and Popularity: The Patriot Minister and London Opinion during the Seven Years' War*. Oxford: Clarendon Press, 1980. Pp. xvi+309. $55.00.

Rev. by Thomas W. Perry in *AHR* 87 (1982): 449.

Pickering, Samuel F., Jr. *John Locke and Children's Books in Eighteenth-Century England*. University of Tennessee, 1981. Pp. 286. $21.00.

Rev. by Francelia Butler in *SAR* 47,iii (1982): 95-97, enthusiastically, as opening up a new avenue of approach. Not seen.

Pitman, Joy, ed. *Manuscripts in the Royal Scottish Museum Edinburgh, Part 1: William Jardine Papers*. Edinburgh: Royal Scottish Museum, 1981. Pp. 46; 17 illus. Free on request.

> Rev. by Paul Lawrence Faber in *AnS* 39 (1982): 97–98. Not seen. Jardine (1800–1874) was an important naturalist.

Powell, Cecilia. "Topography, Imagination and Travel: Turner's Relationships with James Hakewill." *Art History* 5 (1982): 408–25; 14 illus.

> On the series of illustrations for Hakewill's *Picturesque Tour of Italy* (1818–20), executed by Turner before he himself had visited Italy.

Punter, David. "1789: The Sex of Revolution." *Criticism* 24 (1982): 201–17.

> On the psycho-sexual aspects of English reactions to the French Revolution.

Purkis, John. *The World of the English Romantic Poets: A Visual Approach*. London: Heinemann, 1982. £12.50.

> Rev. in *CritQ* 24,iii (1982): 93.

Rapp, Dean. "The Left-Wing Whigs: Whitbread, the Mountain and Reform, 1809–1815." *JBS* 21 (1982): 35–66.

> One of the most interesting and careful accounts of Regency politics I've read in many a year. It will be of definite use to genuine students of the period—those willing to climb mountains. (T.L.A.)

Rashid, Salim. "Adam Smith's Rise to Fame: A Reexamination of the Evidence." *ECent* 23 (1982): 64–85.

> Relying on periodical reviews, Rashid argues that the prevailing view that Smith's ideas were victorious before 1790 is false.

Reid, John Phillip. *In Defiance of the Law: The Standing-Army Controversy, the Two Constitutions, and the Coming of the American Revolution*. University of North Carolina Press, 1981. Pp. vii+287. $20.00.

> Rev. by Caroline Robbins in *PMHB* 106 (1982): 129–31, who finds that Reid has written "a brilliant and stimulating book" which uses the standing-army controversy to show how "the parliamentary supremacy established in and after 1689

created an eighteenth century constitution often lacking in precision, and often at odds with the older system of customary restraints upon arbitrary power." Also rev. by John S. Semonche in *NEQ* 55 (1982): 293-95, who finds that the book at times "lacks sharpness and analytical clarity."

Reynolds, Graham, introd. and comm. *Constable with His Friends in 1806*. 5 vols. Trianon Press and Genesis Publications. £138.00.

    Rev. by Judy Egerton in *BM* 124 (Dec. 1982): 773. Not located.

Robertson, David. *Sir Charles Eastlake and the Victorian Art World*. Princeton University Press, 1978. Pp. xvii+468; 203 plates (2 in color). $50.00.

    Rev. by William Pressly in *ArtB* 64 (1982): 519-20.

Rosenthal, Michael. "Copies after Constable." *BM* 124 (Oct. 1982): 629-33; 11 illus.

    Copies by Archdeacon John Fisher, in a sketchbook now at the Huntington Art Gallery.

Royle, Edward, and James Walvin. *English Radicals and Reformers 1760-1848*. Brighton: Harvester; University Press of Kentucky, 1982. Pp. 233. $18.50.

    Rev. by I.J. Prothero in *TLS*, Jan. 21, 1983, p. 65, as a fairly meager narrative.
    A very swift survey of "the complex and meandering course of radicalism from the days of Wilkes ... to those of Chartism," too often a digest of digests; yet fairly up to date, and frankly "pursued with Whig-like energy" (181). Biases are also Whig-like and Namierian. (On pp. 46-48 we are told that *"local* circumstances" determine the very "nature of British politics," not only their peculiar shape.)
    Odd characters such as "Mirabaud" and "Gilray" appear, and class divisions are called "divides." (D.V.E.)

Rubinstein, W.D. *Men of Property: The Very Wealthy in Britain since the Industrial Revolution*. Rutgers University Press, 1981. Pp. 261. $22.00.

    Rev. by W.L. Guttsman in *AHR* 87 (1982): 1390-91 as "the first comprehensive study of major wealth holders in Britain.... The author has studied the social and economic data relating to 1,439 millionaires and half-millionaires ... who died between 1809 and 1939."

Schweizer, Paul D. "John Constable, Rainbow Science, and
English Color Theory." *ArtB* 64 (1982): 424-45.

Scull, Andrew T. *Museums of Madness: The Social Organization
of Insanity in Nineteenth-Century England.* New York: St.
Martin's Press, 1979. Pp. 275. $17.95.

Rev. by George K. Behlmer in *AHR* 87 (1982): 780-81.

Shattock, Joanne, and Michael Wolff, eds. *The Victorian
Periodical Press: Sampling and Soundings.* Leicester University Press and University of Toronto Press, 1982. Pp. xxx+
400. £28.00; $65.00 Canadian.

Rev. by Christopher Kent in *VPR* 15 (1982): 143-49.

Shelton, George. *Dean Tucker and Eighteenth-Century Economic
and Political Thought.* New York: St. Martin's Press, 1981.
Pp. 289. $25.00.

Rev. by Stephen Baxter in *AHR* 87 (1982): 449-50.
Not seen.

Sherman, Claire Richter, ed., with Adele M. Holcomb. *Women
as Interpreters of the Visual Arts, 1820-1979.* Westport,
Ct.: Greenwood Press, 1981. Pp. xxiv+487. $35.00.

Rev. by Helene E. Roberts in *VS* 25 (1982): 512-14.
Not seen.

Siegfried, Robert, and Robert H. Dott, Jr., eds. *Humphry Davy
on Geology: The 1805 Lectures for the General Audience.*
University of Wisconsin Press, 1980. Pp. xliv+170.

Rev. by Gordon L. Herries Davies in *AnS* 39 (1982): 109-
10: "The chief subjects that he covered are theories of the
earth, the origin of rocks, the character of basalt, the
formation of mineral veins, and the nature of volcanoes."
Four of the ten lectures are devoted to theories of the
earth from Hindu cosmology to James Hutton.

Stock, R.D. *The Holy and the Daemonic from Sir Thomas Browne
to William Blake.* Princeton University Press, 1982. Pp.
395. $27.50.

Yeats's saint ("holy") and drunkard ("daemonic") are
extreme terminals of religious activity which have been
ignored by rationalists ("whigs"), including those who
dominate twentieth-century criticism. Stock traces the
ubiquity of the extremes through the seventeenth and eighteenth centuries and concludes that the Enlightenment has

been given an undeserved good press: "something has indeed
occurred ... in the interval between Browne and Blake; but
what happened may have been an astringency or contradiction,
rather than enlargement or advance." The section on Blake
is considerably oversimplified, e.g., "One wonders, indeed,
if Blake were not hiding something from himself," and "Despite
the last line of *Vala*, the 'dark religions' continued to
haunt him; and one suspects, from his poetry, that he rather
enjoyed the haunting." I sympathize with Stock's project to
enlighten us about the irrational, but anyone who judges
Milton and *Jerusalem* to be merely "supplementary" to *The
Four Zoas* has not given a thorough enough reading to Blake's
struggles with his terrors. (M.T.S.)

Taigakon, Fami-Maria. *The Rediscovery of Greece: Travellers
and Painters of the Romantic Era*. London: Thames and Hudson,
1981.

On a show at the Fine Art Society in London.

Tait, A.A. *The Landscape Garden in Scotland, 1735-1835*.
Edinburgh University Press, 1980. £12.00.

Rev. by Kenneth Woodbridge in *Apollo* 116 (1982): 350-51.

Temple, Nigel. *John Nash and the Village Picturesque*. Allan
Sutton, 1979. £12.00.

Rev. by Kenneth Woodbridge in *Apollo* 115 (1982): 135.

Tennant, R.C. "The Anglican Response to Locke's Theory of
Personal Identity." *JHI* 43 (1982): 73-90.

Law against Locke. (T.L.A.)

Thornton, Robert. *Temple of Flora*, ed. Ronald King. London:
Weidenfeld and Nicolson, 1981. £18.50.

Rev. by Humphrey Brooke in *Apollo* 115 (1982): 133.

Tilly, Louise A., and Charles Tilly, eds. *Class Conflict and
Collective Action*. (New Approaches to Social Science History,
1.) Beverly Hills, Cal.: Sage, 1981. Pp. 260. $20.00; $9.95
paper.

Rev. by Iorwerth Prothero in *AHR* 87 (1982): 1052-53.
Not seen, but includes an essay by Frank Munger on Lan-
cashire popular protest, 1750-1830.

Townsend, Dabney. "Shaftesbury's Aesthetic Theory." *JAAC* 41
(1982-83): 205-13.

Turner, Michael. *English Parliamentary Enclosure: Its Historical Geography and Economic History.* (Studies in Historical
Geography.) Folkestone, England: Dawson; Hamden, Ct.: Archon,
1980. Pp. 247. $22.50.

   Rev. by Donald M. McCloskey in *AHR* 87 (1982): 450-51.

Turpin, John. "John Hogan, Irish Sculptor, 1800-58." *Apollo*
115 (1982): 98-103.

Van Dijk, Maarten. "John Philip Kemble and the Critics." *TN*
36 (1982): 111-18.

Walthew, Kenneth. "Captain Manby and the Conflagration of the
Palace of Westminster." *HT* 32 (Apr. 1982): 21-25; illus.

   Manby's proposals for fire protection continued to fall
on deaf ears even after the destruction of Parliament in
1834.

Wilkinson, Lise. "'The Other' John Hunter, M.D., F.R.S. (1754-
1809): His Contributions to the Medical Literature, and to
the Introduction of Animal Experiments into Infectious
Disease Research." *NRRS* 36 (1982): 227-41.

Williams, Karel. *From Pauperism to Poverty.* Boston: Routledge
and Kegan Paul, 1981. Pp. 383. $60.00.

   Rev. by Anthony Brundage in *AHR* 87 (1982): 451-52.
Not seen.

Witt, John. *William Henry Hunt (1790-1864): Life and Work.*
London: Barrie and Jenkins, 1982. Pp. 264; 113 illus. £35.00.

   Rev. by Graham Reynolds in *TLS*, June 25, 1982, p. 688.

Wright, Catherine Morris. "The Keats-Shelley Association: A
Personal History, Part Two." *KSJ* 31 (1982): 37-63.

   More on the Association, 1909-1944.

Yapp, M.E. *Strategies for British India: Britain, Iran and
Afghanistan, 1798-1850.* Oxford: Clarendon Press, 1980.
Pp. viii+682. $118.00.

   Rev. by Richard Millman in *JMH* 54 (1982): 352-54, as
"excellent"; by Francis Robinson in *EHR* 97 (1982): 155-57.
Not seen.

See also Jacob ("General 2. Environment"); Clarke and Penny ("English 4. Knight"); Reed ("English 4. William Wordsworth").

Reviews of books previously listed:

BREWER, John, and John Styles, eds., *An Ungovernable People: The English and Their Law in the 17th and 18th Centuries* (see *RMB* for 1980, p. 35), rev. by Peter Clark in *EHR* 97 (1982): 374-76; CHERRY, Conrad, *Nature and Religious Imagination: From Edwards to Bushnell* (see *RMB* for 1981, p. 40), rev. by Rowland Sherrill in *JR* 62 (1982): 206-08; FETTER, Frank W., *The Economist in Parliament; 1780-1868* (see *RMB* for 1981, p. 41), rev. as "masterly" by Samuel Hollander in *VS* 25 (1982): 505-07; by David Roberts in *JMH* 54 (1982): 109-11; FINLEY, Gerald, *Landscapes of Memory: Turner as Illustrator to Scott* (see *RMB* for 1981, pp. 42, 127, 139), rev. by Karl Kroeber in *SLJ* 9 (1982): supp. 16, pp. 13-17; GARLAND, Martha McMackin, *Cambridge Before Darwin: The Ideal of a Liberal Education 1800-1860* (see *RMB* for 1981, p. 42), rev. by John D. Root in *AHR* 87 (1982): 1389, who finds its conclusion overstated; by Richard Yeo in *AnS* 39 (1982): 94-95; GORDON, Barry, *Economic Doctrine and Tory Liberalism, 1824-1830* (see *RMB* for 1980, p. 39), rev. by David Roberts in *JMH* 54 (1982): 109-11; HALSBAND, Robert, *The Rape of the Lock and Its Illustrations 1714-1896* (see *RMB* for 1980, p. 39), rev. by Morris R. Brownell in *ECS* 16 (1982): 90-93; HELENIAK, Kathryn Moore, *William Mulready* (see *RMB* for 1981, p. 42), rev. by Anne Rorimer in *ArtB* 64 (1982): 518-19; HUME, Robert D., ed., *The London Theatre World, 1660-1800* (see *RMB* for 1980, p. 40), rev. by Lance Bertelsen in *ECS* 16 (1982): 98-101, as "an incisive summary of the state of the art"; LOUDON, J.H., *James Scott and William Scott, Bookbinders* (see *RMB* for 1981, p. 36), rev. by Miriam M. Foot in *BC* 31 (1982): 378-79; NEALE, R.S., *Class in English History, 1680-1850* (see *RMB* for 1981, p. 46), rev. caustically by David Philips in *EHR* 97 (1982): 856-58; by Peter N. Stearns in *AHR* 87 (1982): 778-79; PAULSON, Ronald, *Popular and Polite Art in the Age of Hogarth and Fielding* (see *RMB* for 1980, p. 43), rev. by Alistair M. Duckworth in *ECS* 16 (1982): 103-08, as "exemplary"; PRESSLY, William L., *The Life and Art of James Barry* (see *RMB* for 1981, p. 47), rev. by Anthony Lacy Gully as a "welcome tonic" in *Albion* 14 (1982): 85-86; by Robert Wark in *BM* 124 (Mar. 1982): 159-60; PRICKET, Stephen, *Romanticism and Religion* (see *ELN* 15, Supp., 42), rev. severely and extensively by E.S. Shaffer in *MLR* 77 (1982): 419-22; RULE, John, *The Experience of Labour in Eighteenth-Century English Industry* (see *RMB* for 1981, p. 50), rev. by S.D. Chapman in *AHR* 87 (1982):

777; THOMAS, William, *The Philosophic Radicals* (see *RMB*
for 1981, p. 52), rev. by J.B. Conacher in *Albion* 14 (1982):
313-15; WATERHOUSE, Ellis, *The Dictionary of British Eighteenth-Century Painters* (see *RMB* for 1981, p. 52), rev. by
Judy Egerton in *BM* 124 (Mar. 1982): 164-66; WEEKS, Jeffrey,
*Sex, Politics, and Society: The Regulation of Sexuality since
1800* (see *RMB* for 1981, p. 53), rev. by Phyllis Grosskurth
in *HT* 32 (June 1982): 60.

Review article:

Gervais, David. *CQ* 10 (1982): 262-71.

On "Turner and the Sublime," an exhibition at the Prints
and Drawings Gallery of the British Museum, 1981, and on
Andrew Wilton's *Turner and the Sublime* (British Museum
Publications, 1980).

3. CRITICISM

Auerbach, Jonathan. "Poe's Other Double: The Reader in the
Fiction." *Criticism* 24 (1982): 341-61.

Backscheider, Paula R., ed. *Probability, Time, and Space in
Eighteenth-Century Literature.* New York: AMS Press, 1982.
$22.50.

A collection of thirteen critical essays, dealing with
"writers equally interested in literature, philosophy, and
science" from Dryden to Austen.
Not seen.

Bellinger, Alan W., and C.B. Jones, eds. *The Romantic Age in
Prose: An Anthology.* (Costerus, New Series, 29.) Amsterdam:
Rodopi, 1980. Pp. vi+159. HFl 30.00.

Rev. by Andrew Nicholson in *YES* 12 (1982): 290-91.

Bentley, G.E., Jr. "The Freaks of Learning: Learned Pigs,
Musical Hares, and the Romantics." *CLQ* 18 (1982): 87-104.

Bornstein, George. "Victorians and Volumes, Foreigners and
First Drafts: Four Gaps in Postromantic Influence Study."
RP&P 6,ii (1982): 1-9.

Bouce, Paul-Gabriel. *Sexuality in Eighteenth-century Britain.*
Manchester University Press, 1982. illus. Approx. £16.50.

Not seen.

Boulger, James D. *The Calvinist Temper in English Poetry*. The
   Hague: Mouton, 1980. Pp. xii+498. $70.50.

   Rev. by Mason I. Lowance, Jr., in *TWC* 13 (1982): 157-58.
   Not seen.

Brinkley, Robert A. "The Dilemma of *Paradise Lost*." *Explorations in Renaissance Culture* 7 (1981): 1-14.

   An analysis of the sovereign rhetoric of Milton's epic and
   of the dilemma with which it confronts "Miltonists like
   Blake." Milton "is 'of the Devil's party' because his God
   is an imitation of the tyrants who--according to *Paradise
   Lost*--imitate Satan."

Brown, Laura. *English Dramatic Form: An Essay in Generic
   History*. Yale University Press, 1981. Pp. xvi+240. $19.50.

   Rev. by James S. Malek in *Criticism* 24 (1982): 183-86.

Campbell, Ian. *The Kailyard: A New Assessment*. Edinburgh:
   Ramsay Head Press, 1981. Pp. 143. £5.25.

   Rev. by Isobel Murray in *SLJ* 9 (1982): supp. 17, pp. 93-94.
   What's new are the commentaries on Scott, Lockhart, Hogg,
   and Galt. Not seen. (T.L.A.)

Chandler, James K. "Romantic Allusiveness." *CritI* 8 (1982):
   461-87.

   "Where Bloom wishes to subsume the Romantic's intentional
   craft into the psychology of influence, I have tried to show
   how the psychology of influence enters the subject matter of
   the Romantic's craft to become part of what he takes for
   granted in his work." Examples of Romantic allusiveness are
   chosen from Coleridge and Wordsworth (alluding to Milton),
   Keats (to Shakespeare), and Shelley (to Wordsworth).

Churchill, Kenneth. *Italy and English Literature 1764-1930*.
   Totowa, N.J.: Barnes & Noble, 1980. Pp. vii+226. $25.00.

   Rev. by David Paroissien in *VS* 25 (1982): 396-97.
   Not seen.

Cieszkowski, Krzysztof A. "The Legend Makers: Chatterton,
   Wallis, and Meredith." *HT* 33 (Nov. 1982): 33-37.

   Summarizes Chatterton's life and mentions several uses
   of the image of the dead young poet in novels, plays, poems,
   and paintings. Includes color illustration of Henry Wallis's
   Death of Chatterton (1856), for which the 27-year-old George

Meredith posed, and black-and-white of Flaxman's *Chatterton drinking from the cup of despair* (ca. 1775).

Cox, Stephen D. *"The Stranger Within Thee": Concepts of the Self in Late Eighteenth-Century Literature*. University of Pittsburgh Press, 1980. Pp. ix+185. $14.95.

  Rev. by Eric Rothstein in *ELN* 20 (1982): 66-68; includes Blake.
  Not seen.

Crews, Frederick. "Criticism Without Constraint." *Commentary* 73 (Jan. 1982): 65-71.

  Crews is harsh but telling on the excesses of those he calls "indeterminist" critics; specifically discussed are Stanley Fish, Jonathan Culler, and especially Geoffrey Hartman. In his final indictment he is prepared to include both himself and his fellow academics: "If shopworn ideas about nothingness and meaninglessness are still allowed to pass for breakthroughs in theory, the fault may lie less in our superstars than in ourselves."

Day, Aidan. "Voices in a Dream: The Language of Skepticism in Tennyson's 'The Hesperides.'" *VN* 62 (1982): 13-21.

  "By contrast with the Romantic stress on the possibilities for some form of rational transcription by the poet of supra-normal experience, the emphasis in Tennyson's poem is that that area of experience lying beyond the rational which is imaged in the life of the Hesperidian Garden is entirely unusable in earthly terms."

Diehl, Joanne Feit. *Dickinson and the Romantic Imagination*. Princeton University Press, 1982. Pp. 205. $18.50.

  Rev. by Rupert Christiansen in *TLS*, Aug. 6, 1982, p. 867, as "a very good book as soon as it shakes free of Bloom's dominating influence. Taking four major 'precursor-figures'-- Wordsworth, Keats, Shelley, and Emerson--Diehl traces out areas of Romantic thought that Emily Dickinson reinterpreted."

DiMarco, Vincent. "Eighteenth Century Suspicions Regarding the Authorship of *Piers Plowman*." *Anglia* 100 (1982): 124-29.

  Suggests that Joseph Ritson thought of the A-text as separate from the B and C versions as early as the 1790s. If so, this is a slight but permanent revision of literary history. (B.C.H.)

DiMarco, Vincent. "Richard Hole and the *Merchant's* and
    Squire's Tales: An Unrecognized Eighteenth-Century (1797)
    Contribution to Source and Analogue Study." *Chaucer Review*
    16 (1982): 171-80.

Eaton, Marcia M. "A Strange Kind of Sadness." *JAAC* 41 (1982-
    83): 51-63.

    Discussing the pleasure we find in works of art which make
    us sad, Eaton also discusses Burke and the sublime. What
    Burke says in connection with fear "transfers to sadness
    without difficulty." Of importance is the control art gives
    us over negative emotions. (R.A.B.)

Emerson, Roger L., Gilles Girard, and Roseann Runte, eds. *Man
    and Nature/L'Homme et la Nature*. (Proceedings of the Canadian
    Society for Eighteenth-Century Studies, vol. 1.) Publications,
    Faculty of Education, University of Western Ontario, 1982.
    Pp. xvi+224; illus. $25.00.

    Nineteen essays, including Richard B. Sher on "Ossian and
    the Scottish Enlightenment" (55-63); James Crombie on "La
    philosophie politique de Kant" (81-92); Gary Kelly on "Auto-
    biography in Rousseau and William Godwin" (93-101); M.E.
    Reisner on "William Blake and Westminster Abbey" (185-98);
    and Howard V. and Charlotte B. Evans on "Women Artists in
    Eighteenth-Century France" (199-207). This last consists of
    a listing, and swift evaluation, of twenty-three women
    artists, six as "Most Successful"; ten as "Moderately Success-
    ful"; seven as "Honorable Mentions." The first six, in their
    time, "were as celebrated as most of the male artists, earned
    as much money, received as favorable reviews, and fulfilled
    the artistic needs of their society."
    The Reisner essay is reviewed below, under "Blake."

Erdman, David V. "Bread, Politics, and Poetry: Morris Eaves
    Interviews David and Virginia Erdman." *SiR* 21 (1982): 277-302.

    One section of *Romantic Texts, Romantic Times: Homage to
    David V. Erdman*. See below, p. 72.

Figes, Eva. *Sex and Subterfuge: Women Novelists to 1850*.
    London: Macmillan, 1982. £12.00.

    Rev. by Kate Kellaway in *New Statesman*, Mar. 19, 1982,
    p. 24; by Kathryn Sutherland in *CritQ* 24,3 (1982): 90-91.
    Examines Austen, Edgeworth, Radcliffe, and Wollstonecraft.

Fischer, Michael. "Marxism and English Romanticism: The Per-
    sistence of the Romantic Movement." *RP&P* 6,i (1982): 27-46.

Fox, Christopher. "Locke and the Scriblerians: The Discussion
   of Identity in Early Eighteenth Century England." *ECS* 16
   (1982): 1-25.

   Imaginative critiques of the problem of identity had begun
   long before the Romantic period.

Gibault, Henri, ed. *Écosse: littérature et civilisation*.
   Publications de l'Université de Grenoble, 1980. Pp. 160.

   Being the transactions of the Scots league of the 1979
   conference of French scholars of British literature. A brief
   review by J.B. Caird in *SLJ* 9 (1982): supp. 17, pp. 96-97
   hints at much of promise. Not seen. (T.L.A.)

Girouard, Mark. *The Return to Camelot: Chivalry and the English
   Gentleman*. Yale University Press, 1981. Pp. 312. $35.00.

Graver, Suzanne. "Modeling Natural History: George Eliot's
   Framing of the Present." *SNNTS* 15:1 (Spring 1983): 26-34.

   "The fact that George Eliot set all but one of her novels
   in historic castback [either near 1800 or around the Reform
   Bill of 1832] suggests not the distancing effects commonly
   ascribed to her retrospective narrations but rather an
   intricately patterned confrontation with the present."

Griffin, Dustin. "Milton and the Decline of Epic in the Eighteenth Century." *NLH* 14 (1982): 143-54.

Harris, Wendell V. *The Omnipresent Debate: Empiricism and
   Transcendentalism in Nineteenth-Century English Prose*.
   Northern Illinois University Press, 1981. Pp. xi+378.
   $22.50.

   Rev. by Karl Beckson in *WHR* 36 (1982): 366-68.

Hayden, John O. *Polestar of the Ancients: The Aristotelian
   Tradition in Classical and English Literary Criticism*.
   University of Delaware Press, 1979. Pp. 237. $16.50; £7.50.

   Rev. by David Bartive in *JEGP* 81 (1982): 102-04, who finds
   the author's "expulsion of Wordsworth and Coleridge from
   the Romantic tradition" and metamorphosis into Aristotelian
   "torchbearers" unconvincing.

Hollander, John. *The Figure of Eden: A Mode of Allusion in
   Milton and After*. University of California Press, 1981.
   Pp. x+155. $17.50.

   Rev. by Susanne Woods in *HLQ* 45 (1982): 85-91.

Hulcoop, John F. "'Nature's Whole Analogies': The Structure
of Some Nineteenth Century Narratives." *DR* 62 (1982): 123-
39.

"Considered as a whole, each one of these narratives
projects nineteenth century man's changing view of nature
as a process of change, unfolding in space without clear
boundaries and in time without a definitive beginning or
end." Examples include *The Prelude* and *Don Juan*.

Kelley, Theresa M. "Proteus and Romantic Allegory." *ELH* 49
(1982): 623-52.

Poets whose adaptations of "the god's traditional powers"
are discussed are Wordsworth, Blake, Coleridge, and Shelley.
Ovid, Ripa's emblems, and Bryant's syncretic mythology provide the background.

King, Everard H. "Beattie's *The Minstrel* and the Scottish Connection." *TWC* 13 (1982): 20-26.

King, James, and Charles Ryskamp, eds. *The Letters and Prose
Writings of William Cowper*. Vol. II: Letters 1782-1786.
Oxford University Press, 1981. Pp. 586; 4 plates. $98.00.

Knights, L.C. *Selected Essays in Criticism*. Cambridge University Press, 1981. Pp. viii+232.

Rev. by Z.A. Usmani in *AJES* 7 (1982): 79-86.
Not seen; but we have relished many of these essays on
first appearance, ranging from Marlowe to James. All teachers
need them; we especially those on Coleridge and early Blake.
To quote Usmani, "Professor Knights is always making us
realize that it is only through our knowledge of the
'irreplaceable uniqueness' of a literary work that our
consciousness is energized" to employ the work of art as
"an open energy-system."

Lehman, David. "Poetry, Verse and Prose: The End of the Line."
Shenandoah 33:2 (1982): 73-93.

In discussing the line separating verse from prose,
Lehman also briefly considers De Quincey on prose composition and Wordsworth through Christopher Ricks's eyes. (R.A.B.)

Levine, George. *The Realistic Imagination: English Fiction
from Frankenstein to Lady Chatterley*. University of Chicago
Press, 1981. Pp. x+357. $25.00; $10.95 paper (1983).

Rev. by William K. Buckley in *SNNTS* 14 (1982): 123-25 and
called "dazzling," "provocative," "original"; by Michael Garra,
with general enthusiasm, in *ASch* 51 (1982): 436-40; by John
Halperin in *SAQ* 81 (1982): 354-56; by Sara Hudson in *SHR* 16
(1982): 363-65; by Juliet McMaster in *MP* 80 (1982): 96-98
as "an important book and a large and far-reaching one";
by Robert M. Polhemus in *ELN* 20 (1982): 74-76; by John
Russell in *SAR* i (1982): 92-96 (calling it "the Realist
imagination"); by L.J. Swingle in *TWC* 13 (1982): 159-61.
    Chapter 2 establishes "The Pattern: *Frankenstein* and
Austen to Conrad." Chapter 3 treats of "*Northanger Abbey:*
From Parody to Novel and the Translated Monster"; Chapter
4, "Sir Walter Scott: History and the Distancing of Desire";
Chapter 5, "Scott and the Death of the Hero." The other
chapters treat of mid-Victorians and post-Victorians, with
an Epilogue on "Lawrence, *Frankenstein*, and the Reversal of
Realism."

Lipking, Lawrence. *The Life of the Poet: Beginning and Ending
    Poetic Careers*. University of Chicago Press, 1981. Pp. 243.
    $20.00.

    Rev. by Donald Davie in *MP* 80:3 (Feb. 1983): 337-40; by
    Joseph Green in *CP* 15,ii (1982): 96-100.
    Includes Blake and Keats. Not seen.

MacKenzie, Raymond N. "Romantic Literary History: Francophobia
    in *The Edinburgh Review* and *The Quarterly Review*." *VPR* 15
    (1982): 42-52.

Marra, Giulio, M.V. Lorenzoni, E. Paganelli, and M. Battilana,
    eds. *Itinerari Negati Momenti della Tradizione Inglese e
    Scozzese Nel Settecento, Letterature Moderne*. Brescia:
    Phideia Editrice, 1981. Pp. 243. Lire 12.000.

    Rev. by Matthew P. McDiarmid in *SLJ* 9 (1982): supp. 17,
    pp. 61-63.
    Called both scrupulous and provocative, the volume includes
    Marilla Battilana's "'The Castaway,' *Caleb Williams, The
    Mysteries of Udolpho*: The Story behind the Page." (T.L.A.)

Marshall, Madeleine Forell, and Janet Todd. *English Congre-
    gational Hymns in the Eighteenth Century*. University Press
    of Kentucky, 1982. Pp. 181. $15.50.

    Four chapters of routine analysis of the hymns of Watts,
    Wesley, Newton, and Cowper are flanked by an introduction
    and conclusion which admit the difficulty of defining the
    genre. A vehement distinction between hymn tradition and

Romanticism is unconvincing because the implicit definition of Romanticism does not go beyond the clichés of sentimentality and love of nature. Stylistic similarities between hymns and the poetry of Blake, Wordsworth, and Shelley add little to the discussion. (M.T.S.)

McFarland, Thomas. "Field, Constellation, and Aesthetic Object." *NLH* 13 (1982): 421-47.

First given at a conference in Houston, Texas, on "English and German Romanticism: Cross-Currents and Controversies," under the title, "Patterns of Parataxis in Anglo-German Cultural Currents." *Echt.* (B.C.H.)

McVeagh, John. *Tradefull Merchants: The Portrayal of the Capitalist in Literature.* London: Routledge and Kegan Paul, 1981. £11.95.

Rev. by Margot Heinemann in *HT* 32 (Apr. 1982): 54. Not seen.

Morgan, Peter F. "Mill and Poetry: The Central Years." *TWC* 13 (1982): 50-56.

Munday, Michael. "The Novel and Its Critics in the Early Nineteenth Century." *SP* 79 (1982): 205-26.

Argues that criticism of novels in our period was, in fact, imaginative and interesting, quite the reverse of what recent writers have suggested. Valuable but not wholly convincing. (B.C.H.)

O'Keefe, Timothy J. *Milton and the Pauline Tradition: A Study of Theme and Symbolism.* Lanham, MD: University Press of America, 1982. Pp. 356. $22.50; $14.00 paper.

Establishes a close dependence of Milton on St. Paul. (Not seen.)

Pedicord, Harry W., and Frederick L. Bergmann, eds. *The Plays of David Garrick.* Vols. I-IV. Southern Illinois University Press, 1980-81. Vol. I: pp. xxxviii+437; $35.00. Vol. II: pp. xviii+385; $35.00. Vol. III: pp. xxvi+469; $50.00. Vol. IV: pp. xviii+472; $50.00.

Rev. by Peter Davison in *Library* 4 (1982): 343-47. The first four of seven volumes.

Pratt, Branwen B. "Charlotte Brontë's 'There was once a little girl': The Creative Process." *AI* 39 (1982): 31-39.

The early writings and fantasies express "her sense of
herself as nurturer rather than the nurtured."

"Professing Literature: A Symposium on the Study of English."
TLS, Dec. 10, 1982, pp. 1355-63; Jan. 7, 1983, pp. 14-15;
Feb. 11, 1983, p. 134.

A symposium in which few toasts were drunk. It was begun
by Paul de Man ("The return to philology"), Rene Wellek
("Respect for tradition"), Anthony Burgess ("The writer among
professors"), Iain McGilchrist ("A pessimist's solution"),
E.D. Hirsch, Jr. ("The contents of English literature"),
Ian Donaldson ("A foreign field"), George Watson ("The
charm of being useless"), Raymond Williams ("Beyond speciali-
zation"), and Stanley Fish ("Professional anti-professional-
ism"). Strong responses by Donald H. Reiman and Kenneth R.
Johnston (and a note by Rodney Pybus) in January drew coun-
ter-fire from Cleanth Brooks and George Watson in February.

Raine, Kathleen. *The Inner Journey of the Poet*. London: Allen
and Unwin. Pp. 208. £9.95.

Rev. by Iain McGilchrist in *TLS*, Oct. 22, 1982, p. 1148,
dismissively.
A collection of essays and lectures; one is about Keats;
Blake, Shelley, and Wordsworth are occasionally invoked.

Robson, John M., and Jack Stillinger, eds. *John Stuart Mill:
Literary Essays and Autobiography*. University of Toronto
Press, 1981. Pp. liv+766. $60.00.

Brief mention in *QQ* 89 (1982): 456-57.
This is the eighteenth volume in the Toronto collected
works. (T.L.A.)

Sandler, Florence. "The Unity of *Felix Holt*." Pp. 137-52 in
Gordon S. Haigh and Rosemary T. VanArsdel, eds., *George
Eliot: A Centenary Tribute*. Totowa, N.J.: Barnes & Noble,
1982.

Though not directly related to Romanticism, this shrewd
correction of "lopsided" views of *Felix Holt, the Radical*
is exemplary in its discrimination among concepts of social
vision. (D.V.E.)

Simpson, K.G. "Rationalism and Romanticism: The Case of Home's
Douglas." *SLJ* 9 (1982): 21-47.

"In Scotland insecurity, allied to that austerity and self-
restraint which are a part of the legacy of Calvinism, led

to the distortion of the Romantic impulse, so that it found expression in extreme form as sentimentalising and nostalgia, the source of what David Daiches has designated the subsequent 'torrent of tartanry.'" Lachin y *garb*. (T.L.A.)

Siskin, Clifford. "Personification and Community: Literary Change in the Mid and Late Eighteenth Century." *ECS* 15 (1982): 371-401.

Smith, Lyle H. "Beyond the Romantic Sublime: Gerard Manley Hopkins." *Renascence* 34 (1982): 173-84.

Spengemann, William C. "Three Blind Men and an Elephant: The Problem of Nineteenth-Century English." *NLH* 14 (1982): 155-73.

By English is meant, not the English language, but the teaching of English in compartments--Romantic, Victorian, American--which the author frowns on.

Stone, Donald D. *The Romantic Impulse in Victorian Fiction.* Harvard University Press, 1980. Pp. viii+396. $17.50.

A substantial introduction of almost fifty pages attempts an overview of Romanticism, arguing a continuing rather than end-stopped phenomenon. Stressing the coexistence of Wordsworthian quiescence and Byronic self-assertion, traditional Conservatism and Promethean radicalism, Stone suggests ways in which the apparent dualism might have found an accommodating framework in a more domestic and communally-oriented Victorian fiction. Scott and Carlyle feature prominently as key figures in the transition. The Waverley Novels, in particular, are seen as encompassing "a Burke-derived loyalty to the structures of political and religious restraint, and an almost Byronic fascination with the disruptive energies of the individual."
Stone also observes the multifarious ways in which leading Romantic writers were perceived both in their own age and Victorian England. The thesis is enlarged with individual chapters on Trollope, Disraeli, Charlotte Bronte, Gaskell, George Eliot, Dickens, and Meredith. More than fifty pages of notes bear witness to an exhaustive course of reading, and Stone must be complimented for having modelled a narrative which, though dense, is always poised and lucid. The book will serve as a useful balance to studies accentuating the "realism" of Victorian fiction, and validly (albeit all too briefly) draws attention to an important and largely neglected watershed in English literature. (P.D.G.)

Sutherland, Kathryn. "The Native Poet: The Influence of
    Percy's Minstrel from Beattie to Wordsworth." *RES* 33 (1982):
    414-33.

Toliver, Harold E. *The Past That Poets Make*. Harvard University
    Press, 1981. Pp. 256.

    Rev. by Moira Megaw in *English* 31 (1982): 172-81.

Vickers, Brian. "The Emergence of Character Criticism, 1774-
    1800." *Shakespeare Survey* 34 (1981): 11-21.

    A useful summary of Coleridge's and Hazlitt's precursors.
    (R.A.B.)

Webster, Sarah McKim. "Circumscription of the Female in the
    Early Romantics." *PQ* 61 (1982): 51-70.

Williams, David. *Cain and Beowulf: A Study in Secular Allegory*.
    University of Toronto Press, 1982. Pp. vii+119. $25.00.

    Rev. by Carl T. Berkhout in *Allegorica* 6,ii (1981): 155-
    57.

See also Boly ("General 3. Criticism").

Reviews of books previously listed:

AERS, David, Jonathan Cook, and David Putner, *Romanticism
and Ideology: Studies in English Writing 1765-1830* (see
RMB for 1981, p. 55), rev. by Sidney Gottlieb in *RP&P* 6,i
(1982): 47-48; by Deborah Gutschera in *HSL* 14 (1982): 80-
81, as worthwhile and sometimes stimulating; ALLEN, Gay
Wilson, *Waldo Emerson: A Biography* (see *RMB* for 1981, p.
56), rev. by Joanne E. Fraser in *PMHB* 106 (1982): 440-42;
by Kenneth S. Lynn in *Commentary* 73 (Mar. 1982): 76-80; by
William H. Pritchard ("Sage Lives," with Joan Abse, *John
Ruskin: The Passionate Moralist*) in *HudR* 35 (1982-83): 619-
27; BUTLER, Marilyn, *Romantics, Rebels, and Reactionaries*
(see *RMB* for 1981, pp. 56-57), rev. by Frank W. Bradbrook in
YES 12 (1982): 295-96; by Tony Boorman in *English* 31 (1982):
150-57; by Raymond N. MacKenzie in *VPR* 15 (1982): 149-51;
by Michael Scrivener in *Criticism* 24 (1982): 286-90;
COOKE, Michael G., *Acts of Inclusion: Studies Bearing on
an Elementary Theory of Romanticism* (see *RMB* for 1979,
p. 52), rev. by E.B. Murray in *RES* 33 (1982): 92-94; by
Frederick W. Shilstone in *SHR* 15 (1981): 264-65; FARRELL,
John P., *Revolution as Tragedy: The Dilemma of the Moderate
from Scott to Arnold* (see *RMB* for 1980, p. 54), rev. in *KSJ* 31

(1982): 210-12; FRY, Paul H., *The Poet's Calling in the English Ode* (see *RMB* for 1980, pp. 55-56), rev. by David R. Anderson in *ECS* 16 (1982): 179-82; by Valden Madsen in *CP* 15,i (1982): 84-87; GREEN, Martin, *Dreams of Adventure, Deeds of Empire* (see *RMB* for 1981, p. 60), rev. by John Batchelor in *RES* 33 (1982): 335-38; JACKSON, J.R. de J., *Poetry of the Romantic Period* (see *RMB* for 1980, pp. 57-58), rev. by Jacques Blondel in *EA* 35 (1982): 334; by Michael G. Cooke in *KSJ* 31 (1982): 206-07; by E.B. Murray in *RES* 33 (1982): 209-13; JACKSON, Wallace, *The Probable and the Marvelous: Blake, Wordsworth, and the Eighteenth-Century Critical Tradition* (see *ELN* 17, Supp., 53), rev. by Leslie Tannenbaum in *ECS* 15 (1982): 463-67; KEITH, W.J., *The Poetry of Nature: Rural Perspectives in Poetry from Wordsworth to the Present* (see *RMB* for 1980, pp. 58-59), rev. by Peter J. Casagrande in *JEGP* 81 (1982): 122-25; by Anne McWhirr in *ArielE* 13,ii (1982): 92-95; LIPKING, Lawrence, ed., *High Romantic Argument: Essays for M.H. Abrams* (see *RMB* for 1981, pp. 63-64), rev. by Jonathan Arac in *TWC* 13 (1982): 147-49; by Spencer Hall in *RP&P* 6,i (1982): 49-51; by Mark Storey in *English* 31 (1982): 157-62; McFARLAND, Thomas, *Romanticism and the Forms of Ruin* (see *RMB* for 1981, pp. 64-65), rev. by P.M.S. Dawson in *MP* 80:3 (Feb. 1983): 321-24; by Lilian R. Furst in *CL* 34 (1982): 281-83; by A.C. Goodson in *ELN* 20 (1982): 70-73; by James A.W. Heffernan in *TWC* 13 (1982): 125-28; McSWEENEY, Kerry, *Tennyson and Swinburne As Romantic Naturalists* (see *RMB* for 1981, p. 65), rev. by Alan Sinfield in *QQ* 89 (1982): 667-70; by Herbert F. Tucker, Jr., in *SiR* 21 (1982): 693-99 as "an eminently worthwhile project that now needs to be pursued and improved in a number of ways"; MELLOR, Anne K., *English Romantic Irony* (see *RMB* for 1980, p. 60), rev. by Frederick W. Shilstone in *SHR* 16 (1982): 73-74; by Peter L. Thorslev, Jr., in *KSJ* 31 (1982): 202-04; POLHEMUS, Robert M., *Comic Faith: The Great Tradition from Austen to Joyce* (see *RMB* for 1981, p. 66), rev. by Peter K. Garrett in *ELN* 20 (1982): 98-101; by Michael Sprinker in *JEGP* 81 (1982): 441-44; PRICKETT, Stephen, ed., *The Romantics* (see *RMB* for 1981, p. 66), rev. by P.M.S. Dawson in *CritQ* 24:2 (1982): 91-92; by Alain Montandon in *Romantisme* 38 (1982): 156-58; PUNTER, David, *The Literature of Terror: A History of Gothic Fictions from 1765 to the Present Day* (see *RMB* for 1980, p. 61), rev. by Benjamin Franklin Fisher IV in *ELN* 20 (1982): 101-03; by Eve Kosofsky Sedgwick in *SiR* 21 (1982): 243-53 as "not adventurous or exacting enough"; REIMAN, Donald H., *The Romantic Context: Poetry 1789-1830* (see *RMB* for 1980, pp. 143-44), rev. by Marilyn Butler in *RES* 33 (1982): 94-97; 7 vols. of this

series rev. by Karina Williamson in *RES* 33 (1982): 480-82;
SIMPSON, David, *Irony and Authority in Romantic Poetry* (see
RMB for 1980, p. 63), rev. by Peter Thorslev, Jr., in *KSJ*
31 (1982): 202-04; TAYLOR, Anya, *Magic and English Romanti-
cism* (see *RMB* for 1979, p. 59), rev. by Denise Degrois in
EA 35 (1982): 219-20; TWITCHELL, James B., *The Living Dead:
A Study of the Vampire in Romantic Literature* (see *RMB* for
1981, p. 68), rev. by C.D.C. in *VP* 20 (1982): 91; by John
Clubbe in *Byron Journal* 10 (1982): 97 as "a superficially
persuasive book likely to mislead the unwary"; TYSON, Gerald
P., *Joseph Johnson: A Liberal Publisher* (see *RMB* for 1979,
p. 60), rev. by Frank H. Ellis in *RES* 33 (1982): 88-90;
WEBB, Igor, *From Custom to Capital: The English Novel and
the Industrial Revolution* (see *RMB* for 1981, p. 69), rev.
by Peter Christmas in *MP* 80 (1982): 214-17 and found disappointing.

Composite reviews:

Curran, Stuart. "Romanticism as Movement." *Review* 4 (1982):
135-57.

Reviews Leopold Damrosch, Jr., *Symbol and Truth in Blake's
Myth* (see *RMB* for 1981, p. 79); Diana Hume George, *Blake
and Freud* (see *RMB* for 1980, p. 77); V.A. De Luca, *Thomas
De Quincey: The Prose of Vision* (see *RMB* for 1980, p. 100);
Tilottama Rajan, *Dark Interpreter: The Discourse of Romanticism* (see *RMB* for 1980, p. 24); Thomas McFarland, *Romanticism and the Forms of Ruin: Wordsworth, Coleridge, and
Modalities of Fragmentation* (see *RMB* for 1981, p. 64).
   Praises each as "a distinguished book"; together they
form "an essential wave of unified scholarly endeavor."
Praises Damrosch's as "a splendid book, an exemplary combination of wide-ranging learning, incisive perception,
and shrewd intelligence," as "one of the subtlest, and at
the same time most unsettling, accounts of Blake's thought."
Praises George as "responsible and perceptive" in the early
chapters, but as not going far enough: he hopes that "in
the sequel she will explain just how Blake got Albion off
the couch." Of De Luca's book, "one may assume that it
will constitute the standard critical statement for some
time." Praises Rajan's as "a new, forceful voice in Romantic criticism," whose deconstructionist revisionism derives
its formulations from the Romantic movement itself. Praises
McFarland as "magisterial," "dazzling," and impressively
learned. Curran concludes: "An academy that sponsors and
nourishes this level of collective intellection, whatever
its problems, is in serious good health. The same must be
said for Romantics studies."

Duckworth, Alistair M. *NCF* 36 (1982): 475-82.

Review of Donald D. Stone's *The Romantic Impulse in Victorian Fiction* (see *RMB* for 1981, p. 68) and of George Levine's *The Realistic Imagination: English Fiction from Frankenstein to Lady Chatterley* (see above, under Levine).

Ferguson, Frances. "Recent Studies in the Nineteenth Century." *SEL* 22 (1982): 707-34.

The journal's annual survey covers recently published editions and a variety of critical, biographical, historical, and interdisciplinary studies.

Kermode, Frank. "Sacred Space." *NYRB*, Oct. 21, 1982, pp. 39-41.

The following books are reviewed: *The New Oxford Book of Christian Verse*, chosen and edited by Donald Davie (Oxford University Press, 1981; pp. 320; $24.95); *The Poems of William Cowper*, ed. John D. Baird and Charles Ryskamp, vol. 1 (see *RMB* for 1980, p. 50); *The Letters and Prose Writings of William Cowper*, ed. James King and Charles Ryskamp, vol. 1, 1750-1781 (see *RMB* for 1979, p. 11) and vol. 2, 1782-1786 (Oxford University Press, 1981; pp. 652; $98.00).

McFarland, Thomas. "Complicated People: Three Studies in the Romantic Sensibility." *YR* 72 (1982): 95-105.

Reviews Grevel Lindop, *The Opium-Eater: A Life of Thomas DeQuincey* (see *RMB* for 1981, p. 112); Kathleen M. Wheeler, *The Creative Mind in Coleridge*, and Oswald Doughty, *Perturbed Spirit: The Life and Personality of Samuel Taylor Coleridge*.

Neve, Michael. "Walking in High Places." *LRB*, Oct. 21-Nov. 3, 1982, pp. 13-14.

A discursive review of books relating Romanticism to the Enlightenment, some specifically to science: *The Ferment of Knowledge*, a collection of essays edited by Rousseau and Porter (listed above under "General 2. Environment"); Thomas McFarland's "marvellously over-the-top" *Romanticism and the Forms of Ruin* (see *RMB* for 1981, pp. 64-65); Trevor Levere's book on Coleridge and science, and Richard Holmes's profile book (both listed below under "Coleridge"); and Winifred Courtney's first Charles Lamb volume (listed under "Lamb"). Lamb takes the reviewer comfortingly down from his heights--and takes up the last third of the review. (D.V.E.)

Rodway, Allan. *BJA* 22 (1982): 281-84.

Review essay on David Morse, *Perspectives on Romanticism*
(Barnes & Noble, 1981; not previously listed in *RMB*) and on
Stephen Prickett, ed., *The Romantics* (see *RMB* for 1981, p.
66).

Festschrift:

Eaves, Morris, ed. *Romantic Texts, Romantic Times: Homage to
David V. Erdman. SiR* 21 (Fall 1982).

A special issue in five sections: "Bread, Politics, and
Poetry: Morris Eaves Interviews David and Virginia Erdman"
(illustrated with photographs); "Essays," by Northrop Frye,
Robert Langbaum, Ronald Paulson, Kenneth Neill Cameron, and
Norman O. Brown; "Inside the Blake Industry: Past, Present,
and Future," ed. Morris Eaves; "Coleridge: The Politics of
the Imagination," ed. Carl Woodring; "Some Recent Romantic
Texts: Reviews," ed. Donald H. Reiman.
See separate entries listed under names of authors or
editors, above ("English 1. Bibliography"; "English 2.
Environment"; "English 3. Criticism") and below ("English
4. Blake," "Coleridge," "Shelley," "Wordsworth").

4. STUDIES OF AUTHORS

AUSTEN

Adams, Timothy Dow. "To Know the Dancer from the Dance: Dance
as a Metaphor of Marriage in Four Novels of Jane Austen."
SNNTS 14 (1982): 55-65.

Northanger Abbey, *Pride and Prejudice*, *Emma*, *Mansfield
Park*.

Barfoot, C.C. *The Thread of Connection: Aspects of Fate in the
Novels of Jane Austen and Others. (Costerus*, 32.) Amsterdam:
Rodopi, 1982. Pp. x+215. Fl. 45.00.

Rev. by F.R. Leavis in *ES* 63 (1982): 189-92.
A monograph.

De Rose, Peter L., and S.W. McGuire, eds. *A Concordance to the
Works of Jane Austen*. 3 vols. New York and London: Garland
Publishing, 1982. Pp. 1645. $250.00.

This concordance is an impressive, expensive demonstration of what a computer can do. Two volumes are taken up by an alphabetical list of significant words (omitting such things as articles), giving for each word a frequency number and quoting in chronological order the contexts of the use, identified by novel title, volume, chapter, and page in the Chapman edition and--for universal reference--paragraph number. Most fascinating are the three appendices in the third volume, which provide an alphabetical list of all words (including those suppressed in the main concordance) with their frequency counts; an auxiliary concordance of "commonly-used adverbs, conjunctions, prepositions, pronouns, verbs, etc." (which gives us, for example, the contexts of the 2018 "when's" in Austen); and a "Frequency Order of All Words," listed in declining order of frequency. I am not sure whether we can build a case for Austen's particularity on her 26,241 "the's" to 13,857 "a's." It is a little sur- prising to learn that "very" ranks high on the list (4066): one wonders whether chiefly in dialogue; but since this is one of the suppressed words, the computer sayeth not. There are pages of words which Austen uses only once: "supernatu- ral" is one; but "romantic" appears twelve times. (J.E.J.)

Gibbon, Frank. "The Antiquarian Connection: Some New Light on *Mansfield Park*." *CQ* 11 (1982): 298-305.

The Nibbs family of Antigua, the author has found, not only "provided Jane Austen with the type of background Sir Thomas [Bertram] would be likely to have had, but also suggested some of the events and characterization of the novel."

Gilson, David. *A Bibliography of Jane Austen*. (The Soho Bibliographies.) Oxford: Clarendon Press, 1982. Pp. xxii+ 877. $110.00.

Rev. by Pat Rogers in *TLS*, Nov. 12, 1982, p. 1242.
This is a major work of scholarship. It began as a second edition of Sir Geoffrey Keynes's 1929 bibliography but out- grew that format and provides much new material, including more information on American editions, on translations, on dramatizations and continuations, and on books owned by Jane Austen. The full description of original editions presents invaluable material on publishing history, reviews, contemporary comments, and sales room records. There are fifty-six pages of facsimiles and nine plates--especially of the 1833 Bentley edition illustrations. The list of biography and criticism is arranged chronologically and

goes to 1978, but is skimpy after 1975. There is a full
index. (J.E.J.)

Grant, John E. "Shows of Mourning in the Text of Jane Austen's
Persuasion." *MP* 80:3 (Feb. 1983): 283-86.

   Proposes two emendations to the received text in a sentence
near the end of chapter 1.

Halperin, John. "Unengaged Laughter: Jane Austen's Juvenilia."
SAQ 81 (1982): 286-99.

Kelly, Gary. "Reading Aloud in Mansfield Park." *NCF* 37 (1982):
29-49.

Koppel, Gene. "The Role of Contingency in *Mansfield Park*: The
Necessity of an Ambiguous Conclusion." *SoRA* 15 (1982): 306-
17.

   To emphasize that human life is governed by contingency,
Austen deliberately frustrates the reader's desire for a
comfortable sense of inevitability.

Leavis, Q.D. "The Englishness of the English Novel." *NUQ* 35
(1981): 148-76.

   A brief discussion of Jane Austen's development as part
of a consideration of how the English Novel came into existence. (R.A.B.)

Monaghan, David, ed. *Jane Austen in a Social Context*. Totowa,
N.J.: Barnes & Noble, 1981. Pp. x+199. $22.50.

   Reviewed by Joel J. Gold in *MP* 80:3 (Feb. 1983): 313-16.
   Editor Monaghan's Introduction sees this collection of
essays as mediating between those critics who make Austen
out a conservative, and those who would have her a subversive, by presenting some papers "actually subversive,"
and some only "apparently subversive." Some are a bit
strained--e.g., Nina Auerbach's ingenious and stimulating
conception of Austen's "double vision" which applies the
Romantic/gothic ideas of imprisonment to domestic situations, casting man as "redeemer/jailer"; and Leroy Smith's
reading of *Mansfield Park* as an antipatriarchal feminist defense of selfhood. Monaghan's own essay more plausibly demonstrates that while Austen's women are intelligent and at least
men's equal, she does not join the feminist rebellion because
she holds the traditional view of woman's role as conservator
of manners. Ann Banfield makes some interesting comparisons
with other nineteenth-century novels regarding the "influ-

ence of place." Showing that although Austen does not deal
with bedroom sex, she reveals more awareness of sexuality
than do her contemporary writers, Jan Fergus provides perhaps
the most helpful explanation yet of the real danger of the
Mansfield Park theatricals. Jane Nardin demonstrates that
Austen's later novels support the Johnsonian work ethic,
and Christopher Kent argues that such details as her awareness of availability and styles of china and muslin qualify
her as a serious historian. The solidest paper is Patricia
Spacks's examination of Austen's generational position in
the light of contemporary advice manuals and little-known
novels. Marilyn Butler and Tony Tanner contribute talks made
to the Jane Austen Society. Butler's paper deals with the
interesting question of the effects of publication of novels
in volumes, but since much depends upon speculation concerning publishers' ignoring authors' intentions, the result
is not very significant. Tanner talks about "inbetween"
characters in *Persuasion* and *Sense and Sensibility*. (J.E.J.)

Moore, Susan. "The Heroine of *Mansfield Park*." *ES* 63 (1982):
139-44.

Rogers, Pat. "Speaking Within Compass: The Ground Covered in
Two Works by Defoe." *SLIm* 15:2 (Fall 1982): 103-13.

Defoe's journeys are set in juxtaposition to the disagreement over "lawlessness" and "compass" in *Mansfield Park*,
vol. I, ch. 9.

Shoben, Edward Joseph, Jr. "Impulse and Virtue in Jane Austen:
Sense and Sensibility in Two Centuries." *HudR* 35 (1982-83):
521-39.

Smithers, David Waldron. *Jane Austen in Kent*. London: Prior,
1981. Pp. 133. £7.95.

Rev. by Elizabeth Jenkins in *S*, Mar. 13, 1982, pp. 24f.
Not seen.

Steele, Pamela. "In Sickness and in Health: Jane Austen's
Metaphor." *SNNTS* 14 (1982): 152-60.

Stewart, Ralph. "Fairfax, Churchill, and Jane Austen's *Emma*."
HSL 14 (1982): 96-100.

Austen's giving some of her characters historical names,
and, more than that, making significant parallels between
her characters and the military generals whose names they
bear, weaken the false appearance of her fictional world
as narrowly parochial.

Stout, Janis P. "Jane Austen's Proposal Scenes and the Limitations of Language." *SNNTS* 14:4 (Winter 1982): 316-26.

See also Maccubbin ("General 2. Environment"); Miller ("General 3. Criticism"); Figes, Levine ("English 3. Criticism").

Reviews of books previously listed:

DE ROSE, Peter L., *Jane Austen and Samuel Johnson* (see *RMB* for 1980, p. 68), rev. by David McCracken in *MP* 80 (1982): 196-97, who finds little new; MONAGHAN, David, *Jane Austen: Structure and Social Vision* (see *RMB* for 1980, p. 69), rev. by F.B. Pinion in *RES* 33 (1982): 484-86; MORGAN, Susan, *In the Meantime: Character and Perception in Jane Austen's Fiction* (see *RMB* for 1980, p. 69), rev. by Robert Lance Snyder in *SNNTS* 14 (1982): 207-11; PARIS, Bernard J., *Character and Conflict in Jane Austen's Novels: A Psychological Approach* (see *RMB* for 1979, p. 67), rev. by F.B. Pinion in *RES* 33 (1982): 484-86; ROBERTS, Warren, *Jane Austen and the French Revolution* (see *RMB* for 1981, p. 74), rev. with disappointment by Christopher Kent in *Clio* 11 (1981-82): 200-01; by Henry Kozicki in *CLS* 19 (1982): 86-88; by F.B. Pinion in *RES* 33 (1982): 90-92; by Andrew Wright in *YES* 12 (1982): 294-95; WILT, Judith, *Ghosts of the Gothic: Austen, Eliot, and Lawrence* (see *RMB* for 1981, p. 75), rev. by Murray Baumgarten in *ELN* 20 (1982): 103-06; by Robert Lance Snyder in *SNNTS* 14 (1982): 207-11.

Composite review:

Roth, Barry. *ECS* 15 (1982): 350-56.

Reviews the following books: David Monaghan, *Jane Austen: Structure and Social Vision*; Susan Morgan, *In the Meantime: Character and Perception in Jane Austen's Fiction*; Warren Roberts, *Jane Austen and the French Revolution*. See *RMB* for 1980, p. 69, and for 1981, p. 74.

BAILLIE, JOANNA

See Zall ("Coleridge").

BECKFORD

Filteau, Claude. *Le Statut narratif de la transgression: essais sur Hamilton et Beckford*. (Etudes, 26.) Sherbrooke: Editions Naamen, 1981. Pp. 200. $18.00.

Freyberger, Ronald. "Eighteenth-Century French Furniture from Hamilton Palace." *Apollo* 114 (1981); 401-09.

   Some references to Beckford's art collecting.

Sherbo, Arthur. "From the *Gentleman's Magazine*: VII. William Beckford's Copy of William Beloe's *Sexagenarian* in the Cambridge University Library." *SB* 35 (1982): 303-05.

   Beckford added four pages of comments on various persons mentioned in the text.

BLAKE

Adams, Hazard. "Post-Essick Prophecy." *SiR* 21 (1982): 400-03.

   See below, Eaves, "Inside the Blake Industry."

Bandy, Melanie. *Mind Forg'd Manacles: Evil in the Poetry of Blake and Shelley*. University of Alabama Press, 1981. Pp. 210. $19.95.

   Rev. by William H. Galperin in *SHR* 16 (1982): 360-62; by William Keach in *TWC* 13 (1982): 142-43. Not seen.

Bentley, G.E., Jr. "Ruthven Todd's Blake Papers at Leeds." *BIQ* 16 (1982): 72-81.

Bertholf, Robert J., and Annette S. Levitt, eds. *William Blake and the Moderns*. State University of New York Press, 1982. Pp. xv+294. $39.50; $14.95 paper.

   The work of resurrecting Blake for the tradition of our literature has not yet been finished; this volume contributes mightily to the task. The thirteen essays here vary in style from plodding to scintillating and in assumed audience from specialist to generalist. In one way or another, all are worth reading: the modernist will surely find something of interest, and Blake scholars may dip in where they have special concerns. Part I traces Blake's influences in modern poets: Yeats, Whitman, Crane, Eliot, Williams, Roethke, Duncan, and Ginsberg. Part II shows

similarities with novelists: Joyce, Lawrence, Cary, and
Lessing. Part III handles more indirect connections with
Marx, Teilhard, and a series of critics, psychologists, and
philosophers.

Several of the essays routinely list borrowings or correspondences throughout the career of the modern writer. Hazard
Adams, in "The Seven Eyes of Yeats," sets down seven important concepts which Yeats studied in Blake and concludes
that Yeats mostly misunderstood Blake. Annette S. Levitt,
in "'The Mental Traveller' in The Horse's Mouth: New Light
on the Old Cycle," quotes from Cary's notebooks to make
clear how his understanding of "The Mental Traveller" helped
to organize the novel whose main character is a Blakean poet.
Jay Parini, in "Blake and Roethke: When Everything Comes
to One," maintains that "Blake remains the single most
important poet for Roethke ... at the ... level of mythopoetic action," especially in The Far Field. Susan Levin,
in "A Fourfold Vision: William Blake and Doris Lessing,"
explores the places where "Lessing's texts intersect with
those of Blake," for example in the idea of contraries in
The Golden Notebook and in the question of insanity in
Briefing for a Descent into Hell.

Other essayists here write with a greater sense of urgency,
perhaps because they penetrate more convincingly into essen-
tials. Thus Alicia Ostriker, in "Blake, Ginsberg, Madness,
and the Prophet as Shaman," begins with Ginsberg's self-
dedication to prophecy in the line of Blake. Her theme is
the poets' need to descend into madness in order to heal,
to submit to Moloch in order to find release from his power.
Myra Glazer, in "Why the Sons of God Want the Daughters of
Men: On William Blake and D.H. Lawrence," concludes with a
poignant similarity between Blake and Lawrence: both failed
to find ways to free themselves from "the male intellect's
terror of feminine power" which they lamented.

The possible tedium of too many similarities is relieved
most refreshingly by Robert F. Gleckner and Robert J. Berthold, who find that Joyce and Duncan accept parts of the
natural world which Blake rejects. In "Joyce's Blake: Paths
of Influence," Gleckner corrects his own earlier article
to conclude that Joyce liked Blake's life more than his
work, and that all his knowledge could have come from Ellis's
The Real Blake. As evidence he gives a chart of correspondences between Ellis's book and Joyce's Trieste lecture on
Blake. Essentially Joyce departs from Blake by accepting
the cycle of generation and the female will, as in Molly's
soliloquy at the end of Ulysses. In "Robert Duncan: Blake's
Contemporary Voice," Berthold stresses a similar departure:

Duncan accepts the literal, actual Dante whom Blake rejects, and he praises the memory which Blake denigrates.

Because they face head-on the question of paradox and apparent contradiction in Blake, the most exciting and ambitious essays in the collection are those by Donald Pease and Leroy Searle. Pease, in "Blake, Whitman, Crane: The Hand of Fire," demonstrates that all three poets try to find ways to combine the "epic form" and the "prophetic vision" which "arise from two completely opposed impulses." He shows Crane struggling with his precursor Eliot much as Blake struggled with Milton, and he shows Whitman in a Blakean quest to combine "the world that *is*" with "the world that *can be*."

Searle, in "Blake, Eliot, and Williams: The Continuity of Imaginative Labor," seems to me the most successful in fulfilling the promise which I hear in the title of the volume. Blake, "an examplary artist," who strives for "comprehensiveness" and "total intelligibility," produces a "generative 'grammar' of imaginative labor." This effort leads to a "state of mental vision which is permanent just as it systematically transforms itself." Yet this is "no paradox, for it is the central principle of imaginative activity." After skillfully exploring the implications of his approach, including much of contemporary criticism, Searle contrasts Eliot's embracing of tradition with Williams's rejection of tradition as both seek for a comprehensive wholeness which is the goal of the true poet.

Probably most intriguing and of most general interest are the three essays in Part III. They assume no specialized knowledge and they provoke wide-ranging thought. Minna Doskow, in "The Humanized Universe of Blake and Marx," shows how both Blake and Marx wanted to achieve full human potential by redefining the subject/world split in Western thought. Their dialectical methods humanize objects and objectify humans in order to transcend that split. Eileen Sanzo, in "Blake, Teilhard, and the Idea of the Future of Man," maintains that Teilhard carries on Blake's millenarian hopes for the future but more successfully incorporates the science which Blake despised.

Useful and provocative, for specialist and non-specialist alike, are the conclusions and implications of William Dennis Horn in "William Blake and the Problematic of the Self." Except for a reductive and distracting digression into Gnosticism, this essay gives a precise and illuminating picture of Blake's Hegelian insight that the self "is not merely a fiction, but ... the original error ... in thought." Horn takes us on an exhilarating tour of Bloom, Freud, Lacan, Hume, and Kant, to demonstrate that Blake was an

"early proponent of the most significant concept in contemporary critical thought": "the painful experience of
abandoning our notion of a nontemporal self."

Altogether this volume far surpasses its modest title:
at one extreme, I might suggest, it proves that modern
literature could not exist without Blake. At the very least,
it supplies ammunition to the Blake scholar who, alas, still
encounters strong doubts (even among Romanticists) that
Blake is worthy of study. As the editors declare in their
introduction ("The Tradition of Enacted Forms"): "Blake
is the most extreme and the most modern of the Romantics."
(M.T.S.)

Bidney, Martin. "Structures of Perception in Blake and Whitman: Creative Contraries, Cosmic Body, Fourfold Vision."
ESQ 28 (1982): 36-47.

"Specifically, each poet produces a psychology of poetic
creativity, showing how creative self-fulfillment depends
on a balance of mental faculties under imagination's
guidance.... Each poet has presented not only a model of
the ideally creative psyche as consisting of pairs of contrasting energies, but also--and simultaneously--a model
of the ideally comprehensive and dynamic religion as consisting of pairs of contrasting mythic figures working in
creative tension with each other, within the mind of Universal Man." Though the puffed jargon of these remarks
qualifies the author for a seat on the Blake Industry
Board, where the name Blake is a word--the only word in
fact--meaning art, what is true of poets here is inseparable
from poetry. Notice too that the poet is said to "produce"--
indicating a definition of creativity masked by too much
Blakean shorthand designed to elevate mechanism as an equal
of an equally unnecessary deconstructionism. (T.L.A.)

Bindman, David. *William Blake: His Art and Times.* New Haven:
Yale Center for British Art; London: Thames and Hudson,
1982. Pp. 192; 233 illus + 21 color plates. $16.00 paper.

Published as the catalogue for exhibitions at the Yale
Center for British Art, 15 Sept.-14 Nov. 1982, and at the
Art Gallery of Ontario, Toronto, 3 Dec. 1982-6 Feb. 1983.
The Blake works chosen are from private as well as institutional collections, a large number American; listed among
the lenders are the Blake scholars G.E. Bentley, Jr.,
Robert N. Essick, and David Bindman. Independently of the
exhibitions, the catalogue serves as an excellent introduction to Blake's art. The quality of reproduction in both
black and white and color is high, and Blake's oeuvre is

represented in all media, from all stages of his career.
Bindman's introductory essay and some of his catalogue
entries usefully illustrate works by Blake's contemporaries,
English and European.

Recommended especially to students of art who may not
know Blake and to readers and students of Blake who know
only his texts. (I.H.C.)

Bishop, Morchard. "William Haley [sic] & His Last Printer."
BC 31 (1982): 187-200.

Hayley's last printer was William Mason, Joseph Seagrave's
successor. Bishop describes a cache of documents including
sixty-nine letters between Hayley and Mason or his wife, and
a number of portraits.

Blondel, Jacques, and Pierre Leyris, eds. *OEuvres* T. III.
Trad. de l'anglais par Pierre Leyris. Paris: Flammarion,
1980. Pp. 432. Fr. 85.00.

Bogan, James. "Blake's Jupiter Olympius in Rees' *Cyclopaedia*."
BIQ 15 (1982): 156-62; 8 illus.

Bogan, James, and Fred Goss, eds. *Sparks of Fire: Blake in a
New Age*. Richmond, Calif.: North Atlantic Books, 1982.
Pp. 552; illus. $12.95 paper.

"Heterogeneous" is an inadequate word for the contents
of this fat collection, whose publication has been blessed
by both public and private grants and gifts. Conventional
scholarly articles (by Roger Easson, Morris Eaves, Albert
Roe, and others) and the relatively few involuntary contributions by Blake himself (quotations and a handful of
designs) are interspersed with a variety of "creative"
work: music, dance scenes, graphics, prose fantasies, and
many poems. Despite the liberal use of his name and in
some instances of what he undoubtedly would have called
plagiarisms, the exhibits have less to do with William
Blake than with the authors and their own cultural present.

Among the contemporary illustrations (which include a
rendering of "The Tyger" as a "poetry comic"), a welcome
exception is the series of paintings of Blake's "life and
works" by Bo Lindberg, who shows that he has an imaginative
understanding of both. (I.H.C.)

Brinkley, Robert A. "Blake and the Prophecy of Satan." *New
Orleans Review* 9:2 (1982): 73-76.

In *Paradise Lost* Milton speaks authoritatively in order to oppose Satan. In Blake's poem *Milton*, the poet of *Paradise Lost* learns that "to oppose Satan is to do Satan's will by perpetuating his authoritative voice."

Brown, Norman O. "The Prophetic Tradition: For David Erdman." *SiR* 21 (1982): 367-86.

This "prophetic tradition" is Islamic, and Brown's new intellectual interest yields a startling hyperbole: "The line from Jesus to Blake goes through Muhammad." More specifically, the connection with Blake is made through one of Brown's secondary authors, Henry Corbin, who has related the Sufi mystic Ibn Arabi to Blake's putative theosophic sources, Paracelsus, Boehme, and Swedenborg.

Butlin, Martin. "A Concordance between William Rossetti's Annotated Lists, W. Graham Robertson's Supplementary List, and Butlin's Catalogue Numbers." *BIQ* 16 (1982): 12-21; illus.

Chayes, Irene H. "Between Reynolds and Blake: Eclecticism and Expression in Fuseli's Shakespeare Frescoes." *BRH* 85 (1982): 139-68; illus.

Defines the eclecticism and expressionism of Fuseli, before he met Blake, as moving between Reynolds and Blake and only properly in focus when we look back from the modern Expressionists, through Blake, to Fuseli "securely lodged in his own time."

Christensen, Bryce J. "The Apple and the Vortex: Newton, Blake, and Descartes." *P&L* 6 (1982): 147-61.

Blake's perception of Newton's philosophy was "radically distorted"; Newton was no mechanist but a spiritualist. But Christensen's judgments on both Newton and Blake are contradicted by Margaret C. Jacob (see "General 2. Environment"). Compare also Beer ("Wordsworth"). (R.A.H.)

Damrosch, Leopold, Jr. "Burns, Blake, and the Recovery of Lyric." *SiR* 21 (1982): 637-60.

Davies, Stephen. "The Aesthetic Relevance of Authors' and Painters' Intentions." *JAAC* 41 (1982-83): 65-76.

In finding that aesthetic understanding of painting and literature is not determined by the painter's and author's intentions, Davies discusses the word "mills" in *Jerusalem*. While the word "could not have referred to the factories

of the industrial revolution" and while "a person who gives
'mills' such a reference is mistaken if he thinks he is giving
the word a reference that Blake would or could have acknowledged," the reader is not mistaken "in thinking that there
is a statement in the poem about the desecration of nature
by factories." The reader "gives the word this reference ...
and he is entitled to do so" because "all poets give up
ownership of their poems when they make the poems public."
But is the purpose of reading necessarily to make a text
one's own? If the reader is entitled to treat a text as
personal property, will the poem be as interesting when the
reader does so? (R.A.B.)

DeLuca, V.A. "'The Unwearied Sun': An Echo of Addison in Blake's
Milton." *ELN* 20 (1982): 8-10.

Eaves, Morris, ed. "Inside the Blake Industry: Past, Present,
and Future." *SiR* 21 (1982): 389-443.

   One section of *Romantic Texts, Romantic Times* (see Eaves,
"English 3. Criticism--Festschrift"). Ten Blake scholars--
David V. Erdman, Robert N. Essick, Hazard Adams, Joseph
Viscomi, W.J.T. Mitchell, Nelson Hilton, Morton D. Paley,
Karl Kroeber, Robert Gleckner, John E. Grant--report on what
has been done, what needs to be done, and what may be done
in the future in Blake studies.

Eaves, Morris. *William Blake's Theory of Art.* (Princeton Essays
on the Arts, 13.) Princeton University Press, 1982. Pp. 217;
3 illus. $18.50; $8.95 paper.

   Rev. by Andrew Lincoln in *TLS*, Feb. 4, 1983, p. 111,
sympathetically but briefly.
   The most noteworthy aspect of this monograph is the
author's method, evidently influenced at some remove by
post-structuralist criticism. By a process of definition
and distinction, reformulation, reduction and equation or
substitution, Eaves moves step by step to a preordained
conclusion: the unity, or "identity," of artist, work, and
audience, which to him is ideally envisioned in Romantic
expressive theory. The logical and semantic sleight of hand
is fascinating, and Enlightenment theory, especially, gains
from a fresh formulation; statements by the other Romantics
tend to support Eaves on the idea of an audience. Blake
himself seems to fit the pattern when his "Christian"
passages can be translated into aesthetic terms. Otherwise,
however, despite Eaves's efforts to turn it into formal
theory, what Blake says or appears to say about art is

limited by variables of occasion or context, or by meanings
not immediately disclosed (e.g., as for "identity"), which
are not taken into account.

Blake's actual works are excluded from consideration and
their absence is felt. Disputing the generations of critics
who have found the execution in Blake's designs inadequate
to the conception, Eaves argues the inseparability of conception and execution only from the standpoint of theory,
not by citing practical examples. The only extended verse
passage (from the closing lines of *Jerusalem*) is quoted
without comment as Eaves's own rhetorical ending, although
it is one with which a study bearing this title might have
been expected to begin.

All in all, this is more properly the exposition of Morris
Eaves's theory of art, a neo-Romantic tour de force which
is more persuasive without than with the persona of William
Blake. (I.H.C.)

Erdman, David V. "A Book to Eat." *BIQ* 15 (1982): 170-75;
8 illus.

Of the text-clutching giant in *Jerusalem* 62 and the little
book, visible in some copies, in *Jerusalem* 99.

Erdman, David V., ed., with commentary by Harold Bloom. *The
Complete Poetry and Prose of William Blake*. Newly revised
edition. Garden City, N.Y.: Anchor Press/Doubleday, 1982.
Pp. xxvi+990; 4 illus. $19.95 paper. University of California
Press, 1982. $29.95 cloth.

For its exemplary textual editing, the revised *Complete
Poetry and Prose* has been awarded the emblem of approval
of the Modern Language Association Committee on Scholarly
Editions; in this case, the approved scholarly edition also
is intended for use in the classroom and on publication was
a book-club selection. Emendations accumulated since the
publication of the first edition (1965; see *ELN* 4, Supp.,
22) have been incorporated in the texts proper. There are
some rearrangements, the most noteworthy being a new Night
the Seventh in *The Four Zoas*, conflated from the previously
separate Nights VIIa and VIIb. All surviving letters written
by Blake now are included in his prose, in place of the
earlier limited selection.

The textual notes have been extensively revised and
updated, and as always Erdman's remarks are worth reading
for their own sake. Regrettably, except for accommodations
to the new arrangements in the texts Harold Bloom's critical
commentary is reprinted with little revision. (I.H.C.)

Erdman, David V. "The Future of Blake Studies." *SiR* 21 (1982): 391-94.

See above, Eaves, "Inside the Blake Industry."

Essick, Robert N. "Blake in the Marketplace 1980-1981." *BIQ* 16 (1982): 86-196; illus.

Essick, Robert N. "Blake Today and Tomorrow." *SiR* 21 (1982): 395-99.

See above, Eaves, "Inside the Blake Industry."

Essick, Robert N., and Morton D. Paley. *Robert Blair's The Grave, Illustrated by William Blake: A Study with Facsimile.* London: Scolar Press; Berkeley, CA: University Press Books, 1982. Pp. x+243; facsimile plus 29 supplementary illus. $90.00.

This new and certainly definitive edition has been prepared with remarkable thoroughness. The facsimile of the 1808 quarto, with Blair's text and Schiavonetti's engravings, is accompanied by a bibliography of subsequent editions, reproductions of Blake's rejected designs, and a catalogue of all the relevant designs, published, rejected, and associated. The discursive sections include an account of the background and history of the poem and a summary of Blair's textual revisions; a plate-by-plate commentary on Blake's designs; and a reconstruction of the episode involving the entrepreneur Cromek and the *Grave* project which is an absorbing contribution to Blake biography.

Where the editors might be faulted is in the relatively little they have to say about the aesthetic consequences of Cromek's choice of Schiavonetti as engraver. It is not only that the published engravings "substitute competence for genius" (53); there is a fundamental incongruity between Schiavonetti's highly finished technique and Blake's often awkward figural style (see, e.g., pl. 3, "The Meeting of a Family in Heaven"), which is as unsettling today as it must have been to contemporary readers. In themselves, too, the designs—even when those Cromek rejected are put back in sequence—are uneven in imaginative appeal. Other considerations aside, Blake seems to have found Blair less inspiring than he had found Young and Gray a decade earlier. (I.H.C.)

Fogel, Aaron. "Pictures of Speech: On Blake's Poetic." *SiR* 21 (1982): 217-42.

Complete with excursions to "London" and Marvell's Appleton House, this is a complex and playful journey into Blake's "morphemic patterning." The Surrey Hills passage in *Jerusalem* (6:14-26) is written in the "'key' of Jerusalem, which is the key of lamentation," because it is full of /r + u/. A question to ask about Golgonooza: "How can you build an ooze?" The fun is weighted with serious inquiries into history, Milton, and marriage, Fogel's intention being to show "the drama of difficult transition from one dialogical state to another." (M.T.S.)

Frye, Northrop. "The Meeting of Past and Future in William Morris." *SiR* 21 (1982): 303-18.

Out of his revaluation of Morris, Frye develops a mini-theory of culture and politics: "cultural developments in time, as in space, seem to go in opposition to the political and economic currents."

Fuller, David. "The Translation of Vision: Reading Blake's *Tiriel*." *DUJ*, n.s. 44 (1982): 29-36.

A sensible approach to the poem as an early expression of Blake's central concerns, this would be a useful addition to an introductory reading list. (R.M.R.)

Gleckner, Robert F. "Blake's Little Black Boy and the Bible." *CLQ* 18 (1982): 205-13.

Must reading for those who have been misled by fashionable misreadings of "The Little Black Boy" which assume that Blake was confused about innocence and experience. (D.V.E.)

Gleckner, Robert F. "Blake's Swans." *BIQ* 15 (1982): 164-69.

Especially of Blake *as* swan, as in *Jerusalem* 11.

Gleckner, Robert F. "A Creed Not Outworn." *SiR* 21 (1982): 431-35.

See above, Eaves, "Inside the Blake Industry."

Gleckner, Robert F. "Edmund Spenser and Blake's Printing House in Hell." *SAQ* 81 (1982): 311-22.

Gleckner finds some impressively convincing sources in Spenser which lead him to read (not *quite* so convincingly) Blake's passage as an allegorical anti-allegory. But as a sample of his great work-in-progress, pursuing Blake through the abysses of *The Faerie Queene*, this is a joy. (D.V.E.)

Gleckner, Robert F. "The Strange Odyssey of Blake's 'The Voice of the Ancient Bard.'" *RP&P* 6,i (1982): 1-25.

Gleckner, Robert F. "W.J. Linton, a Latter-day Blake." *BRH* 85 (1982): 208-27; illus.

Gleckner sees an atavism of Blake in the career of Linton, poet, politician, essayist, and engraver in the mid-Victorian era.

Gourlay, Alexander S., and John E. Grant. "The Melancholy Shepherdess in Prospect of Love and Death in Reynolds and Blake." *BRH* 85 (1982): 169-89; illus.

A Reynolds painting, of Anne Dashwood before marriage, is found to share several motival "particulars" with the title-page portrait of Blake's Thel.

Grant, John E. "Blake in the Future." *SiR* 21 (1982): 436-43.

See above, Eaves, "Inside the Blake Industry."

Grant, John E. "Some Drawings Related to Blake's *Night Thoughts* Designs: The Coda Sketch and Two Pictures not Previously Connected with the Series." *BIQ* 16 (1982): 7-11; illus.

Greenberg, Mark L. "The Rossettis' Transcription of Blake's Notebook." *Library* 4 (1982): 249-72.

This intends a complete collation of the transcript with remarks on the transcriber's "creativity" and we are thankful for it. (T.L.A.)

Gully, Anthony Lacy. "Mr. B. and the Cherubim: A Critical Examination of William Blake's *A Descriptive Catalogue* of 1809." *Phoebus* 1: *A Journal of Art History* (1980): 23-45.

Hilton, Nelson. "Becoming Prolific Being Devoured." *SiR* 21 (1982): 417-24.

See above, Eaves, "Inside the Blake Industry."

James, Jerry. "UCSC Acquires Collection of Poet's Works." Santa Cruz *Sentinel*, May 1, 1983; interview.

The UCSC library has acquired the "entire archive of Trianon Press," including hand-corrected negatives and hand-cut stencils, of forty Trianon titles, about half of works by Blake, the others including works by Aldous Huxley, Robert Graves; art works by Cezanne and Chagall; there are also engravings for twenty-one books never published, including Brueghel, Turner, Pissarro.

Johnson, Mary Lynn. "Observations on Blake's Paintings and Drawings (Based on Butlin's Catalogue Raisonne)." *BIQ* 16 (1982): 4-6.

    Several identifications, recurrent motifs, and analogues noted, e.g., the six toes of Goliath and, after the Fall, the Angel of the Divine Presence.

Johnson, Mary Lynn, and John E. Grant. "The Norton Critical Edition of Blake: Addenda and Corrigenda." *BIQ* 16 (1982): 107-10.

Kroeber, Karl. "Infirm Perswasion." *SiR* 21 (1982): 429-30.

    See above, Eaves, "Inside the Blake Industry."

Lincoln, Andrew. "Blake's Lower Paradise: The Pastoral Passage in *The Four Zoas*, Night the Ninth." *BRH* 84 (1981): 470-78.

    A close reading, which sheds light directly--and also on the predicament of Thel.

Lucie-Smith, Edward. "The Fiery Vision of William Blake Is Burning Bright." *The Smithsonian* 13 (Sept. 1982): 50-59; illus.

Minnick, Thomas L., and Detlef W. Dörrbecker. "Blake and His Circle: A Checklist of Recent Scholarship." *BIQ* 16 (1982): 111-20.

Mitchell, W.J.T. "Dangerous Blake." *SiR* 21 (1982): 410-27.

    See above, Eaves, "Inside the Blake Industry."

Natoli, Joseph P. *Twentieth-Century Blake Criticism: Northrop Frye to the Present*. New York and London: Garland Publishing, Inc., 1982. Pp. xxvi+327. $45.00.

    An annotated bibliography, "primarily designed for college students," covering the years 1947-1980 and limited to books, journal articles, reviews, and dissertations on record in English. Its value as a research tool is enhanced by the classification of the entries under eleven different subheadings, including some unusually specific ("Symbols and Themes," "Style and Form," "Sources and Analogues").

Paley, Morton D. "What Is to Be Done?" *SiR* 21 (1982): 425-27.

    See above, Eaves, "Inside the Blake Industry."

Raine, Kathleen. "Blake: The Poet as Prophet." *E&S* 35 (1982): 66-83.

   Nothing new here. Blake is closer to Sufism than to Christianity, which is reduced to "naive Evangelical piety." Raine does insist on the influence of Swedenborg, an influence she thinks has been "virtually disregarded" in academic circles. (R.M.R.)

Raine, Kathleen. *The Human Face of God: William Blake and the Book of Job.* London and New York: Thames & Hudson, 1982. Pp. 320. £20.00.

   Rev. by Morton D. Paley in *BM* 124 (Dec. 1982): 772-73. Not seen.

Read, Dennis M. "Blake's 'Tender Stranger': *Thel* and Harvey's *Meditations.*" *CLQ* 18 (1982): 160-67.

Read, Dennis M. "The Context of Blake's 'Public Address': Cromek and the Chalcographic Society." *PQ* 60 (1981): 69-86.

   The London Chalcographic Society, formed in 1807 and dissolved in 1811, drew the wrathful fire of Blake's unpublished "Public Address," and its history is central to the tale of Cromek's role in Blake's career. Yet its very existence has been unknown and doubted until now. And happily Dennis Read has found not only the fact but extensive documentation in six articles in the *Examiner.* Particulars include Cromek's secretaryship and his alliance with Robert Hunt, Blake's "Hand." (D.V.E.)

Read, Dennis M. "Practicing 'The Necessity of Purification': Cromek, Roscoe, and *Reliques of Burns.*" *SB* 35 (1982): 306-19.

   The story, well told, of R.H. Cromek's editorial difficulties with Burns's friends and family, who were determined that nothing "discreditable" should be published. *Schadenfreude* for Blakeans. (R.M.R.)

Reiman, Donald H., and Christina Shuttleworth Kraus. "The Derivation and Meaning of 'Ololon.'" *BIQ* 16 (1982): 82-85.

   Important for reading *Milton.* (D.V.E.)

Reisner, M.E. "William Blake and Westminster Abbey." Pp. 185-99 in *Man and Nature/L'Homme et la Nature* (listed above, p. 61).

Adds to previous research some striking details of costume,
etc., adapted by Blake from Abbey monuments, supporting the
seriousness of Blake's claim of faithfulness "to authentic
monuments" in his Canterbury Pilgrims. Details of the Par-
doner's costume are shown, and helpfully discussed, as
are details in the portrayal of the Wife of Bath and the
Prioress. But, alas, relying on misreadings in Kiralis, who
makes out both these women as whores (leaving no one to be
Jerusalem in the age of Chaucer), and accepting Keynes's
misquotation of Notebook page 85 (conflating "Female Will"
and "Queens of England"--whereas Blake moved on from mention
of the "Female Will" to describe the good "Kings & Queens
of England" as nurturing spirits) also silently omitting
Blake's positive reference to the Prioress as "truly grand
and really polite" and elegant with "the beauty of our
ancestors" which did not decline "till after Elizabeth's
time" (*D. Cat.*, p. 12), Reisner unhappily achieves a clearly
erroneous application of his particulars. (D.V.E.)

Rivero, Albert J. "Typology, History, and Blake's *Milton.*"
JEGP 81 (1982): 30-46.

Rumsby, R.L. "Trinities of 'The Tyger.'" *CQ* 11 (1982): 316-28.

A close reading of three patterns of imagery.

Stock, R.D. *The Holy and the Daemonic from Sir Thomas Browne
to William Blake.* Princeton University Press, 1982. Pp.
395. $27.50.

Rev. by Robin Robbins in *TLS*, Sept. 24, 1982, p. 1046,
as a dim and ridiculous book which scholars and students
"should waste no time in reading." Not seen.

Tannenbaum, Leslie. *Biblical Tradition in Blake's Early
Prophecies: The Great Code of Art.* Princeton University
Press, 1982. Pp. xii+373. $25.00.

While Northrop Frye continues to extend his Blakean biblical scheme into wider applications (see *The Great Code*),
Leslie Tannenbaum follows up more directly on Frye's lead
in *Fearful Symmetry* and tries "to understand what Blake
meant when he said that the Bible is the Great Code of
Art." Lamenting the dearth of studies of eighteenth-century
biblical exegesis, Tannenbaum insists that "we cannot talk
meaningfully about Blake and the Bible without talking
about Blake and biblical tradition" because "Blake's canon
was an intentional imaginative re-creation of the Bible,
conditioned by his recognition of traditional interpretation

of Scripture and by his own reworking of those interpretations." Chapter IV, the best in the book, defines the difficult concept of typology, and concludes: "By defining Christ
as the Imagination, Blake adopts as his subject the typological process itself."

Tannenbaum's research is penetrating and his presentation
of it clear and convincing; however, the application of
his findings to the Lambeth books in chapters V-X does not
measure up to the brilliance of chapters I-IV. Like Frye,
Tannenbaum writes more strongly when he is generalizing
than when he is particularizing. And like Frye, he cannot
fit his subject into one book. His final pages point forward:
"*The Book of Los* ... contains ... a prospect of the road
leading to *Jerusalem*" in which Blake will "simultaneously
fulfil and annihilate the great code of art." I prophesy
that the forthcoming book on the late prophecies, much
better raw material for Tannenbaum's smithing, will fulfill
the promise dangled so tantalizingly in this volume. (M.T.S.)

Viscomi, Joseph. "The Workshop." *SiR* 21 (1982): 404-09.

See above, Eaves, "Inside the Blake Industry."

See also Maccubbin ("General 2. Environment"); Mell ("English
1. Bibliography"); Paulson ("English 2. Environment");
Kelley, Lipking, Stock, composite review by Curran ("English
3. Criticism"); Johnson, Randel ("Coleridge"); Higonnet
("German 2. General").

Reviews of books previously listed:

AULT, Donald, *Visionary Physics: Blake's Response to Newton*
(see *ELN* 13, Supp., 28), rev. by A.A. Ansari in *AJES* 7
(1982): 92-100; BENTLEY, G.E., Jr., ed., *William Blake's
Writings* (see *RMB* for 1979, pp. 69-70), rev. by E.J. Rose
in *SiR* 21 (1982): 509-14; BUTLIN, Martin, *The Paintings and
Drawings of William Blake* (see *RMB* for 1981, pp. 78-79),
rev. by Michael Ferber in *YR* 71 (1982): ix-xii; with great
care by Jean H. Hagstrum in *MP* (1982): 445-51, concluding,
despite a few disagreements, "that this work is thoroughly
reliable and highly suggestive"; by Peter Parker in *New
Statesman*, Jan. 29, 1982; by Peter Quennell in *Apollo* 15
(1982): 295; by Irene Tayler in *AJ* 42 (1982): 66-69; by
Jerrold Ziff in *ArtB* 64 (1982): 673-75; DAMROSCH, Leopold,
Jr., *Symbol and Truth in Blake's Myth* (see *RMB* for 1981,
pp. 79-80), rev. by Hazard Adams in *MP* 80:3 (Feb. 1983):
316-20 with admiring disagreement; by Jacques Blondel in
EA 35 (1982): 332-33, favorably; by Morris Eaves, critically,

in *JEGP* 81 (see next page); by Robert Gleckner in *SiR* 21
(1982): 666-74 with vigorous contention and extravagant
praise ("the best book on Blake in recent years"); DUNBAR,
Pamela, *William Blake's Illustrations to the Poetry of
Milton* (see *RMB* for 1980, p. 74), rev. by J. Karl Franson
in *MiltonQ* 15 (1981): 99-101; by Jean-Jacques Mayoux in *EA*
35 (1982): 216-17, favorably; ERDMAN, David V., et al., eds.,
William Blake's Designs for Edward Young's Night Thoughts
(see *RMB* for 1980, p. 75), rev. by Detlef W. Dörrbecker in
BIQ 16 (1982): 130-39, with "gratitude ... mingled with
resentment for the editors' and publisher's sheer careless-
ness" (on the false assumption that "serious" efforts were
not made to improve the quality of the plates); by Jean H.
Hagstrum in *ECS* 15 (1982): 339-44, in considerable detail;
by Robert Halsband in *JEGP* 81 (1982): 576-77; by W.J.T.
Mitchell in *MP* 80 (1982): 198-295, who finds fault with
the interpretation of the designs; by Morton D. Paley
in *SiR* 21 (1982): 674-82, who finds (quite truly) that
"the reproductions often fail to convey the overall quali-
ties of the originals" and who fears that the forthcoming
commentary volumes will be too narrowly iconographical
in interpretation; by Dennis Welch and Joseph Viscomi,
closely and extensively, in *PQ* 60 (1981): 539-42; also by
Viscomi in *Fine Print* 8,ii (1982): 49-50; ESSICK, Robert N.,
William Blake Printmaker (see *RMB* for 1981, pp. 81-82),
rev. by Dennis M. Read in *TWC* 13 (1982): 139-41; GALLANT,
Christine, *Blake and the Assimilation of Chaos* (see *RMB* for
1979, p. 73), rev. in *AJES* 6 (1981): 107-13; by Thomas J.J.
Altizer in *Journal of the American Academy of Religion*,
Sept. 1979, pp. 485-86; by Stephen D. Cox in *ECS* 15 (1982):
205-09; GEORGE, Diana Hume, *Blake and Freud* (see *RMB* for
1980, p. 77), rev. by Zachary Leader in *SiR* 21 (1982): 683-
89 as "admirable"; by Brian Wilkie, favorably, in *JEGP* 81
(1982): 115-18; KEYNES, Geoffrey, ed., *The Letters of William
Blake*, 3rd ed. (see *RMB* for 1980, p. 79), rev. by Jacques
Blondel in *EA* 35 (1982): 331-32; by Sheila M. Smith in
BJA 22 (1982): 90-91; LEADER, Zachary, *Reading Blake's
"Songs"* (see *RMB* for 1981, pp. 84-86), rev. by Jacques
Blondel in *EA* 35 (1982): 333-34; by Mary Lynn Johnson in
JEGP 81 (1982): 572-76; PALEY, Morton D., *William Blake*
(see *ELN* 17, Supp., 68), rev. by Kenneth Garlick in *Apollo*
115 (1982): 510.

Review articles:

Ackland, Michael. "Blake and His Analysts." *SoRA* 14 (1981):
    302-07.

Reviews Diana Hume George, *Blake and Freud* (see *RMB* for
1980, p. 77), and Leopold Damrosch, Jr., *Symbol and Truth
in Blake's Myth* (see *RMB* for 1981, pp. 79-80).

Eaves, Morris. *JEGP* 81 (1982): 438-41.

A severe examination of "the brittle backbone of Damrosch's
argument" (i.e., a "rigid antithesis of wish and reality")
in *Symbol and Truth in Blake's Myth* (see listing above)
which ends with praise for "several fine passages of interpretation" and despite weaknesses in the primary argument
"essentially sound introductions to some problematical areas
of Blake's thought."

Essick, Robert N. *BIQ* 16 (1982): 22-65; illus.

A review of Martin Butlin's *Paintings and Drawings of
William Blake* (see *RMB* for 1981, pp. 78-79) as "one of the
finest" catalogues raisonnés "ever written on any artist,"
which every Blake scholar should read "word for word, cover
to cover." (The same should be said of this review, which
goes informatively and critically through all the thirty-
two categories of Butlin's work, pointing out discoveries,
making other ones--positive or negative--and instructing
all of us while demonstrating "that there is room enough
in this catalogue for all of us to ride our hobbyhorses.")
A most valuable critique. (D.V.E.)

Grant, John E. "Who Shall Bind the Infinite and Arrange It in
Libraries? [The Uses of Bentley's] *William Blake's Writings*
and *Blake Books*." *PQ* 61 (1982): 277-304.

(The bracketed words in the essay title were dropped in
PQ.)
(For previous listings of the Bentley *Writings* see *RMB* for
1979, pp. 69-70; *RMB* for 1980, p. 84; of *Blake Books*, see
ELN 16, Supp., 27-28; *RMB* for 1979, p. 81; *RMB* for 1980,
p. 84.)
While focusing on G.E. Bentley's two publications, Grant
in an extensive and detailed critique takes occasion to
examine and compare seven recent textual and/or pictorial
editions and to refer to eight other editions or studies--
as well as important recent reviews of some of these. After
an opening section "On the Value of Information in Blake
Studies," Grant moves on to "Descriptions, Representations,
and Reproductions of Illuminated Printing," and then "How
Blake Ought to be Edited," "The Reliability and Accessibili-
ty of Bentley's Data," "What Bentley Tells About *Songs of
Innocence and of Experience*," "Reporting Pictorial Details

in" the *Songs*, and finally "Looking Forward to Seeing What Has
Been Accomplished." Conclusion: "It is the artist's part
to give form to airy nothings, 'with bounds to the Infinite
putting off the Indefinite / Into most holy forms of
Thought' ... and it is the editor-bibliographer's part to
make it plain that the Indefinite has indeed been put off.
This, in most respects, Bentley has done." (D.V.E.)

Vaughan, William. "Blake and the Interpreters." *Art History* 5
(1982): 106-09.

Discusses Pamela Dunbar, *William Blake's Illustrations to
the Poetry of Milton*; David Erdman, et al., *William Blake's
Designs for Edward Young's Night Thoughts: A Complete Edition*; and Martin Butlin, *The Paintings and Drawings of
William Blake* (see *RMB* for 1980, pp. 74 and 75, and for
1981, p. 78). Vaughan is most favorable toward Dunbar's
"perceptive aligning of pictorial character and meaning."

BURKE

Dowling, William C. "Burke and the Age of Chivalry." *YES* 12
(1982): 109-24.

Rizvi, Dr. S.N.A. *The Sociology of the Literature of Politics:
Edmund Burke.* 2 vols. (SSEL, Romantic Reassessment, 197.)
University of Salzburg, Austria, 1982. Pp. 431.

A long "sociological approach" to Burke, admired as a
"supporter of good against evil," in eleven chapters. Burke
had many ideas; he wrote about many things; he used many
words. These have never been examined so solemnly. Rizvi
has even searched the first hundred pages of the *OED* for
Burke's "uses of certain words" that the *Dictionary* has
"accepted." (Rizvi gives the entry dates but fails to note
that five of the first six examples--I stopped there--are
uses first "accepted" at dates averaging a hundred years
earlier.) (D.V.E.)

Weinsheimer, Joel. "Burke's *Reflections*: On Imitation as
Prejudice." *SHR* 16 (1982): 223-32.

Burke's arguments against originality, in both politics
and literature, defend "prejudice" as a rational adherence
to principles and tastes founded on past experience.

See also Pendleton ("English 1. Bibliography"); Paulson
("English 2. Environment"); Eaton ("English 3. Criticism");
Butler ("Godwin").

Review of book previously listed:

FREEMAN, Michael, *Edmund Burke and the Critique of Political Radicalism* (see *RMB* for 1981, p. 92), rev. by Paul Gottfried in *ECS* 16 (1982): 214-16, severely.

BYRON

Bone, J. Drummond. "On 'Influence,' and on Byron's and Shelley's Use of *Terza Rima* in 1819." *KSMB* 32 (1982): 38-48.

On the dangers and difficulties of influence studies and on *terza rima* in *Prophecy of Dante* and *West Wind*.

Byron Journal 10 (1982).

Dr. Kiriakoula Solomou writes on "The Influence of Greek Poetry on Byron" (4-19); concentrating on both Byron's classical debts and his knowledge of modern Greek poetry in so short a space restricts her inquiry, but several perceptions are of interest. Nancy M. Goslee's "Pure Stream from a Troubled Source: Byron, Schlegel and Prometheus" (20-36) makes a real contribution by reminding us of John Black's 1815 translation of Schlegel's study of Aeschylus and connecting it to Byron's lyric. Hermann Fischer writes on "Metre and Narrative Rhetoric in Byron" (38-53), concluding: "I think the fashionable 'metrical tale' as characterized in my introductory remarks proved so exceedingly well suited to Byron's genius because its heterogeneity as a genre between classical tradition and romantic taste offered Byron the chance of being at once individual and realistic in content and universal in language." Work on Byron's manipulation of Scott's forms carefully leads us to this conclusion of an essay of value and definite interest. Charles J. Clancy's "Death and Love in Byron's *Sardanapalus*" (55-71) does not cite Manning and McGann's *Fiery Dust*, preferring to work out a reading along the love-death lines of Paulino Lim's *The Style of Lord Byron's Plays* (Salzburg, 1973). "Byron's Intelligence Mission to Greece" (72-74) by Kyriakos H. Metaxas, and Nancy Brownlow's "Edward Noel Long--A Portrait for Newstead" (76-78) are for aficionados only. The brief reviews of this volume are cited under their subjects, and though short many have important suggestions to make. The Byron Society has made genuine strides with Vol. 10. (T.L.A.)

Clubbe, John, and Ernest Giddey. *Byron et la Suisse: Deux
Études*. Geneva: Librairie Droz, 1982. Pp. 182.

> We are grateful to Librairie Droz for making a review copy
> of this work available. In it Giddey writes on "La Renommée
> de Byron à Genève et dans le Canton de Vaud (1816-1924)"
> (61-182). From this it is clear that Giddey's essay in the
> Trueblood volume is the preface to a longer and better-docu-
> mented study now available. Clubbe gives a good introduction
> on Hobhouse and Byron, which well recognizes that Hobhouse
> rightly merited Byron's personal regard, and prefaces
> Clubbe's transcription from manuscript of Hobhouse's journal
> of the alpine tour of 1816. Those who know the letterpress
> version in *Recollections of a Long Life* will be both sur-
> prised and richly rewarded. We can only hope that Clubbe's
> transcript is made available in the *Byron Journal*. (T.L.A.)

Craig, Jane Melbourne. "George Chapman's *The Conspiracy and
Tragedy of Charles Duke of Byron*." *SEL* 22 (1982): 271-83.

> Useful for *all* Byronists. (T.L.A.)

Cunningham, John. *The Poetics of Byron's Comedy in Don Juan*.
(SSEL, Romantic Reassessment, 106.) University of Salzburg,
Austria, 1982. Pp. x+???. $13.50.

> My copy of Prof. Cunningham's work ends in mid-sentence
> on p. 240. This may reflect either a faulty copy, or an
> SSEL decision to publish the work in two volumes. Whatever,
> I have no notes, etc., nor does the index exactly clarify
> this problem. What we do have here is a reading of *Don Juan*
> in two parts, both inspired by Auden's thinking on the poem,
> and less than that thinking in the main: "To be poetic is
> to be figurative, for by metaphors a poet grasps unsuspected
> likenesses between disparate objects, by them he intuits
> the meaning of his subject, by them he transforms it and
> reveals its color. Byron's curious stylistic trait of
> throwing up one figure after another as he circles around
> a character or a situation trying to define it indicates
> how similes and metaphors display the richness of individual
> objects; thereby, figurative language renews one's percep-
> tion of the plenitude of experience." Part one of Cunning-
> ham's study uses *Don Juan* to work back toward a Byron poetic
> along the lines of the quotation. Part two turns this poetic
> upon two features of *Don Juan* to (1) challenge the poem's
> pessimism by finding comedy where others find irony, and
> (2) uncover its religious impulse: "No critic has demon-
> strated that, by means of writing poetry, Bryon perceives
> in the tedium of life earnests of the ecstatic joy of eternity

and that *Don Juan* is, in several important respects, a
religious poem," and we may add that all poetry is a form
of prayer. Cunningham has ideas about *Don Juan*; he has
sat down with the variorum 2nd edition (much less so with
its variants) and put his ideas to work; in the course of
doing so he punishes Ridenour as straw man, and gives McGann
a small spanking for *Don Juan in Context* without taking up
its challenge; Manning is not mentioned. The result is a
disjointed reading, truer by far to Cunningham than to Byron,
and one that needs editing and compression. But in the midst
of all the opera, hedged and choked, a provocative theme
can be glimpsed. I should like to see the work rewritten
and republished by an American university press. (T.L.A.)

Davis, Kenneth W. "Lord Byron's Letter to J.J. Coulmann."
N&Q 29 (1982): 210-11.

Counters Marchand in *BLJ* on the date--July [7?]--arguing
for July 10--cf. July 12 in Prothero. (T.L.A.)

Gunn, Peter, ed. *Lord Byron: Selected Prose*. Baltimore: Penguin
Books, 1972, reprinted 1982. Pp. 570. $5.95.

Listed to note availability--no change since 1972. (T.L.A.)

Hirsch, B.A. "The Erosion of the Narrator's World View in
Childe Harold's Pilgrimage, I-II." *MLQ* 42 (1981): 347-68.

Hogg, James, ed. *Romantic Reassessment* 81:3 (SSEL). Salzburg,
Austria, 1982. Pp. 83. $12.50.

I found 81:2 in *RMB* for 1981, p. 62. This adds Erwin A.
Storzl, "Stylistic Media of Byron's Satire" (3-23); Ernest
Giddey, "Borrowings from Foreign Languages in Byron's
Poetry with Special Reference to *Don Juan*" (24-36); Brigitte
Lohmar, "Byron's Pilgrimage in Criticism: The Reviews of
Don Juan 1819-1824" (37-63); and "'English Bards' and After-
wards: Byron as a Critic of His Contemporaries" (64-83) by
Michael G. Sargent.
Storzl provides a useful appreciation of the *range* of
stylistic devices at work in Byron's satiric verse. Giddey
makes us appreciate Byron's fascination with language as a
consequence of this catalogue. Lohmar works over Wain's
collection of contemporary reviews, and has William Haller's
"Lord Byron and the British Conscience" (*Sewanee Review*
24 [1916]: 7) in mind; she is surprised at the connection
of negative social reaction and negative literary judgment.
Sargent's survey connects modern understandings of Byron's
targets with their satiric portraits. All in all a better
than average collection. (T.L.A.)

Howell, Margaret J. *Byron Tonight: A Poet's Plays on the
19th Century Stage.* Vancouver: M.J. Howell (1310 W. 10th
Ave., Vancouver V6H 1J6), 1982. Pp. 224; 16 illus. $30.00,
autographed. (Littlehampton, Sussex: George Philip & Son;
also Springwood Books, Windlesham, Surrey: £7.95.)

Rev. by Leslie A. Marchand in *Byron Journal* 10 (1982):
89-90.
The story of the Victorian actor-managers adapting a
popular poet's closet dramas to the melodramatic and
spectacular requirements of the contemporary theatre. Not
seen.

Lawton, David. "The Corsair Reaches Port." *Opera News* 46,xx
(June 1982): 16-18, 42.

About the first American performances of Verdi's 1848
opera based on Byron's poem. Discusses the appeal of the
poem, which in Italy alone had already been set to music
four times before Verdi.

Marchand, Leslie A., ed. *Byron's Letters & Journals.* Vol.
XII: Index. *The Trouble of an Index.* London: John Murray;
Harvard University Press, 1982. Pp. 166. $15.00.

Vols. I-XI are carefully appreciated by Jack Stillinger
in *SiR* 21 (1982): 514-23; Vol. X is reviewed by Elizabeth
Longford in *Byron Journal* 10 (1982): 85-86; Vol. XI is
reviewed by William St. Clair in *Byron Journal* 10 (1982):
86-89, and by Andrew Rutherford in *DUJ* 43 (1982): 314.

Marchand, Leslie A., ed. *Lord Byron: Selected Letters and
Journals.* London: Murray; Harvard University Press, 1982.
Pp. v+400. $17.50.

Rev. by Kathy O'Shaughnessy in *New Statesman,* Dec. 10,
1982, pp. 28f.

Martin, Philip W. *Byron: A Poet before His Public.* Cambridge
University Press, 1982. Pp. x+253. $37.50; $11.95 paper.

Rev. by John Bayley ("Byron and the 'Lively Life'") in
NYRB, June 2, 1983, pp. 25-32, generally taking his cue
for a long review essay, but mentioning Martin only
briefly as one of "the few" good modern Byron critics (p.
32).
"This book was researched before McGann's new edition of
Byron's poetry was produced," and in this sense it comes
at the end of a critical line, not a beginning. Manning's
study was also unavailable to the author, which further

discounts the value of the opus, for Manning's work is very
much a beginning. But Martin's back is turned because he
wants not a new start, but an end, as he examines: *Childe
Harold* I-IV, the Turkish Tales, the *Prisoner of Chillon*,
Manfred, three Historical tragedies, *Cain*, and *Don Juan*--
the last in forty-seven pages. The thesis begins with a
saving grace: "The blindness, and one is tempted to say
wilful blindness, of Byron's readers testified to the extent
of their control over his product, but his loss of artistic
independence was compensated for by the attractions of the
image they had fashioned for him. Thus at the beginning of
his career Byron was confronted by an unsophisticated reading public that was tempting him to produce material through
which this image could be sustained or strengthened. This,
obviously, makes the critic's task an awkward one." The
task is awkward because the "sense received when reading
much of Byron's verse is not so much 'How well he plays
his part!' nor even (conversely) 'He doesn't mean it really
and of that he is aware' as 'He fails to convince me and
himself that he means it here, but he thinks he might, he
thinks he could do.' And within this kind of response, we
may concern ourselves with the degree of Byron's conviction."
This kind of third degree gets Martin in trouble when he
writes of *Childe Harold* (and specifically II: 95-96): "As
a child of his time who knows all about St Preux and Werther
even if he knows nothing about Wordsworth, he feels compelled
to provide his poetry with an emotional dimension. The
ambivalence involved in the attempt to create this dimension,
however, causes us to wonder whether Byron is capable of
feeling any of the emotions which form a part of his act."
"Us" here has to be a modern audience at best--the audience
of Byron's day had no doubt at all. Martin's progressive
negativism takes him further and further away from Byron's
public and nearer and nearer to our own. Thus the gap
widens: "The most damaging aspect of Byron's tragedies from
a historical point of view is that their presentation of
the neo-classical Stoic is in want of a political reference....
This factor alone may not make Byron's dramas bad any more
than it makes Alfieri's good, but to take account of it is
to begin to identify the want of conviction that can be
detected in the continuous retreats into rhetoric and
tableaux. The absence of a political situation in England
in 1820 that could promote real excitement from the dramatic
presentation of high-minded sacrificial conduct means that
the gestures of Byron's tragedies must be regarded as
fundamentally aesthetic rather than political. That is to
say, they were offered purely as a demonstration against
the condition of the contemporary stage. As such they are

insufficiently felt to create around them an artistic
context through which they could succeed." Well, shut my
Tocqueville, burn the censored text of *Marino Faliero*,
and ignore the opening-night audience reaction! It was
Drinkwater who wrote that Byron was as crazy as his audience
but smarter. (T.L.A.)

McGann, Jerome J., ed. *Lord Byron: The Complete Poetical
Works*. Clarendon Press, Oxford University Press, 1980-81.
Vol. II: pp. viii+464; Vol. III: pp. x+498. $98.00 each;
$59.00 each in paper.

Vol. I reviewed by Carl Woodring in *KSJ* 31 (1982): 207-
09; by Malcolm Kelsall in *Byron Journal* 10 (1982): 80-81;
by Frederick L. Beatty in *SiR* 21 (1982): 518-23; by Jack
Stillinger in *JEGP* 81 (1982): 125-29; by Neil Fraistat
in *TWC* 13 (1982): 152-54; see also *RMB* for 1981, p. 89;
Vol. II reviewed by J. Drummond Bone in *Byron Journal* 10
(1982): 81-82; Vols. I-II by C. Bergerolle in *EA* 35 (1982):
337; Vols. I-III by James Chandler in *MP* 80 (1982): 208-
11; by J. Drummond Bone in *MLR* 78 (1983): 154-57.
Of the reviews, Bone's longer critique is central, provid-
ing both questions and answers, and corrections; Woodring
has many minor criticisms of format and rejects some coup-
lets and two epigrams; Fraistat offers a few proof corrections; Beatty a great deal more; and Stillinger writes:
"As an admirer of precision, however, I think perhaps the
work in both manuscript and proofs was not sufficiently
checked." But it is Kelsall, who asks (of *Hints from Horace*):
"But in matters of topical satire is there not a strong
case for printing the text closest to the events (1811)
and not the doctored afterthoughts of another decade?"
and Bone writing: "There would appear to be an awful
muddle over the copy-text used for Canto IV [*Childe Harold's
Pilgrimage*]" who raise the most serious issues. I think it
no heresy to suggest that editing Byron's poetry would
exceed the difficulty of editing his letters. The letters
took a lifetime. For a single individual to attempt the
poems and plays in twenty years at the most is a Herculean--
no, I have to say Promethean--action; despite the work on
Don Juan and other poems already completed. The great
misfortune is that the manuscript situation did not allow
for an organized team effort for a twenty-five-year period.
Other editions come to mind, and the corrections and
emendations of the unfolding text will continue; let us
hope for the widest debate. Surely we will get a detailed
errata in the final volume, just as we certainly gain
immeasurably from the present volumes. (T.L.A.)

Melikian, Anahid. *Byron and the East*. Beirut: American Univer-
    sity Press (now distributed by Syracuse University Press),
    1977. Pp. 124. $13.00.

    Not seen.

Pieske, Christa. "Mazeppa, exemple d'une illustration murale."
    GBA 100 (Sept. 1982): 85–86.

    On interpretations of Byron's poem in painting, sculpture,
    and engraving.

Raphael, Frederic. *Byron*. London and New York: Thames & Hudson,
    1982. Pp. 224. $18.95.

    A review by Richard Deveson in the *New Statesman* (Aug.
    20, 1982, p. 20) says it all: "This is not a book that the
    world badly needed." (T.L.A.) Rev. by Michiko Kakutani in
    NYT, Nov. 4, 1982, p. C23, as unscholarly; by Peter Quennell
    in *S*, Aug. 7, 1982, pp. 20f.
    Only listed but not mentioned separately in John Bayley's
    long review article noted above under Martin.

Rosa, George M. "Byronism and 'Babilanisme' in *Armance*." *MLR*
    77 (1982): 797–814.

    Stendhal's Octave suffers from Byronic impotence in the
    style of the *Corsair*'s Conrad. (T.L.A.)

Sharma, Kavita A. *Byron's Plays: A Reassessment*. (SSEL, Poetic
    Drama & Poetic Theory, 69.) University of Salzburg, Austria,
    1982. Pp. iv+222. (No index.) $13.50.

    The SSEL series, despite its difficulties, has served
    Byron scholars in America and England by publishing the work
    of a younger generation of critics writing abroad. Last
    year SSEL gave us Dr. Kushwaha's first-rate study of Byron's
    dramas, and this year it follows with Dr. Sharma's success-
    ful reassessment. Again we note that Dr. Sharma has brought
    his research up to the present moment, unlike earlier scholars
    publishing in this series. However, reference to both Kush-
    waha and to Tandom's recent work on the plays is needed.
    Dr. Sharma gives us a brief introduction to Byron the drama-
    tist, followed by the two major sections of the study on the
    historical plays and the metaphysical works. Each of these
    sections has its own introduction and conclusion. The read-
    ing is eminently sensible throughout both sections. Finally,
    Dr. Sharma gives us a separate chapter on *Werner* that goes
    beyond his earlier readings. The book's conclusion repeats
    the insistence that the thrust of the historical plays is

political, and that of the metaphysical dramas "questions
God's ways to man." But it does not synthesize these tasks
as Bostetter, writing on the "Politics of Paradise" and
borrowing Byron's phrase, did. (T.L.A.)

Sherbo, Arthur. "From the *Gentleman's Magazine*: VI. The Text
and Canon of Byron's Poems." *SB* 35 (1982): 301-03.

Ten poems by or attributed to Byron appeared in the magazine from 1812 to 1824, some of which contain significant
variations from the received texts.

Stark, Myra. "The Princess of Parallelograms, or the Case of
Lady Byron." *KSJ* 31 (1982): 118-35.

Poor Malcolm Elwin takes an undeserved drubbing in this
somewhat dated piece whose author prefers a portrait of Lady
Byron as Florence Nightingale. What it all comes down to
is this: "A 'lesser life' hers may be, but her life had a
reality of its own: it deserves to be seen." (T.L.A.)

Steffan, T.G., E. Steffan, and W.W. Pratt. *Lord Byron: Don
Juan*. Yale University Press, 1982. Pp. 759. $25.00; $8.95
paper.

This is a reprint of the 1973 Penguin edition, itself
reprinted in 1977. Four changes in the text result from the
recent availability of the proofs of cantos I and II. Additions to the notes post-1977 are given on pp. 756-59.
(T.L.A.)

Trueblood, Paul G., ed. *Byron's Political and Cultural In-
fluence in Nineteenth-Century Europe: A Symposium*. Atlantic
Highlands, N.J.: Humanities Press; London: Macmillan, 1981.
Pp. xx+210. $30.00; £15.00.

Listed in *RMB* for 1981, p. 102.
Rev. by Hermione de Almeida in *KSJ* 31 (1982): 210-12; by
D.H. Reiman in *SAQ* 81 (1982): 478-79; by Allen Rodway in
N&Q 29 (1982): 366-67; by Ian Scott-Kilvert in *Byron Journal*
10 (1982): 95-96.
Contents: Douglas Dakin, "The Historical Background";
William Ruddick, "Byron and England"; Robert Escarpit,
"Byron and France"; Cedric Hentschel, "Byron and Germany";
E.G. Protopsaltis, "Byron and Greece"; Giorgio Melchiori,
"Byron and Italy"; Juliusz Zulawski, "Byron and Poland";
F. de Mello Moser, "Byron and Portugal"; Nina Diakonova
and Vadim Vacuro, "Byron and Russia"; Estaban Pujals,
"Byron and Spain"; Ernest Giddey, "Byron and Switzerland";
Paul G. Trueblood, "Byron and Europe." Though he ends quot-

ing Byron on "Words are things," Dakin's is a good period-
history summary--though the Atlantic tradition (or connection) is missing. Ruddick's work is on the persistence of
Byron's ideals--not the politics of his day. Escarpit finds
only a figurative connection to the revolution of 1848.
Hentschel finds Byron's Hellenism significant for German
idealism. "Byron and Greece" concentrates on the last days,
rather than the days ahead. Melchiori finds Byron a catalyst
of *Risorgimento*. Diakonova is more concerned with literary
influence, and Pushkin in particular, and for Giddey see
under Clubbe above. In conclusion Trueblood summarizes all
the essays, and adds them up to his point: Byron's connection of the new nationalism and the spirit of ancient
liberty is the source of Byron's political persistence. But
always this union needs to be understood in the context
of Pocock's monumental study of the roots of the Atlantic
republican tradition in Florentine political thought.
(T.L.A.)

Wellens, Oskar. "Francis Hodgson: Reviewer of Byron in the
    'Critical Review.'" *NM* 83 (1982): 203-09.

    Assigns reviews of *Childe Harold's Pilgrimage* (June 1812),
Giaour (July 1813), and the *Bride of Abydos* (July 1813)
to Hodgson, on the basis of internal evidence carefully
elucidated, while adding to our understanding of the shift
to ultra-conservative judgments following 1815. (T.L.A.)

See also Graham, Tsigakon ("General 2. Environment"); Raizis,
Sadowska-Guillon ("General 3. Criticism"); Aitken ("English
1. Bibliography"); Hulcoop ("English 3. Criticism"); Minor
("Clare"); Hemmings ("French 1. General"); MacGregor
("French 2. Girodet"); Rosa ("French 2. Stendhal").

Reviews of books previously listed:

BURNETT, T.A.J., *The Rise and Fall of a Regency Dandy:
The Life and Times of Scrope Berdmore Davies* (see *RMB* for
1981, p. 92), rev. by Martin R. Davies in *Byron Journal*
10 (1982): 92-93; by Peter W. Graham ("A Dandy in Amber")
in *SAQ* 81 (1981): 455-61; by Andrew Sanders in *HT* 32 (Feb.
1982): 56; DE ALMEIDA, Hermione, *Byron and Joyce through
Homer: Don Juan and Ulysses* (see *RMB* for 1981, pp. 93-95),
rev. by Arnold Goldman in *Byron Journal* 10 (1982): 90-92,
with criticism; ditto by K.E. Marre in *MFS* 28 (1982):
267-68; by Michael Seidel in a composite review in *YR* 71
(1982): 604-11; by Frederick W. Shilstone in *SAR* 47,iii
(1982): 77-80; MANNING, Peter J., *Byron and His Fictions*

(see *ELN* 17, Supp., 72), rev. by Ian Scott-Kilvert in *YES* 12 (1982): 296-98; MARCHAND, Leslie A., ed., *Byron's Letters and Journals*, 11: 1823-24 (see *RMB* for 1981, pp. 99-100), rev. by Betty T. Bennett in *TWC* 13 (1982): 151-52; and by Frederick W. Shilstone in *SCR* 15,i (1982): 129-31; RANDOLPH, Francis Lewis, *Studies for a Byron Bibliography* (see *RMB* for 1980, p. 89), rev. by J. Drummond Bone in *YES* 12 (1982): 298-99; by Theodore Hofmann, as "essential," in *BC* 31 (1982): 257-58; TRUEBLOOD, Paul Graham, ed., *Byron's Political and Cultural Influence in Nineteenth-Century Europe: A Symposium* (see *RMB* for 1981, p. 102), rev. by Donald H. Reiman in *SAQ* 81 (1982): 478-79.

Composite review:

Jack, Ian. "Byron Refreshed." *Review* 4 (1982): 1-17.

Reviews Leslie A. Marchand, ed., *Byron's Letters and Journals* 12 vols. (see above) and Jerome J. McGann, ed., *Lord Byron: The Complete Poetical Works*, Vols. I-III (see above). Jack praises the format and accuracy of Marchand's work, but has several "minute and niggling criticisms" about mistakes in Latin and sometimes inadequate annotations. Although he finds McGann's chronological arrangement of the poetry unwise, he praises the edition highly, especially the commentary.

Review article:

Spender, Stephen. "Statesman Manqué." *NR*, year-end issue, 1982, pp. 32-36.

Includes comments on Frederic Raphael, *Byron* (see above) and *Lord Byron: Selected Letters and Journals*, ed. Leslie A. Marchand (see above).

CARLYLE

Baker, Lee C.R. "Carlyle's Secret Debt to Schiller: The Concept of Goethe's Genius." *VN* 61 (1982): 21-22.

"Few scholars have recognized Thomas Carlyle's debt to Friedrich Schiller." The short list grows. (T.L.A.)

Bennett, J.A.W. *The Humane Medievalist and Other Essays in English Literature and Learning, from Chaucer to Eliot.* Ed. Piero Boitani. Rome: Edizioni di Storia e Letterature, 1982. Pp. 410. L25,000,00.

Rev. by Stephen Medcalf in *TLS*, Apr. 1, 1983, pp. 317-18.
Contains a chapter on "Carlyle and the Medieval Past."
Not seen.

Cate, George Allan, ed. *The Correspondence of Thomas Carlyle
and John Ruskin.* Stanford University Press, 1982. Pp. x+251;
12 illus. $28.50.

Cate's edition includes 115 letters from Ruskin to Carlyle
and 39 from Carlyle to Ruskin. Of these, 80 of the former
and 12 of the latter are published for the first time. As
we might expect, we learn more about Ruskin than Carlyle,
the more so because Carlyle's letters date mostly from the
early and middle years of the relationship. Nevertheless,
Carlyle's letters are almost all of substantial length
and content.

In Carlyle's early and middle letters, a typical pattern
finds him beginning with thanks for some gift--cigars,
brandy, flowers for Jane Welsh. The tone is hearty, jocular,
and gruffly affectionate to Ruskin. Carlyle then moves on
to a serious topic of common interest, such as Durer's
engravings or geology, Carlyle's style is sturdy, secure,
and laced with earthy metaphors.

The few later letters show his deep concern at Ruskin's
declining mental health. We sense this concern in a passage
of troubled praise in one of the hitherto unpublished
letters: "In fact it becomes clearer to the world than ever
that there is but one Ruskin in the world; an unguidable
man, but with quantities of lightning in the interior of
him, which are strange and probably dangerous to behold.
Well, well; unguidable to outsiders you surely are; and
you justly may pretend to spend your own lightning in the
way you find suitablest to this wildly anarchic condition
of affairs. Continue only for a quarter of a century yet
as you may fairly hope to do; there will be something of
result visible, something of combustion, kindling here and
there in the dark, boundless belly of our Chaos; and mean-
while the clang of the silver bow will be cheering to all
the select of men." A few lines later he concludes: "With
all my heart I wish you noble victory and success" (190).

The fifty-eight-page introduction is helpful on biography
but has little on the nature of their intellectual relationship. However, the publication of new material is certainly welcome, and the book includes a useful index.
(R.A.H.)

Harris, Kenneth Marc. *Carlyle and Emerson: Their Long Debate.*
Harvard University Press, 1978. Pp. 194. $12.50.

Rev. by Bruce Kuklick in *JHP* 19 (1981): 515.

Le Quesne, A.L. *Carlyle*. Oxford University Press, 1982. Pp.
99. $12.95/£5.50; £1.25 paper.

    Rev. by Rosemary Ashton in *TLS*, Sept. 24, 1982, p. 1046,
as an excellent survey, full of "illuminating sketches and
stimulating hints for further reading"; by Ian Campbell in
SLJ 9 (1982): supp. 17, pp. 91–92, as making *too much* sense.
Not seen.

Tarr, Rodger L. "Carlyle's Incidental Montage: *The Guises* and
the Theory of Transcendent Historicism." *VN* 61 (1982): 8–11.

    "To use the words of Eugene O'Neill, Carlyle writes from
'tears and blood.'" (T.L.A.)

Tarr, Rodger L. "Emendation as Challenge: Carlyle's 'Negro
Question' from Journal to Pamphlet." *PBSA* 75 (1981): 341–45.

    The attack on telescopic philanthropy became more pro-
vocative in the revised version.

Tarr, Rodger L., and Carol Anita Clayton. "'Carlyle in America':
An Unpublished Short Story by Sarah Orne Jewett." *AL* 54
(1982): 101–15.

    Carlyle meets Thoreau at Walden Pond and Emerson in Con-
cord on a secret visit to America. Jewett's story is more
evidence of the pervasive influence of Carlyle on American
writers.

Taylor, Beverly. "Carlyle's Historical Imagination: Untrue
Facts and Unfactual Truths." *VN* 61 (1982): 29–31.

    Reminds us of Scott's influence. (T.L.A.)

See also Morris, Waddington ("General 3. Criticism"); Aitken
("English 1. Bibliography"); Stone ("English 3. Criticism").

Reviews of books previously listed:

    CLUBBE, John, ed., *Froude's Life of Carlyle* (see *RMB* for
1979, p. 89), rev. by J.R. Watson in *DUJ*, n.s. 44 (1982):
92–93; DIBBLE, Jerry A., *The Pythia's Drunken Song: Thomas
Carlyle's "Sartor Resartus"* (see *ELN* 17, Supp., 76–77),
rev. by Marshall Brown in *CRCL* 9 (1982): 287–93.

CLARE

Lessa, Richard. "Time and John Clare's Calendar." *CritQ* 24:1 (1982): 59-71.

The only escape Clare allows from the drudgery of country life is into memories of a happier past.

Minor, Mark. "Clare, Byron, and the Bible: Additional Evidence from the Asylum Manuscripts." *BRH* 85 (1982): 104-26.

Clare's manuscript additions to Byron's *Hebrew Melodies* are here discussed for the first time. Minor calls particular attention to the genuine impact on Clare's poetry not only of Byron's poems but of the Old Testament sources of the "Hebrew Melodies."

Robinson, Eric, and Richard Fitter, eds. *John Clare's Birds*. (Illustrated by Robert Gillmore.) Oxford University Press, 1982. Pp. xxii+105; 25 illus. $16.50.

Rev. by Redmond O'Hanlon in *TLS*, Jan. 21, 1983, p. 70, who is severe on Fitter for passing over Clare's mistakes of bird lore and for making several of his own.
Clare described 145 British birds from observation, also 135 species of plants. This gathering of his notes, poems, and "natural history letters" about birds has considerable charm.
"Birds increasingly become, as Clare matures as a poet, a quality of his environment" modified as he grows "more and more concerned to stress ... particularity and ... limits" (ix). (D.V.E.)

Strickland, Edward. "Conventions and Their Subversions in John Clare's 'An Invite to Eternity.'" *Criticism* 24 (1982): 1-15.

According to Strickland, the poem is "concerned more than anything else with articulating [Clare's] difficulties and his doubts about his ability to go on as a poet."

Review of book previously listed:

TIBBLE, Anne, and R.K.R. Thornton, eds., *The Midsummer Cushion* (see *RMB* for 1980, p. 94), rev. by Patricia M. Ball in *YES* 12 (1982): 300-01.

COBBETT

Lemrow, Lynne. "William Cobbett's Journalism for the Lower
    Orders." *VPR* 15 (1982): 11-26.

Spater, George. *William Cobbett: The Poor Man's Friend.*
    2 vols. Cambridge University Press, 1982. Illus. $49.50.
    Rev. by Ronald Blythe in *NYRB*, June 10, 1982, pp. 29-30;
    by David Bromwich in *NR*, Dec. 13, 1982, pp. 29-34; by
    J.F.C. Harrison in *TLS*, June 25, 1982, pp. 685-87, as "a
    plain, workmanlike job" that Cobbett would have approved
    of; by Gertrude Himmelfarb in *The New Criterion* 1 (Oct.
    1982): 42-50, calling attention to the negative aspects
    of Cobbett's complex character; by Richard Ingrams in *S*,
    May 1, 1982, p. 20; by Brian Martin in *New Statesman*,
    May 14, 1982, p. 26, as "a major achievement"; by John W.
    Osborne in *AHR* 87 (1982): 1387-88, with some disappointment
    for its interpretation but praise for its wealth of new
    material; in *PBSA* 76 (1982): 506f.; by Sam Pickering in
    SR 90 (1982): xc-xciv.
       There have been many biographies of Cobbett, but none
    so ample, so sturdily keeping abreast of the Porcupine,
    and so generously giving a chronological sampling of the
    strong words of a man who was all his life busy writing--
    an estimated twenty million words in print! Cobbett was
    also busy with his feet, and his voice, and we are well
    served by George Spater's Boswellian faithfulness to all
    these movements of his hero. A clear, sympathetic narrative
    reporting, properly emphasizing (as in the subtitle) the
    positive features of those movements--with an occasional
    parenthetical grin or wincing at an outrageous self-por-
    trait or sudden decamping, whereby Cobbett kept the initia-
    tive through most of the swings and bloody upsettings of
    Anglo-French-American history from Revolution to Reform
    Bill: this is the best way to keep "The Poor Man's Friend"
    on our library shelves. For political diagnoses we still
    have C.D.H. Cole's *Life* (while Spater draws upon much new
    material) and the many pages in E.P. Thompson's *Making
    of the English Working Class* in which we are shown how
    Cobbett was often "right in his description of causes but
    wrong in his conclusions." And most of us will be happier
    with making our own evaluations than accepting the insis-
    tence (in John W. Osborne's *Thought and Times*, 1966) that
    Cobbett must be regarded primarily as a reactionary.
       The end-papers map "Cobbett's Corner of England"; Gillray
    caricature prints supply many of the fifty-two illustra-
    tions, saving the biographer from conflict of interest.
    An excellent work. (D.V.E.)

COLERIDGE

Brisman, Leslie. "Coleridge and the Supernatural." *SiR* 21 (1982): 123-59.

   In this tour-de-force (see especially pp. 148-50) Bris-man argues for "Coleridge's romanticism as a form of radical Protestantism." Coleridge's "view of the relation of miracles to faith may be regarded as the very center of his religious thought"; if miracles were regarded as evidence for faith, then the senses would take priority. Instead, "the whole project of the domestication of the sublime ... the 'theology' as well as the style of the conversation poems, for example--is the expression in poetry of the imitation of Christ," who is the copresence of signifier and signified. Avoiding simple reduction to repetitions of "the One Life idea," Brisman explores the complex implications of his thesis and concludes by applying it to *The Rime of the Ancient Mariner*. (M.T.S.)

Christensen, Jerome. "Once an Apostate Always an Apostate." *SiR* 21 (1982): 461-64.

   See below, Woodring, "Coleridge: The Politics of the Imagination."

Christopher, Joe R. "The Ancient Mariner Baptised: A Study of New Birth in Parts V and VI of *The Rime of the Ancient Mariner*." *SCB* 42 (1982): 117-19.

Doughty, Oswald. *Perturbed Spirit: The Life and Personality of Samuel Taylor Coleridge*. Fairleigh Dickinson University Press, 1981. Pp. 365. $40.00.

   Rev. by Thomas McFarland (see below, p. 115).

Fischer, Michael. "Morality and History in Coleridge's Political Theory." *SiR* 21 (1982): 457-60.

   See below, Woodring, "Coleridge: The Politics of the Imagination."

Gravil, Richard. "A New Conversation Poem by Coleridge?" *ChLB* 37 (1982): 94-98.

   A sympathetically eloquent reading of "The Pains of Sleep" as fulfilling the requirement of the complexities of daring to "commune with our very and permanent self" (*The Friend*). Convincing. (D.V.E.)

Harding, Anthony John. "Inspiration and the Historical Sense in 'Kubla Khan.'" *TWC* 13 (1982): 3-8.

Jackson, H.J. "Coleridge's Collaborator, Joseph Henry Green." *SiR* (1982): 160-79.

Traces the friendship between Coleridge and Green: the two men met at least once a week from 1818 to 1834, and Green acted as Coleridge's literary executor after his death.

Jackson, H.J. "Coleridge's 'Maxilian.'" *CL* 33 (1981): 38-49.

An item of comparative literature, because the source of Coleridge's "The Historie and Gests of Maxilian" has been discovered (by Cyrus Hamlin) to be E.T.A. Hoffmann's "Der goldne Topf." Jackson discusses briefly Coleridge's checkered relations with *Blackwood's*, which published a first part of "The Historie," and gives a clear text of a manuscript fragment, hitherto unpublished, of a second part. Neglects the human side of Coleridge's gest/jest as a parody of his own magazine, *The Friend*. (D.V.E.)

Johnson, Barbara. "Teaching as a Literary Genre." *YFS*, no. 63 (1982): iii-vii.

The editor's preface to an issue titled *The Pedagogical Imperative: Teaching as a Literary Genre*, as well as an analysis of the relationship between poem and gloss in "The Rime of the Ancient Mariner." Both are pedagogical, the Mariner in the poem teaching the Wedding Guest, the gloss teaching the reader. The poem, however, dramatizes discontinuities in rational logic and suggests that one aspect of teaching is the compulsion to repeat what is not understood. The gloss, in contrast, represents the traditional pedagogical impulse to explain, to fill in discontinuities with causal explanations and moral judgments. Interesting, but we can learn a good deal more about this theme in Mann's *Doctor Faustus*. (R.A.H.)

Johnson, Mary Lynn. "Coleridge's Prose and a Blake Plate in Stedman's *Narrative*: Unfastening the 'Hooks & Eyes' of Memory." *TWC* 13 (1982): 36-38.

Levere, Trevor. "S.T. Coleridge and the Human Sciences: Anthropology, Phrenology, and Mesmerism." In M.P. Hanen, M.J. Osler, and R.G. Weyant, eds., *Science, Pseudo-Science and Society*. Wilfrid Laurier University Press, 1980. Pp. x+307. $7.50.

The volume is reviewed by R. Paul Thompson in *QQ* 89 (1982):

915-18. For more on Levere see *RMB* for 1981, p. 107, and above, p. 48. (T.L.A.)

Maiorino, Giancarlo. "A Voice of Its Own Birth: Bruno and the Foundations of Coleridge's Poetics." *CLS* 19 (1982): 296-318.

Argues persuasively that "beyond general references to Platonism and Pantheism, the remarkable modernity of Bruno's philosophy of literature influenced Coleridge's conception of art often to an extent not less important than, and at times positively prior to, contemporary German sources." Thus Maiorino, as compared to McFarland (*Coleridge and the Pantheistic Tradition*), shifts the weight of influence from Schelling toward Bruno. A helpful essay, though the relationship between a poetics of organic unity and Pantheism, suggestively discussed by McFarland, is left unexplored. (R.A.H.)

Marks, Emerson R. *Coleridge on the Language of Verse.* (Princeton Essays in Literature.) Princeton University Press, 1981. Pp. xii+117. $9.50.

Rev. by Edward Kessler in *TWC* 13 (1982): 122-23.

In this pleasantly printed little book, the offshoot of a longer study, Coleridge's views on poetic diction and prosody are reexamined in relation to his version of mimetic theory, with illuminating results. His special status in modern criticism, too, which he acquired through the New Critics, is enhanced by the parallels and affinities the author finds between his (Coleridge's) thought and that of the linguistic and structuralist theorists of the past half-century, especially the members of the Prague School. (I.H.C.)

Miall, David S. "The Meaning of Dreams: Coleridge's Ambivalence." *SiR* 21 (1982): 57-71.

"Did Coleridge have a theory of dreams?" No, but he had insights of "depth and complexity." Comparing Coleridge's ideas and those of earlier speculators--including Hobbes, Hartley, Darwin, and especially Andrew Baxter--Miall concludes that Coleridge was no Freud or Jung. He retained an ambivalence about whether the best and the worst of dreams could issue from a unified self, an ambivalence typical of all aspects of his inquiry into the laws of the mind. (M.T.S.)

Mileur, Jean-Pierre. *Vision and Revision: Coleridge's Art of Immanence.* University of California Press, 1982. Pp. xi+184. $19.00.

Rev. by John Beer in *TLS*, Dec. 17, 1982, p. 1389, as scarcely worth the effort reading.

Another testimony to Coleridge's modernity. "Revision" in
the title refers not only to his later reworking of his
best-known poems but also and more especially to his evolution from "self-alienation" as a poet to ultimate "self-
recognition" as an interpreter of the Bible. The names
alluded to, the terminology employed, and the now familiar
combinations of disciplines and themes--hermeneutics,
"textuality," and psychoanalysis, together with "belated-
ness" and "revision" itself--identify the author as an
eclectic follower of current schools of criticism which some
admirers of the Romantics may still deplore.

Not a few of Mileur's conceptual formulations seem at the
moment to darken rather than elucidate the long-standing
Coleridgean problems; on the level of sentence and paragraph, this is not a book that is easy to read. Yet other
formulations do genuinely clarify Coleridge's subtleties
of thought and statement by subtleties of the author's
own, which earlier criticism could not provide. Although in
their basic outlines the standard readings of the poems are
largely preserved (an exception is Mileur's reinterpretation
of "To William Wordsworth"), they now are brought together
with his prose in a new, unifying perspective that long has
been needed. (I.H.C.)

Modiano, Raimonda. "Metaphysical Debate in Coleridge's Political Theory." SiR 21 (1982): 465-74.

See below, Woodring, "Coleridge: The Politics of the
Imagination."

Moffat, Douglas. "Coleridge's Ten Theses: The Plotinian
Alternative." TWC 13 (1982): 27-31.

In Ch. XII of the Biographia "what has been dismissed as
bad Schelling is, in fact, rather good Plotinus."

Perlis, Alan D. "Coleridge and Conrad: Spectral Illuminations,
Widening Frames." JNT 12 (1982): 167-76.

In "The Rime of the Ancient Mariner" and Heart of Darkness
multiple-frame narratives and chiaroscuro descriptions
serve to raise questions about the nature of truth.

Randel, Fred V. "Coleridge and the Contentiousness of Romantic
Nightingales." SiR 21 (1982): 33-55.

With some help from Blake and much help from Milton,
Randel analyzes Coleridge's "The Nightingale" to show that
it is both agonistic and organic. Coleridge's poem is a
"rebellious son" to Milton, a "senior sibling" to Words-

worth, and a "generative father" to Keats, in whose great
praise the article concludes. (M.T.S.)

Salinger, Leo. "Shakespeare and the Ventriloquists." *Shakespeare Survey* 34 (1981): 51-59.

A discussion of Coleridge and *Hamlet* which does not consider a "faded portrait of the melancholy prince" but
Coleridge's "general statements about Shakespeare's methods
of characterization," in particular, the "I" representative.
(R.A.B.)

Sitterson, Joseph C., Jr. "'The Rime of the Ancient Mariner'
and Freudian Dream Theory." *PLL* 18 (1982): 17-35.

A useful critique of the "invalid assumption" which underlies most psychoanalytic interpretations of Coleridge's
poem. They tend to treat it as a dream and ignore "the sort
of coherence in the poem which nonpsychoanalytic interpretation finds there" but which Freud does not find characteristic of dreams themselves. The dreamlike quality of
the poem does not make it a dream but involves the presence
as in dreams of what Freud calls "primary process thinking."
(R.A.B.)

Stephens, Fran Carlock. "An Autograph Letter of S.T. Coleridge."
RES 33 (1982): 298-302.

Storch, Rudolf F. "The Politics of the Imagination." *SiR* 21
(1982): 448-56.

See below, Woodring, "Coleridge: The Politics of the
Imagination."

Swiatecka, M. Jadwiga. *The Idea of the Symbol: Some Nineteenth
Century Comparisons with Coleridge.* Cambridge University
Press, 1980. Pp. viii+213. $26.95.

Rev. by Hazard Adams in *JR* 62 (1982): 312-14; by J.
Robert Barth, S.J., in *SiR* 21 (1982): 703-07 as "not a
wholly satisfying book" but "an interesting and potentially
very useful one"; by John L. Mahoney in *TWC* 13 (1982):
124-25.

Talmor, Sascha. "Fancy and Imagination in Coleridge's Poetics."
DUJ, n.s. 43 (1982): 233-40.

"The difference between fancy and imagination is, in the
final count, simply the difference between good and less
good poetry, appraised on the basis of their words, word
order, and structure."

Tyler, Luther. "Coleridge & Co.: A Review Essay." *SCR* 14,ii (1982): 116-28.

A longish essay (and in punishingly small print) on recent books by Hill, Kessler, Marks, and McFarland from 1978 on.

Watson, Kenneth. "Coleridge's Use of Notes." *RP&P* 6,ii (1982): 11-22.

Wellens, Oskar. "John Payne Collier: The Man Behind the Unsigned *Times* Review of 'Christabel' (1816)." *TWC* 13 (1982): 68-72.

Wheeler, Kathleen M. *The Creative Mind in Coleridge's Poetry.* Harvard University Press, 1981. Pp. ix+198. $15.00.

Rev. by P.M.S. Dawson in *CritQ* 24:2 (1982): 87-88; by Anthony John Harding in *MLQ* 43 (1982): 181-85; by Arden Reed in *TWC* 13 (1982): 116-18. Not seen.

Woodring, Carl, ed. "Coleridge: The Politics of the Imagination." *SiR* 21 (1982): 447-74.

One section of *Romantic Texts, Romantic Times* (see Eaves, "English 3. Criticism--Festschrift"). Four authors--Rudolf Storch, Michael Fischer, Jerome Christensen, Raimonda Modiano--discuss Coleridge's metaphysics and political philosophy, touching on his definition of imagination, theory of symbolism, dialectic of polarity, and "apostasy."

Zall, P.M. "The Cool World of Samuel Taylor Coleridge: Joseph Lancaster's System." *TWC* 13 (1982): 91-93.

Zall, P.M. "The Cool World of Samuel Taylor Coleridge: The Question of Joanna Baillie." *TWC* 13 (1982): 17-20.

See also Berridge, Morrell ("English 2. Environment"); Chandler, Kelley, Vickers ("English 3. Criticism"); Higgonet ("German 2. Criticism"); Wheeler ("German 3. Tieck").

Reviews of books previously listed:

CHRISTENSEN, Jerome, *Coleridge's Blessed Machine of Language* (see *RMB* for 1981, pp. 57-58), rev. by Peter J. Manning, enthusiastically, in *TWC* 13 (1982): 112-14; COBURN, Kathleen, *Experience into Thought: Perspectives in the Coleridge Notebooks* (see *RMB* for 1980, p. 94), rev.

by Geoffrey Little in *RES* 33 (1982): 482-84; EVEREST, Kelvin, *Coleridge's Secret Ministry: The Context of the Conversation Poems, 1795-98* (see *RMB* for 1980, p. 95), rev. by Reeve Parker as not "convincing," in *TWC* 13 (1982): 119-20; by P.M. Zall in *ECS* 15 (1982): 362-64; JACKSON, J.R. de J., *Samuel Taylor Coleridge, Logic*, No. 13 of *The Collected Works of Samuel Taylor Coleridge* (see *RMB* for 1981, p. 107), rev. by Raimonda Modiano in *TWC* 13 (1982): 108-12; KESSLER, Edward, *Coleridge's Metaphors of Being* (see *RMB* for 1979, p. 93), rev. by W.J.B. Owen in *RES* 33 (1982): 214-16; by Stephen Prickett in *YES* 12 (1982): 291-93; SULTANA, Donald, ed., *New Approaches to Coleridge: Biographical and Critical Essays* (noted, but not reviewed, in *RMB* for 1981, p. 109), rev. by Rosemary Ashton in *TWC* 13 (1982): 120-22; WHALLEY, George, ed., *Marginalia I* (see *RMB* for 1980, pp. 96-97), rev. by J. Robert Barth, S.J., in *TWC* 13 (1982): 106-08; by Denise Degrois in *EA* 35 (1982): 474-75; by Elinor Shaffer in *SiR* 21 (1982): 531-40; WHEELER, Kathleen, *Sources, Processes and Methods in Coleridge's "Biographia Literaria"* (see *RMB* for 1980, pp. 97-98), rev. by John Colmer in *AUMLA* 57 (1982): 79-81; by John W. Wright in *TWC* 13 (1982): 114-16.

Composite review:

McFarland, Thomas. "Complicated People: Three Studies in Romantic Sensibility." *YR* 72 (1982): 95-105.

Review essay on recent studies of Coleridge by Grevel Lindop (see *RMB* for 1981, p. 112), Oswald Doughty, and Kathleen Wheeler (*RMB* for 1980, p. 97).

THE CRITICAL REVIEW

See Wellens ("Byron").

DARWIN

King-Hele, Desmond, ed. *The Letters of Erasmus Darwin.* Cambridge University Press, 1981. Pp. xxxii+363; 51 illus. $95.00.

Rev. by Donald M. Hassler in *TWC* 13 (1982): 137-38. Not seen.

DE QUINCEY

Bilsland, John W. "De Quincey's Critical Dilations." *UTQ* 52
    (1982): 79-93.

    Although the "dilations" occasionally are distorting, "they
    always derive from De Quincey's own deeply felt and pro-
    foundly personal experiences, and ... convey a vivid sense
    of his insights as a sympathetic and imaginative reader."

Wilner, Joshua. "Autobiography and Addiction: The Case of
    DeQuincey." *Genre* 14 (1981): 493-503.

    Uses the anonymous *Confessions* to test Philippe Lejeune's
    theory of the importance of proper names in defining auto-
    biography.

See also Berridge ("English 2. Environment"); composite
    review by Curran ("English 3. Criticism").

Reviews of books previously listed:

    DE LUCA, V.A., *Thomas De Quincey: The Prose of Vision* (see
    RMB for 1980, p. 100), rev. by John R. Nabholtz in *ELN* 20
    (1982): 68-70; by Robert Lance Snyder in *SAR* 46:4 (1981):
    67-70; LINDOP, Grevel, *The Opium-Eater: A Life of Thomas
    DeQuincey* (see *RMB* for 1981, p. 112), rev. by Betty Abel
    in *ContR* 239 (Dec. 1981): 331-32; by Bill Ruddick in *ChLB*
    37 (1982): 101-03, as needed and well done; by J.R. Watson
    in *CritQ* 24,ii (1982): 13-17.

DYER

Wickham, D.E. "'Amicus Redivivus' Repertus: A New Discovery
    about George Dyer." *ChLB* 38 (1982): 114-16.

    Wickham, archivist of the Clothworkers' Company, finds
    that Dyer's university career was supported by an exhibi-
    tion (worth £10 a year) from the Clothworkers' Company
    trust fund.

EDGEWORTH

See Figes ("English 3. Criticism").

Reviews of book previously listed:

COLVIN, Christina, ed., *Maria Edgeworth in France and Switzerland: Selections from the Edgeworth Family Letters* (see *RMB* for 1980, p. 101), rev. by J. Lough in *FS* 36 (1982): 209; by George O'Brien in *YES* 12 (1982): 288-89; by F.B. Pinion in *RES* 33 (1982): 90-92.

EDINBURGH REVIEW

See MacKenzie ("English 3. Criticism").

THE ENGLISHMAN'S MAGAZINE

Prance, Claude A. "*The Englishman's Magazine*." *ChLB* 37 (1982): 98-101.

A brief account of this short-lived magazine of Edward Moxon (Apr. to Oct. 1831), unsuccessful *despite* help from Lamb.

THE EXAMINER

See Read ("Blake").

GALT

See Aitken ("English 1. Bibliography"); Campbell ("English 3. Criticism").

THE GENTLEMEN'S MAGAZINE

See Sherbo ("Byron").

GODWIN

Bentley, G.E., Jr. "Copyright Documents in the George Robinson Archive: William Godwin and Others 1713-1820." *SB* 35 (1982): 67-110.

The documents provide an informative record of an important publisher's business dealings with his writers, Godwin prominent among them.

Butler, Marilyn. "Godwin, Burke, and *Caleb Williams.*" *EiC* 32 (1982): 237-57.

Palacio, Jean de. *William Godwin et son monde intérieur.* Presses universitaires de Lille (diffusion: Les Belles Lettres), 1980. Pp. 220. Fr. 63.00.

Rev. by Jean Gillet in *Romantisme* 37 (1982): 125-26; by Peter Marshall in *EA* 35 (1982): 335-36, as disappointing. Not seen.

See also Emerson et al., Marra et al. ("English 3. Criticism"); Hyde, Scrivener ("Shelley, P.B.").

Reviews of book previously listed:

LOCKE, Don, *A Fantasy of Reason: The Life and Thought of William Godwin* (see *RMB* for 1980, p. 102), rev. by James H. Averill in *TWC* 13 (1982): 138-39; by R.L. Brett in *RES* 33 (1982): 340-41; by Mitzi Myers in *ECS* 16 (1982): 77-79 and found wanting.

THE GOTHIC NOVEL

Beer, Gillian. "'Our unnatural No-voice': The Heroic Epistle, Pope, and Women's Gothic." *YES* 12 (1982): 125-51.

Lewis, Paul. "Mysterious Laughter: Humor and Fear in Gothic Fiction." *Genre* 14 (1981): 309-27.

Borrows "incongruity theory" from psychology to develop a system of structural classification based on the balance of humor and fear in the novels (including *Northanger Abbey*). A useful exercise. (R.M.R.)

Noske, Frits. "Sound and Sentiment: The Function of Music in the Gothic Novel." *M&L* 62 (1981): 162-75.

Ann Radcliffe in particular used music as a plot device, a way of expressing strong feeling, and an indicator of moral character. (Charlotte Dacre and Lewis also mentioned.)

Tracy, Ann B. *The Gothic Novel, 1790-1830: Plot Summaries and Index to Motifs*. University Press of Kentucky, 1981. Pp. viii+216. $14.00.

Rev. by Coral Ann Howells in *VPR* 15 (1982): 81-82.

See also Frew ("English 2. Environment"); "Godwin"; "Lewis"; "Radcliffe."

Reviews of book previously listed:

MacANDREW, Elizabeth, *The Gothic Tradition in Fiction* (see *RMB* for 1981, p. 114), rev. by Frederick Garber in *CLS* 19 (1982): 394-96 with tempered praise; by Terry Heller in *ArQ* 38 (1982): 87-89.

Composite review:

Gresham, Stephen. *SHR* 16 (1982): 70-71.

Reviews Elizabeth MacAndrew, *The Gothic Tradition in Fiction* (see *RMB* for 1981, p. 114); Judith Wilt, *Ghosts of the Gothic: Austen, Eliot, and Lawrence* (see *RMB* for 1981, p. 75); David Punter, *The Literature of Terror: A History of Gothic Fictions from 1765 to the Present Day* (see *RMB* for 1980, p. 61); and James B. Twitchell, *The Living Dead: A Study of the Vampire in Romantic Literature* (see *RMB* for 1981, p. 68).

HAZLITT

Albrecht, W.P. "Structure in Two of Hazlitt's Essays." *SiR* 21 (1982): 181-90.

Focusing on the "metonymic substitutions" in "On Going on a Journey" and "Why Distant Objects Please," Albrecht shows that the second part of each essay reverses the first part, and suggests that his methods may be useful for studying more complex essays such as "The Indian Jugglers" and "On the Fear of Death." (M.T.S.)

Jones, Stanley. *The Second Mrs. Hazlitt—A Problem in Literary Biography*. University College of Swansea, 1982. Pp. 17.

Investigates "a literary mystery," the identity of Hazlitt's second wife.

Ready, Robert. *Hazlitt at Table*. East Brunswick, N.J.:
Associated University Presses, 1981. Pp. 126. $13.50.

Rev. by Joel Haefner in *ChLB* 38 (1982): 116-19 as
failing, from obscure verbiage and up-beat jargon, to
keep its critical feet on the ground; by Ralph M. Wardle
in *KSJ* 31 (1981): 223-24.
Not seen.

Story, Patrick. "'William Hazlitt's *Spirit of the Age* and
Sir William Allan': A Correction." *KSJ* 31 (1982): 29-30.

Marcia Allentuck's article "William Hazlitt's *Spirit of
the Age* and Sir William Allan: A Commentary," *KSJ* 30 (1981):
29-33, prompts Story to note that he had already published
Allan's commentary in *The Wordsworth Circle* in 1970. Following Story's "Correction" is Allentuck's "Response" (pp.
30-31).

Verdi, Richard. "Hazlitt and Poussin." *KSMB* 32 (1981): 1-18.

Argues that Hazlitt was instrumental in effecting the
change of taste that led to regarding Poussin "less as a
learned and philosophical painter than as a profoundly
lyrical and emotional one." Also counters (pp. 15n.-16n.)
Ian Jack's contention that Poussin's paintings specifically
inspired Keats's poetry.

Wells, Stanley. "Shakespeare in Hazlitt's Theatre Criticism."
ShS 35 (1982): 43-56.

Useful for its strong partiality to Hazlitt not Hunt.
(T.L.A.)

See also Vickers ("English 3. Criticism"); Prochazka ("French
2. Stael").

Review of book previously listed:

KEYNES, Geoffrey, *Bibliography of William Hazlitt* (see
RMB for 1981, p. 116), rev. by Theodore Hofmann in *BC*
31 (1982): 248, 251.

HOGG

Groves, David. "Parallel Narratives in Hogg's *Justified
Sinner*." *SLJ* 9:2 (1982): 37-44.

"Hogg's faith in the possibility of an authentic middle way, however, is conveyed through the sustained structural parallel, through irony which undermines the pretensions and extreme positions of both narrators, through the choric roles of Bessy Gillies and Samuel Scrape, and finally through the antithetical character development of the two narrators." Argued. (T.L.A.)

Laughlan, William F., ed. *James Hogg's "Highland Tours."* Hawick: Byways Books, 1981. Pp. viii+160. £1.95.

> Rev. by Douglas Gifford in *SLJ* 9 (1982): supp. 17, pp. 84-89.
> A selection for bicyclists that remembers. (T.L.A.)

Morris, Patricia. "A Periodical Paternity Claim: Pringle vs. Hogg." *ESA* 25 (1982): 55-58.

> A sharp critique of Hogg's claim to be originator of *Blackwood's*. (T.L.A.)

Parr, Norah. *James Hogg at Home.* Dollar: Douglas Mack, 1980. Pp. viii+142.

> Rev. by Douglas Gifford in *SLJ* 9 (1982): supp. 17, pp. 84-89.
> A domestic biography by a distant great granddaughter. (T.L.A.)

Smith, Nelson C. *James Hogg.* (Twayne's English Authors.) Boston: Twayne Publishers, 1980. Pp. 188. $11.95.

> Rev. by Douglas Gifford in *SLJ* 9 (1982): supp. 17, pp. 84-89.

See also Aitken ("English 1. Bibliography").

KEATS

Bowe, Nicola Gordon. "The Miniature Stained Glass Panels of Harry Clarke." *Apollo* 115 (1982): 111-13.

> Including one on Keats's *Eve of St. Agnes*.

Chambers, Jane. "'For Love's Sake': *Lamia* and Burton's Love Melancholy." *SEL* 22 (1982): 583-600.

> Chambers uses Burton effectively to provide a context in which the characters seem to behave more intelligibly,

but she doesn't convince this reader that Apollonius was
motivated by love melancholy. All in all, she probably takes
the poem more seriously than Keats did. (R.M.R.)

Coldwell, Joan. "'Meg Merrilies': Scott's Gipsy Tamed." *KSMB*
32 (1981): 30-37.

Goslee, Nancy M. "Phidian Lore: Sculpture and Personification
in Keats's Odes." *SiR* 21 (1982): 73-85.

The central figures in "Indolence," "Psyche," "Melancholy,"
and "Autumn" are "images of a longed-for sculptural, mythic,
and unself-conscious wholeness of the human, the artificial,
and the natural," but they lose presence as they are per-
sonified, reduced to abstract names, by a modern consciousness. Goslee's idea, a good one, is almost hidden by the
heavy scaffolding borrowed from A.W. Schlegel, Angus Fletcher,
Geoffrey Hartman, and Paul Fry. (R.M.R.)

Lovell, Ernest J., Jr., and John Clubbe. "Keats the Humanist."
Kentucky Review 3 (1982): 3-18.

Affectionate, fairly routine appreciation of Keats's
mind and personality, with special attention to the reli-
gious-ethical dimension. Lovell nudges Keats a little too
far in the direction of Christianity and doesn't make clear
how a Christian background could nourish Keats's "non-
dogmatic" personality while turning Wordsworth into a
bully. (R.M.R.)

Ogden, James, and A. Jonathan Bate. "Shakespeare and the
'Nightingale': Two Comments." *English* 31 (1982): 134-41.

More Shakespearean echoes in the ode.

Pascal, Richard. "Faulkner's Debt to Keats in *Light in
August*: A Reconsideration." *SoRA* 14 (1981): 161-67.

A defensible argument--that borrowed images are not
necessarily "allusions" to be understood only by reference
to their original context--is undermined by a simplistic
reading of "Ode on a Grecian Urn" as a celebration of
"other-worldly beauty and truth." Faulkner understood
the poem better than Pascal does. (R.M.R.)

Patterson, Charles I., Jr. "The Monomyth in the Structure
of Keats's *Endymion*." *KSJ* 31 (1982): 64-81.

Defends the unity of Keats's plot by pointing out parallels with the universal myth of the hero, as presented in

Joseph Campbell's *The Hero with a Thousand Faces*. A useful exercise, with only occasional signs of strain, as in the easy identification of the Indian maid with Proserpine. (R.M.R.)

Peterfreund, Stuart. "Keats's Debt to Maturin." *TWC* 13 (1982): 45-49.

Rand, Richard. "o'erbrimm'd." *OLR* 5:1-2 (1982; double issue): 37-58.

From the *OLR* conference at Southampton University. In this guerilla action against literary criticism's "policing" of its terms, Rand shows that Keats's "To Autumn," supposedly a "pure" and "perfect" canonical work, is actually a translation. "Autumn has read her Keats attentively, and has translated him with exceptional fidelity and shrewdness." Well, someone is shrewd, but not necessarily faithful. How much does this have to do with Keats or with poetry? Rand tries to "let the word 'translation' spread to a fuller semantic range, towards the limit (if such a limit indeed exists) of its semantic potential." Fun to read, but as Rand admits in the Question and Answer period, "I'm not particularly translating Keats, as much as I'm translating Derrida." (M.T.S.)

Ryan, Robert M. "The Fall of One of the Noblest Men Alive: Benjamin Bailey, Archdeacon of Colombo." *BRH* 85 (1982): 9-26; illus.

Ryan reconstructs the mournful story of the man Keats called one of the noblest. What Keats saw as Bailey's nobility may have gone to his head when he found himself only the Archdeacon and not the Bishop--of Colombo. (D.V.E.)

Sitterson, Joseph C. "Narrator and Reader in *Lamia*." *SP* 79 (1982): 297-310.

If readers respond uncertainly to the poem it is because the narrator, a shifting, subtle, ironic figure, deliberately frustrates stock responses, forcing us to recognize that misery and heartbreak originate in human desire, in human nature. An important article for its insistence, generally persuasive, on the complexity of the narrator. (R.M.R.)

Walker, Carol Kyros. "*Lamia* as Theatre Art." *KSJ* 31 (1982): 105-17.

A pleasant, informative essay, arguing that Keats's experience of pantomime and ballet must have influenced "a
poem so rich in flights, pursuits, mythological characters,
transformations, benevolent and hostile agents, and artificial setting." Romantic ballet had not yet taken shape
but, as Walker reminds us, Lycius, Apollonius, and Lamia
might easily be identified as prototypes of Prince Siegfried,
Von Rothbart, and that metamorphic swan. Gracefully executed.
(R.M.R.)

Wolfson, Susan J. "Keats the Letter-Writer: Epistolary Poetics."
RP&P 6,ii (1982): 43-62.

Yost, George. "Keats's Halfway Zone." PQ 60 (1981): 95-103.

A useful reminder of all the dim lights, distant sounds,
drowsy reveries, coy women, and other examples of the half-
concealed that Keats used to provoke the reader's imaginative cooperation. (R.M.R.)

Zak, William F. "To Try That Long Preserved Virginity: Psyche's
Bliss and the Teasing Limits of the Grecian Urn." KSJ 31
(1982): 82-104.

Psyche represents "the androgynous poetic soul generatively
'possessing' itself in its marital intercourse with the
world," while the Urn maintains a "teasing 'attitude' of
maidenly protest and adolescent obliviousness to everything
but itself." But Zak is really more serious than that. And
this would be a much better essay if he had abandoned the
sexual gimmick (a labored extension of a barely perceptible
metaphor in Keats's "Mansion" letter) and given us only his
splendid discussion of "Ode on a Grecian Urn," a very
impressive demonstration of reading and reasoning ability,
and a major contribution to criticism of the poem. (R.M.R.)

See also Diehl ("General 3. Criticism"); Randel ("Coleridge");
Verdi ("Hazlitt").

Reviews of books previously listed:

GRADMAN, Barry, Metamorphosis in Keats (see RMB for 1981,
p. 119), rev. by Carol L. Bernstein in TWC 13 (1982): 154-
57; by Leon Waldoff in KSJ 31 (1982): 220-22; SHARP, Ronald
A., Keats, Skepticism, and the Religion of Beauty (see RMB
for 1979, pp. 104-05), rev. by Anne Elliott in RES 33
(1982): 370-71; by Spencer Hall in SHR 15 (1981): 266;
STILLINGER, Jack, ed., The Poems of John Keats (see ELN 17,

Supp., 90-91), rev. by John Barnard in *SiR* 21 (1982): 541-46.

KNIGHT

Clarke, Michael, and Nicholas Penny, eds. *The Arrogant Connoisseur: Richard Payne Knight 1751-1824.* Manchester University Press, 1982. Pp. x+190, incl. 59 plates, 11 in color. £30.00; £9.50 paper.

A finely illustrated catalogue (pp. 125ff.) of a Knight exhibition at the Whitworth Art Gallery in 1982 is preceded by seven essays, three by Penny, one by Clarke, one by Claudia Stumpf, and two by Peter Funnell, constituting in substance and judgment the first serious book on Payne Knight, correcting two centuries' accumulation of legend, misinformation, and silence.

The Society of Dilettanti, a dining club whose constitution forbade being "serious in earnest," sponsored expeditions to the Mediterranean undertaken by men such as Sir William Hamilton and Knight and Charles Townley and d'Hancarville, who backed up their "armchair anthropology and comparative mythology" (5) with serious investigation and collecting of evidence of "the symbolic language of antiquity" (semiots, note). Knight, exploring the summit of Etna, took careful samples of the ash for Hamilton, a "keen volcanologist." Their joint volume on *The Worship of Priapus* (1786) exhibited physical evidence of the survival of pagan phallic cults in engravings "which would raise an eyebrow even today" (57) and the "big toes" shown were deposited in the British Museum, today safely out of sight.

Serious in a different field was Knight's didactic poem *The Landscape*--its wisdom resisted in his day--toward the end of which we should not be surprised to find Knight defending Byron's *Cain* (17) nor to learn that he was admired by Peacock (57). Publication in 1805 of Knight's *Analytical Inquiry into the Principles of Taste* precipitated an interesting controversy. Indeed, Knight "was rarely out of controversy, whether he was editing Homer, writing his *Discourse on the Worship of Priapus* or undervaluing the Elgin marbles." These pithy chapters are of great help, but let us hope that Clarke and his associates will move on to a full biography. (D.V.E.)

LAMB

Coates, John. "Lamb's Bias in *Specimens of the English Dramatic Poets*." *ChLB* 39 (1982): 125-38.

Courtney, Winifred F. *Young Charles Lamb 1775-1802*. New York University Press, 1982. Pp. xviii+411; illus. $30.00.
Rev. by Marilyn Butler in *Sunday Times* (London), Aug. 29, 1982; by Richard Holmes in *Times* (London), Sept. 23, 1982; by Jonathan Keates in *TLS*, Nov. 26, 1982, p. 1315; by Peter Quennell in *Financial Times*, Aug. 14, 1982; by Geoff Walden in *Citizen Register* (Ossining), Dec. 26, 1982. (See also the composite review by Michael Neve, listed above under "General 3. Criticism.")
Most of the reviewers seem pleased to be reminded of Charles Lamb, some nostalgically; confronted with a biography written out of devotion to the subject and to the truth, hence "a book that is extremely detailed, and not governed by a clear theme" (thus Neve), all find themselves retelling the tale of "the day of horrors," and then recognizing the "toughness" of Lamb's character and, with Winifred Courtney's help, shaking off the sentimentality which they, or others, had wrapped around Lamb and his writing and talking. Quennell ends "beginning to revise the rather prejudiced opinion of Lamb's character and adult gifts that once I shared with Cyril Connolly." Keates, still defining Lamb as a "shambling hobbledehoy," concedes that this study "proposes and justifies a closer identification of the works with their ... creator than any demanded so far." Holmes sees the appeal of this book "in the extraordinary circle of friends" which made Lamb "a sort of Maypole of literary London." Butler finds Courtney "a shrewd and knowledgeable biographer" but dismisses as "bizarre" the idea "that Lamb was strong on politics." (This fits with Butler's insistence, elsewhere, that Blake's "apotheoses of Pitt and Nelson" had to be worshipful and patriotic because of the prevailing "ideology.") Neve, not committed to the one-ideology thesis, accepts as an important novelty in this book "the use made of some political writings of the young Lamb" to place him "more firmly than before in the culture of metropolitan radical journalism, with its dash of Godwinian ideas and mild Jacobin sympathies."
Yes, it is a challenging biography, written by a challenge-taker: the next dare being to find a title for Volume Two. (D.V.E.)

Hill, Alan G. "Lamb and Wordsworth: The Story of a Remarkable Friendship." *ChLB* 37 (1982): 85-92.

Monsman, Gerald. "Confessions of a Prosaic Dreamer: Charles Lamb's Critique of the Poetic Sublime." *Criticism* 24 (1982): 159-73.

Nath, Prem. "Charles Lamb's 'The Two Races of Men' and Chapters 2-4 of the Third Book of Dr. Francis Rabelais." *PQ* 61 (1982): 101-04.

A hitherto unnoticed source for Lamb's essay on the "two distinct races, the men who borrow, and the men who lend," is shown to be Rabelais' chapter in which Panurge "praiseth the Debtors and Borrowers." Not only are there several close borrowings, but "both Rabelais and Lamb feel convinced that the borrowing-lending activity spreads a necessary and welcome warmth on human existence."

Riehl, Joseph E. "Charles Lamb's *Mrs. Leicester's School* Stories and Elia: The Fearful Imagination." *ChLB* 39 (1982): 138-43.

Ruddick, William. "'The Great Un-hanged': Charles Lamb through the Eyes of His Scottish Contemporaries." *ChLB* 40 (1982): 149-58.

An informative, witty survey of the history of Lamb's reputation in Scotland.

Saxena, D.C. "The Autobiographical Content of Lamb's Letters." *ChLB* 40 (1982): 158-63. (To be continued.)

Reviews of book previously listed:

PARK, Roy, ed., *Lamb as Critic* (see *RMB* for 1980, p. 108), rev. by J.H. Alexander in *YES* 12 (1982): 293-94; by Joel Haefner in *PQ* 61 (1982): 365-67; by W.J.B. Owen in *RES* 33 (1982): 486-88.

LEWIS

See Le Tellier ("General 3. Criticism"). *See also* listings under "Gothic Novel."

LOCKHART

Kestner, Joseph. "John Gibson Lockhart's *Matthew Wald* and
   Emily Bronte's *Wuthering Heights*." *TWC* 13 (1982): 94-96.

MATURIN

See Le Tellier ("General 3. Criticism"); Peterfreund ("Keats").

MEDWIN

See Raizis ("General 3. Criticism").

PEACOCK

Prickett, Stephen. "Peacock's *Four Ages* Recycled." *BJA* 22
   (1982): 158-66.

   Sees Peacock as being aesthetically in advance of the
Romantics whom he satirized. A fresh perspective. (B.C.H.)

See also Butler, Polhemus ("English 3. Criticism").

Reviews of book previously listed:

   BUTLER, Marilyn, *Peacock Displayed: A Satirist in His Context* (see *RMB* for 1979, p. 109), rev. by Tonette Bond in
   SHR 15 (1981): 267; by David Gallon in *RES* 33 (1982): 343-
   44.

QUARTERLY REVIEW

See MacKenzie ("English 3. Criticism").

RADCLIFFE

See Figes, Marra et al. ("English 3. Criticism"); "The Gothic
   Novel."

SCOTT

Alexander, J.H. *Marmion: Studies in Interpretation and Composition.* (SSEL.) University of Salzburg, Austria, 1981. Pp. xv+257.

Rev. by Jill Rubenstein in *SLJ* 9 (1982): supp. 17, pp. 82-84.
Not seen, but of clear import. (T.L.A.)

Alexander, J.H. "The Year's Work in Scottish Literary Studies 1980: Scott." *SLJ* 9 (1982): 37-40.

Anderson, James. *Sir Walter Scott and History with Other Papers.* Edinburgh: Edina Press, 1981. Pp. viii+200. £6.75.

This derives from an exceptionally diligent dissertation, presented at Edinburgh in 1965, for which the author deservedly received a Carnegie award. The dissertation spanned the whole range of Scott's historical writing--including his antiquarian work, and formal histories--as seen against a full background of Scottish historiographical activity in the later eighteenth century. In celebrating such worthy progenitors as William Robertson and Lord Hailes it usefully drew attention to a much firmer intellectual origin for Scott's view of history than those more wispy ancestral figures (e.g., Whitaker and Sharon Turner) previously mentioned by literary historians. At the time one expected an imminent publication; but Anderson quickly hived off the more immediately approachable part of his findings, featuring Scott's use of history in the novels, in a series of articles for *SSL* (1966-68). What represented in many ways the more substantial product of Anderson's labors was thus left behind.

The present volume presents mostly a shortened version of the thesis, unfortunately pruned most severely in those areas left unpublished. A tendency to trade in tangible details is thus made to look even more angular in Anderson's now historically compressed opening chapters on formal historiography. The main body reproduces, without significant alteration, the *SSL* articles--Anderson, as there, illustrating at length the range of Scott's historical knowledge, his extraordinary powers of assimilation, and some of the more discernible ways in which "fact" was converted for the purposes of "fiction." Again Anderson's method tends to place undue emphasis on novels, such as *Old Mortality*, with a more obvious source in historical documentation. An entirely new "Postscript" is markedly

strident in resisting "historicist" and/or Romantic interpretation. The idea that Scott saw "man as the Product of
his Natural and Social Environment" is dismissed more extremely than before as "sublime mysticism and nonsense."
And if the novels made concessions to historicity, it was
mainly owing to a "public ... too knowing to accept in
fiction mediaeval knights who behaved like Regency bucks."
The latter offers an unusual elevation of Scott's audience
at his expense.

The book also retains a long appendix detailing Scott's
citation of historical sources, which in this newly lightened
format seems over-heavy. Anderson also adds a number of
essay-pieces ("Other Papers"), the product presumably
of his subsequent work on Scott. Almost perversely desultory
in some of their titles (one is headed "Scott's Works: Odd
points of interest: topography, etc."), these fail noticeably in their attempt to combine trenchancy and non-de-
liberateness. Some interesting possibilities are touched
on--for instance, Scott's immersion in Smollett--but
Anderson's tendency to belabor all criticism later than
Andrew Lang is for the most part embarrassing. By making
available a substantial body of research, however, this
publication will be welcome. (P.D.G.)

Berger, Dieter A. "'Damn the Mottoe': Scott and the Epigraph."
Anglia 100 (1982): 373-96.

Crawford, Thomas. *Walter Scott*. Edinburgh: Scottish Academic
Press; Columbia University Press, 1982. $6.50 paper.

Largely a reissue, under a different banner ("Scottish
Writers Series"), first published in 1965. Includes, however, new material on the ballads, longer poems, and *The
Heart of Midlothian*. Also noteworthy for an updated final
chapter, offering a magisterial view of Scott criticism in
this century. (P.D.G.)

Crouzet, Michel, ed. *Waverley, Rob-Roy, La Fiancée de
Lammermoor*. (Bouquins.) Paris: Robert Laffont, 1981.
Pp. 993.

Fleischner, Jennifer B. "Class, Character and Landscape in
Old Mortality." *SLJ* 9:2 (1982): 21-36.

"There is a great deal of travelling from place to place
in *Old Mortality*, a novel filled with exiles and wanderers....
Differences in social position are imaged by differences
in perspective.... In a novel whose travellers are exiles,

wanderers, itinerant soldiers and prisoners of war,
travelling becomes a metaphor for inevitable social movement." Cleishbotham and the wrong side of the tracks. (T.L.A.)

Hewitt, David, ed. *Scott on Himself: A Selection of the
Autobiographical Writings of Sir Walter Scott.* Edinburgh:
Scottish Academic Press; Columbia University Press, 1981.
Pp. xxx+298. £6.50; $15.00.

> Rev. by Robert C. Gordon in *SLJ* 9 (1982): supp. 16, pp.
> 11-13, who finds the collection more satisfying than Lock-
> hart.
> A compilation apparently with a dual purpose. On one
> level, Hewitt presents an anthology of Scott's autobiographi-
> cal writing, incorporating a full version of the Ashestiel
> "Memoir" (previously only available imperfectly as the
> first chapter in Lockhart's *Life*) with a varied selection
> from the letters, prefaces, and *Journal*. A cogent intro-
> duction explores carefully the variety of masks and tones
> employed by Scott in addressing both his correspondents
> and audience. Hewitt also examines Scott's habit of defining
> himself through a social persona, entertains the possi-
> bility that this might have helped conserve deeper imagin-
> ative impulses, but denies any extreme form of Romantic
> "self-examination." At the same time, Hewitt offers a
> working illustration of the opportunities open to a modern
> editor of Scott. Reference to the MS. of the Ashestiel
> "Memoir"--a fairly recent acquisition by the National
> Library of Scotland--allows him to identify three distinct
> stages of composition, while integrating into the main text
> elements presented by Lockhart only in the form of notes.
> Hewitt argues convincingly in favor of the superior value
> of the second editions of Scott's longer poems, and an
> eclectic use of the first edition, Magnum Opus, and MS.
> (where available) in the case of the novels. Lastly he
> attempts a more exact transcription of part of the *Journal*,
> working from Scott's holograph in the Pierpont Morgan
> Library rather than the spotted photostat consulted by
> W.E.K. Anderson. Here, as with transcriptions from MS.
> letters, punctuation and editorial emendation are kept to
> a Spartan minimum. Readers wishing to refer to the corres-
> pondence or *Journal* will probably still go to the established,
> more "complete" and "readable" editions of Grierson and
> Anderson. But Hewitt's selection advertises only too clear-
> ly the weight of Scott manuscripts now readily accessible
> and the sophisticated editorial techniques waiting their
> reproduction. (P.D.G.)

Horward, Donald D. "Napoleon, His Legend, and Sir Walter
Scott." *SHR* 16 (1982): 1-13.

The *Life of Napoleon* was as biased against the Emperor
as the publications that created the Legend were in his
favor.

Klepetar, Steven F. "Levels of Narration in *Old Mortality*."
TWC 13 (1982): 38-45.

Lamont, Claire, ed. *Sir Walter Scott. Waverley: Or, 'Tis
Sixty Years Since.* Oxford: Clarendon Press, 1981. Pp.
xlii+470. $59.00.

Rev. by J.H. Alexander in *SLJ* 9 (1982): supp. 17, pp.
76-81.

By far the most complete and accomplished edition of a
Scott novel yet. Attempts to free *Waverley* from some of
the encrustations which attached to it as the flag-bearer
to Cadell's Magnum Opus edition in 1829. Lamont uses the
rare first edition of 1814 for her copy text, making a
number of emendations from surviving parts of the MS.
but accepting the authority of subsequent editions and the
Magnum only infrequently. Scholarly comprehensiveness,
however, dictates the addition of the Magnum introductions
and notes in its wake. Lamont's own notes, bearing witness
to her exhaustive research, are invariably apposite and
never showy. Her introduction covers efficiently Scott's
composition of the novel, its probable sources, and the
history of the text since the first edition. With an over-
haul of the Waverley Novels long overdue, there could be
no better illustration of the pitfalls and rewards likely
to be experienced in such an undertaking.

Two slight qualifications. Though one appreciates Lamont's
desire to present a text as close as possible to that intended by Scott for his original readers, the Magnum
version—which differs substantively on almost every page—
does on occasions appear to offer fuller and superior
readings which Lamont ideally should have at least noted.
Secondly, notwithstanding Lamont's interesting conjecture
about an intermediate period of composition in 1810, the
introduction is perhaps less clear than it might have
been on Scott's completion of the novel before publication
in July 1814. His letters to J.B.S. Morritt, immediately
afterwards, could be taken to indicate that much of one
of the world's most momentous books was written in a very
short dash. (P.D.G.)

McMaster, Graham. "Realism and Romance in *The Heart of Midlothian*." *CQ* 10 (1982): 202-18.

McMaster, Graham. *Scott and Society*. Cambridge University Press, 1982. Pp. 253. $39.50.
Rev. by Neil Berry in *English* 31 (1982): 146-50; by John Henry Raleigh in *NCF* 37 (1982): 233-36.

By interpreting Scott's fiction as a reflection of tensions and instabilities endemic in his own Regency world, this major study makes a decided stand against the orthodox "historicist" approach to the Waverley Novels. In an introductory comparison between *Waverley* (1814) and *Redgauntlet* (1824), McMaster finds the former predominantly "optimistic" in its interpretation of social development and "diachronic" in structure, the latter often disturbingly fragmented and "symbolical" in expression. In spite of the occasional whiff of special pleading, this leads tellingly to the central issue of why such differences should exist in two novels which ostensibly share the common theme of Jacobinism.

The middle section of the book is concerned with the nature and eventual vulnerability of Scott's theoretical view of society and more conscious political credo. The origin of several of his presuppositions is successfully sought in the Scottish "philosophical history" of the later eighteenth century, which McMaster rightly considers a continuing--even increasingly diverse--influence on Scott's generation. McMaster also breaks new ground by suggesting ways in which Scott's view was tested and stretched by the practical issues of his day, as well as through contact with the ideas of more contemporary spokesmen such as Malthus and Ricardo. He also offers an astute account of Scott's working politics, successfully countering popular notions of Scott as a sentimental Tory and neo-feudalist by drawing attention to the strictly contemporary nature of much of his Pittite Toryism, bolstered as it was by a fluid and apparently impregnable "patronage" system in early nineteenth-century Scotland.

McMaster's main thesis is that Scott's ideology came under increasingly disturbing pressure as Britain's economic and social problems burgeoned after Waterloo. The decisive year was 1819, Scott's response to Peterloo bringing a new shrillness to his political writing. Here again McMaster sometimes gives the impression of arguing too strenuously for victory. Scott's riposte to James Ballantyne on the "Manchester massacre" in the *Edinburgh Weekly Journal* (which an appendix reproduces in full) is a more stable echo of current Tory attitudes than per-

haps McMaster realizes. McMaster, too, tends to under-
estimate the comparative prosperity and stability of the
early 1820s, which would only have reinforced Scott's feeling that his actions in 1818-20 had been correct. Yet a
distinct shift in tone is evident in Scott's writing at this
time, and McMaster's dogged pursuit of his goal offers one
level of valid interpretation.

The final section presents a survey of the full gamut of
Waverley Novels, arguing a largely unchecked movement from
diachrony and "realism" to a more disturbingly "synchronic"
symbolism. By now McMaster's penchant for schematization
is rampant, as novels are forced (sometimes kicking) into
five developmental "groups." Often uncompromisingly compressed,
McMaster's analysis is frequently reminiscent of Francis
Hart's *Scott's Novels* (1966)--an obvious influence; though
an effort is also made to assimilate more recent forms of
advanced psychological and linguistic interpretation. While
claiming to avoid over-narrow "evaluative" judgments, by
elevating the allegedly more "diverse" later novels McMaster
inevitably casts a shade on "realistic" favorites such as
Waverley and *Rob Roy*. This will not find easy credence
among those readers lately brought back to Scott via the
vigor and freshness of the early "Scottish" novels.

The severity of McMaster's argumentation is not quite
matched by scholarly accuracy. The use of J.G. Tait's
edition of *The Journal*, instead of W.E.K. Anderson's in-
finitely preferable modern revision, suggests a thesis not
entirely updated, while some quotations--particularly from
MSS. in the National Library of Scotland--are badly garbled.
Surely over-priced even by today's standard, and making
few concessions to its readers, this book will not make
friends lightly. But it is an important study, and makes
a significant step toward that long-standing desideratum--
a first-rate book on Scott. (P.D.G.)

Scott, Paul Henderson. *Walter Scott and Scotland*. Edinburgh:
William Blackwood, 1981. Pp. xii+99. £5.95.

Claiming to pick up where Edwin Muir (in *Scott and Scotland* [1936]) left off, Scott writes lucidly and succinctly
about the peculiarly Scottish elements in his subject's
upbringing. Chapters on Scott's childhood in the Borders,
training at Edinburgh High School, and attendance at Edinburgh College are all first-rate and bear marks of being
matched by the author's personal experience. The book also
includes a useful account of the influence of the Scottish
Enlightenment--emphasizing the effects of its broader at-
mosphere and tone on Scott's historical imagination. (It

is interesting to observe how reference to the Enlightenment in this way, once a brave unorthodoxy, is rapidly becoming something of a set-piece.) The author also rightly stresses the complex feelings still current in Scott's time concerning Scotland's loss of independence, and points to ways in which such emotions might be said to suffuse the poems and novels. But logic becomes severely strained when the book goes one step further to identify Scott with profoundly anti-Unionist opinions. The writer plucks out apparently quasi-nationalist statements from their broader settings--for example, comments by characters in novels which, when seen fully, seem more whining than patriotic-- and, conversely, ignores an at least equally strong "British" dimension. The interesting relationship between "Scottish" and "British" elements in Scott--a fallow yet rewarding field--is left mostly untouched.

One statement, to the effect that Scott only expressed qualified or begrudging acceptance of the Union, is manifestly wrong. In the final paragraph of his *Description of the Regalia of Scotland* (1819), a pamphlet guide, Scott's praise was unequivocal ("blessing the wise decrees of Providence, which, after a thousand years of bloodshed, have at length indissolubly united two nations, who, speaking the same language, professing the same religion, and united in the same interests, seem formed by GOD and Nature to compose one people.") Admittedly it is Scott's purplest prose that is so employed, and he was hardly likely to propound difficult politics to a mixed and ill-defined audience (in more select circles, he could be waspish enough on similar subjects). But this still leaves the question of why Scott should enlist such noticeably Scottish emblems in so distinctly a "British" cause. I suspect the writer's "nationalist" Scott is as much an anachronism as the Unionist appeaser reviled by MacDiarmid and revered by Trevor-Roper. (P.D.G.)

Scott, Paul Henderson, ed. *Sir Walter Scott: The Letters of Malachi Malagrowther.* Edinburgh: William Blackwood, 1981. Pp. xxxiv+185. £4.95.

Rev. by Peter Garside in *SLJ* 9 (1982): supp. 17, pp. 73-76.

Scott Newsletter. No. 1, Autumn 1982. Aberdeen University. Pp. 16.

Subscriptions (£2.00/$5.00) to: Business Manager, Dr. David Hewitt, Department of English, University of Aberdeen, Old Aberdeen AB9 2UB, Scotland.

Sutherland, Kathryn. "Walter Scott's Highland Minstrelsy and His Correspondence with the Maclean Clephane Family." *SLJ* 9 (1982): 48-66.

Examines a number of unpublished sources that comment on Scott after Jacobite songs in the Highlands. (T.L.A.)

Walker, Eric G. *Scott's Fiction and the Picturesque*. (SSEL, Romantic Reassessment, 108.) University of Salzburg, Austria, 1982. Pp. 79. $12.50.

An interesting topic, its potential by no means fully realized here. Walker gathers together Scott's more obvious statements on the picturesque and comments sensibly. He also makes fairly orthodox suggestions about Scott's "metonymic" use of landscape to suggest contrasting historical situations, while arguing more fitfully that Scott's strongest instinct was to go beyond the set or static "picturesque." A discursive chapter on *The Bride of Lammermoor* is allowed to stray too widely from the matter directly in hand. Walker fails to consider the possibility of deeper "ideological" elements in contemporary theorists such as Uvedale Price, and gives an inadequate sense of the firmness with which Scott could deploy topography as a sophisticated socio-historical correlative. A fullish bibliography fails to include Alistair Duckworth's model essay, "Scott's Fiction and the Migration of Settings," *SLJ*, 7,i (1980): 97-112; also my own "*Redgauntlet* and the Topography of Progress," *SoRA* (1977): 155-73, and "*Waverley*'s Pictures of the Past," *ELH*, 44 (1977): 659-82. (P.D.G.)

Wilson, A.N. *The Laird of Abbotsford. A View of Sir Walter Scott*. Oxford University Press, 1980. Pp. xiv+197. £8.95.

Listed in *RMB* for 1981, p. 128.

Wilson consciously reverts to an older tradition of critical biography, taking as his model earlier compendiums of the life and works such as John Buchan's *Sir Walter Scott* (1932) and Hesketh Pearson's *Sir Walter Scott: His Life and Personality* (1954). Unfortunately this also involves an overcharged, and ultimately self-defeating, assault on current Scott scholarship—or rather, Wilson's patently exaggerated version of this. (In reality, one hardly feels threatened by the spectre of "learned journals teeming with critical assessments of *The Talisman*.") Though considered in most respects "perfectly odious," J.G. Lockhart is the main provider of the book's biographical materials, Wilson often further dramatizing and streamlining elements in the *Life* which ideally would have benefited from more careful and

skeptical treatment. Pointedly playing for the gentlemen
rather than the professionals, Wilson addresses a common
readership which at best sounds decidedly antiquated (one
which keeps "Percy's *Reliques*, not Scott's *Minstrelsy*, on
the bedside table"). His own speaking voice can also seem
unduly mannered (Jeanie Deans's character "shines out of
her dumpy little countenance," George IV stands "ludicrously
obese" in his kilt). At least one chapter ("Scott's Religion") struggles in the face of the evident barrenness
of its subject. Wilson's criticism, too, is capable of
verging on the banal—"slapdash" in detail, *The Monastery*
still "has some wonderful characters and some great scenes."
Nevertheless, a novelist himself, Wilson can write stylish-
ly and has some moments of genuine insight. His commentary
on the poetry, with stress on the imaginative impulse behind
the novels, to some extent helps recreate the enraptured
response of Scott's earliest readers. The book will undoubtedly draw attention back to the Scott legend, but
offers little of lasting scholarly value. (P.D.G.)

See also Aitken ("English 1. Bibliography"); Finley ("English
2. Environment"); Campbell, Levine, Stone ("English 3.
Criticism"); Coldwell ("Keats"); Sturrock ("Wordsworth");
Ward ("German 2. General"); Ambrose ("Italian 1. General").

Reviews of books previously listed:

BROWN, David, *Walter Scott and the Historical Imagination*
(see *RMB* for 1980, p. 113), rev. by John Henry Raleigh in
YES 12 (1982): 289-90; LASCELLES, Mary, *The Story-Teller
Retrieves the Past: Historical Fiction and Fictitious
History in the Art of Scott, Stevenson, Kipling, and Some
Others* (see *RMB* for 1980, p. 115), rev. by Jane Millgate
in *RES* 33 (1982): 213-14; REED, James, *Sir Walter Scott:
Landscape and Locality* (see *RMB* for 1980, p. 115), rev. by
Karl Kroeber in *SLJ* 9 (1982): supp. 16, pp. 13-17; TULLOCH,
Graham, *The Language of Walter Scott* (see *RMB* for 1980,
p. 117), rev. by George Bourcier in *EA* 35 (1982): 334-35;
by Claire Lamont in *SLJ* 9 (1982): supp. 17, pp. 71-73.

SHELLEY, MARY

Alderman, Ralph M. "Mary Shelley and Washington Irving Once
More." *KSJ* 31 (1982): 24-28.

   "From 1823 to 1830 Irving's attitude toward Mary Shelley ...
was distant and reserved."

Foust, R.E. "Monstrous Image: Theory of Fantasy Antagonists."
  Genre 13 (1980): 441-53.

  Uses *Frankenstein* to illustrate a theory of the antagonist
  as "autochthonic doppelgänger," representing one side of
  the primordial schism between civilization and nature, and
  wreaking earth's revenge against the rationalism that had
  subdued it.

McInerney, Peter. "*Frankenstein* and the Godlike Science of
  Letters." *Genre* 13 (1980): 455-75.

  Readers who can endure the tiresome wordplay about
  creation and authorship will find some important points
  being made about Walton's narrative. (R.M.R.)

Seed, David. "'Frankenstein'--Parable or Spectacle?" *Criticism*
  24 (1982): 327-40.

Sunstein, Emily W. "Shelley's Answer to Leslie's *Short and
  Easy Method with the Deists* and Mary Shelley's Answer,
  'The Necessity of a Belief in the Heathen Mythology to
  a Christian.'" *KSMB* 32 (1981): 49-54.

  Transcribes and provides context for Mary's incomplete
  MS.

See also Levine ("English 3. Criticism"); "The Gothic Novel."

Reviews of books previously listed:

  BENNETT, Betty T., ed., *The Letters of Mary Wollstone-
  craft Shelley*, vol. 1 (see *RMB* for 1980, pp. 118-19),
  rev. by Doucet Devin Fischer in *SiR* 21 (1982): 523-30;
  by Richard Holmes in *NYTBook Review*, May 18, 1980, p. 14;
  by William St. Clair in *Byron Journal* 10 (1982): 93-95;
  GILBERT, Sandra M., and Susan Gubar, *The Madwoman in the
  Attic: The Woman Writer and the Nineteenth-Century Literary
  Imagination* (see *RMB* for 1979, p. 113), rev. by Penny
  Boumelha in *RES* 33 (1982): 345-47; KETTERER, David,
  *Frankenstein's Creation: The Book, the Monster, and Human
  Reality* (see *RMB* for 1979, p. 114), rev. by Rosemary Jack-
  son in *YES* 12 (1982): 301-02; by Stephen Prickett in *RES*
  33 (1982): 216-18; LEVINE, George, and U.C. Knoepflmacher,
  eds., *The Endurance of Frankenstein: Essays on Mary Shelley's
  Novel* (see *RMB* for 1979, pp. 114-15), rev. by Rosemary
  Jackson in *YES* 12 (1982): 301-02; by Stephen Prickett
  in *RES* 33 (1982): 216-18.

Review article:

Johnson, Barbara. "My Monster/My Self." *Diacritics* 12,ii
   (Summer 1982): 2-10.

A review article focusing on *Frankenstein*: "In order to
prove herself worthy of her parentage, Mary, paradoxically
enough, must thus usurp the parental role and succeed in
giving birth to *herself* on paper. Her declaration of existence as a writer must therefore figuratively repeat the
matricide that her physical birth all too literally entailed."
A provocative psychoanalysis, in which Percy and Byron
take a bit of a licking. (R.A.H.)

SHELLEY, P.B.

Allott, Miriam, ed. *Essays on Shelley*. Totowa, N.J.: Barnes &
   Noble Books, 1982. Pp. xviii+286. $28.50.

In her introduction ("Attitudes to Shelley: The Vagaries
of a Critical Reputation") to this volume, Miriam Allott
usefully details the Victorian responses to Shelley, indirectly preparing us, however, for the vagaries of her
associates' critical essays that follow. These essays,
some much better than others, are arranged "more or less
according to the chronological order of the principal works
chosen for discussion." David Seed's "Shelley's 'Gothick'
in *St. Irvyne* and After" rambles and summarizes a bit too
much: a more controlled analytical approach, if one is
possible for these early works, is needed to redeem or explain Shelley's experiments with the Gothic. Vincent Newey's
"The Shelleyan Psycho-Drama: 'Julian and Maddalo'" offers
not much new but convincingly presents the poem as a
dramatic monologue in which an older Julian chastizes the
younger and naive Julian for his inadequate "credal optimism." Michael Worton's quite good "Speech and Silence
in *The Cenci*" takes us beyond the action of the drama and
freshly examines its theme of the efficacy of language:
not only the rape but most of the action is *reported*; words
are used to affirm identity, to structure thought, and to
veil or unveil reality; and the dialogue explicitly inter-
relates thought with word with thing. Kenneth Muir's
"Shelley's Magnanimity," pleasant enough, tells us what we
already know: that *Prometheus Unbound* "is related to other
works written between October 1818 and December 1819."
Ann Thompson's "Shelley's 'Letter to Maria Gisborne': Tact
and Clutter" nicely juxtaposes Shelley's intimate "Letter"
to the more formal and contrived verse epistles of other

poets but then "argues" (mainly by way of summary) only
the "tact" and "generosity" of the poem's tone. Brian
Nellist's excellent "Shelley's Narratives and 'The Witch
of Atlas'" argues that most narrative, but especially
Shelley's, in principle and practice befits skepticism or
at least pluralism. Looking at many of Shelley's poems,
Nellist tells us much about Shelley's unorthodox transitions,
his non-traditional temporal sequences, and his reversed or
equivocal conclusions. Then Nellist turns to the Witch and
argues that "the method of narration rather than the object
of narration ... gives the poem its centre." Geoffrey Ward's
"Transforming Presence: Poetic Idealism in Prometheus Unbound and Epipsychidion" labors more than necessary to
propose that "Shelley's writing is vehement in its subversion of dualism and hierarchy within perception, politics,
and philosophy." Bernard Beatty's "The Transformation of
Discourse: Epipsychidion, Adonais, and Some Lyrics" finely
distinguishes, as Byron did by way of the owl and the nightingale, the language of discourse and language of lyricism
that coexist in Shelley's major poetry. Frequently, Shelley's
lyrical lines "dissolve the logic of sentence construction
and imply another model for human consciousness than that
provided by discourse." Beatty is also good on Shelley's
artistic use of discursive language and rhetorical speed.
Finally, Miriam Allott's "The Reworking of a Literary Genre:
Shelley's 'The Triumph of Life'" explicates Shelley's last
poem by reference to its antecedents in Petrarch (and
others) and to its five-part structure. The volume is usefully indexed for those seeking specific reference to
Shelley's works. (C.E.R.)

Bennett, Betty T., and Alice Green Fredman. "A Note on the
    Dating of Shelley's 'The Triumph of Life.'" KSJ 31 (1982):
    13-15.

    Convincing evidence that lines 41-46 were drafted on or
    after 27 May 1822. (C.E.R.)

Buehrens, David P. "Difference Sweet Where Discord Cannot
    Be: Marital Felicity and the Structure of Shelley's Pro-
    metheus Unbound." MSE 8,iii (1982): 27-35.

    "In the Asia-Prometheus bond of his great psychodrama,
    therefore, Shelley from the immediate anguish of bitter
    personal sorrow achieved perhaps his grandest 'transform-
    ing image,' his most sublime approximation of that noble
    ideal," writes Buehrens, with Erich Segal in mind. (T.L.A.)

Burwick, Frederick. "The Language of Causality in *Prometheus Unbound.*" *KSJ* 31 (1982): 136-58.

This essay does many good things: e.g., explains Shelley's "and speech created thought"; reconciles Shelley's "Mind cannot create [matter]" with his belief in a mind that does create "words and signs"; and clarifies the meanings of and relations between Shelley's (and Prometheus's) "doing" and "suffering." (C.E.R.)

Butler, Marilyn. "Myth and Mythmaking in the Shelley Circle." *ELH* 49 (1982): 50-72.

Cameron, Kenneth Neill. "Shelley as Philosophical and Social Thinker: Some Modern Evaluations." *SiR* 21 (1982): 357-66.

Shelley scholars of the past half-century are evaluated according to one criterion: how well they have recognized that "beneath the symbolic complexities of his poetry there is a solid philosophical and socio-political base."

Cundiff, Paul A. *Robert Browning: Compiler of the Shelley Concordance*. Tampa, Fla.: [Privately Printed], 1982. Pp. 30. [Available from author at 7010B Santa Ana Drive, Tampa, Fla. 33617.]

Lacking a preliminary background on or explanation of the Brownings' infatuation with and uses for Shelley's poetry, this monograph will not interest or help Shelley scholars. What Browning critics will think of it remains to be seen. Cundiff's thesis is "that Robert Browning compiled the [a?] Shelley concordance before he met Elizabeth Barrett, that they employed his compilation to identify disguised allusions to Shelleyan thought in their 1845-46 letters, and that the absence of the poet's name on the published title page [of the 1892 concordance??] is a subterfuge." With that brief thesis, Cundiff immediately launches into letters #189-192 (4 and 6 Jan. 1846) from *The Letters of Robert Browning and Elizabeth Barrett Browning* (I, 355-69) and "demonstrates" with overwhelming detail that the Brownings covertly used the words from Shelley's poetry (primarily *Swellfoot the Tyrant*) to inform their four letters with Shelleyan phrases and ideas. Why, how, or if this was done is less than certain. (C.E.R.)

Dawson, P.M.S. "Shelley and the *Improvvisatore* Sgricci: An Unpublished Review." *KSMB* 32 (1981): 19-29.

Shelley's review, in Italian, of Sgricci's 22 Jan. 1821 performance of a tragedy on Hector is here usefully tran-

scribed and translated. Shelley's judgments here have parallels in the Defence. (C.E.R.)

Hogle, Jerrold E. "Shelley's Poetics: The Power as Metaphor."
KSJ 31 (1982): 159-97.

A brilliant albeit difficult essay that challenges many
traditional interpretations of Shelley's ontology, episte-
mology, aesthetic, and ethic. If readers demur through the
first half of this article, they should struggle through
to Parts III and IV ("The Social Affect" and "The Voice of
Resistance and the Voice of Tumult") where Hogle is the most
persuasive and clear in his argument. Hogle rejects the idea
of an objectively Platonic or a subjectively Aristotelian
or empirical constant or essence or center or principle
in the matrix of Shelley's thought. Rather, rereading the
major and familiar passages of A Defence of Poetry, Hogle
argues that the matrix is only a matrix: Shelley's only constant is the inconstancy or transference or substitution or
shifting ground or transformation provided by metaphor.
Dualism and monism dissolve here into the ground of all
being--the inescapable and shifting and yet-to-be appre-
hended relations of center and circumference, subject and
object, thought and thing, self and other. Only by these
metaphoric relations is there speech and thought and poetry
and self and society. Shelley, Hogle argues, tried to teach
us this in his Defence; and here Hogle tries again, with a
decentered peroration to his argument respecting both
Shelley's metaphoric ideas on metaphor and Hogle's own
reflections upon them. (C.E.R.)

Hyde, Michael W. "Notes on Shelley's Reading of Godwin's
Enquirer." KSJ 31 (1982): 15-24.

A series of parallels between Godwin's and Shelley's
statements, with emphasis on Shelley's reworking or correcting Godwin.

Jost, François. "Anatomy of an Ode: Shelley and the Sonnet
Tradition." CL 34 (1982): 223-46.

Keach, William. "Shelley, Rhyme, and the Arbitrariness of
Language." RP&P 6,ii (1982): 23-42.

Shelley's artistry has received considerable attention
in the last few years. Keach, analyzing rhyme in passages
of The Triumph of Life and Mont Blanc, adds to our appreciation of Shelley as arbiter of the arbitrariness of language.
(C.E.R.)

Lucas, Timothy R. "The Old Shelley Game: Prometheus and Pre-
destination in Burgess' Works." *MFS* 27:3 (Autumn 1981):
465-78.

Perrin, Jean. "La symbolique de *Prometheus Unbound* et *Les
Structures anthropologiques de l'imaginaire*." *EA* 35 (1982):
26-38.

Phillips, Jane E. "Lucretian Echoes in Shelley's 'Mont Blanc.'"
CML 2 (1982): 71-93.

Although some of the echoes here adduced are certainly
not the result of influence, Phillips' outline of the
numerous similarities does suggest that Shelley was to some
degree indebted to Lucretius (whom he reread in July 1816)
for his "conceptualization of experience in metaphor," his
"combination and association of poetic images," and his
"forceful arrangements of sound and sense." (C.E.R.)

Pollin, Burton R. "More Music for Shelley's Poetry." *KSJ* 31
(1982): 31-36.

Sixty-five more settings to add to the 1,309 in Pollin's
Music for Shelley's Poetry (1974).

Schell, John F. "A Harmony of Visions: The Moon and Earth
Figures in 'Prometheus Unbound,' Act IV." *ArielE* 13,ii
(1982): 35-45.

Schulze, Earl. "The Dantean Quest of *Epipsychidion*." *SiR* 21
(1982): 191-216.

Disputes Frank McConnell's 1971 opinion that Shelley's
ironies lead to despair over the inadequacy of language.
Rather, says Schulze, they are a "means to an esthetic
poise." Both exploiting and changing the terms of his
Dantean sources, Shelley renews the power of metaphor, and,
by means of a fully humanized form of transcendence, confronts and resolves the problems of *Alastor*. (M.T.S.)

Scrivener, Michael Henry. *Radical Shelley: The Philosophical
Anarchism and Utopian Thought of Percy Bysshe Shelley*.
Princeton University Press, 1982. Pp. xiii+354. $30.00.

After McNiece's, Guinn's, Dawson's, and others' books,
Scrivener's analysis of Shelley's politics (and ethics)
might seem superfluous—but it makes quite good reading
and complements much that has gone before. Challenging
and illuminating are the beginning and ending of the book,
where either the context of anarchism or a redefinition

of Shelley's ethical idealism forces Scrivener to extend
himself and our understanding of Shelley. The middle chapters,
however, tend to repeat what is already known about Shelley's
utopian thought. The best parts of the first three chapters
("Visionary Radicalism and Radical Culture"; "The Making of
a Philosophical Anarchist [1809-1813]"; "Romanticism and
Religion [1814-1817]") present Shelley as an heir of Godwin
who, "more than any other radical, influenced Shelley's
political philosophy"--both writers are utopian rather than
revolutionary theorists whose advocacy of a gradual transformation of man and society separated them from the more
radical political philosophers, whom Scrivener uses for context. (Four of Godwin's novels, by the way, are separately
analyzed on pp. 22-32 as expressions of epistemological
doubt.) Scrivener is also good in distinguishing Shelley
from Godwin: "the former is much more activist than the
latter, more eager to intervene socially with philosophical
insights [and associations], and more willing to risk the
dangers of revolution." Of special interest is Scrivener's
extended discussion, in anarchist terms or contexts, of
usually ignored works: e.g., *Zastrozzi*, where the "fates
of the characters prefigure the difficulty the Shelleyan
idealist will encounter"; *A Declaration of Rights*, "Shelley's
most extreme attempt to popularize radical ideas and to
translate anarchist ideals into a form potentially understandable to an extensive audience"; *A Refutation of Deism*;
Alastor, which investigates by way of the narrator and the
poet "the plight of the solitary rebel, the aristocratic
dissenter, who can choose whether to be aristocratic or
egalitarian, apolitical or political, uninvolved or activist,
pamphleteer or poet"; and *Essay on Christianity*, a fragment
that Scrivener wishes to retitle "God, Christ, and Equality."
In the fourth chapter ("The Hermit of Marlow [1817]"), an
excellent contemporary context glosses *A Proposal for Putting
Reform to the Vote*, and contemporary resonances are found
in *Laon and Cythna*. With *Laon and Cythna*, however, and with
the many middle works discussed in the fifth chapter ("*Prometheus Unbound* in Context [1818-1820]"), Scrivener is more
content to summarize Shelley's utopianism than to explain
it in terms of Godwin or political events. Consequently,
this long chapter (pp. 140-246) on such diverse works as
Rosalind and Helen, *Euganean Hills*, *Julian and Maddalo*,
Mask of Anarsky, and even *A Philosophical View of Reform*
lacks the brilliance of the rest of the book. Scrivener
could have eliminated his brief discussions of some less
relevant works and extended his analysis of philosophical
anarchism in others: e.g., more could have been done with
The Cenci, linking the paternalism in Italy to that in

England or showing that Beatrice's revenge was a morally wrong revolutionary act. Summary also dominates some of the sixth chapter ("Defending the Imagination [1820-1821]"), but the analyses of *Adonais* and then of *Hellas* and *The Triumph of Life* in the final chapter ("An Ethical Idealism [1821-1822]") are excellent. Joining those critics who judge that these three poems continue (or at worst modify) Shelley's meliorism rather than contradict it, Scrivener persuasively argues that Shelley in 1821-22 merely accommodates his libertarianism to an increasing understanding of historical progress. In *Hellas*, Shelley "sets out again to write poetry that will serve the interests of a specific political cause without either compromising his ethical idealism or tainting the cause with an unnecessary radicalism." The ideal outside of time at the end of *Hellas*, rather than suggesting Shelley's desire to transcend the world, seems to be no more escapist than the Temple of the Spirit in *Laon and Cythna*--both serve as beacons to any future progress in time. Such a "mediation of the Ideal" is also to be found in *Charles the First*, given ten pages of sensible explication in this last chapter. (C.E.R.)

States, Bert O. "Standing on the Extreme Verge in *King Lear* and Other High Places." *GaR* 36 (1982): 417-25.

A few pages on Beatrice's description of the precipice in *The Cenci*.

White, Harry. "Relative Means and Ends in Shelley's Socio-Political Thought." *SEL* 22 (1982): 613-31.

See also Diehl, Raizis ("General 3. Criticism"); Graham ("English 2. Environment"); Kelley ("English 3. Criticism"); Bandy ("Blake"); Bone ("Byron"); Prochazka ("French 2. Stael"); Higonnet ("German 2. Criticism").

Reviews of books previously listed:

ABBEY, Lloyd, *Destroyer and Preserver: Shelley's Poetic Skepticism* (see *RMB* for 1980, pp. 121-22), rev. by John Buxton in *RES* 33 (1982): 488-90; by P.M.S. Dawson in *YES* 12 (1982): 299-300; CRONIN, Richard, *Shelley's Poetic Thoughts* (see *RMB* for 1981, pp. 132-34), rev. by John Freeman in *KSMB* 32 (1981): 59-62; by Jerrold E. Hogle in *KSJ* 31 (1982): 212-14; DAWSON, P.M.S., *The Unacknowledged Legislator: Shelley and Politics* (see *RMB* for 1980, pp. 122-23), rev. by John Buxton in *RES* 33 (1982): 488-90; by Donald H. Reiman in *KSJ* 31 (1982): 214-16; DUFFY, Edward,

*Rousseau in England: The Context of Shelley's Critique of
the Enlightenment* (see *RMB* for 1980, p. 124), rev. in French
by R. Trousson in *CLS* 19 (1982): 396-98, who finds it routine
on Rousseau, valuable on Shelley; FOOT, Paul, *Red Shelley*
(see *RMB* for 1981, p. 134), rev. by Patrick Story in *KSJ* 31
(1982): 218-20; HALL, Jean, *The Transforming Image: A Study
of Shelley's Major Poetry* (see *RMB* for 1981, p. 134), rev.
by Tonette L. Bond in *SHR* 16 (1982): 72-73; by C. Castan in
AUMLA 58 (1982): 196-98; by P.M.S. Dawson in *KSJ* 31 (1982):
216-18; by Dwight McCawley in *CollL* 9 (1982): 72-73.

SMITH, HORACE

See Raizis ("General 3. Criticism").

SOUTHEY

Manogue, Ralph Anthony. "Southey and William Winterbotham:
   New Light on an Old Quarrel." *ChLB* 38 (1982): 105-14.

   Hitherto neglected evidence enables Manogue to give us
a biographical portrait of the man who kept the unpublished
manuscript of Southey's "Wat Tyler" for twenty-three years,
the Reverend William Winterbotham, friend and partner of
the radical publisher James Ridgway. (D.V.E.)

Review of book previously listed:

   BERNHARDT-KABISCH, *Robert Southey* (see *ELN* 17, Supp., 102),
   rev. by Jean Raimond in *EA* 35 (1982): 218-19.

SPENCE

Dickinson, H.T., ed. *The Political Works of Thomas Spence*.
   Newcastle Upon Tyne: AVERO, 1982. Pp. xviii+124; illus.
   £5.75 paper., postpaid.

   Selections from sixteen of Spence's pamphlets and sixteen
of his songs, ranging from 1782 to 1807?, though his busy
times were the 1790s. (Illustrated with the famous profile
of 1810 and eighteen title pages.)
   Spence explains himself pretty well, especially in "The
Case of Thomas Spence" (1792) and "The Important Trial of
Thomas Spence" (1803). (We are mercifully spared the versions
in his own phonetic alphabet.) The editor supplies a brisk

but valuable introduction and bibliography, and he stresses both Spence's penetration--his "greater awareness than nearly all of his radical contemporaries of the economic sources of political power" and his more extensive vision of a welfare state than that outlined by Paine--and the survival of his ideas, evidence (often neglected) that some radicals did keep alive the reform campaign and maintain associations, despite illegality, with "small groups of like-minded men."

For any Romanticist who does not know Spence, here is a fine opportunity to make his merry acquaintance. (D.V.E.)

WOLLSTONECRAFT

Carners, Guillermo. "Francisca Ruiz de Larrea de Böhl de Faber y Mary Wollstonecraft." *HR* 50 (1982): 133-42.

Pénigault-Duhet, Paule. "Passion, raison et déraison chez les héroïnes de Mary Wollstonecraft." Pp. 131-41 in *La Passion dans le monde anglo-américain aux XVII*[e] *et XVIII*[e] *siècles.* Université de Bordeaux, 1979.

Poovey, Mary. "Mary Wollstonecraft: The Gender of Genres in Late Eighteenth-Century England." *Novel: A Forum on Fiction* 15 (1982): 111-26.

A genre which promotes feeling and expression, in themselves traps for women, will inevitably fail if a writer hopes to show female autonomy positively. Thus when Wollstonecraft turned to the novel structure for political purposes, she exposed contradictions between her political insights and her "finer sensations." Textual hesitations and an ambiguity in narrative perspective which plunge the narrator continually into "romantic expectations which ... society annexed to female sexuality," and a narrative continually broken at critical, affective moments are the result.

The narrator (Wollstonecraft?) who is also caught between political realism and sentimental idealism is a victim as much as Maria whose court defense affirms that feelings cannot solve the problem of spiritual impoverishment in bourgeois society. The attempt to create a myth of the autonomous self to signal the inadequacies of empirical and rationalist philosophies fails; all relationships are sexually degrading. (M.F.)

Topliss, Iain. "Mary Wollstonecraft and Maria Edgeworth's Modern Ladies." *Etudes Irlandaises* 5 (Dec. 1981): 13-31.

Vlasopolos, Anca. "Mary Wollstonecraft's Mask of Reason in *A Vindication of the Rights of Woman*." *DR* 60 (1980): 462-71.

See also Figes ("English 3. Criticism").

Reviews of books previously listed:

TODD, Janet, *Women's Friendship in Literature* (see *RMB* for 1980, p. 131), rev. by Terry Castle in *ECS* 16,xi (1982): 86-90; TYSON, Gerald P., *Joseph Johnson: A Liberal Publisher* (see *RMB* for 1979, p. 60), rev. by O.M. Brack, Jr., in *ECS* 15,iv (1982): 484-85.

WORDSWORTH, DOROTHY

Reviews of book previously listed:

HOMANS, Margaret, *Women Writers and Poetic Identity: Dorothy Wordsworth, Emily Bronte, and Emily Dickinson* (see *RMB* for 1981, p. 145), rev. by Betsy Colquitt in *CollL* 9 (1982): 77-78; by Arlyn Diamond in *JEGP* 81 (1982): 270-74; by Susan Gubar in *YR* 71 (1982): 446-53; by Elizabeth K. Helsinger in *MP* 80 (1982): 99-100; by Wendy Martin in *TWC* 13 (1982): 135-36; by Roy Andrew Miller in *YR* 71 (1982): 446-58.

WORDSWORTH, WILLIAM

Abbey, Lloyd. "Michael." *QQ* 89 (1982): 550-59.

A *poem*, deliberately reenacting Wordsworth's, but in a jungle setting on the island of Timor in the East Indies. The tone can be gathered from the opening lines: "If from the dumps of Dili you turn east / to climb past Portuguese colonial wrecks,".... The villain is not London destroying Luke, but (guess who?) Suharto firebombing a village after a visit from Kissinger (who else?) in 1975, thus destroying the equivalent of the Sheepfold. Keep your gin up, and reread *Mutiny on the Bounty*. (B.C.H.)

Averill, James H. "The Shape of *Lyrical Ballads* (1798)." *PQ* 60 (1981): 387-407.

Baker, Jeffrey. "Prelude and Prejudice." *TWC* 13 (1982): 79-86.

A stinging attack on the editorial and critical principles behind the Norton edition of *The Prelude*, an edition which Baker sees as animated by a distaste for Christianity and by modishly leftish politics. Baker finds four categories of changes in the 1850 version and claims real superiority on poetic, as well as on philosophical, grounds in comparison with earlier versions. "The modern reader recognizes easily that evangelical piety is an almost insuperable obstacle to sound literary judgment, but he may not recognize that its opposite represents an equal difficulty" (p. 86). An impressive case; for a different assessment, see Robert Young's "Reply," below. (B.C.H.)

Bement, Peter. "Simon Lee and Ivor Hall: A Possible Source." *TWC* 13 (1982): 35-38.

Suggests that Wordsworth encountered a poem by Evan Evans (1731-1788), written in Welsh but translated into English and circulated in manuscript, "On Seeing the Ruins of Ivor Hael's Palace ... in Monmouthshire," Ifor Hael (Ivor the Generous) being the patron of the famous medieval poet Dafydd ap Gwilym. Wordsworth visited Thomas Pennant in North Wales in 1791 or 1793; Pennant was Evan Evans's benefactor. The Welsh connection is interesting, and largely unexplored. (B.C.H.)

Bialostosky, Don. "Narrative Diction in Wordsworth's Poetics of Speech." *CL* 34 (1982): 305-29.

Argues that Wordsworth, like Plato, defined narrative as an imitation of speech, whereas Coleridge was more aligned with Aristotle's theory that it is an imitation of action. By the poetics of Aristotle and Coleridge, therefore, the Lyrical Ballads are failures, "but if we recognize the distinctive principle of a poetics of speech, we may find terms in which to appreciate them...."

Bialostosky, Don H. "Narrative Irony and the Pleasure Principle in 'Anecdote for Fathers' and 'We Are Seven.'" *JEGP* 81 (1982): 227-43.

Cosgrove, Brian. "Wordsworth's Moonlight-Poetry: Poetry and the Sense of the 'Uncanny.'" *ArielE* 13,ii (1982): 19-32.

Davies, Hunter. *William Wordsworth: A Biography*. New York: Atheneum, 1980. $17.95.

Rev. by Doris Grumbach in *New York Times Book Review*, Dec. 14, 1980, p. 11.

Dawson, William P. "The Perceptual Bond in 'Strange Fits of Passion.'" *TWC* 13 (1982): 96–97.

Frosch, Thomas R. "Wordsworth's 'Beggars' and a Brief Instance of Writer's Block." *SiR* 21 (1982): 619–36.

Psychoanalysis, with some evidence and much conjecture, which attempts to "reconstruct the interior drama" of the making of the poem "Beggars," as the story moved from Dorothy's journal to William's imagination. (M.T.S.)

Gravil, Richard. "*Lyrical Ballads* (1798): Wordsworth as Ironist." *CritQ* 24:4 (1982): 39–57.

Masterful demonstration of the poet's complex uses of irony in his attempt to educate a corrupt reading public. An important article. (R.M.R.)

Harding, Anthony John. "Field of Vision: Hugh Hood and the Tradition of Wordsworth." *CL* 94 (1982): 85–94.

Wordsworthian influence in a modern Canadian writer.

Johnston, Kenneth R. "Wordsworth and *The Recluse*: The University of Imagination." *PMLA* 97 (1982): 60–82.

Kelley, Theresa M. "Spirit and Geometric Form: The Stone and the Shell in Wordsworth's Arab Dream." *SEL* 22 (1982): 563–82.

Langbaum, Robert. "Wordsworth's Lyrical Characterizations." *SiR* 21 (1982): 319–39.

On Wordsworth's "border" figures, those at the "minimum level of consciousness" between nature and humanity, who are characterized by the narrators' visual impressions rather than by their own speech. "Resolution and Independence," "The Old Cumberland Beggar," "The Idiot Boy," and similar poems are discussed.

Liu, Alan. "'Shapeless Eagerness': The Genre of Revolution in Books 9–10 of *The Prelude*." *MLQ* 43 (1982): 3–28.

Magnuson, Paul. "The Articulation of 'Michael'; or, Could Michael Talk?" *TWC* 13 (1982): 72–79.

McCracken, David. "Wordsworth on Human Wishes and Poetic
Borrowing." *MP* 79 (1982): 386-99.

McFarland, Thomas. "Wordsworth on Man, on Nature, and on Human
Life." *SiR* 21 (1982): 601-18.

A crisp and clear deconstruction of the famous triple
phrase from the Prospectus to *The Recluse*. "Though inauthentic
with regard to the possibilities of a poem that would set
forth a philosophical system [as imagined by Coleridge]
[it] was authentic in terms of Wordsworth's idiosyncratic
development.... it is a fitting, paradoxical beginning to
a poem vast in design and import, but unachieved and broken
in fact." (M.T.S.)

McFarland, Thomas. "Wordsworth's Best Philosopher." *TWC* 13
(1982): 59-68.

A study of "the variety and pervasiveness of Wordsworth's
tendency to introduce blocking elements into the flow of
his greatest passages" (p. 62), especially into the *Ode*.
McFarland identifies the best philosopher as Hartley Coleridge and makes interesting comments on the nature of
originality in Wordsworth, a poet in whom the details are
everywhere derivative but the effect startlingly new: such
originality derives, not from priority, but, according to
Hazlitt, from intensity. An important article. (B.C.H.)

Owen, W.J.B. "The Charm More Superficial." *TWC* 13 (1982):
8-16.

Pirie, David B. *William Wordsworth: The Poetry of Grandeur
and Tenderness*. New York and London: Methuen, 1982. Pp.
301. $29.95.

Rev. by Kathryn Sutherland in *CritQ* 24:3 (1982): 77-81;
by Cedric Watts in *TLS*, Sept. 24, 1982, p. 1046, as sometimes
strained but "generally proficient, lucid, strenuous, and helpful." See also composite review by Jackson, below, p. 154.

Proffitt, Edward. "'Though Inland Far We Be': Intimations of
Evolution in the Great Ode." *TWC* 13 (1982): 88-90.

Reed, Mark L. "Constable, Wordsworth, and Beaumont: A New
Constable Letter in Evidence." *ArtB* 64 (1982): 481-83.

Sent by Constable to Wordsworth in 1836, with a copy of
his *Various Subjects of Landscape ... intended to display ...
the chiar'oscuro of nature* (1833), this letter reveals that

Constable was first led to read Wordsworth by Beaumont,
probably in late 1801 or early 1802, and that Wordsworth
likely attended one of Constable's lectures on English
landscape in London in May or June 1836. An important link.
(B.C.H.)

Ruddick, Bill. "'Adding to Wordsworth': Norman Nicholson's
Sea to the West and *The River Duddon* Sonnets." *CritQ* 24:2
(1982): 53-59.

"Two poets, both conscious of increasing difficulty in
finding fresh material and the imaginative energy to give
it sustained poetic expression, find comfort in natural
forces which seem akin to their sense of the quenchless
vitality inherent within the human mind."

Schneider, Steven. "An Interview with Louis Simpson." *TWC*
13 (1982): 99-104.

A conversation about Simpson's love of Wordsworth.

Sturrock, J. "Sigismonda and Ghismonde: Wordsworth and Scott
on Dryden and Boccaccio." *ES* 63 (1982): 134-38.

Thomas, Gordon K. "Wordsworth's Iberian Sonnets: Turncoat's
Creed?" *TWC* 13 (1982): 31-34.

Young, Robert. "A Reply: To 'Prelude and Prejudice,' by
Jeffrey Baker." *TWC* 13 (1982): 87-88.

See also Alpers, Boly, Bromwich, Diehl, Hassler, Pike, Pocock
("General 3. Criticism"); Beckett ("English 2. Environment");
Hulcoop, Kelley, Sutherland ("English 3. Criticism"); Randel
("Coleridge"); Rosenblum ("French 1. General"); Prochazka
("French 2. Stael"); Higonnet ("German 2. Criticism").

Reviews of books previously listed:

BAKER, Jeffrey, *Time and Mind in Wordsworth's Poetry* (see
RMB for 1980, p. 135), rev. by James A.W. Heffernan in *SiR*
21 (1982): 253-58 as "distinctly illuminating" (composite
review includes Devlin: see below); BETZ, Paul F., ed.,
Wordsworth's Benjamin the Waggoner (see *RMB* for 1981, pp.
145-47), rev. by Paul Magnuson in *TWC* 13 (1982): 130-32;
by Donald H. Reiman (with Jonathan Wordsworth, et al.,
The Prelude 1799, 1805, 1850 [see *RMB* for 1979, p. 134]) in
SiR 21 (1982): 502-09; by Mary Wedd in *ChLB* 39 (1982): 143-
45, noting the fitness of the dedication to Lamb; DARLINGTON,

Beth, ed., *The Love Letters of William and Mary Wordsworth*
(see *RMB* for 1981, p. 147), rev. by John Stewart Collis in
S, Apr. 3, 1982, pp. 24f.; DEVLIN, D.D., *Wordsworth and the
Poetry of Epitaphs* (see *RMB* for 1981, p. 148), rev. by James
A.W. Heffernan in *SiR* 21 (1982): 253-58 as good on Wordsworth's audiences, but, for the most part, careless (composite
review includes Baker: see above); HILL, Alan G., ed., *The
Letters of William and Dorothy Wordsworth, V, The Later
Years, Part 2, 1829-1834* (see *RMB* for 1980, pp. 137-38),
rev. by James H. Averill in *SiR* 21 (1982): 496-501; SHERRY,
Charles, *Wordsworth's Poetry of the Imagination* (see *RMB*
for 1981, p. 152), rev. by Judith W. Page in *MP* 80 (1982):
205-08; WÜSCHER, Hermann J., *Liberty, Equality, and Fraternity
in Wordsworth, 1791-1800* (see *RMB* for 1980, pp. 141-42),
rev. by Michael Friedman in *TWC* 13 (1982): 133-35; by Mary
Moorman in *DUJ*, n.s. 43 (1982): 312-14.

Review articles:

Bayley, John. "Family Man." *NYRB*, Feb. 18, 1982, pp. 13-15.

Discussion based on the recent editions of Wordsworth correspondence by Beth Darlington: *The Love Letters of William
and Mary Wordsworth*, and *My Dearest Love: Letters of William
and Mary Wordsworth, 1810*. See *RMB* for 1981, pp. 147 and 148.

McSweeney, Kerry. "The Hiding Places of Wordsworth's Power."
QQ 89 (1982): 113-30.

An essay review of Averill's *Wordsworth and the Poetry of
Human Suffering* (see *RMB* for 1980, p. 133) and Lipking's
edition, *High Romantic Argument: Essays for Meyer Abrams*
(see *RMB* for 1981, p. 63). Finding Averill's study excellent,
McSweeney quotes its understanding of spots of time: "The
important thing is not what the child felt, but *that* he
felt.... The essential element of the spot of time is the
mind's recapitulation of a scene that death has endowed with
significance." McSweeney then writes: "That is to say, in
the spots of time sequence Wordsworth locates power not in
possible sublimity but in pathos, not in the mind's mastery
of external things but in human suffering and the response
of the child's imagination to it, not in the early bright-
ness of the mother-child bond but in the anxiety of visionary
dreariness." *Fallings from us* is the phrase in Wordsworth
which most eludes. (T.L.A.)

Composite reviews:

Averill, James H. Review in *JEGP* 81 (1982): 119–22.

Deals somewhat favorably with John A. Hodgson, *Wordsworth's Philosophical Poetry 1797–1814* (see *RMB* for 1981, pp. 149–50) and hostilely with Charles Sherry, *Wordsworth's Poetry of the Imagination* (see *RMB* for 1981, pp. 152–54).

Jackson, Rosemary. "The Human Abstract: Wordsworth, Ruskin and 'Art.'" *Encounter* 58 (June–July 1982): 81–86.

Reviews the following: David B. Pirie, *William Wordsworth: The Poetry of Grandeur and of Tenderness* (London and New York: Methuen, 1982; pp. 301; £14.95), together with David Aers, Jonathan Cook, and David Punter, *Romanticism and Ideology: Studies in English Writing, 1765–1830*; *The Romantics*, ed. Stephen Prickett; Elizabeth Gunn, *A Passion for the Particular: Dorothy Wordsworth, A Portrait*; *The Love Letters of William and Mary Wordsworth*, ed. Beth Darlington. (See *RMB* for 1981, pp. 55, 66, 145, and 147, respectively.) Also considered: John Dixon Hunt, *The Wider Sea: A Life of John Ruskin* (New York: Viking; London: Dent, 1982) and *New Approaches to Ruskin*, ed. Robert Hewison (London & Boston: Routledge and Kegan Paul, 1981).

FRENCH

(Compiled by Mary Ellen Birkett, Smith College;
Alfred G. Engstrom, University of North Carolina;
Eugene F. Gray, Michigan State University; Jon B.
Hassel, University of Arkansas; James S. Patty,
Vanderbilt University; Albert B. Smith, Jr., Uni-
versity of Florida; Emile J. Talbot, University of
Illinois at Urbana-Champaign)

1. GENERAL

*L'Accademia delle Scienze di Torino e la cultura franco-
piemontese dell'età napoleonica.* Atti della giornata di
studio promossa dall'Accademia delle Scienze di Torino
in collaborazione con l'Associazione Universitaria Italo-
Francese. 27 marzo 1969. Turin: Accademia delle Scienze,
1977. Pp. 129.

Rev. by Carlo Cordié in *SFr* 25 (1981): 567-68.
Stendhal, Ginguené, and Balzac are treated.

Agulhon, Maurice. *The Republic in the Village: The People of
the Var from the French Revolution to the Second Republic.*
Trans. Janet Lloyd. Cambridge University Press, 1982. Pp.
348. $44.50.

Translation of a work originally published in 1970 (see
ELN 10, Supp., 71).

Agulhon, Maurice. "Le sang des bêtes. Le problème de la protection des animaux en France au XIXe siècle." *Romantisme*
31 (1981): 81-109.

Ajame, Pierre, and Marion Brucker. *300 héros et personnages
du roman français d'Atala à Zazie.* Paris: Balland, 1981.
Pp. 400. Fr. 89.00.

Rev. by Claude Coustou in *NRF* 349 (Feb. 1, 1982): 128-29.

Andries, Lise, ed. *Robert le Diable et autres récits.* (Stock plus; série Moyen Age, 60.) Paris: Stock, 1981. Pp. 240. Fr. 31.50.

Five texts, in their nineteenth-century form, from the "littérature de colportage": *Robert le Diable, Richard sans peur, Jean de Paris, Pierre de Provence et la belle Maguelonne,* and *Grisélidis.*

Angrand, Pierre. "'Liste alphabétique des peintres d'un talent remarquable,' 1824." *GBA* 100 (Nov. 1982): 178-82.

A document listing the names of painters, sculptors, and engravers, with comments on their work, considered to have been intended as a guide for the young vicomte de La Rochefoucauld when he took charge of the Département des Beaux-Arts.

Antoine, Régis. *Les Ecrivains français et les Antilles, des premiers Pères Blancs aux Surréalistes Noirs.* Paris: G.P. Maisonneuve et Larose, 1978. Pp. 430.

Rev. by G. Cesbron in *NCFS* 9 (1981): 289-91.

According to the above review, Chapter 4 ("1794-1848, le déploiement littéraire, d'une abolition à l'autre") treats Hugo (*Bug-Jargal*), l'abbé Grégoire, Madame de Staël, Sismondi, Schoelcher, Lamartine (*Toussaint Louverture*).

Ashbrook, William. *Donizetti and His Operas.* Cambridge University Press, 1982. Pp. 744. £25.00.

Rev. by Michael Tanner in *TLS*, Sept. 24, 1982, p. 1038.

Auster, Paul, sel. and ed. "Notebooks of Joseph Joubert." *The New Criterion* 1 (Dec. 1982): 17-31.

Extracts from the voluminous daily writings of "a writer of the first order" who "spent his whole life preparing himself for a work that never came to be written."

Baillio, Joseph. "Quelques peintures réattribuées à Vigée Le Brun." *GBA* 99 (Jan. 1982): 13-26; 20 illus.

Barbier, Frédéric. "Le commerce international de la librairie française au XIXe siècle (1815-1913)." *RHMC* 28 (1981): 94-117.

Barbier, Frédéric. "Les ouvriers du livre et la révolution industrielle en France au XIXe siècle." *Revue du Nord,* Jan.-Mar., 1981, pp. 189-205.

Barblan, Marc-A. *Journalisme médical et échanges intellectuels au tournant du XVIIIe siècle: le cas de la "Bibliothèque britannique" (1796-1815)*. Avant-propos de Jean Starobinski. (Archives des Sciences, vol. 30, fasc. 3.) Geneva, 1977. Pp. 116.

    Rev. by Michel Gilot in *RHL* 80 (1980): 118; by John Lough in *FS* 34 (1980): 345.

Bassan, Fernande. "Ecrivains-voyageurs français en Terre Sainte après Chateaubriand: Didot, Forbin, Marcellus, et al." *NCFS* 10 (1981-82): 37-44.

Baticle, Jeannine, and Cristina Marinas. *La Galerie espagnole de Louis-Philippe au Louvre, 1838-1848*. (Notes et Documents des Musées de France, 4. Ministère de la Culture.) Paris: Editions de la Réunion des Musées Nationaux, 1982. Pp. 308. Fr. 100.00.

    Rev. by Germain Bazin in *L'OEil* 323 (June 1982): 71; by Jonathan Brown in *BM* 949 (Apr. 1982): 250-51.

Bellet, Roger. "Le sang de la guillotine et la mythologie de Jean Hiroux (1830-1870)." *Romantisme* 31 (1981): 63-76.

Bergot, François. "Le blanc et le noir, ou la vérité romantique de Géricault." *L'OEil* 322 (May 1982): 28-35.

    On Géricault's prints, many of which are well reproduced here. The author's key point: Géricault "se sert du trivial pour atteindre au sublime: à ce génie fait de *poésie* et de *vérité*, suffirent le blanc et le noir."

Bertier de Sauvigny, Guillaume de. *La France et les Français vus par les voyageurs américains, 1814-1848*. Paris: Flammarion, 1982. Pp. 432. Fr. 120.00.

    Rev. by the author in *RDM*, Sept. 1982, p. 761.

Bianchini, Angela. *Voce Donna, Momenti strutturali dell' emancipazione femminile*. Milan: Valentino Bompiani, 1979. Pp. 277.

    Rev. by Antoinette Roubichou in *Friends of George Sand Newsletter*, 4,ii (1981): 62.

Biermann, Karlheinrich. *Literarische-politische Avant-garde in Frankreich. 1830-1870. Hugo, Sand, Baudelaire und Andere*. Stuttgart: Kohlhammer, 1982. Pp. 320. DM 82.00.

Blaze de Bury, Henri. *Musiciens contemporains.* (Les Introuvables.)
Plan-de-la-Tour: Editions d'Aujourd'hui, 1982. Pp. 290. Fr.
88.00.

  Reprints the edition of Paris (Michel Lévy), 1856.

Boime, Albert, Charles Rosen, and Henri Zerner. "'The Unhappy
Medium': An Exchange." *NYRB*, Oct. 21, 1982, pp. 49-51.

  Boime's reply to Rosen and Zerner's review (*NYRB*, May 27,
1982) of his *Thomas Couture and the Eclectic Vision* (see
RMB for 1981, p. 161), with their rebuttal. The nub of this
quarrel is the application of the term "neo-conservative"
to the present revival of interest in academic painting and
l'art pompier.

Bowman, Frank Paul. "La circulation du sang religieux à
l'époque romantique." *Romantisme* 31 (1981): 17-35.

Brady, Patrick. "Memory and Form: The Textual Status and
Function of Literary Recollection." *NCFS* 10 (1982): 199-214.

  Illustrations are taken from a number of the major Romantic
writers.

Brahimi, Denise. *Arabes des Lumières et bédouins romantiques.*
Paris: Le Sycomore, 1982. Pp. 230. Fr. 89.00

Braun, Sidney D. "Lilith: Her Literary Portrait, Symbolism,
and Significance." *NCFS* 11 (1982-83): 135-53.

  After sketching the Biblical and para-Biblical background
of the Lilith legend, Braun turns to nineteenth- and twentieth-century French literature. The Romantic period provides
little material (scattered references in Vigny's *Journal d'un
poète*, a few lines from Hugo's *La Fin de Satan*).

Broglie, Gabriel de. *L'Orléanisme: la ressource libérale de
la France.* Paris: Librairie académique Perrin, 1981. Pp.
411. Fr. 75.00.

  Rev. by Pierre de Boisdeffre in *RDM*, July 1981, pp. 48-51.

Brosse, Monique. "Le statut des langues étrangères dans la
fiction maritime du Romantisme." Pp. 431-41 in *Etudes de
langue et de littérature françaises offertes à André Lanly*.
Nancy: Publications de l'Université de Nancy II, 1980.
Pp. xvi+593.

Brunel, Pierre. *Vincenzo Bellini*. Paris: Fayard, 1981. Pp.
432. Fr. 129.00.

Rev. by V. Del Litto in *SC* 24 (1981-82): 219-20; by Edith
Weber in *RH* 541 (1982): 243.

Brunet, Etienne. *Le Vocabulaire français de 1789 à nos jours*.
3 vols. (Classiques.) Geneva: Slatkine, 1982. Fr. 1271.00.

Bujnicki, Tadeusz. "Roman historique du XIXe siècle. Problèmes
de structure." Pp. 69-79 in *Le Genre du roman. Les genres
de romans*. (Publications de l'Université de Picardie.)
Paris: Presses universitaires de France, 1981. Pp. 160.
Fr. 75.00.

Bullen, Barrie. "The Source and Development of the Idea of
the Renaissance in Early XIXth Century French Criticism."
MLR 76 (1981): 311-22.

Contests the view (W.K. Ferguson, Lucien Febvre) that
Burckhardt and Michelet "invented the Renaissance," seeking--
rather successfully--to show that "the historical concept
was well established in the French mind" well before these
two great historians made their contributions. The evidence
adduced is primarily from the art-historical writings of
Seroux d'Agincourt, Artaud de Montor, and Paillot de Monta-
bert; the key texts date from the Empire and early Restoration. (J.S.P.)

Cabanis, Pierre-Jean-Georges. *On the Relations between the
Physical and Moral Natures of Man*. 2 vols. Trans. Margaret
Duggan Saidi; ed. George Mora. Johns Hopkins University
Press, 1982. $28.50.

Chevalley, Sylvie. "Rachel et les écrivains romantiques."
Romantisme 38 (1982): 117-26.

The great tragedian's personal and literary relations
with Janin, Musset, Lamartine, and Vigny (whose hope to
have her star in *Le More de Venise* and *Chatterton* was never
realized). The author regards all this as "l'histoire des
rendez-vous manqués entre Rachel et les écrivains romantiques." Yet, she claims, Rachel could have been "l'inspira-
trice d'un nouveau romantisme."

Christout, Marie-Françoise. "La Féerie romantique au théâtre
de *La Sylphide* (1832) à *La Biche au bois* (1845), choréo-
graphies, décors, trucs et machines." *Romantisme* 38 (1982):
77-86.

On the effort, occasionally successful, to create a fairy-
tale fantastic in the production of Romantic ballets. The
author focuses on several of the best examples, notably
Giselle.

Cipollaro Andreoli, Olga. "Paris et le Romantisme." *Francia*
18 (Jan.-Mar. 1981): 82-98.

Claudon, Francis. *Encyclopédie du romantisme.* (Encyclopédie
des Arts.) Paris: Somogy, 1980. Pp. 290. Fr. 85.00.

Cobb, Richard. *Promenades: An Historian's Appreciation of
Modern French Literature.* Oxford University Press, 1980.
Pp. 160. $16.98.

Cogniat, Raymond. *Le Romantisme.* Paris: Septimus (Weber-
Diffusion), 1982. Pp. 208. Fr. 119.00

    An art book; one hundred reproductions.

Cohen, William B. *The French Encounter with Africans: White
Responses to Blacks, 1530-1880.* Indiana University Press,
1980. Pp. xix+360. $22.50.

    Rev. by Michael T. Ryan in *JMH* 54 (1982): 117-19, who
finds that the book is "a competent introduction" and that
what it "lacks in richness and subtlety it gains in scope."

Conlon, John J. *Walter Pater and the French Tradition.* Buck-
nell University Press, 1982. Pp. 176. $21.50.

Curtis, Jean-Louis. *La France m'épuise.* Paris: Flammarion,
1982. Pp. 216. Fr. 50.00.

    Rev. by Pierre de Boisdeffre in *RDM*, June 1982, pp. 668-
69.
    Pastiches of Chateaubriand, Balzac, Stendhal, and others.

Dédéyan, Charles. "Laennec et les écrivains de son temps."
Pp. 245-59 in *Laennec. 1781-1826* (Special Issue of *Revue
de Palais de la Découverte* 22 [Aug. 1981]).

D'Hulst, Lieven, José Lambert, and Katrin Van Bragt. "Littérature et traduction en France (1800-1850): état des travaux."
Pp. 301-07 in Zoran Konstantinović, et al., eds., *Literary
Communication and Reception. Communication littéraire et
réception. Literarische Kommunikation und Rezeption.* Proceedings of the IXth Congress of the International Comparative Literature Association/Actes du IXe Congrès de l'Associ-

ation internationale de Littérature comparée. Innsbruck,
1979. (Innsbrucker Beiträger zur Kulturwissenschaft, Sonder-
heft 46.) Innsbruck, 1980. Pp. 436.

Duchange, Ernest. "Sur deux cartes de visite de grimaciers à
Paris (XVIIIe et XIXe siècle)." *GBA* 100 (Sept. 1982): 79-84;
5 illus.

Illustrations of facial expressions.

Dupont-Jones, Louisa. *Pierrot-Watteau: A Nineteenth-Century
Myth*. (Etudes littéraires françaises, 23.) Tübingen: Gunter
Narr, 1982. Pp. 140.

Egbert, Donald Drew. *The Beaux-Arts Tradition in French Architecture: Illustrated by the Grands Prix de Rome*. Ed. David
Van Zanten. Princeton University Press, 1980. Pp. 217.
$22.50.

Rev. by R.D. Middleton in *ArtB* 64 (1982): 340-42.

El Nouty, Hassan. *Théâtre et pré-cinéma: essai sur la probléma-
tique du spectacle au XIXe siècle*. Paris: Nizet, 1978. Pp.
301. Fr. 64.20.

Rev. by Steven M. Taylor in *NCFS* 9 (1981): 276-78.

Emsley, Clive. "The French Police in the 19th Century." *HT* 32
(Jan. 1982): 22-27.

"The framework for the police of nineteenth-century France
emerged out of the reorganisations of the Revolution and
Napoleon."

Faletti, Heidi E. "A.W. Schlegel on Spanish Drama and the
Romanticism of the Romance Literatures in France." Pp. 16-
25 in Frederick C.H. García, ed., *Papers on Romance Literary
Relations Presented at the Romance Literary Relations Group
of the Modern Language Association*. West Point: Department
of Foreign Languages, United States Military Academy, 1982.
Pp. 32.

Schlegel "contributed meaningfully to the specifically
Hispanic mainstream of literature and theory in the romanti-
cism of France through his timely and concise studies on
Spanish drama," especially with respect to the *Préface de
Cromwell*. The author tries to prove too much in too little
space. (J.S.P.)

Farwell, Beatrice. *French Popular Lithographic Imagery, 1815-1870. Lithographs and Literature*, Vol. I. (Chicago Visual Library.) University of Chicago Press, 1981. Pp. x+104. Rev. by Thérèse Dolan Stamm in *NCFS* 11 (1982-82): 183-85. See *GBA* 1366 (Nov. 1982): "Chronique des Arts," p. 20. This first volume (of twelve) deals with the relationship between lithography and the works of Balzac, Flaubert, Baudelaire, Hugo, and Sue.

Felkay, Nicole. "La librairie et la presse de 1825 à 1845. Documents inédits. Première partie: années 1825-1829 (incluses)." *Revue Française d'Histoire du Livre* 29 (Oct.-Dec. 1980): 685-99.

Ferment, Claude. "Le caricaturiste Traviès. La vie et l'oeuvre d'un 'Prince du Guignon.'" *GBA* 99 (Feb. 1982): 63-78.

Festa-McCormick, Diana. "The Myth of the *Poètes Maudits*." Pp. 199-215 in Robert L. Mitchell, ed., *Pre-text/Text/Context: Essays on Nineteenth-Century French Literature*. Ohio State University Press, 1980. Pp. xi+284.

The author's account transcends French literature, to include the literary depiction of Tasso. From the French Romantic period, most crucial is Vigny's treatment of Gilbert, Chatterton, and Chénier.

Fischer, Jan O. "Poésie et société en France au XIXe siècle." *Philologica Pragensia* 24 (1981): 196-99.

A review of the papers given at the symposium held in Wuppertal, Apr. 13-15, 1981.

Fox, Robert. "Learning, Politics and Polite Culture in Provincial France: The Sociétés savantes in the XIXth Century." *Historical Reflections/Réflexions historiques* 7 (1980): 543-64.

Frölich, Juliette. "La Norvège et le XIXe siècle français." *Romantisme* 32 (1981): 124-26.

On the activities of the Institut français of the University of Oslo.

Gabaudam, Paulette. *El Romanticismo in Francia, 1800-1850.* (Serie Manuales universitarios.) Salamanca: Ediciones Universidad de Salamanca, 1979. Pp. 688. Pes. 750.00.

Gaigneron, Axelle de. "Le romantisme illustré." *Connaissance des Arts* 363 (May 1982): 70-75.

Brief discussion of Romantic book illustrations (prints in general are also treated) as a reflection of the age and as presage of our own time.

Gallaher, John G. *The Students of Paris and the Revolution of 1848.* Southern Illinois University Press, 1980. Pp. xx+128. $9.95.

Rev. by John J. Baughman in *The Historian* 44 (1981-82): 102-03.

Garavini, Fausta. "Province et rusticité: esquisse d'un malentendu." *Romantisme* 35 (1982): 73-89.

The Romantic taste for local color, buttressed by a traditionalistic reaction against centralization, led to a revival of interest in provincial cultures. But tensions between Paris and "la province" remained: "le Romantisme aime le populaire et le rustique, non le provincial et le dialectal." Balzac, and, especially, George Sand are the key figures in the earlier part of this account of the conflict.

García Felguera, María de los Santos, ed. *Imagen romántica de España.* 2 vols. Madrid: Ministerio de Cultura, 1981. Pes. 1000.00.

Rev. by Raleigh Trevelyan in *BM* 949 (Apr. 1982): 251. Catalogue of a show (Oct.-Nov. 1981) given at the Palacio de Velázquez. Many items reflect French interest in (and exploitation of) the imagery of Romantic Spain. An article on Mérimée is included among the accompanying materials (five letters written in 1830).

García Martínez, J.A. "La imagen de España y el romanticismo." *Universidad* (Santa Fe), Jan.-Apr. 1979, pp. 53-78.

Gasnault, François. "Bal, délinquance et mélodrame dans le Paris romantique: l'affaire de la 'Tour de Nesle' (1844)." *RHMC* 29 (1982): 36-69.

A psycho-social examination of the interplay of theater, dance-hall, and "real life," apropos of a scandal in which young working-class criminals took the names of characters from Dumas's famous melodrama.

Gasnault, François. "Les salles de bal du Paris romantique;
décors et jeux des corps." *Romantisme* 38 (1982): 7-18.

Gavoty, Bernard. *Liszt. 1: Le Virtuose, 1811-1848.* Paris:
Julliard, 1980. Pp. 358. Fr. 70.10.

Rev. by Edith Weber in *RH* 541 (1982): 245.

*Le Génie de la forme: mélanges de langue et littérature offerts
à Jean Mourot.* Presses universitaires de Nancy, 1982. Pp.
651.

Pertinent articles: René Pomeau, "Chateaubriand personnage
de roman en 1812" (369-75); Jacques Chaurand, "Autour du
mot *gothique* et de son emploi chez Chateaubriand" (377-88);
René Guise, "Chateaubriand et la 'femme enthousiaste' de
Beauvais" (389-98); Yves Le Hir, "Le réseau nocturne dans
Volupté de Sainte-Beuve" (rev. in the present *RMB*) (399-407);
Pierre Larthomas, "Hugo linguiste" (409-17); Monique Brosse,
"Robinson [Crusoé] romantique" (419-27); Marcel Graner, "Le
jugement en appel: la critique stendhalienne, 1846-1856"
(443-52); Anny Detalle, "Barbey d'Aurevilly disciple de
Laclos dans *Une vieille maîtresse*?" (461-66); Marie-Christine
Cousinat-Haro, "Alexandre Dumas en Russie: un carnet de
voyage inconnu" (467-76); Pierre-Georges Castex, "Chateau-
briand et Villiers de l'Isle-Adam" (509-18).

Les Gens de médecine vus au milieu du XIXe siècle. (Errance.)
Paris: Armand Colin, 1982. Pp. 112. Fr. 95.00

Contemporary descriptions by writers, with twenty-nine
illustrations by Gavarni, Grandville, and Charlet.

Gerbod, Paul. "La scène parisienne et sa représentation de
l'histoire nationale dans la première moitié du XIXe siècle."
RH 539 (1981): 3-30.

A valuable synthesis, revealing, first, that only a small
percentage of plays had historical themes. In general, more
recent periods were favored over earlier ones; i.e., the
Middle Ages and Renaissance were not as popular as we
usually say. Contemporary events grew ever more popular
(Napoleon, the Spanish and Greek expeditions, etc.). Kings,
princes, and great military leaders and heroes dominate
the stage. In general, the civic virtues are proclaimed
and popular prejudices (Anglophobia, for example) are reinforced. (J.S.P.)

Gilroy, James P. *The Romantic Manon and Des Grieux. Images of Prévost's Heroine and Hero in Nineteenth-Century French Literature.* Preface by Gita May. (English Series, 5.) Sherbrooke: Naaman, 1980. Pp. 160. $15.00.

Gregory, David. "The Influence of French Socialism on the Thought of Karl Marx, 1843-45." Pp. 242-51 in *Proceedings of the Sixth Annual Meeting of the Western Society for French History. 9-11 November 1978, San Diego, California.* Santa Barbara: Western Society for French History, 1979. Pp. 384.

This study "stresses the continuity between French socialism under the July Monarchy and the earliest, quasi-Romantic formulation of Marxism in the mid-1840s, and it concludes that Marxism before 1847 was little more than a synthesis of ideas suggested by earlier French theorists." The Saint-Simonians, Fourier, Leroux, Proudhon, Sismondi, and lesser figures are prominent in this account of the genesis of Marx's ideas.

Gross, Robert Allen. "Ingres' Celtic Fantasy *The Dream of Ossian.*" *The Rutgers Art Review* 2 (1981): 43-48.

On the pictorial, literary, and biographical sources of the painting.

Guibert, Noëlle. "Le XIXe siècle des décors. Des fonctions sous des mots." *Comédie-Française* 99 (May 1981): 23-35.

Gusdorf, Georges. *Les Sciences humaines et la pensée occidentale.* T. IX: *Fondements du savoir romantique.* (Bibliothèque scientifique.) Paris: Payot, 1982. Pp. 480. Fr. 150.00.

Rev. by Marc-Mathieu Münch in *Romantisme* 38 (1982): 153-55.

Guth, Paul. *Histoire de la littérature française.* T. II: *De la Révolution à la Belle Epoque.* (Flammarion Grand Format.) Paris: Flammarion, 1980. Pp. 796.

Hardouin-Fugier, Elisabeth. *Louis Janmot. 1814-1892.* Presses universitaires de Lyon, 1982. Pp. 360. Fr. 140.00.

Hausmann, Franz Josef. "Gesprochene Sprache im *Trésor de la langue française.*" *ZfSL* 92 (1982): 220-32.

Based on Vols. I-VIII of the *Trésor.*

Hector Moreau (1801-1872), architecte de la transparence. Paris: L'Equerre (Diffusion: Garnier), 1980. Pp. 190. Fr. 110.00.

Hemmings, F.W.J. "A Focal Figure in the Romantic Fraternité
des Arts: Sardanapalus." Pp. 1-12 in *Literature and Society:
Studies in Nineteenth and Twentieth Century French Literature Presented to R.J. North*. Birmingham: John Goodman &
Sons, 1980. Pp. vii+247. £14.00.

On the Sardanapalus theme as treated by Byron, Delacroix,
and Berlioz. Emphasis is on Delacroix; Hemmings shows that,
though the painter surely knew Byron's play and the classical
sources, he essentially invented his subject: "it arose
from the very depths of the artist's being."

Höfner, Eckhard. *Literarität und Realität. Aspekte des Realis-
musbegriffs in der französischen Literatur des 19. Jahrhunderts*. (Studia Romanica, 38.) Heidelberg: Winter, 1980.
Pp. 337. DM 84.00.

Holme, Bryan, ed. *Grandville's Animals: The World's Vaudeville*.
New York and London: Thames and Hudson, 1981. Pp. 63.
$4.95.

Rev. by Louise Collis in *Art & Artists* 184 (Jan. 1982):
47-48.

Houston, John Porter. "Romantic Prose." Pp. 177-203 in John
Porter Houston, *The Traditions of French Prose Style: A
Rhetorical Study*. Louisiana State University Press, 1981.
Pp. xii+278.

In this chapter of Houston's suggestive survey (which is
preceded by a chapter on Chateaubriand and followed by one
on Flaubert), general (period) stylistic traits are derived
from a brief examination of passages by Hugo, Michelet,
Gautier, Balzac, Stendhal (who is treated at greatest
length), Nerval, Bertrand, and Baudelaire. It emerges from
this study that dominant features of Romantic prose style
are elaborate and unusual comparisons, multiplicity and
mixing of genres, and, especially, transcendence of mimesis,
even in historical fiction. (J.S.P.)

Humilière, Jean-Michel. *Louis Blanc (1811-1882)*. (Aux Sources
du Socialisme.) Paris: Editions ouvrières, 1982. Pp. 168.
Fr. 45.00.

Jarrassé, Dominique. "1831 ou la spéculation sur l'architecture." *Monuments historiques* 123 (Oct.-Nov. 1982): 72-76.

A study of the *prix de Rome* competition in architecture
for that year, with some fine illustrations, reinforces the

impression that the hold of Neo-Classicism over official
architectural doctrine was all-powerful.

Join-Dieterle, Catherine. "Evolution de la scénographie à
l'Académie de musique à l'époque romantique." *Romantisme*
38 (1982): 65-76.

On the transformation of stage design at the Paris Opera.
The development closely paralleled that of literary and
artistic taste: by 1850 the Neo-Classical sets of the Empire
period had given way to highly "realistic" ones showing
architecture or landscapes well adapted to such productions
as *Les Huguenots* (e.g., the Château de Chenonceaux) and
Gustave III (which featured a gloomy forest scene). There
are several good illustrations, poorly reproduced.

Jordan, Ruth. *Nocturne: A Life of Chopin*. London: Constable,
1978. Pp. 286. £6.95.

Rev. by Alan Walker in *M&L* 60 (1979): 361-62.

Jurt, Joseph. "Der Mythos des Juden in der französischen
Literatur und Publi-Zistik des 19. Jahrhunderts." Pp. 166-
95 in Simon Lauer, ed., *Kritik und Gegenkritik in Christen-
tum und Judentum*. Bern, Frankfurt-am-Main, and Las Vegas:
Peter Lang, 1981. Pp. 223.

Kavanagh, Thomas M. "Rousseau's *Le Lévite d'Ephraïm*: Dream,
Text, and Synthesis." *ECS* 16:2 (Winter 1982-83): 141-61.

Kimpel, Ben D., and T.C. Duncan Eaves. "Ezra Pound's Use of
Sources as Illustrated by His Use of Nineteenth-Century
French History." *MP* 80 (1982-83): 35-52.

In *The Cantos*, Pound often refers to nineteenth-century
French historical writings and memoirs dealing with Napoleon
(Talleyrand, Madame de Rémusat, Princess Lieven, the
Duchesse de Dino, Madame de Genlis, Thiers).

Kluck, Frederick J. "Charles Gleyre and the French Romantics."
NCFS 10 (1982): 228-43.

On the literary level, the main point made concerns the
artist's "emotional affinity with Alfred de Vigny."

Krakovitch, Odile. "Les romantiques et la censure au théâtre."
Romantisme 38 (1982): 33-43.

Follows the history of censorship through the period 1830-
50, with some attention to individual cases involving Nerval,

Hugo, Dumas, *Robert Macaire*, Balzac (*Vautrin*), and Sue. As for the period of heaviest censorship (1835-48): "La censure symbolisa, plus encore que durant la période précédente, la classe au pouvoir" (i.e., the *haute bourgeoisie*).

Kremer-Marietti, Angèle. *Le Positivisme*. (Que sais-je?, No. 3034.) Paris: Presses universitaires de France, 1982. Pp. 128. Fr. 18.50.

Lacassin, Francis. *Vampires de Paris*. (Maîtres de l'Etrange et de la Peur.) Paris: Union générale d'Editions, 1981. Pp. 250. Fr. 46.70.

> Rev. by Louis-Vincent Thomas in *ASSR* 52,ii (1981): 245. Texts by Gautier and Dumas are included.

Lacoste-Veysseyre, C. *Les Alpes romantiques: le thème des Alpes dans la littérature française de 1800 à 1850*. 2 vols. (Biblioteca del Viaggio in Italia, 4.) Geneva: Slatkine, 1981. Sw.Fr. 130.00.

Lafont, Robert. "Le 'Midi' des troubadours: histoire d'un texte." *Romantisme* 35 (1982): 25-48.

> On the elaboration of the myth of the troubadours, which, as centuries passed, grew away from the texts of their poetry. In the early nineteenth century, Fabre d'Olivet, Stendhal (*De l'amour*), and Sismondi (*De la littérature du Midi de l'Europe*) furnish the most important variants.

La Fournière, Xavier de. *Alexis de Tocqueville, un monarchiste indépendant*. Paris: Librairie académique Perrin, 1981. Pp. 381. Fr. 70.10.

> Rev. by Maurice Bouvier-Ajam in *Europe* 637 (May 1982): 244-45; by Georges Dethan in *Revue d'Histoire Diplomatique* 95 (1981): 98-99.

Lambert, José. "Théorie de la littérature et théorie de la traduction en France (1800-1850) interprétées à partir de la théorie du polysystème." *Poetics Today* 2,iv (1980-81): 161-70.

Leca, Ange-Pierre. *Et le choléra s'abattit sur Paris, 1832*. Paris: Albin Michel, 1982. Pp. 228. Fr. 79.00.

L'Ecuyer Lacroix, Sylvia. "Joseph d'Ortigue et la linguistique de la musique." *Etudes littéraires* 15 (1982): 11-31.

A brief account of the musician's life and a summary of his ideas. As for his literary relations, he was a friend of Lamennais and underwent some influence from Nodier. The author sees in d'Ortigue "le pionnier de la sémiologie et de la philologie musicales."

Lefrançois, Thierry. *Daumier*. (Tout.) Paris: Flammarion, 1982. Pp. 96. Fr. 20.00.

Leniaud, Jean-Michel. *Jean-Baptiste Lassus (1807-57) ou le temps retrouvé des cathédrales*. (Bibliothèque de la Société française d'Archéologie.) Geneva: Droz, 1981. Pp. 296. Fr. 270.00.

Rev. by Robin Middleton in *BM* 952 (July 1982): 456-57. This predecessor and collaborator of Viollet-le-Duc is best remembered as the first editor of Villard de Honnecourt's notebook (1858).

Le Normand, Antoinette. *La Tradition classique et l'esprit romantique: les sculpteurs de l'Académie de France à Rome de 1824 à 1840*. Rome: Edizioni dell'Elefante, 1981. Pp. 378.

Rev. by Jacques de Caso in *Romantisme* 37 (1982): 117-19; by Neil McWilliam in *Oxford Art Journal* 4,ii (1981): 60-62; by Nicholas Penny in *Art History* 5 (1982): 246.

Liszt, Franz. *Des bohémiens et de leur musique en Hongrie*. (Les Introuvables.) Plan-de-la-Tour: Editions d'Aujourd'hui, 1982. Pp. 348. Fr. 108.00.

Reproduces the text of the edition of Paris, 1859.

Lough, John. *The Philosophes and Post-Revolutionary France*. Clarendon Press, Oxford University Press, 1982. Pp. 284. £19.50.

Rev. by L.A. Siedentop in *TLS*, Oct. 8, 1982, p. 1108.

Lubac, Henri de. *La Postérité spirituelle de Joachim de Flore*. T. II: *De Saint-Simon à nos jours*. Paris: Lethielleux, 1982. Pp. 512. Fr. 210.00

Rev. by Henri Crouzet, S.J., in *Bulletin de Littérature Ecclésiastique* 83 (1982): 156-57; by Jean Séguy in *ASSR* 53,ii (1982): 325; by Elisabeth Guibert Sledziewski in *Romantisme* 36 (1982): 99-100.

French figures treated in this second volume are Cousin, Fourier, Lamennais, Buchez, Leroux, George Sand, Michelet, and Quinet. (The earlier volume [see *RMB* for 1980, p. 210] included discussion of Joseph de Maistre and Ballanche.)

Luciani, Gérard. "Mythes et images de Venise chez les voyageurs
français entre 1750 et 1850." *Bulletin de l'Université de
Savoie, Département d'Italien* 4 (Oct. 1979): 57-83.

See résumé by Anna Galliano in *Bollettino del Centro
interuniversitario di Ricerche sul Viaggio in Italia* 1,ii
(1980): 121-22.

Luciani, Gérard. "Venise et les voyageurs français de la
première moitié du XIXe siècle." Pp. 109-20 in Emanuele
Kanceff and Gaudenzio Boccazzi, eds., *Voyageurs étrangers
à/Foreign Travellers in/Viaggiatori stranieri a/Venezia.*
Actes du Congrès de l'Ateneo Veneto, 13-15 octobre 1979.
(Biblioteca del Viaggio in Italia, Studi, Bibliothèque du
Voyage en Italie, Etudes, 9.) Geneva: Slatkine, 1981. Pp.
253.

A rather rapid overview of the subject, with no one writer
really featured; Daru, Paul de Musset, Gautier, Lady Morgan,
Stendhal, Chateaubriand, George Sand, and Charles Didier
are cited once or twice each. Major themes which emerge are
morality, nostalgia for the past, love of the picturesque;
major images are "Venise ... ville déchue," "Venise-femme,"
"Venise anadyomène," and "la gondole funèbre."

Lyman, Thomas W. "Saint-Sernin, Viollet-le-Duc et la théorie
de l'harmonie des proportions." *GBA* 100 (Dec. 1982): 227-39.

Draws on unpublished documents to combat the claim that
Viollet-le-Duc's restoration of the Romanesque church in
Toulouse was carried out in the light of the theory of
proportion expressed in the article on that subject in his
Dictionnaire raisonné.

Martel, Philippe. "Les historiens du début du XIXe siècle et
le Moyen Age occitan: Midi éclairé, Midi martyr ou Midi
pittoresque." *Romantisme* 35 (1982): 49-71.

A survey of the dominant images of medieval Occitania
projected by Sismondi, Guizot, Augustin Thierry, Fauriel,
Mary Lafon, Henri Martin, and Michelet. Ideological (i.e.,
political and religious) interpretations of these views
are offered, e.g., the reaction to the Albigensian Crusade.

Martin, Marc. "Journalistes parisiens et notoriété (vers 1830-
1870). Pour une histoire sociale du journalisme." *RH* 539
(1981): 31-74.

A statistical analysis of the profession, using two editions of Vapereau's *Dictionnaire des contemporains* (1858,
1870) as the basic source.

Mayeur, Françoise. *Histoire générale de l'enseignement et de l'éducation en France*. T. 3: *De la Révolution à l'Ecole républicaine*. Paris: Nouvelle Librairie de France, 1982. Pp. 683.

Rev. by Eugen Weber in *TLS*, Mar. 4, 1983, pp. 219-20.

Mazzotta, Gabriele. "L'illustrazione romantica." *L'Esopo* 9 (Mar. 1981): 9-20.

On French book illustrations, 1830-50.

McManners, John. *Death and the Enlightenment: Changing Attitudes to Death among Christians and Unbelievers in Eighteenth-Century France*. Oxford University Press, 1982. Pp. 619. $29.95.

Rev. by Robert Darnton ("The Art of Dying") in *NYRB*, May 13, 1982, pp. 8-12.

McWilliams, Neil. "David d'Angers and the Panthéon Commission: Politics and Public Works under the July Monarchy." *Art History* 5 (1982): 426-46.

On the controversy over David's Panthéon frieze (it contained such controversial figures as Voltaire, Rousseau, Manuel, and Lafayette). By 1837 the régime had moved away from the liberalism which had permitted David to get the commission. He stood his ground when the minister called for changes. The episode reveals the tensions and problems involved in "offical commissioning policy of the period."

Merle, Roger. *Armand Barbès, un révolutionnaire romantique*. Toulouse: Privat, 1978. Pp. 280. Fr. 54.00.

Michel, Arlette. "Jules Verne et la science romantique." Pp. 117-24 in *Colloque d'Amiens (11-13 novembre 1977), Jules Verne, écrivain du XIXe siècle, II: filiations, rencontres, influences*. (La Thésothèque, 5.) Paris: Minard (Lettres modernes), 1980. Pp. 109. Fr. 50.00.

Middleton, Robin, ed. *The Beaux-Arts and Nineteenth-Century French Architecture*. MIT Press, 1982. Pp. 272. $29.95.

According to a notice in *TLS*, June 18, 1982, p. 675, among the eleven essays on architecture as taught at the Ecole des Beaux-Arts from 1819 to 1968 is one on Hugo.

Miquel, Pierre. *Eugène Isabey (1803-1886). La marine au XIXe siècle*. 2 vols. Maurs-la-Jolie: La Martinelle, 1982. Fr. 1400.00.

Rev. by Germain Bazin in *L'OEil* 327 (Oct. 1982): 64. According to Bazin, Isabey prolonged the Romantic spirit in painting (he compares him to Dumas).

Miquel, Pierre. *Félix Ziem, 1821-1911.* 2 vols. Maurs-la-Jolie: La Martinelle, 1978. Fr. 980.00.

Rev. by René Jullian in *Apollo*, June 1982, pp. 510-11.

Morse, David. *Perspectives on Romanticism: A Transformational Analysis.* London: Macmillan, 1981. Pp. xiii+310. £15.00.

Rev. by Paul Hamilton in *TLS*, Mar. 19, 1982, p. 322.

Mozet, Nicole. "Yvetot vaut Constantinope. Littérature et géographie en France au XIXe siècle." *Romantisme* 35 (1982): 91-114.

On the socio-economic implications of the nineteenth-century interest in "la province": "Cessant d'être seulement lieu d'exil et d'ennui, elle s'est transformée, par la grâce de la gravure et de la description, documentaire et littéraire, en un espace à explorer, à inventorier, à admirer--et quelquefois à acheter." Balzac is the principal source of Mozet's material for the earlier part of the century; George Sand and Stendhal also furnish some.

Nanquette, Claude. *Les Grands Interprètes romantiques.* Paris: Fayard, 1982. Pp. 32. Fr. 135.00.

Photographs of the "stars."

Newman, Edgar Leon. "Lost Illusions: The Regicides in France During the Bourbon Restoration." *NCFS* 10 (1981-82): 45-74.

Thick with facts and figures about the treatment of and reaction to the Regicides who survived into the Restoration period, Newman's study gives a graphic picture of their fate. (J.S.P.)

Nicolas, Anne. "L'esthétique impossible. Les *Poétiques* françaises du XIXe siècle." *Langue française* 49 (Feb. 1981): 5-13.

Orr, Linda. "Tocqueville et l'histoire incompréhensible: *L'Ancien Régime et la Révolution.*" *Poétique* 49 (Feb. 1982): 51-70.

Pagliano Ungari, Graziella. "La nouvelle et son encadrement au XIXe siècle." *Kwartalnik Neofilologiczny* (Warsaw) 27 (1980): 375-84.

Parent-Lardeur, Françoise. *Les Cabinets de lecture. La lecture publique à Paris sous la Restauration.* (Bibliothèque historique.) Paris: Payot, 1982. Pp. 208. Fr. 85.00.

The first book-length study of the subject, this solid treatment is carried out in the *Annales* manner. (J.S.P.)

Perrot, Philippe. *Les Dessus et les dessous de la bourgeoisie. Une histoire du vêtement au XIXe siècle.* Paris: Fayard, 1981. Pp. 349. Fr. 69.00.

Rev. by Barbara T. Cooper in *NCFS* 11 (1982-83): 199-200; by Philip Thody in *TLS*, Oct. 16, 1981, p. 1199.

Pistone, Danièle. "Réflexions sur l'évolution du public musical parisien." *Romantisme* 38 (1982): 19-23.

On the growth and democratization of the musical public in Paris; in fact, "au public a succédé la masse, la foule."

Piwinska, Maria. "Le vieillard désespéré et l'histoire." *Romantisme* 36 (1982): 3-14.

On the Romantic transformation of the idea of old age.

Pourvoyeur, Robert. "Jules Verne et le romantisme musical." Pp. 155-68 in *Colloque d'Amiens (11-13 novembre 1977), Jules Verne, écrivain du XIXe siècle, II: filiations, rencontres, influences.* (La Thèsothèque, 5.) Paris: Minard (Lettres modernes), 1980. Pp. 109. Fr. 50.00.

Quatremère de Quincy, Antoine Chrysostome. *Essai sur la nature, le but et les moyens de l'imitation dans les beaux-arts.* Ed. L. Krier and D. Porphyrios. Brussels: Archives d'Architecture moderne, 1980. Pp. xxxiv+xii+436+18.

Rev. by Jean-Claude Lebensztejn in *Critique* 37 (1982): 3-21.
A reproduction of the edition of 1823.

Radisich, Paula Rea. "Eighteenth-Century Plein-Air Painting and the Sketches of Pierre-Henri de Valenciennes." *ArtB* 64 (1982): 98-104.

Ramos Ortega, Francisco. "La fortuna del Cid en el romanticismo francés." *Revista de Literatura* 43,lxxxv (1981): 37-58.

Rancière, Jacques. *La Nuit des prolétaires.* Paris: Fayard, 1981. Pp. 451. Fr. 89.00

Rev. by Harry L. Butler in *FR* 56 (1982-83): 500-01.

Writing from the perspective of "althusserian marxism,"
Rancière examines the literary efforts of radicalized French
workers of the nineteenth century, in the words of the above
review, "to disengage, perception by perception, the workers'
rising consciousness with respect to work, bosses, class
solidarity, collective actions, etc., and to reveal the
errors in the idealistic movements' attempts to organize
communities in which labor and the collective good would
be the driving values rather than individualism and greed."

Raoul, Valerie. *The French Fictional Journal: Fictional
Narcissism/Narcissistic Fiction.* University of Toronto Press,
1980. Pp. 158. $12.50.

Rev. by Lynn Kettler Penrod in *FR* 56 (1982-83): 471-72.
Though emphasis is on post-Romantic examples, Madame de
Krüdener, Lamartine, Nodier, Sainte-Beuve, and Senancour
are discussed in passing. As the author explains, she is
studying the "interferences" of two literary codes, that
of the "fictional journal" and that of the novel (the conventions of the latter, she says, subjugate those of the
diary). The approach is semiotic and specifically inspired
by Genette.

Ray, Gordon N. *The Art of the French Illustrated Book, 1700-
1914.* 2 vols. Cornell University Press, 1982. $185.00.

Réizow, Boris. "Le Romantisme dans la littérature italienne
et française au début du XIXe siècle." Pp. 505-12 in Béla
Köpeczi et al., eds., *Actes du VIIIe Congrès de l'Association internationale de Littérature comparée. Proceedings
of the 8th Congress of the International Comparative Literature Association. T. I: Trois grandes mutations littéraires:
Renaissance, Lumières, Début du vingtième siècle.* Stuttgart:
Bieber, 1980. Pp. 1005.

Rheims, Maurice. "Le nu, jusqu'au trouble de l'âme et des
corps." *Connaissance des Arts* 350 (Apr. 1981): 52-57.

On the rise of sensuality in nude sculpture during the
nineteenth century, from the academism of Thorvaldsen to
the expressionism of Rodin.

Rosenblum, Nancy L. "Romantic Militarism." *JHI* 43 (1982):
249-68.

Writers from French literature predominate (Constant,
Chateaubriand, Stendhal, Musset, Vigny), but Wordsworth,
J.S. Mill, and W. von Humboldt are also discussed.

Rosenthal, Donald A. "Ingres, Géricault and 'Monsieur Auguste.'"
BM 124 (Jan. 1982): 9-14; 5 illus.

Jules-Robert Auguste (1789-1850), painter and sculptor,
and his relations with the two artists named.

Rossard, Janine. *Pudeur et romantisme. Mme Cottin, Chateaubriand, Mme de Krüdener, Mme de Staël, Baour-Lormian, Vigny,
Balzac, Musset, George Sand.* Paris: A.-G. Nizet, 1982. Pp.
126. Fr. 80.00.

The titles of the individual chapters of this study of
sexual modesty in French Romantic literature--a sequel to
her earlier work, *Une clef du romantisme: la pudeur* (see
ELN 15, Supp., 91)--usually reveal the thrust of each:
"Passions et tensions pudiques dans *Claire d'Albe*"; "La
pudeur chez M. de Chateaubriand"; "Rayons pudiques dans
Valérie"; "Défendre l'amour: Mme de Staël dans *Corinne*";
"Une pudeur en forme" [Baour-Lormian]; "Le comte de Vigny
et la pudeur"; "Le lys de Balzac"; "L'enfant terrible de
la pudeur" [Musset]; "George Sand: pudique ou impudique?"
Rossard's present study aims at throwing light on the psychology of the period (whereas the earlier one was written from
the standpoint of literary history). The result is a set of
graceful and perceptive essays, whether studying individual
works (*Claire d'Albe, Valérie, Corinne, Le Lys dans la
vallée*) or exploring on a broader front (Chateaubriand,
Baour-Lormian, Vigny, Musset, Sand). (J.S.P.)

Rude, Fernand. *Les Révoltes des canuts, 1831-1834.* (Petite
Collection Maspero, Histoires.) Paris: Maspero, 1982. Pp.
205. Fr. 25.00.

Rev. by Maurice Agulhon in *Romantisme* 38 (1982): 161-62.

Saint-Gerand, Jacques-Philippe. "Un aspect de la langue française au XIXe siècle: le *Journal grammatical* de 1835 et sa
fonction sociologique." *FM* 49 (1981): 337-57.

An examination of the contents of this periodical for
the year 1835 reveals "les complexités d'une époque de
mutation sociale, ... l'instabilité, ... la recherche tâton-
nante d'une société en quête de valeurs intellectuelles
qui fixent l'évolution trop rapide des réalités matérielles."
The Romantics were severely criticized in this journal dedicated to preserving the "édifice régulier et majestueux"
of the French language.

176   French / 1. General

Sandoz, Marc. *Cahiers Théodore Chassériau*, T.I. Paris:
Editart/Librairie des Quatre Chemins, 1982. Pp. 44. Fr. 80.00.

Seaton, Beverly. "French Flower Books of the Early Nineteenth
Century." *NCFS* 11 (1982-83): 60-71.

An able sketch of the rise of a genre usually ignored or
despised but which flourished vigorously in the period 1810-
20. The author succeeds in showing that such books "represent aspects of thought on the relationship between nature
and man, and attitudes towards the study of nature itself."
The rising interest in botany and gardening, the vogue of
descriptive poetry à la James Thomson, the influence of
Rousseau, and the elaboration of a "language of flowers"
form the background against which the genre developed. No
influence of this genre, however, is suggested on "serious"
literature. (J.S.P.)

Shaw, Marjorie. "In Search of a Dramatic Image in Nineteenth
Century France." Pp. 23-28 in *Literature and Society:
Studies in Nineteenth and Twentieth Century French Literature
Presented to R.J. North*. Birmingham: John Goodman & Sons,
1980. Pp. vii+247. £14.00.

The actual performance record of Romantic dramatists is
shown to be rather poor--only Musset has had any substantial
number of performances.

Slama, Béatrice. "Femmes écrivains." In Jean-Paul Aron, ed.,
Misérable et glorieuse: la femme au XIXe siècle. Paris:
Fayard, 1980. Pp. 248. Fr. 53.95.

Soldini, Jean. "Luigi Canonica et la leçon des architectes
révolutionaires." *GBA* 99 (Mar. 1982): 95-100; 7 illus.

Starobinski, Jean. *1789. The Emblems of Reason*. Trans. Barbara
Bray. University Press of Virginia, 1982. Pp. 298. $24.95.

On David, Fuseli, Goya, Mozart, Boullée, et al.

Stavan, Henry Anthony. *Le Lyrisme dans la poésie française de
1760 à 1820. Analyse et textes de quelques auteurs*. The
Hague and Paris: Mouton, 1972. Pp. 226.

Rev. by William F. Edmiston in *Diderot Studies* 20 (1981):
366-68.

Stone, John, and Stephen Mennell, eds. and trans. *Alexis de
Tocqueville on Democracy, Revolution and Society: Selected*

Writings. (The Heritage of Sociology Series.) University of
Chicago Press, 1980. Pp. x+391. $27.50.

Rev. by Max Beloff in *Encounter*, Feb.-Mar. 1981, pp. 85-86.

Storey, Robert. "Tha Pantomime of Jean-Gaspard Deburau at the
Théâtre des Funambules (1819-1846)." *Theatre Survey* 23 (1982):
1-29.

A solidly-researched effort to get at the reality of Deburau's
theater (as against, say, the "Baptiste" of *Les Enfants du
paradis*, which repeats the Jules Janin view of him). The
various types of pantomime he produced are described and
differentiated; his different Pierrots are discussed. The
author goes in for a certain amount of psychologizing.
(J.S.P.)

Sydow, Bronislav-Edouard, ed. *Correspondance de Frédéric Chopin.*
3 vols. Paris: La Revue Musicale/Editions Richard-Masse,
1982. Fr. 360.00.

Talleyrand, Charles-Maurice de. *Mémoires, 1754-1815.* Ed. Paul-
Louis and Jean-Paul Couchoud. (Les Mémorables.) Paris: Plon,
1982. Pp. 832. Fr. 150.00.

Taylor, baron Isidore, ed. *Voyages pittoresques et romantiques
dans l'ancienne France: Dauphiné.* Marseille: Jeanne Laffitte--
Les Mots doux, 1982. Pp. 246. Fr. 3000.00

Ternois, Daniel. *Ingres.* Paris: Fernand Nathan, 1980. Pp. 80.
Fr. 119.00.

Thomas, Edmond. *Voix d'en bas. La poésie ouvrière du XIXe
siècle.* (Actes et Mémoires du Peuple.) Paris: Maspero, 1979.
Pp. 464. Fr. 80.00.

Rev. by Pierre Brochon in *RHL* 81 (1981): 801-02.

Thompson, Patrice. "Essai d'analyse des conditions du spectacle dans le Panorama et le Diorama." *Romantisme* 38 (1982):
47-64.

Most useful are the sketch of the history of these institutions and the description of the facilities and their
functioning (some not too spectacular illustrations are included). These give way to "une grille de lecture des
rapports entre spectacle et spectateur qui [peut] situer
plus exactement le panorama et le diorama synchroniquement
par rapport aux autres types de machines spectaculaires."
(J.S.P.)

Thuillier, Guy. *Bureaucratie et bureaucrates en France au XIXe siècle.* (Hautes Etudes médiévales et modernes, 38.) Geneva: Droz, 1980. Pp. xx+672. Sw.Fr. 100.00.

Rev. by Howard Machin in *JMH* 53 (1981): 733-34.

Tocqueville, Alexis de. *De la démocratie en Amérique.* Ed. François Furet. 2 vols. (Garnier-Flammarion, 353-354.) Paris: Garnier-Flammarion, 1981. Fr. 9.39 (each vol.).

Tsigakou, Fani-Maria. *The Rediscovery of Greece: Travellers and Painters of the Romantic Era.* London: Thames and Hudson, 1981. Pp. 208. £16.00.

Rev. by Hugh Lloyd-Jones in *TLS*, Feb. 12, 1982, p. 157.

Viallaneix, Paul, and Jean Ehrard, eds. *Nos ancêtres les Gaulois.* Actes du Colloque international de Clermont-Ferrand. Clermont-Ferrand: Association des Publications de la Faculté des Lettres et Sciences humaines de Clermont-Ferrand, 1982. Pp. 492. Fr. 180.00.

At the heart of this symposium (June 23-25, 1980) is a series of articles dealing with numerous aspects of the life and history of the Gauls as reflected in the literature, the visual arts, the scholarship (and pseudo-scholarship), and political theorizing of the pre-Romantic and Romantic age: Jean Balcou, "La Tour d'Auvergne, théoricien breton du mythe gaulois" (107-13); Jacques Gury, "Nos ancêtres les Gaulois dans le décor pittoresque dans le dernier tiers du XVIIIe siècle" (119-26); Edouard Guitton, "Duclos, Roucher, Chateaubriand et la cueillette du gui" (127-38); Béatrice Didier, "Le mythe des Gaulois chez Chateaubriand" (144-52); Jean-Maurice Gautier, "L'épisode de Velléda dans *Les Martyrs* de Chateaubriand" (153-61); Jacques Joly, "'Oltre ogni umana idea': le mythe, la tragédie, l'opéra dans la *Norma* de Bellini" (165-76); Ceri Crossley, "William Price: druide contestataire" (177-81); Bernard Tanguy, "De la gallomanie au nationalisme breton" (187-93); Jean-Yves Guiomar, "Quand les bretonistes répudièrent la Gaule (1840-1850)" (195-201); Claudine Lacoste, "Les Gaulois d'Amédée Thierry" (203-09); Christian Croisille, "Michelet et les Gaulois ou les séductions de la patrie celtique" (211-19); Pierre Michel, "Mythe barbare et mythe gaulois de 1789 à 1848" (221-29); Rémi Mallet, "Henri Martin et les Gaulois: histoire et mythe" (231-44).

Balcou unearths and rehabilitates La Tour d'Auvergne's *Origines gauloises* (1791). Gury dicsusses "picturesque" gardens, real and literary, e.g., at Ermenonville, where

an altar in Gallic style was set up by the Marquis de Girardin
(Rousseau's patron). Guitton provides a source study of a
famous episode in *Les Martyrs*, showing the influence of
Roucher's *Les Mois* and tracing the literary treatment of
this theme to its ultimate source, Pliny. Didier, leaving
the Velléda episode to another speaker, studies the general
impact of Gallic myth and history in Chateaubriand and relates
his literary and historical discussions of the Gauls to his
deepest personal preoccupations. Gautier looks at the Velléda
episode from several points of view: sources (Livy, Tacitus),
autobiography, treatments of the theme in painting, sculpture, music, and later literature (e.g., traces in Nerval
and Verlaine). Joly's subject is, essentially, the transformation of Soumet's tragedy (and other sources) into
Bellini's opera. Crossley resurrects the curious figure of
William Price (1800-93), militant partisan of the Druids,
of Chartism, and of cremation (who had no direct impact on
French literature). Tanguy traces the rise of Breton nationalism from the Académie celtique, under Napoleon, through
the fundamental work of Hersart de La Villemarqué, de Courson, La Borderie, and Joseph Loth. Guiomar follows the debate
over the indigenous (Armorican) vs. insular (i.e., British
and Welsh) origins of the Breton race and language and especially of the "matière de Bretagne," through the works of
Hersart de La Villemarqué, Aurélien de Courson, Amédée
Thierry, Arthur de La Borderie, and other historians; the
crux of the debate was the disputed mass migration of Britons
to Armorica in late Roman times. Focusing on one of these
figures, Thierry (*Histoire des Gaulois*, 1828), Lacoste brings
out the special point of view and contribution of the
brother of the more famous Augustin Thierry: his insistence
on the convergence of the two ideas, nation and race, and
his synthesis of a Gallic national character, principal
source of the people and culture of modern France. Croisille
wishes to point out Michelet's originality in giving the
Gauls an important place in his *Histoire de France*, quanti-
tatively and--more importantly--qualitatively; he summarizes
Michelet's image of the Gauls and brings out the historian's
inner struggle betwen his Celticism and his effort, as a
"scientific" historian, to give an objective assessment of
the place of the various racial groups from which the French
nation sprang. Michel parts company from the rest of these
papers by offering, rather than scholarly research, a
dithyramb on the theme of the identification, in revolutionary tradition, of the bourgeois liberals with the Gauls
and of the enemies of the Revolution with the Barbarians
(internally, the proletariat; externally, the Austrians,

Cossacks, and other "Huns"); after 1830, Michelet can
identify with the Barbarian (Fourier, however, denounced
Civilization as barbaric; Saint-Simon pinned the label on
Liberals, i.e., Capitalists). In short, Michel reveals the
polyvalence of the contrast Gaul/Barbarian. Mallet's study
of Henri Martin as propagator of the Gallic myth reveals
this historian to be not merely "le celtomane du XIXe siècle"
by following the evolution of his treatment of the Gauls
through the successive editions of his influential *Histoire
de France*.
      All of these studies represent solid scholarship; even
Michel's grows out of his large-scale 1981 work, *Un Mythe
romantique: les barbares 1789-1848* (see *RMB* for 1981, p.
166). Their presentation was punctuated with interesting
"debates" (pp. 115-17, 139-40, 143-44, 183-85, 247-49);
their publication here is accompanied by several valuable
illustrations from nineteenth-century documents. (J.S.P.)

Viatte, Auguste. "Le Romantisme." Pp. 26-42 in Auguste Viatte,
      Histoire comparée des littératures francophones. (Nathan-
      Université.) Paris: Fernand Nathan, 1980. Pp. 215. Fr. 77.00.

      Rev. by Gilles Gingras in *Etudes Canadiennes* 10 (1981):
      241; by Henri Lafon in *Le Français dans le Monde* 163 (Aug.-
      Sept. 1981): 16-17.

Vier, Jacques. "La poésie catholique dans le romantisme breton."
      La Pensée catholique 189 (Nov.-Dec. 1980): 91-97.

Vigier, Philippe. *La Vie quotidienne en province et à Paris
      pendant les journées de 1848*. (Vie quotidienne.) Paris:
      Hachette, 1982. Pp. 448. Fr. 72.00.

Wald Lasowski, Patrick. *Syphilis. Essai sur la littérature
      française du XIXe siècle*. (Les Essais, 219.) Paris: Galli-
      mard, 1982. Pp. 165. Fr. 72.00.

      Stendhal and Balzac are the authors treated from the
      Romantic era.

Waquet, François. *Les Fêtes royales sous la Restauration ou
      l'Ancien Régime retrouvé*. (Bibliothèque de la Société fran-
      çaise d'Archéologie, 14.) Paris: Arts et Métiers graphiques,
      1982. Pp. 210. Fr. 150.00.

Wechsler, Judith. *A Human Comedy. Physiognomy and Caricature
      in 19th-Century Paris*. Foreword by Richard Sennett. Univer-
      sity of Chicago Press, 1982. Pp. 208. $29.95.

Rev. by Michael Neve in TLS, Sept. 17, 1982, p. 991.
Balzac, Deburau, Monnier, Daumier, and Baudelaire figure
prominently in this study.

Wick, Peter A., ed. The Court of Flora: Les Fleurs Animées.
The Engraved Illustrations of J.-J. Grandville. New York:
George Braziller, 1981. Pp. 72.
Twenty pages of introduction to fifty-two plates.

Wild, Nicole, ed. Aubert et l'opéra romantique. Catalogue de
l'exposition du centenaire. Paris: Mairies des 13e et 3^e
arrondissements, 1982. Pp. 63.

Williams, John R., ed. Physionomie du Théâtre de l'Odéon.
Columbia, S.C.: French Literature Publication Co., 1982.
$3.95.

Text of an anonymous manuscript of the early 1840s,
including caricatures and describing productions at the
Odéon. There are also portraits of Mademoiselle Georges
and Marie Dorval.

Wilson, James D. The Romantic Heroic Ideal. Louisiana State
University Press, 1982. Pp. xii+223. $18.50.

Though focused on American Romanticism, this attempt to
define the Romantic heroic idea mentions several French
Romantic heroes in passing and Chateaubriand's René rather
often.

See also Heartz ("General 2. Environment"); Blondel, Guillaud,
Punter ("English 2. Environment").

Reviews of books previously listed:

ALEXANDRIAN, Sarane, Le Socialisme romantique (see RMB for
1979, p. 136), rev. by Mireille Bossis in RHL 81 (1981):
797-98; ALLEN, James Smith, Popular French Romanticism (see
RMB for 1981, pp. 157-58), rev. by Mary Ellen Birkett in
Degré Second 6 (July 1982): 207-08; by Robert T. Denommé
in FR 55 (1981-82): 575-76; by Thomas Gretton in FS 36 (1982):
223-24; by Maurice Larkin in ESR 12 (1982): 489-91; by James
S. Patty in KRQ 29 (1982): 215-16; BAUDE, Michel, and Marc-
Mathieu Münch, eds., Romantisme et religion (see RMB for
1981, pp. 158-60), rev. by Volker Kapp in RF 93 (1981):
463-65; by Emile Poulat in ASSR 52,ii (1981): 191; BETH-
LENFALVAY, Marina, Les Visages de l'enfant dans la littéra-

ture française du XIXe siècle (see RMB for 1979, pp. 138-
39), rev. by Clayton Alcorn in FR 54 (1980-81): 598; BOIME,
Albert, Thomas Couture and the Eclectic Vision (see RMB for
1981, p. 161), rev. by Colin Bailey in Oxford Art Journal
4 (1981): 55-56; by Anita Brookmer in BM 932 (Nov. 1980):
768-71; by Ekkehard Mai in Pantheon 40 (1982): 76-77; by
Charles Rosen and Henri Zerner in NYRB, May 27, 1982, pp. 49-
54; by Pierre Vaisse in Kunst Chronik, Feb. 1982, pp. 71-76; by
Eugen Weber in JIH 12 (1981-82): 703-05; BOURGEOIS, René,
L'Ironie romantique (see ELN 13, Supp., 66), rev. by Serge
Bisarello in LR 36 (1982): 360-62; BOWMAN, Frank Paul, Le
Discours sur l'éloquence sacrée à l'époque romantique (see
RMB for 1980, pp. 147-48), rev. by Pierre Aubéry in NCFS 9
(1981): 257-59; by P.J. Bayley in FS 36 (1982): 76-77; by
Danielle Menozzi in RHE 77 (1982): 149-53; BRESSOLETTE,
Claude, L'Abbé Maret (see RMB for 1980, p. 148), rev. by
Louis Le Guillou in CMenn 13 (1981): 61; BROMBERT, Victor,
The Romantic Prison (see ELN 15, Supp., 83-84; 17, Supp.,
112), rev. by Bert O. States in HudR 32 (1979): 617-20;
BROOKNER, Anita, Jacques-Louis David (see RMB for 1980, p.
149), rev. by Thomas Crow in Art History 5 (1982): 109-17;
by Marc Jordan in The Connoisseur 835 (Sept. 1981): 8-9;
by Marina Warner in Encounter, Apr. 1981, pp. 67-69; BURTON,
June K., Napoleon and Clio (see RMB for 1980, p. 149), rev.
by M.S. Anderson in The Historian 43 (1980-81): 431-32;
CLAUDON, Francis, L'Idée et l'influence de la musique chez
quelques romantiques français (see RMB for 1980, p. 150),
rev. by Philippe Berthier in Romantisme 35 (1982): 137-39;
DEL LITTO, V., ed., Le Journal intime et ses formes littéraires (see RMB for 1979, p. 142), rev. by Frank P. Bowman
in RHL 82 (1982): 499-501; ECOLE NATIONALE SUPERIEURE DES
BEAUX-ARTS, CHAPELLE DES PETITS-AUGUSTINS, Le Voyage d'Italie
d'Eugène Viollet-le-Duc (see RMB for 1980, p. 152), rev. by
Gianni Carlo Sciolla in Bollettino del Centro interuniversitario di Richerche sul Viaggio in Italia 1,ii (1980): 127;
FELTEN, Hans, Französischen Literatur unter der Julimonar-
chie (1830-1848) (see RMB for 1980, p. 153), rev. by Mechthild Albert in SC 25 (1982-83): 479-81; FISCHER, Jan O.,
"Epoque romantique" et réalisme (see RMB for 1980, p. 153),
rev. by Horst Heintze in BRP 19 (1980): 355-56; by Jean
Pérus in Europe 623-624 (Mar.-Apr. 1981): 278-81; FRIED,
Michael, Absorption and Theatricality: Painting and Beholder
in the Age of Diderot (see RMB for 1981, p. 163), rev. (with
Else Marie Bukdahl, Diderot, Critique d'Art) by Philip
Conisbee in BM 124 (July 1982): 455-56; by Lionel Gossman
in French Forum 7 (1982): 271-75; FURST, Lilian R., Counter-
parts (see ELN 16, Supp., 82-83), rev. by Robert S. Tate in

SAR 47 (1982): 116-17; FUSCO, Peter, and H.W. Janson, eds.,
The Romantics to Rodin (see *RMB* for 1980, pp. 153-54), rev.
by Neil McWilliam in *Oxford Art Journal* 4,ii (1981): 60-62;
GUITTON, Henri, ed., *Missions et démarches de la critique*
(see *ELN* 15, Supp., 89, 115), rev. by Yvonne Bellenger in
O&C 6,ii (1981): 153-58; by Margaret Groves in *RR* 71 (1980):
98-100; HOWARTH, W.D., *Sublime and Grotesque* (see *ELN* 14,
Supp., 63-64), rev. by Hana Jechová in *RBPH* 59 (1981): 721-
22; IMBS, Paul, ed., *Trésor de la langue française*, T.V.
(see *ELN* 16, Supp., 84), rev. by H.J. Wolf in *RF* 93 (1981):
179-84; JORDAN, David P., *The King's Trial: The French Revolu-
tion vs Louis XVI* (see *RMB* for 1979, p. 146), rev. by Alfred
J. Bingham in *MLJ* 66 (1982): 91-92; KENNEDY, Emmet, *A
"Philosophe" in the Age of Revolution: Destutt de Tracy and
the Origins of "Ideology"* (see *RMB* for 1979, p. 147), rev.
by Aram Vartanian in *JHP* 19 (1981): 512-15; LANGE, Wolf-
Dieter, ed., *Französische Literatur des 19. Jahrhunderts*, I:
Romantik und Realismus (see *RMB* for 1980, p. 156), rev. by
Donald P. Haase in *NCFS* 10 (1982): 360-61; by Siegbert
Himmelsbach in *RHL* 82 (1982): 928-30; LEJEUNE, Philippe,
Le Pacte autobiographique (see *ELN* 15, Supp., 89), rev. by
John Cruickshank in *FS* 36 (1982): 367-68; MANSEL, Philip,
Louis XVIII (see *RMB* for 1981, p. 166), rev. by Guillaume
de Bertier de Sauvigny in *RHMC* 28 (1981): 690-93; by P.G.
in *RH* 541 (1982): 200; MAY, Georges, *L'Autobiographie* (see
RMB for 1980, p. 158), rev. by Paul J. Archambault in *Sym-
posium* 36 (1982): 182-85; by John Cruickshank in *FS* 36
(1982): 367-68; by Nanette Christine Le Coat in *MLN* 97
(1982): 993-97; McCARTHY, Mary, *Ideas and the Novel* (see
RMB for 1980, p. 158), rev. by Philip Stevick in *MFS* 27
(1981-82): 748-49; PICHOIS, Claude, *La Littérature française*,
T. 13 (see *RMB* for 1979, pp. 149-50), rev. in *Bulletin des
Etudes Parnassiennes* 2 (1981): 45-56; by James S. Patty in
FR 54 (1980-81): 469-70; PORTER, Laurence M., *The Literary
Dream in French Romanticism* (see *RMB* for 1979, pp. 151-52,
211), rev. by Susan Noakes in *SiR* 21 (1982): 114-18; PORTER,
Laurence M., *The Renaissance of the Lyric in French Romanti-
cism* (see *ELN* 17, Supp., 117), rev. by Willi Hirdt in *ZfSL*
92 (1982): 267-69; QUEMADA, Bernard, ed., *Trésor de la langue
française du XIXᵉ et du XXᵉ siècle (1789-1960)*, T. VIII (see
RMB for 1981, p. 169), rev. by Veikko Väänänen in *NM* 83
(1982): 216-17; RAYMOND, Marcel, *Romantisme et rêverie* (see
RMB for 1979, p. 152), rev. by Hana Jechová in *RLC* 56 (1982):
219-20; RENOUVIER, Charles, *Manuel républicain de l'homme
et du citoyen* (see *RMB* for 1981, p. 169), rev. by Pierre
Guiral in *RH* 541 (1982): 201-02; by Eugene Schulkind in *FS*
36 (1982): 84; RICHARD, Jean-Pierre, *Microlectures* (see *RMB*

for 1979, p. 153), rev. by Michel Collot in *RHL* 82 (1982):
329-31; by Jeannine Jallat in *Littérature* 42 (May 1981):
123-27; SABATIER, Robert, *Histoire de la poésie française*,
T. 5 (see *ELN* 16, Supp., 87), rev. by Jean-Paul de Nola in
SFr 25 (1981): 367; SCHLEIFER, James T., *The Making of Tocqueville's "Democracy in America"* (see *RMB* for 1980, p. 162),
rev. by Max Beloff in *Encounter*, Feb.-Mar. 1981, pp. 86-87;
SCHNACK, Arne, *Animaux et paysages dans la description des
personnages romanesques (1800-1845)* (see *RMB* for 1980, p.
163), rev. by Mary Ellen Birkett in *NCFS* 9 (1981): 259-60;
STANTON, Domna C., *The Aristocrat as Art* (see *RMB* for 1980,
p. 164), rev. by Emilien Carassus in *RHL* 82 (1982): 936-37;
by Yves Hersant in *XVIIe Siècle* 33 (1981): 267-68; STAUM,
Martin S., *Cabanis: Enlightenment and Medical Philosophy
in the French Revolution* (see *RMB* for 1980, p. 164), rev.
by Thomas E. Kaiser in *JMH* 54 (1982): 121-23; TISON-BRAUN,
Micheline, *Poétique du paysage* (see *RMB* for 1981, p. 170),
rev. by Marie-Claude Charras in *RLMC* 35 (1982): 80-83;
WEISBERG, Gabriel P., *The Realist Tradition* (see *RMB* for
1981, p. 172), rev. by Jean-Paul Bouillon in *Romantisme*
37 (1982): 119-20; by Marjorie Schreiber Kinsey in *NCFS* 11
(1982-82): 186-88.

Composite reviews:

Penny, Nicholas. "The Classical Tradition and the Garden Orna-
ment." *Art History* 5 (1982): 243-46.

Review of Antoinette Le Normand, *La Tradition classique et
l'esprit romantique* (Rome: Edizioni dell'Elefante, 1981;
pp. 378; 99 illus.; approx. £25.00); and François Souchal,
*French Sculpture of the 17th and 18th Centuries--The Reign
of Louis XIV*, vol. I (London: Faber, 1977).

Whitely, Jon. *BM* 124 (Nov. 1982): 773-74.

Review of Maurice Serullaz, *Delacroix* (see *RMB* for 1981,
p. 193), and Daniel Ternois, *Ingres* (Paris: Fernand Nathan,
1982; pp. 192; 426 illus., 86 col. pls.; Fr. 149.00.).

Wrigley, Richard. "Ways of Seeing at the Salon." *Art History*
5 (1982): 358-63.

The following books are discussed: Else Marie Bukdahl,
Diderot, critique d'art (Copenhagen: Rosenhilde & Bagger,
1980, vol. I; pp. 558; 127 illus.; £13.75); Michael Fried,
*Absorption and Theatricality: Painting and Beholder in the
Age of Diderot* (see *RMB* for 1981, p. 163); Helena Zmijewska,
La Critique des salons en France du temps de Diderot (1759-

89) (Warsaw: Wydamnictwa Universytetu Warsawskiego, 1980; pp. 292; 82 illus.)).

Review article:

Crow, Thomas. "'Gross David, with the Swoln Cheek.'" *Art History* 5 (1982): 109-17.

A severe critique of Anita Brookner, *Jacques-Louis David* (see *RMB* for 1980, p. 149), demonstrating the author's shortcomings point by point.

2. STUDIES OF AUTHORS

AGOULT

Bellas, Jacqueline. "Liszt et la fille de Madame O.... Documents inédits." *Littératures* 2 (Fall 1980): 133-40.

Gigarella, Jean. "Marie d'Agoult amoureuse ou bas bleu?" *Marseille* 124 (1980): 89-94.

AMIEL

Monnier, Philippe M. "Le dossier Amiel: bilan et perspectives d'un siècle de recherches." *Romantisme* 32 (1981): 91-99.

An *état présent* of study and criticism on Amiel.

Review of book previously listed:

GAGNEBIN, Bernard, and P.M. Monnier, eds., *Journal intime* (see *ELN* 17, Supp., 121), rev. by Jean-Louis Chrétien in *Critique* 37 (1982): 251-64.

AZAÏS

Baude, Michel. "Un théâtre populaire: le théâtre du Montparnasse d'après le journal inédit de P.-H. Azaïs." *Romantisme* 38 (1982): 25-32.

Covers the period 1821-38 (the theater was founded in 1819).

Reviews of book previously listed:

BAUDE, Michel, *P.-H. Azaïs, témoin de son temps* (see *RMB* for 1981, p. 175), rev. by Frank Paul Bowman in *Romantisme* 35 (1982): 143-44; by Jean-René Derré in *RHL* 82 (1982): 921-23.

BALLANCHE

Derré, Jean-René. *Dossier de la Ville des expiations de Ballanche.* Avec des textes inédits de Ballanche. Paris: Editions du CNRS, 1982. Pp. 136. Fr. 60.00.

Michel, Arlette, ed. *Le Vieillard et le jeune homme.* (Les Classiques de la Politique.) Paris: Garnier, 1981. Pp. 158.

Rev. by A.J.L. Busst in *FS* 36 (1982): 481-82; by Jacques Julliard in *Le Nouvel Observateur*, Jan. 23-29, 1982, p. 57; by P. Michel in *Romantisme* 36 (1982): 101-02.

Murphy, Susan. "Pierre-Simon Ballanche and Victor Hugo's *Quatrevingt-treize.*" Pp. 141-44 in A. Maynor Hardee, ed., *Authors and Philosophers.* (French Literature Series, VI.) University of South Carolina, 1979.

A three-stage structure in the novel parallels Ballanche's tripartite theory of human destiny, from primitive unity, through division and fall, to spiritual unity, so that Murphy senses Ballanche's presence in Hugo's view of history.

Paulson, William R. "Ballanche ou le traducteur caché." *NCFS* 9 (1981): 159-70.

Ballanche's theory of speech (*parole*) and its ramifications in his views on language, myth, and poetry and in his own writing.

See also Annales Benjamin Constant 2 ("Constant, B.").

Reviews of book previously listed:

La Ville des expiations (see *RMB* for 1981, p. 176), brief rev. in *BCLF* 435 (Mar. 1982): 352; by A.J.L. Busst in *FS* 36 (1982): 481-82; by Arlette Michel in *Romantisme* 36 (1982): 100-01.

BALZAC

Adamson, Donald. *Balzac: Illusions perdues.* (Critical Guides
to French Texts.) London: Grant and Cutler, 1982. Pp. 90.

Ambrière, Madeleine, ed. *La Peau de chagrin.* (Lettres françaises.) Paris: Imprimérie nationale, 1982. Pp. 432. Fr.
260.00.

L'Année balzacienne 1981. Paris: Garnier, 1981. Pp. 403

Contains: R. Guise, "Balzac et la presse de son temps"
(7-36); J. Ott, "Honoré de Balzac" par Henry James (II)
(37-52); G. Sagnes, "Tentations balzaciennes dans le manuscrit de *L'Education sentimentale*" (53-64); M. Andreoli,
"Quelques perspectives de lecture sur une nouvelle de
Balzac: *La Paix du ménage*" (65-122); R. Chollet, "Balzac
journaliste: le tournant de 1830" (123-38); M. Ménard, "Une
esthétique du rire: Balzac et l'arabesque comique" (139-68);
N. Mozet, "A propos d'une thèse sur la province balzacienne:
quelques problèmes de méthode" (169-92); J. Gale, "Le jar-
din de Monsieur Grandet" (193-204); J. Frölich, "Le texte
initial: la description du boudoir de Mme du Tillet dans
Une Fille d'Eve" (205-24); C. Vercollier, "Le lieu du récit
dans les nouvelles encadrées de Balzac" (225-36); C. Dédéyan,
"Balzac et Astolphe de Custine à Vienne" (237-44); C. Schopp,
"Le tombeau d'Honoré de Balzac" (245-54); P. Mustière,
"La mise en fiction de l'histoire dans *Béatrix*. Propositions
et hypothèses de travail" (255-66); R. Butler, "Dessous
économiques dans *La Comédie humaine*: les crises politiques
et la spéculation" (267). Reviews and Bibliography.

L'Année balzacienne 1982. Paris: Garnier, 1982. Pp. 357.

Contains: P.A. Perrod, "Nouveaux documents sur l'affaire
Peytel: la genèse d'une erreur judiciaire" (7-30); F.
Letessier, "Balzac et Lamartine" (31-62); J.L. Steinmetz,
"Balzac et Pétrus Borel" (63-76); R. Guise, "Balzac et la
presse de son temps: le romancier devant la critique fémi-
nine" (77-106); R. de Cesare, "Sur le comte Guidoboni-
Visconti. Documents inédits" (107-30); M. Lichtle, "Balzac
à l'école du droit" (131-50); T. Bodin, "Balzac poète"
(151-66); A.M. Bijaoui-Baron, "La bureaucratie balzacienne.
Aux sources d'un thème et de ses personnages" (167-80);
M. Labouret-Grare, "L'aristocrate balzacienne et sa
toilette" (181-94); P. Mustière, "Sur *Un début dans la vie*.
Jeu du hasard, espace de l'occasion, roman de l'intempestif"
(195-210); P. Berthier, "Autopsie d'un petit journal:

Chérubin (1834-1835)" (211-26); P. Danger, "La castration dans *La Peau de chagrin*" (227-46); A. Lorant, "Pulsions oedipiennes dans *Le Lys dans la vallée*" (247-56); C. Ménage, "Balzac paysagiste: *la Grenadière*" (257-72); R. Fortassier, "Le Limousin vu par Balzac" (273). Reviews and Bibliography.

Bandegans, André. "Fascinations et nostalgies balzaciennes dans *Modeste Mignon*: du propos à l'effet." *Bulletin de l'Académie Royale de Langue et Littérature Françaises* 58 (1980): 20-55.

Barricelli, Jean-Pierre. "The Social and Metaphysical Rebellions of Vautrin and the 'Innominato.'" *The Comparatist* 5 (1981): 19-29.

Bernard, Claude E. "A propos de *La Peau de chagrin* d'Honoré de Balzac: comment le sens vient au texte." *NCFS* 10 (1982): 244-67.

Besser, Gretchen Rous. "Historical Intrusions into Balzac's Fictional World." Pp. 76-84 in *Historical Figures in French Literature*. (French Literature Series, Vol. VIII.) Dept. of Foreign Languages and Literatures, University of South Carolina, 1981. Pp. 146.

Brooks, Peter. "Narrative Transaction and Transference (Unburying *Le Colonel Chabert*)." *Novel* 15 (1982): 101-10.

Castex, Pierre-Georges, ed. *La Comédie humaine*. T. XI: *OEuvres philosophiques. Etudes analytiques*. (Bibliothèque de la Pléiade.) Paris: Gallimard, 1980.

    Rev. by R. Quinsat in *RHL* 82 (1982): 299-303.

Daugherty, Sarah B. "*The Golden Bowl*: Balzac, James and the Rhetoric of Power." *TSLL* 24 (1982): 68-81.

Eisensweig, Uri. "L'instance du policier dans le romanesque. Balzac, Poe et le mystère de la chambre close." *Poétique* 51 (1982): 279-302.

    Compares *Maître Cornélius* with Poe's *Rue Morgue*.

Frappier-Mazur, Lucienne, et al. *Colloque Balzac, juillet 1980, Cerisy-la Salle. Balzac, l'invention du roman*. (Colloque de Cerisy.) Paris: Belford, 1982. Pp. 288. Fr. 79.00.

Greet, Anne Hyde. "Picasso and Balzac: *Le Chef-d'oeuvre inconnu*."
The Comparatist 6 (1982): 56-66.
On Picasso's etchings and woodcuts (1931). Twelve illustra-
tions.

Laszlo, Pierre. "Production d'énergie romanesque: *La Peau de
chagrin*." *MLN* 97 (1982): 862-71.

Lock, Peter. "Text Crypt." *MLN* 97 (1982): 872-89.
Basically psychoanalytical study which explains the idea
of the *secret* encoded in the text and the strategies of
defenses used to protect the secret, with particular reference to *La Grande Bretèche*.

McCarthy, Mary Susan. *Balzac and His Reader: A Study of the
Creation of Meaning in La Comédie humaine*. University of
Missouri Press, 1982. Pp. 176. $18.00.

Monographie de la presse parisienne. Précédé de *Minigraphie
de la presse parisienne* de Guy Hocoquenghem. Paris: Hallier/
Albin Michel, 1981. Pp. 202. Fr. 35.00.

Mozet, Nicole. *La Ville de province dans l'oeuvre de Balzac*.
L'espace romanesque: fantasmes et idéologie. Paris: C.D.U.
et SEDES, 1982. Pp. 332.

Rev. by André Vanoncini in *Romantisme* 38 (1982): 158-60.

Pasco, Allan H. "Balzac and the Art of the Macro-Emblem in
Splendeurs et misères des courtisanes." *ECr* 22 (1982): 72-81.

Pasco, Allan H. "Image Structure in *Le Père Goriot*." *French
Forum* 7 (1982): 224-34.
Very interesting article which argues that the unity of
the novel is to be found in the image of degraded love in
all its forms. (J.B.H.)

Pickup, Ian. "Causality and Determinism in Balzac: The 'Law'
of Diminishing Possibilities." *ML* 62 (1981): 196-200.

Serper, Arie. "Les personnages de Balzac et de Zola." *Les
Cahiers Naturalistes* 56 (1982): 37-45.

Stary, Sonja G. "Balzac's Cold-hearted Coquettes: The Link
between Foedora, Antoinette and Valérie." *Degré Second* 6
(July 1982): 101-20.

See also L'Accademia delle Scienze di Torino, Curtis, Farwell,
Garavini, Mozet, Wald Lasowski, Wechsler ("French 1.
General"); Bolster ("Gautier"); Smith ("Lerminier"); The George Sand
Papers, Présence de George Sand 13 and 14 ("Sand"); Goebler-
Lingens ("Stendhal").

Reviews of books previously listed:

BARBÉRIS, Pierre, Le Colonel Chabert (see RMB for 1981, p.
177), rev. by O. Heathcote in FS 36 (1982): 482; EITEL,
Wolfgang, Balzac in Deutschland (see RMB for 1980, p. 172),
rev. by G. Kaiser in GRM 32 (1982): 370-76; FESTA-McCORMICK,
Diana, Balzac (see RMB for 1979, p. 162), rev. by C. Smet-
hurst in FS 36 (1982): 339; LE HUENEN, Roland, and Paul
Perron, Balzac: Sémiotique du personnage romanesque (see
RMB for 1980, p. 173), rev. by C. Coates in FR 55 (1982):
907; PRENDERGAST, Christopher, Balzac. Fiction and Melodrama
(see ELN 17, Supp., 126), rev. by A. Lacy in RR 73 (1982):
262-64; VAN ROSSUM-GUYON, Françoise, et al. Balzac et les
Parents pauvres (see RMB for 1981, p. 180), rev. by A.
Jourdain in Romantisme 36 (1982): 113-15; by D. Kelly in
RR 73 (1982): 264-65.

Review article:

Van Schendel, Michel. "Balzac: de l'oeuvre au texte." UTQ 51
(1982): 112-24.

Long review of two books by Roland Le Huenen and Paul Perron,
Le Roman de Balzac and Balzac: Sémiotique du personnage
romanesque.

BARBEY D'AUREVILLY

Mickel, Emmanuel, Jr. "Barbey d'Aurevilly and Fromentin:
Classical Aesthetic Values in a Romantic Context." Symposium
35 (1981-82): 292-306.

Petit, Jacques, ed. Correspondance générale, T. I: 1824-1844.
(Annales littéraires de l'Université de Besançon, 247.)
Paris: Les Belles Lettres, 1981. Pp. 254. Fr. 125.00.

Rev. by Luigi Tundo in Culture Française (Bari) 28
(1981): 60-67.

BAUDELAIRE

Composite review:

Wood, Michael. "Beautiful and Damned." *NYRB*, Dec. 2, 1982,
pp. 16-20.

Reviewing F.W.J. Hemmings, *Baudelaire the Damned: A Biography*
(London: H. Hamilton; New York: Scribner's, 1982; pp. 251;
$17.95); Rosemary Lloyd, *Baudelaire's Literary Criticism*
(Cambridge University Press, 1981; pp. 338; $59.95); and
Charles Baudelaire, *Les Fleurs du Mal*, trans. Richard Howard
(Brighton: Harvester Press; Boston: Godine, 1982; pp. 365;
$22.50).

BERANGER

Gaxotte, Pierre. "Béranger, monument historique." *Le Spectacle
du Monde/Réalités* 234 (Sept. 1981): 81-84.

BERLIOZ

Bailbé, Joseph-Marc. "Berlioz lecteur de Chateaubriand."
Société Chateaubriand: Bulletin 23 (1980): 9-13.

Barzun, Jacques. *Berlioz and His Century: An Introduction to
the Age of Romanticism*. University of Chicago Press, 1982.
Pp. 448. $8.95 paper.

An abridgment of Barzun's now classic, two-volume study
(1956).

Bloom, Peter Anthony. "Berlioz à l'Institut Revisited." *Acta
Musicologica* 53 (1981): 171-99.

A heavily documented account of the composer's election
to the Académie des Beaux-Arts (1856) and his activities
as a member.

Boyer, Alain. *Berlioz*. Paris: Mengès, 1982. Pp. 350. Fr. 65.00.

Clavaud, Monique, ed. *Carnets intimes d'Hector Berlioz*.
Villeurbanne: Monique Clavaud, 1982. Pp. 60. Fr. 35.00.

Fauquet, Joël-Marie. "Hector Berlioz et l'Association des
Artistes musiciens. Lettres et documents inédits." *Revue
de Musicologie* 67 (1981): 211-36.

Langford, Jeffrey. "Berlioz, Cassandra, and the French Operatic
    Tradition." *M&L* 62 (1981): 310-17.

    On Berlioz's reasons for enhancing the role of Cassandra
    (as against Virgil's account), foremost among them being
    the influence of the finale of Rossini's *Le Siège de Corinthe*.
    Thus *Les Troyens* is a paradoxical blend of the traditional
    and the innovative.

Piatier, François, ed. *Les Soirées de l'orchestre*. (Stock+
    Plus, série: Musique.) Paris: Stock, 1980. Pp. 480. Fr. 25.00.

Raby, Peter. *Fair Ophelia: A Life of Harriet Smithson Berlioz*.
    Cambridge University Press, 1982. Pp. 216. £12.95.

    Rev. by Anita Brookner in *TLS*, Dec. 17, 1982, pp. 1395-
    96.

Silex, N⁰ 15: *Hector Berlioz*. Grenoble: Silex (Distributor:
    Presses universitaires de Grenoble), 1980. Pp. 140. Fr.
    35.00.

See also Hemmings ("French 1. General"); Mitzman ("Michelet");
    Singer (Sand").

Review of book previously listed:

PIATIER, François, *"Benvenuto Cellini" de Berlioz ou le
    mythe de l'artiste* (see *RMB* for 1979, p. 167), rev. by
    Pierre Citron in *Romantisme* 35 (1982): 140.

Composite review:

Quennell, Peter. *S*, Nov. 27, 1982, pp. 27-28.

    Review of Peter Raby, *Fair Ophelia: A Life of Harriet Smith-
    son Berlioz* (Cambridge University Press, 1982) and David
    Cairns, ed., *The Memoirs of Hector Berlioz*.

BONALD

Klinck, David M. "From Catholic Traditionalism to Social
    Catholicism: A Comparison of the Attitudes of Louis de
    Bonald and Félicité Lamennais to Industrialization (Abstract).
    P. 274 in *Proceedings of the Sixth Annual Meeting of the
    Western Society for French History. 9-11 November 1978,
    San Diego, California*. Santa Barbara: Western Society for
    French History, 1979. Pp. 384.

It appears that Lamennais was slightly less negative than Bonald (see comments by Stanley Mellon, pp. 286-87).

OEuvres complètes. 15 vols. Geneva: Slatkine Reprints, 1982. Sw.Fr. 1350.00.

Reprint of the editions of Paris, 1817-1843.

Petyx, Vincenza. "Stato selvaggio e rivoluzione in Louis Gabriel de Bonald." *Atti della Accademia delle Scienze di Torino.* II. *Classe di Scienze morali, storiche e filologiche* 113,i-ii (1979): 57-79.

See discussion by Carlo Cordié in *SFr* 25 (1981): 565-66.

Reedy, W. Jay. "Conservatism and the Origins of the French Sociological Tradition: A Reconsideration of Louis de Bonald's Science of Society." Pp. 264-73 in *Proceedings of the Sixth Annual Meeting of the Western Society for French History. 9-11 November 1978, San Diego, California.* Santa Barbara: Western Society for French History, 1979. Pp. 384.

Bonald should not be seen as a major source of the Saint-Simonian and Comtean effort to create a science of society: his theocratic views are the obstacle to such an interpretation (that of Robert Nisbet) (see comment by Stanley Mellon, pp. 284-86).

See also Petyx ("Maistre, J. de").

BOREL

Pompili, Bruno. "Un articolo di Pétrus Borel su Pierre Bayle e sulla condizione dello scrittore." *SFr* 25 (1981): 258-66.

On Borel's article which appeared in the *Revue de Paris* on Aug. 10, 1845.

Reviews of books previously listed:

POMPILI, Bruno, ed., *Critica degli spettacoli: feuilletons du "Commerce"* (see *RMB* for 1980, p. 180), rev. by Carlo Cordié in *SFr* 25 (1981): 179; by Rosemary Lloyd in *FS* 36 (1982): 339-41; by Jean-Luc Steinmetz in *RHL* 81 (1981): 794-96; POMPILI, Bruno, ed., *Opera polemica* (see *RMB* for 1980, p. 180), rev. by Carlo Cordié in *SFr* 25 (1981): 375-76; by Rosemary Lloyd in *FS* 36 (1982): 339-41; by Jean-Luc Steinmetz in *RHL* 81 (1981): 794-96.

BRILLAT-SAVARIN

Roudaut, Jean, ed. "Mythologie gastronomique (Méditation, XXX)."
NRF 346 (Nov. 1, 1981): 182-91.

BRIZEUX

Review of book previously listed:

RIO, Joseph, ed., Marie (see RMB for 1980, p. 180), rev. by
Hervé Kerbourc'h in Itinéraires 250 (Feb. 1981): 173-77.

CAPEFIGUE

Stewart, Harry F. "Capefigue: An Historical Source for Jean
Genet's Fantasies." RomN 22 (1981-82): 254-58.

CHARRIÈRE

Lettres écrites de Lausanne. Trois femmes. Lettres de Mistriss
Henley. Lettres neuchâteloises. Romans. Paris: Le Chemin
vert, 1982. Pp. 352. Fr. 72.00.

   Rev. by Louise Herlin in NRF 357 (Oct. 1, 1982): 115-16.

Reviews of books previously listed:

CANDAUX, Jean-Daniel, et al., eds., OEuvres complètes (see
RMB for 1980, p. 180), rev. (Vol. I) by Margaret Bruyn Lacy
in ECS 16 (1982-83): 96-98; COURTNEY, C.P., A Preliminary
Bibliography of Isabelle de Charrière (see RMB for 1980,
p. 180), rev. by Dennis Wood in MLR 77 (1982): 453-54.

CHATEAUBRIAND

Dubé, Pierre H. "Harmony in Les Aventures du dernier Abencérage:
The Voyage as Metaphor." RUO 51 (1981): 705-13.

Gillet, Jean. "Chateaubriand, Volney et le sauvage américain."
Romantisme 36 (1982): 15-26.

   For Chateaubriand the noble Indian recalled the Roman
virtues, and the Indian warriors seemed like Homeric heroes.
Volney found in the Indians the same savagery he found in

the Greeks and insisted that the cult for this quality was a
natural result of the barbarous violence of the French and
American revolutions. For Volney, nights in the American
wilderness were ruined by horse-flies and mosquitoes. (Amus-
ingly, there is not a single mosquito in *Atala*.) For Chateaubriand, the Indians' poor social and political organization
marked a decadence caused by European influence rather than
Volney's natural state of savagery; but for Chateaubriand
America with its vast space still seemed a place of "primitive freedom."

Kadish, Doris Y. "Symbolism of Exile: The Opening Description
in *Atala*." *FR* 54 (1980-81): 358-66.

Le Hir, Yves. "Des 'Martyrs' de Chateaubriand au 'Rivage des
Syrtes,' de J. Gracq." *IL* 34 (1982): 121-22.

McIvor, Gordon K. *Images du paradis perdu: Chateaubriand et
l'Amérique*. Montpellier: Université Paul Valéry, 1980. 516
feuillets dactylographiés.

   Rev. by Raymond Lebègue in *Société Chateaubriand: Bulletin*
23 (1980): 74-75.

Ormesson, Jean d'. *Mon Dernier Rêve sera pour vous. Une
Biographie sentimentale de Chateaubriand*. Paris: Lattès,
1982. Pp. 445. Fr. 65.00.

   Rev. by Patrick Lindsay Bowles in *TLS*, Nov. 5, 1982, p.
1222.

   The six chapters of the book concern Chateaubriand's
mistresses and friends: Charlotte Ives, Pauline de Beaumont,
Delphine de Custine, Natalie de Noailles, Cordélia de
Castellane, and Hortense Allart.

Redman, Harry, Jr. "Aux pieds du maître: Le jeune Gustave
Flaubert admirateur de Chateaubriand." *NCFS* 10 (1981-82):
291-300.

Riberette, Pierre, ed. *Correspondance générale*. Tome III:
1815-1820. Paris: Gallimard, 1982. Pp. 553.

   Rev. by George D. Painter in *TLS*, July 16, 1982, p. 762.

Société Chateaubriand: Bulletin 23 (1980).

   Includes, among others, the following articles and notes:
Joseph-Marc Bailbé, "Berlioz lecteur de Chateaubriand"
(9-13); Pierre Riberette, "Une lettre inédite de Chateau-

briand à Madame Récamier (1834)" (21-24 with two MS
photographs); Michèle Maréchal-Trudel, "Chateaubriand et
Venise: un amour de tête" (30-34); Brian Rogers, "Nodier
lecteur de Chateaubriand" (including as an appendix an
unpublished *dialogue burlesque* by Nodier between Atala
and Chactas during the great storm) (44-51); Harry Redman,
Jr., "Un cierge au fond du sac diplomatique--Chateaubriand
à Rome en 1829 (Billet inédit)" (60-62); Fernand Letessier,
"Pages retrouvées de Victor Hugo sur Chateaubriand" (76);
various reviews of recent books on Chateaubriand (listed
elsewhere in the present bibliography); bibliography of
letters, MSS, works, etc.

See also Curtis, Luciani, Viallaneix, Wilson ("French 1.
General"); Henry ("Chênedollé"); Soria ("Spanish 2. General").

Reviews of books previously listed:

COELHO, Alain, ed., *Pensées* ... *et premières poésies* (see
RMB for 1980, p. 181), rev. by l'abbé André Wartelle in
Société Chateaubriand: Bulletin 23 (1980): 71; DENUX,
Roger, *La Terrible Course de Chateaubriand* (see *RMB* for
1980, p. 181), rev. by Pierre Riberette in *Société Chateau-
briand: Bulletin* 23 (1980): 72-73; GILLET, Jean, *Les "Para-
dis perdus" dans la littérature française de Voltaire à
Chateaubriand* (see *ELN* 15, Supp., 86-87), rev. by Tanguy Logé
in *LR* 35 (1981): 161-63; LEBÈGUE, Raymond, *Aspects de
Chateaubriand* (see *RMB* for 1980, p. 182), rev. by Pierre
Clarac in *Société Chateaubriand: Bulletin* 23 (1980): 69-70;
by Francine Dugast-Portes in *AnBret* 88 (1981): 560-61; by
Pierre Riberette in *RHL* 81 (1981): 1013-14; RIBERETTE,
Pierre, ed., *Correspondance générale*, T. 2 (see *RMB* for
1980, pp. 182-83), rev. by Raymond Lebègue in *Société
Chateaubriand: Bulletin* 23 (1980): 71-72.

CHÉNEDOLLE

Henry, Jacques. "Chateaubriand et Chênedollé au château de
Fervaques." *Précis analytique des Travaux de l'Académie
des Sciences, Belles-Lettres et Arts de Rouen* (1977), pp.
63-79.

COESSIN

Riberette, Pierre. "Un réformateur du XIXe siècle et ses
disciples: François-Guillaume Coessin." Pp. 161-79 in *1848.*
Les Utopismes sociaux. Utopie et action à la veille des
journées de février. Préface de Maurice Agulhon. (Société
d'Histoire de la Révolution de 1848 et des Révolutions du
XIXe Siècle.) Paris: C.D.U.-SEDES, 1981. Pp. 290. Fr. 121.84.

COLET

Aruta Stanpacchia, Annalise. "Louise Colet a Napoli." *Francia*
17 (July-Dec. 1981): 43-61.

Bellet, Roger, ed. *Femmes de lettres au XIXe siècle: autour*
de Louise Colet. Presses universitaires de Lyon, 1982. Pp.
320. Fr. 65.00.

COMTE

Berrêdo Carneiro, Paulo E. de, and Paul Arbrousse-Bastide,
eds. *Correspondance générale et confessions.* T. V: *1849-1850.*
Paris: Archives positivistes/Vrin, 1982. Pp. 452. Fr. 210.00.

Kremer-Marietti, Angèle. *L'Anthropologie positiviste d'Auguste*
Comte. Geneva: Slatkine, 1981. Pp. 576. Fr. 80.00.

Kremer-Marietti, Angèle. *Le Projet anthropologique d'Auguste*
Comte. Paris: C.D.U. et SEDES, 1981. Pp. 112. Fr. 34.00.

    Rev. by Annie Petit in *Romantisme* 36 (1982): 96-97.

McLaverty, James. "Comtean Fetishism in *Silas Marner*." *NCF*
36 (1981-82): 318-36.

Regozini, Georg Maria. *Auguste Comtes "Religion der Menschheit"*
und ihre Ausprägung in Brasilien. Eine religiongeschichtliche
Untersuchung über Ursprung, Werden und Wesen der "positivis-
tischen Kirche" Brasiliens. Frankfurt-am-Main: Lang, 1977.
Pp. 240.

    Rev. by Antoine Lion in *ASSR* 53,ii (1982): 347.

Schmaus, Warren. "A Reappraisal of Comte's Three-State Law."
History and Theory 21 (1982): 248-66.

    An attempt to rehabilitate Comte by refuting attacks on
his "law," e.g., those of Karl Popper.

Standley, Arline Reilein. *Auguste Comte.* (Twayne World Authors
Series, 625.) Boston: Twayne Publishers (G.K. Hall), 1981.
Pp. 178. $14.95.

See also Kremer-Marietti ("French 1. General"); Battail
("Littré").

CONSTANT, A.-L.

Tilby, Michael. "Rabelais vu par Gobineau et l'abbé Constant."
SFr 25 (1981): 299-304.
Apropos of Gobineau's "Les Conseils de Rabelais" (1847)
and Constant's *Rabelais à la Basmette.* The latter cannot be
a reply to Gobineau (for chronological reasons) but, probably,
to Leroux's *Lettres sur le Fouriérisme.*

CONSTANT, B.

Aguet, Jean-Pierre. "Benjamin Constant, député de Strasbourg,
parlementaire sous la monarchie de juillet (juillet-décembre 1830)." Pp. 79-125 in *Autour des "Trois glorieuses"
1830. Strasbourg, Alsace et la liberté.* Actes du colloque
de Strasbourg, 16-18 mai 1980. (Publications de la Société
savante d'Alsace et des régions de l'Est. Recherches et
documents, 31.) Strasbourg: Istra, 1982.

Annales Benjamin Constant 2 (1982).

    Contents: Pierre Deguise, "Hommage à Pierre Cordey"
(1-2); Jean-Pierre Aguet, "Benjamin Constant parlementaire
sous la monarchie de Juillet (juillet-décembre 1830)" (3-
45); Louis Trenard, "Benjamin Constant et les libéraux
lyonnais" (47-71); Henri Grange, "De l'influence de Necker
sur les idées politiques de Benjamin Constant" (73-80);
Kurt Kloocke, "Benjamin Constant et Mina von Cramm: documents inédites" (81-109); Simone Balayé, "Une lettre inédite
de Benjamin Constant à Madame Talma" (111-12); Henri Zalis,
"*Adolphe*: le prolongement d'un état d'âme" (113-15); Waclaw
Szyszkowski, "La notion d'intimité chez Benjamin Constant"
(117-21); "Comptes rendus" (123-28); "Chronique" (129-30).
    The emphasis in this miscellany of studies, notes, and
reviews is clearly on the political and intellectual aspects
of Constant's life and work. Aguet studies in great detail
Constant's participation in the debates of the Assembly.
Trenard's study of Constant's relationship with such Lyonnais
liberals as Camille Jordan and de Gérando brings into

the network the more literary figures of Madame de Staël,
Madame de Krüdener, Ballanche, and, on the sentimental
level, Madame Récamier. Grange traces the influence of
Necker's ideas about the separation of executive and legis-
lative powers on Constant's *Fragments d'un ouvrage abandonné
sur la possibilité d'une Constitution républicaine dans un
grand pays*. Kloocke's score of unpublished documents, duly
annotated, concerning Constant and his first wife shed light
on the autobiographical sources of *Cécile* and even on his
narrative techniques. Constant's letter to Madame Talma
(Apr. 14, 1804) is the only one known on his side of this
correspondence. Szyszkowski links Constant's ideas on individual liberty to modern theories of the right to privacy.
Kloocke reviews Simone Balayé's *Madame de Staël: Lumières
et liberté* and takes the occasion to publish a letter
addressed to Madame de Staël by a certain Audibert (July 10,
1789). The "Chronique" which closes this issue of the *Annales*
deals with the plans for the publication of the complete
works of Constant. (The first volume of these *Annales*, the
individual articles in which are discussed below by author,
appeared in 1980 as part of the *Cahiers Vilfredo Pareto/
Revue Européenne des Sciences Sociales*.)

Benton, Robert J. "Political Expedience and Lying: Kant vs
Benjamin Constant." *JHI* 43 (1982): 135-44.

In the essay "Ueber ein vermeintes Recht, an Menschen-
liebe zu lügen," Kant's criticism of Constant (in response
to the latter's "Des réactions politiques") is that "Constant
makes political expediency more fundamental in principle
than *Recht*, and in doing so undermines the foundations of
politics itself."

Bowman, Frank P. "Nouvelles lectures d'*Adolphe*." *Cahiers
Vilfredo Pareto/Revue Européenne des Sciences Sociales*
50 (May 1980): 27-42.

Penetrating survey of criticism of *Adolphe*, covering the
years 1968-1978, with suggestions for further research.
(E.F.G.)

Callot, Emile-François. "La conception du chef de l'Etat
chez Benjamin Constant et ses rapports au régime politique."
Annales de la Faculté de Droit de l'Université Jean Moulin
(1982): 31-67.

Cordey, Pierre. "Benjamin Constant et la guerre." *Revue
Militaire Suisse* 126 (1981): 58-68.

A summary of Constant's attitudes on the subject.

Cordey, Pierre. "Benjamin Constant, Gaetano Filangieri et la *Science de la législation.*" *Cahiers Vilfredo Pareto/Revue Européenne des Sciences Sociales* 50 (May 1980): 55-79.

On the origins and composition of Constant's *Commentaire sur l'ouvrage de Filangieri.*

Cordey, Pierre. "Les *Cahiers Benjamin Constant.* Tables 1955-1967." *Cahiers Vilfredo Pareto/Revue Européenne des Sciences Sociales* 50 (May 1980): 209-15.

Cours de politique constitutionnelle. 2 vols. Geneva: Slatkine Reprints, 1982. Sw.Fr. 250.00.

Reprint of the edition of Paris, 1872.

Courtney, C.P. *A Bibliography of Editions of the Writings of Benjamin Constant to 1833.* London: Publications of the Modern Humanities Research Association, 1982. Pp. xxxiv+270. £33.50.

Deguise, Pierre. "Nouvel état présent des études sur Benjamin Constant." *Cahiers Vilfredo Pareto/Revue Européenne des Sciences Sociales* 50 (May 1980): 9-25.

Covers the period 1967 to 1980.

Delbouille, Paul. "Une edition d'*Adolphe* à Vienne en 1817." *CahiersS* 29-30 (1981): 155-57.

Dodge, Guy H. *Benjamin Constant's Philosophy of Liberalism, a Study in Politics and Religion.* University of North Carolina Press, 1980. Pp. xii+194. $16.50.

Rev. by E. Harpaz in *RHL* 82 (1982): 127-31.
A good examination of Constant's views on despotism, popular sovereignty, constitutionalism, religion, and political economy, with an attempt to place Constant in a modern perspective. (E.F.G.)

Ehrard, Jean. "De Meilcours à Adolphe, ou la suite des Egarements." *SVEC* 190 (1980): 101-17.

Fornerod, Françoise. "Guy de Pourtalès et la première Société des Amis de Benjamin Constant." *Cahiers Vilfredo Pareto/ Revue Européenne des Sciences Sociales* 50 (May 1980): 201-07.

Gonin, Eve. *Le Point de vue d'Ellénore. Une Réécriture d' "Adolphe."* Paris: José Corti, 1981. Pp. xiii+197. Fr. 75.00.

Rev. by Simone Balayé in *Romantisme* 38 (1982): 160-61; by
N. King in *FS* 36 (1982): 477-78.

The central portion of this book, which departs from common
practice by concentrating on Ellénore rather than Adolphe,
consists of Ellénore's imagined confessions to the priest
who visits her just before her death. The reader may well
question the justification for rewriting an acknowledged
masterpiece, but the author, in the last section of her
book, makes some useful comments about Constant's manner of
depicting Ellénore and about the latter's moral and social
situation. (E.F.G.)

Guerci, Luciano. *Libertà degli antichi e libertà dei moderni:
Sparta, Atene e i "philosophes" nella Francia del Settecento.*
(Esperienze, 51.) Naples: Guida, 1979. Pp. 283. L. 8500.00.

Harpaz, Ephraïm. "Benjamin Constant polémiste; étude de quelques articles." *Cahiers Vilfredo Pareto/Revue Européenne
des Sciences Sociales* 50 (May 1980): 43-53.

Constant's use of irony in his polemical articles.

Harpaz, Ephraïm, ed. *L'Esprit de conquête; La Liberté des
anciens et des modernes.* (Les Classiques de la Politique.)
Paris: Garnier Frères, 1981.

Harpaz, Ephraïm. "Une lettre inconnue de Benjamin Constant
à Napoléon (janvier 1815)." *Revue de la Bibliothèque Nationale*
3 (Mar. 1982): 27-34.

Hoffmann, Paul. "Benjamin Constant critique de Jean-Jacques
Rousseau." *RHL* 82 (1982): 23-40.

Concerns Constant's attempt to expose the contradictions
between Rousseau's theory of freedom and the totalitarian
practices which flow from the same presuppositions.

Hofmann, Etienne. "Lettres de Benjamin Constant à Louis-
Ferdinand et à Thérèse Huber (1798-1806)." *CahiersS* 29-30
(1981): 77-122.

Hofmann, Etienne. "Les relations de Benjamin Constant avec les
milieux économiques de l'Alsace, lors de son mandat de
député de Strasbourg, 1827-1830." Pp. 139-49 in *Autour des
"Trois glorieuses" 1830. Strasbourg, Alsace et la liberté.*
Actes du colloque de Strasbourg, 16-18 mai 1980. (Publications de la Société savante d'Alsace et des régions de
l'Est. Recherches et documents, 3.) Strasbourg: Istra,
1982.

Holmes, Stephen. "Liberal Uses of Bourbon Legitimism." *JHI*
43 (1982): 229-48.

Kelly, George Armstrong. "Constant Commotion: Avatars of a
Pure Liberal." *JMH* 54 (1982): 497-518.

"If the history of 'modern liberty' ... began in some
sense with Hobbes's radical modifications of the justification of the classical *civitas*, it was not only incrementally,
but decisively, changed by Constant, who expands and endorses
many of Hobbes's values and insists with him, on the *necessity* of the political, to protect men from each other, but
who rejects utilitarian arguments as they pertain to man's
free navigation in the large sphere exempt from politics."
Kelly here attempts to discover just why he believes Constant to be a special water-shed figure, in the course of
a re-examination of much recent work on Constant, and we
profit from the attempt. (T.L.A.)

King, Norman, and Jean-Daniel Candaux. "La correspondance
de Benjamin Constant et de Sismondi (1801-1830)." *Cahiers
Vilfredo Pareto/Revue Européenne des Sciences Sociales* 50
(May 1980): 81-172.

Thirty-five letters of Constant to Sismondi, eight letters
from Sismondi to Benjamin Constant, Rosalie de Constant,
Charles Pougens, and Claude Hochet.

Kloocke, Kurt. "Documents inédits ou peu connus de et sur
Benjamin Constant." *SFr* 25 (1981): 459-71.

Texts of letters to Ludwig Robert, Karl August Böttiger,
notes to Goethe, Sophie von Schardt, and Charlotte von
Schiller, and some correspondence concerning Constant's
nomination to the Academy of Sciences at Göttingen.

Kloocke, Kurt. "Une étude littéraire inachevée de Benjamin
Constant: les 'Fragments d'un essai sur la littérature dans
ses rapports avec la liberté.'" *Cahiers Vilfredo Pareto/
Revue Européenne des Sciences Sociales* 50 (May 1980): 173-
200.

Publication of Constant's manuscript, preserved in the
Bibliothèque Nationale, with commentary.

Kloocke, Kurt. "Nihilistische Tendenzen in der französischen
Literatur des 18. Jahrhunderts bis zu Benjamin Constant.
Beobachtungen zum Problem des 'Ennui.'" *DVLG* 56 (1982):
576-600.

Good discussion of expressions of ennui in eighteenth-century France. The young Constant is specifically mentioned on pages 583-88. (E.F.G.)

Leuilliot, Paul. "Benjamin Constant député de Strasbourg et Alsace." Pp. 39-78 in *Autour des "Trois glorieuses" 1830. Strasbourg, Alsace et la liberté.* Actes du colloque de Strasbourg, 16-18 mai 1980. (Publications de la Société savante d'Alsace et des régions de l'Est. Recherches et documents, 31.) Strasbourg: Istra, 1982.

Peterson, Carla. "Constant's Adolphe, James's 'The Beast in the Jungle,' and the Quest for the Mother." *ELWIU* 9 (1982): 224-39.

The point of comparison between the two tales is Abrams' summary of the prodigal son myth and the failure of language to provide redemption or self-revelation.

Starobinski, Jean. "Benjamin Constant et l'éloquence." *Cadmos* 3 (Winter 1980): 26-42.

Constant felt that individual liberty could only be guaranteed by a representative government. For the latter to exist, the free circulation of ideas was essential.

Violi, Carlo. "Constant e la 'nouvelle philosophie' tedesca. Una polemica con Kant." *Quaderni dell'Istituto Galvano della Volpe* 3 (1981): 1-64.

Winkler, Markus. "La distinction entre les anciens et les modernes chez Constant, Schiller et Frédéric Schlegel." *Etudes de Lettres* (Oct.-Dec. 1982): 59-84.

See also Corredor, Hofmann ("Staël").

Reviews of books previously listed:

CHICOTEAU, Christine, *Chère Rose, A Biography of Rosalie de Constant* (see *RMB* for 1981, p. 188), rev. by R.B. Leal in *AUMLA* 56 (1981): 259-60; FAIRLIE, Alison, *Imagination and Language* (see *RMB* for 1981, p. 189), rev. by J. Cruickshank in *FS* 36 (1982): 225-26; HARPAZ, Ephraïm, ed., *Recueil d'articles (1795-1817)* (see *ELN* 17, Supp., 131), rev. by H. Gouhier in *Revue des Travaux de l'Académie des Sciences Morales et Politiques* 132 (1979): 443; HARPAZ, Ephraïm, ed., *Recueil d'articles (1820-1824)* (see *RMB* for 1981, p. 189), rev. by M.A. Wégimont in *NCFS* 10 (1981-82): 361-62; HOFMANN,

Etienne, ed., *Bibliographie analytique* (see *RMB* for 1981,
p. 189), rev. by P. Deguise in *FR* 55 (1981-82): 682-83;
by E. Harpaz in *RHL* 82 (1982): 132-33; by N. King in *MLR*
77 (1982): 212; HOFMANN, Etienne, ed., *Les Principes de
politique* (see *RMB* for 1981, p. 189), rev. by P. Deguise
in *RHL* 82 (1982): 918-21; by A. Schnegg in *Musée neuchâtelois*
18 (1981): 195-96; by M. Winkler in *RF* 94 (1982): 122-30;
LOWE, David K., *Constant. An Annotated Bibliography of
Critical Editions and Studies* (see *RMB* for 1980, p. 187),
rev. by C. Cordié in *SFr* 24 (1980): 361-62; by K. Kloocke
in *RJ* 31 (1980): 237-38.

Composite review:

Kelly, George Armstrong. "Constant Commotion: Avatars of a
Pure Liberal." *JMH* 54 (1982): 497-518.

Review of books by Gauchet (see *RMB* for 1981, p. 188),
Guerci (see above), Harpaz (see *RMB* for 1981, p. 189), and
Hofmann (see *RMB* for 1981, p. 189).

CORBIERE

Roudaut, Jean. "Les deux Corbières." Pp. 295-320 in Jean
Roudaut, *Ce qui nous revient. Autobiographie.* (Le Chemin.)
Paris: Gallimard, 1980. Pp. 462. Fr. 95.00.

COURIER

Longus. *Daphnis et Chloé ou les Pastorales.* (Les Introuvables.)
Plan-de-la-Tour: Editions d'Aujourd'hui, 1982. Pp. 174.
Fr. 52.00.

Reproduces the edition of Paris (Alphonse Lemerre), 1878;
the text is Courier's revision of Amyot's translation (the
notorious ink-spill occurred in connection with Courier's
work on this edition).

CUSTINE

See Gimenez ("Spanish 2. General").

Comte, Gilbert. "A propos de.... Eugène Delacroix ou l'inconnu
paradoxal." *Revue de la Bibliothèque Nationale* 1,ii (Dec.
1981): 96-98.

Based on a recent edition of Delacroix's *Journal* (see
Joubin, *infra*). The author stresses the painter's intellectual honesty.

Enckell, Pierre. "L'écrivain." *NL*, Nov. 26, 1981, p. 43.

Johnson, Lee. "Delacroix's Road to the Sultan of Morocco."
Apollo, Mar. 1982, pp. 186-89.

Traces the genesis of *The Sultan of Morocco and His Entourage* through a close study of the painter's North African
sketchbooks and by comparison with photographs of the site
today.

Joubin, André, and Régis Labourdette, eds. *Journal, 1822-1863*.
Préface de Hubert Damisch. (Les Mémorables.) Paris: Plon,
1981. Pp. xxxvi+942. Fr. 102.80.

Rev. by André Bourin in *RDM*, Nov. 1981, pp. 421-25.

Kliman, Eve Twose. "Delacroix's Lions and Tigers: A Link
between Man and Nature." *ArtB* 64 (1982): 446-66.

A conversation with Taine (1863) and passages from the
Journal are used to provide "the framework of thought behind
Delacroix's preoccupation with the lion and tiger.... Delacroix saw the lion and tiger not only as embodiments of
nature, but as simpler reflections of the good and evil in
man."

Lobet, Marcel. "Ecriture et peinture dans le *Journal* d'Eugène
Delacroix." *Bulletin de l'Académie Royale de Langue et de
Littérature Françaises* 59 (1981): 224-37.

Disjointed generalities on the interrelationship of Delacroix's literary work and his painting, focused, of course,
on the *Journal*. "Ecriture et peinture ont, chez Delacroix,
la même vibration, la même fébrilité, le même frémissement
du créateur qui veut donner forme et vie à la conscience
et à l'inconscient, à ces correspondances où les idées et
les couleurs se répondent sur les plages illimitées de
l'indicible." (J.S.P.)

Sérullaz, Maurice. *Delacroix.* Paris: Fernand Nathan, 1981.
    Pp. 208. Fr. 139.20.

See also Hemmings, Rosenthal, Whitely ("French 1. General");
    Johnson ("Dumas"); *Présence de George Sand* 15 ("Sand").

Reviews of books previously listed:

JOHNSON, Lee, *The Paintings of Eugène Delacroix* (see *RMB*
    for 1981, p. 193), rev. by Norman Bryson in *FS* 36 (1982):
    211-12; by Paul Joannides in *Art History* 5 (1982): 348-52;
    WELLINGTON, Hubert, ed., *The Journal of Eugène Delacroix*
    (see *RMB* for 1980, p. 189), rev. by Marina Warner in
    Encounter, Apr. 1981, pp. 69-71.

DELAVIGNE

Athanassoglou, Nina. "Un tableau d'inspiration philhellénique
    à Saint-Omer: *La mort du jeune diacre* de Vincent-Nicolas
    Raverat." *Revue du Louvre* 31 (1982): 21-26.

    This painting (1824) takes its subject from a poem in
    Les Messéniennes.

Ramos Ortega, Francisco. "La fortuna del Cid en el romanticismo
    francés." *Revista de Literatura* 43 (Jan.-June 1981): 37-58.

    Delavigne's *La Fille du Cid* (1829) is among the works
    discussed.

DELECLUZE

Gaxotte, Pierre. "Etienne-le-satisfait." *Le Spectacle du Monde*
    223 (Oct. 1980): 97-100.

DENIS

Baldran, Jacqueline. "Ferdinand Denis et le Brésil." *Re-
    cherches et Etudes Comparatistes Ibéro-Françaises de la
    Sorbonne Nouvelle* 1 (1979): 29-41.

DESCHAMPS

Pelletier, Monique. "Un témoin de la jeunesse des Romantiques, Mme A.D., muse et poète." *BduB* 1982-II, pp. 157-65. On Anna Daclin (née Gaudriot), who seems to have been the "mystérieux amour" in Emile Deschamps's life. A few glimpses into the Romanticism of the Restoration years.

DIDIER

See Luciani ("French 1. General").

DUMAS

Acté. (La Bibliothèque oubliée.) Paris: France-Empire, 1980. Pp. 272. Fr. 32.00.

Callais, François. "Un rendez-vous de la gastronomie et de la littérature au milieu du XIXe siècle. Alexandre Dumas et Vuillemot à l'hôtel de la Cloche." *Bulletin de la Société Historique de Compiègne* 27 (1980): 183-95.

Le Collier de la reine. 2 vols. (1000 Soleils Or.) Paris: Gallimard, 1980. Fr. 23.70 each vol.

Davidson, Alan, ed. *Dumas on Food. Selections from "Le Grand Dictionnaire de Cuisine."* London: The Folio Society, 1978; University Press of Virginia, 1982. Pp. 327. $17.50.

D'Hulst, Lieven. "Le voyage allemand de Nerval et Dumas en 1838." *Etudes Nervaliennes et Romantiques* 3 (1981): 53-57.

Isabel de Bavière. 2 vols. (Les Grands Romans historiques.) Geneva: Faurot, 1979. Fr. 31.80 each vol.

Johnson, Lee. "Delacroix, Dumas and 'Hamlet.'" *BM* 124 (1982): 717-21.

Krakovitch, Odile. "Manuscrits des pièces d'Alexandre Dumas et procès verbaux de censure de ces pièces conservés aux archives nationales." *RHL* 82 (1982): 638-46.

Mankowitz, Wolf. *Mazeppa. The Lives, Loves and Legends of Adah Isaacs Menken. A Biographical Quest.* London: Blond and Briggs, 1982. Pp. 270. £10.95.

Rev. by John Stokes in *TLS*, Aug. 20, 1982, p. 901.
In this well-documented, illustrated account of the
colorful career of the American performer (or "centauresse"
as Maurois calls her) Adah Menken, brief mention is made
of her friendship with the aging Dumas, along with passing
mention of Sand and Gautier. (E.F.G.)

Munro, Douglas. *Alexandre Dumas Père. A Bibliography of Works
Published in French 1825-1900.* (Garland Reference Library
of the Humanities, 257.) New York: Garland, 1981. Pp. xiii+
391.

Schopp, Claude. "Les excursions de Dumas sur les bords du
Rhin (1838). Restitution chronologique." *Etudes Nervaliennes
et Romantiques* 3 (1981): 59-71.

Schopp, Claude. "La jeunesse d'Alexandre Dumas, 1817-1821.
Adèle et Aglaé, ou la recherche du temps perdu." *Bulletin
de la Société des Amis d'Alexandre Dumas* 10 (1982): 21-25.

Schopp, Claude, ed. *Lettres d'Alexandre Dumas à Mélanie Waldor.*
(Centre de Recherches, d'Etudes et d'Editions de Correspon-
dances du XIXe Siècle.) Paris: Presses universitaires de
France, 1982. Pp. 208. Fr. 160.00.

Les Trois Mousquetaires. 2 vols. (Le Temps d'un Livre, 30-31.)
Paris: Magnard, 1982. Fr. 21.15 each vol.

See also Gasnault, Lacassin, Miquel ("French 1. General");
Menarini ("Hugo, V."); *Etudes Nervaliennes et Romantiques* 3
("Nerval"); Gimenez ("Spanish 2. General").

Reviews of books previously listed:

ADLER, Alfred, *Dumas und die böse Mutter* (see *RMB* for 1980,
p. 189), rev. by C. Cordié in *SFr* 25 (1981): 176-77;
NEUSCHÄFER, H.-J., *Populärromane im 19. Jahrhundert von
Dumas bis Zola* (see *ELN* 17, Supp., 134), rev. by P.J. Whyte
in *FS* 36 (1982): 89-91.

FABRE D'OLIVET

Tappa, Gilbert, ed. *Miscellanea Fabre d'Olivet.* I-IV. (Collection Bélisane.) Nice: Galerie Noir et Blanc, 1978. Pp. 66.
Fr. 70.00.

Rev. by Jean Senelier in *SFr* 24 (1980): 525.
Reprints the following works: *Oratorio à l'occasion de
la fête du sacre de S.M. l'Empereur, Prédictions politiques,
Idamore ou le Prince africain,* and *Vers à mes amis pour le
jour de ma fête.*

See also Lafont ("French 1. General").

FAURIEL

See Denis ("Staël"); Fauriel ("Italian 2. Manzoni").

FERRIERE

Tilby, Michael. "Autour de Samuel Cramer: quelques remarques
sur Baudelaire et Théophile de Ferrière." *LR* 36 (1982):
59-73.

Finds a greater and more interesting relationship than
Pommier had admitted between *La Fanfarlo* and Ferrière's
Il Vivere: contes de Samuel Bach (1835). The core of the
affinity is "leur commun désir de sonder les paradoxes
d'une conception de l'artiste importante et nouvelle."

FEVAL

*Contes de Bretagne: Le Joli Château.-Anne des îles.-La Femme
blanche des marais.* (Bibliothèque celtique.) Paris: Jean
Picollec, 1980. Pp. 284. Fr. 58.55.

FLAUBERT

"Bibliomanie" et autres textes, 1836-1839. (Traversée du XIXe
Siècle.) Paris: J.-C. Godefroy, 1982. Pp. 260. Fr. 56.00.

L'Education sentimentale: première version; Passion et Vertu.
(GF, 339.) Paris: Garnier-Flammarion, 1980. Pp. 376. Fr.
13.05.

Unwin, T.A., ed. *Trois Contes de jeunesse.* (Textes littéraires,
41.) University of Exeter, 1981. Pp. xxi+76. £2.00.

Reviews of book previously listed:

BEM, Jeanne, *Désir et savoir dans l'oeuvre de Flaubert* (see
RMB for 1981, p. 197), rev. by A. Fairlie in *FS* 36 (1982):
214; by E. Gray in *FR* 55 (1981-82): 554-55; by A. Israël-
Pelletier in *NCFS* 10 (1981-82): 150-51.

FORNERET

OEuvres. Précédées d'un texte d'André Breton. Geneva: Slatkine
Reprints, 1980. Pp. 286. Fr. 50.00.

FORTOUL

Lacoste, Claudine. "La mise en scène romanesque des idées
politiques de Rousseau." Pp. 118-27 in *Rousseau et Voltaire
en 1978. Actes du colloque international de Nice (juin 1978).*
(Etudes rousseauistes et Index des OEuvres de J.-J. Rousseau,
Série C: Etudes diverses, 1.) Geneva: Slatkine, 1981. Pp.
384.

FOURIER

Guarneri, Carl J. "Importing Fourierism to America." *JHI* 43
(1982): 581-94.

On the simplification and modification of Fourier's ideas
as they were adapted to an American context by Brisbane,
Ripley, and Godwin. His "uncompromising secularism and anti-
nationalism" had to be moderated.

Sombart, Nicolas. "De Madame de Staël à Charles Fourier."
CahiersS 29-30 (1981): 31-61.

The crucial facts brought out here are that Fourier sent
her a copy of *Théorie des quatre mouvements* (1808), that
she was the only *individual* so favored, and that she replied
in a letter, published in 1905 but unknown to Staëliens.
It seems that Fourier saw in Madame de Staël "L'anti-Napoléon"
and a symbol of female liberation. But there is no proof
that she read his book; in any case, she failed to live up
to his expectations.

Spencer, Michael C. *Charles Fourier.* (Twayne World Author
Series, 578.) Boston: Twayne Publishers (G.K. Hall), 1981.
Pp. 184. $14.50.

Rev. by Ceri Crossley in *FS* 36 (1982): 478.

As Fourier's life is so little known, Spencer condenses the essential facts into five pages and moves on to a densely packed discussion of Fourier's ideas, which are organized thematically. Spencer manages to take Fourier seriously and to treat his doctrines objectively and completely. In addition to the expected scholarly apparatus, there is a useful brief glossary of terms, the words to which Fourier gave his own peculiar meaning. Spencer's book is now the best available introduction in English to Fourier's thought. (J.S.P.)

Tundo, Laura. "Péguy e Fourier, ricerca di analogia." *Quaderno Filosofico* (Lecce) 4 (1980): 73-88.

See also Gregory, Viallaneix ("French 1. General"); Tilby ("Constant, A.-L."); Goldstun ("Saint-Simon").

Reviews of books previously listed:

MONETI, Maria, *La Meccanica delle passioni* (see *RMB* for 1980, p. 191), rev. by Carlo Cordié in *SFr* 25 (1981): 371; NATHAN, Michel, *Le Ciel des Fouriéristes* (see *RMB* for 1981, pp. 198-99), rev. by Jean-Claude Fizaine in *Romantisme* 36 (1982): 103-05.

FRAYSSINOUS

Mortier, Roland. "Une théologie politique sous la Restauration." Pp. 93-107 in Guy Cambier, ed., *Christianisme d'hier et d'aujourd'hui: hommages à Jean Préaux*. Brussels: Editions de l'Université, 1979. Bel.Fr. 565.00.

GAUTIER

Bolster, Richard, ed. *La Vie de Balzac racontée par Théophile Gautier*. Paris: La Pensée universelle, 1981. Pp. 128. Fr. 32.00.

Already listed without commentary (under "Balzac") in *RMB* for 1981, p. 178. Bolster presents the text of Gautier's long article on Balzac published in the Spring of 1858. The edition is of limited value compared to Claude-Marie Senninger's *Honoré de Balzac par Théophile Gautier* (see *RMB* for 1980, p. 195), which presents not one but all of Gautier's

critical articles on Balzac, together with a fully documented
study of the Gautier-Balzac association and with abundant
notation. (A.B.S.)

Brown, Marilyn. "Ingres, Gautier, and the Ideology of the
Cameo Style of the Second Empire." *Arts Magazine* 56 (Dec.
1981): 94-99.

Contemporary reactions to Ingres's painting, *Apotheosis
of Napoleon I* (1855), reflect their authors' political
attitudes. Gautier's statements on the work, as well as his
practice of the "poetic cameo," lead Brown to judge him a
conservative in both art and ideology. Gautier is represented
as showing bad faith, professing indifference to politics
while implicitly supporting the imperial regime of Napoleon
III.

Bulletin de la Société Théophile Gautier 4 (1982).

Material and administrative affairs of the Société.

Burnett, David Graham. "The Architecture of Meaning: Gautier
and Romantic Architectural Visions." *French Forum* 7 (1982):
109-16.

Deals with poems from *La Comédie de la mort* in which
architectural imagery predominates. Gautier here is primarily
concerned with the function of poetry. Though he may express
hopelessness regarding the possibility of any meaning in the
poem ("Portail") or go to the other extreme, viewing the
poem as the bearer of universal truth ("Notre-Dame"), he
more often recognizes that there is no essential meaning,
that there are only momentary truths, fleeting and quickly
lost.
The general question of Gautier's ideas on meaning remains
unanswered. Professor Burnett would make a valuable contribution by pursuing a response throughout Gautier's production. (A.B.S.)

Le Capitaine Fracasse. Paris: France Loisirs, 1982. Pp. 493.
Fr. 42.00.

Cirillo, Valeria De Gregorio. "Il doppio in *Mademoiselle de
Maupin*." *Annali Istituto Universitario Orientale, Napoli,
Sezione Romanza* 22 (1980): 359-95.

A not very clear study of parallelisms and oppositions
in both the form and the content of the novel. The conclusion (for which recognition of doubling was scarcely neces-

sary): in *Mademoiselle de Maupin* Gautier evokes his own experience in search of full satisfaction. Reality cannot offer a sense of abundant pleasure, because it is transitory. Even art is a meager compensation, doomed as it is to deal only with appearances. (A.B.S.)

Dulmet, Florica. "A propos d'une réédition: *Mademoiselle de Maupin.*" *Ecrits de Paris* 406 (Oct. 1980): 89-99.

The re-edition, presumably Robichez's (see *RMB* for 1980, pp. 194-95), is not mentioned. Dulmet prefers to give an impressionistic review of Gautier's life. Nothing new or stirring. (A.B.S.)

Hering, Doris. *Giselle and Albrecht: American Ballet Theatre's Romantic Lovers.* With performance photographs by Fred Fehl. Brooklyn: Dance Horizons, 1981. Pp. 191. $30.00.

Rev. by George Dorris in *Dance Chronicle* 5 (1982): 113-16.

Killick, Rachel. "Gautier and the Sonnet." *Essays in French Literature* 16 (1979): 1-16.

The (surprisingly slight) place of the sonnet in Gautier's poetry; his (essentially conservative) ideas on the form; his (relatively unsuccessful) practice as a sonneteer; and his contribution to the evolution of the sonnet in France: he led the next generation to confuse technical correctness and perfection, so to see the composition of a "correct" sonnet as the height of artistic achievement.

Lacoste, Claudine, ed. *Exposition Théophile Gautier et les artistes de son temps.* Montpellier: Imprimerie de recherche, Université Paul Valéry, 1982. Pp. 35.

Catalog of paintings exhibited at the Musée Fabre in Montpellier at the time of a Gautier colloquium, Sept. 15-18, 1982. Lacoste accompanies the entry for each painting with Gautier's comment on the work.

Lévy-Delpla, Laurence. *Le Roman de la momie de Théophile Gautier.* (Textes pour Aujourd'hui.) Paris: Larousse, 1980. Pp. 159.

Running commentary on the story. A *fiche pédagogique* contains a *lexique* of Egyptian terms, indications on Gautier's and contemporaries' interest in ancient Egypt, an introduction to Egyptian civilization, notes on Gautier's life and works, an analysis of the characters and the structure of the novel, and a discussion of the relationship between *Le Roman de la momie* and the historical novel.

Lyons, Margaret. "Judith Gautier and the Soeurs de Notre-
Dame de Miséricorde: A Comment on *Spirite*." Pp. 56-65 in
C.A. Burns, ed., *Literature and Society: Studies in Nine-
teenth- and Twentieth-Century French Literature Presented
to R.J. North*. University of Birmingham, John Goodman and
Sons, 1980. Pp. vii+247. £14.00.

Demonstrates that, while Carlotta Grisi may have inspired
the conception of *Spirite*, Gautier's daughter too made a
major contribution to the story, specifically to those episodes having to do with Lavinia's entry into convent life.

Mademoiselle de Maupin. Préface de Françoise d'Eaubonne.
Geneva: Famot, 1980. Pp. xx+335.

Partie carrée. (Coll. Demain et son Double.) Paris: J.-M.
Laffont, 1982. Pp. 328. Fr. 89.00.

Picot, Jean-Pierre. "Lewis, Hoffmann, Gogol, Gautier: du
statut de l'identité au cérémonial de la mort dans le
récit fantastique." *Littératures* 5 (Spring 1982): 19-35.

The discussion, insofar as Gautier is concerned, deals
with *Le Chevalier double* and *Avatar*. For Picot, the fantastic
tale is a form particularly apt for representing psychological phenomena. The demonstration reaches the (all too
obvious) conclusion that the *récit fantastique*--any literary
work, for that matter--is "un mensonge qui dit la vérité"
(p. 34). (A.B.S.)

Pieyre de Mandiargues, André, ed. *Spirite. Nouvelle fantastique*.
(Traversée du XIXe Siècle.) Paris: J.-C. Godefroy, 1982.
Pp. 196. Fr. 52.00.

Robichez, Jacques. "Théophile Gautier conteur." *FSSA* 10 (1981):
51-56.

Text of a paper presented in Pretoria at a colloquium
on the evolution of narrative works since the time of Romanticism. Robichez is concerned with the balance in novels
between the events of the story and the various (often
subtle) intrusions by the author. Gautier was a frequent
intruder, but his intrusions diminished between *Mademoiselle
de Maupin* and *Le Capitaine Fracasse*, an indication that he
was following a general trend.

Le Roman de la momie. (1000 Soleils d'Or.) Paris: Gallimard,
1979. Pp. 288. Fr. 23.70.

Roos, Jacques. "Un idéaliste méconnu: Théophile Gautier."
    Pp. 27-32 in Jacques Roos, Etudes de littérature générale
    et comparée. Paris: Editions Ophrys, [1979]. Pp. 141.
    Gautier's idealism, which Roos seeks to rehabilitate,
exploits beauty as a means to achieve spiritual satisfaction.

Savalle, Joseph. Travestis, métamorphoses, dédoublements:
    essai sur l'oeuvre romanesque de Théophile Gautier. (La
    Thèsothèque, 11.) Paris: Minard, 1981. Pp. 259. Fr. 126.00.
    The architecture secrète of Gautier's fictional works.
Consideration of the three motifs listed in the title leads
Savalle to take Gautier's stories and novels as a series of
attempts by the protagonists to achieve a sense of unity
through love. Only Spirite represents success in the quest:
Gautier recognizes that happiness derives from a spiritual
orientation, not from the materialism of earlier works.
Savalle sees in the stories a pervasive autobiographical
element. Gautier was describing attempts to escape remorse
and despair dating back to early amorous disappointments.
    Though his biographical hypotheses are debatable, Savalle's
conclusions regarding Gautier's interest--the question of
happiness--are well-founded and his thematic approach proves
its usefulness. (A.B.S.)

Snell, Robert. Théophile Gautier: A Romantic Critic of the
    Visual Arts. Oxford: Clarendon Press, 1982. Pp. 273.
    Rev. briefly in GBA 124 (Oct. 1982), Supp., pp. 23-24;
by Norman Bryson in TLS, July 2, 1982, p. 722.
    Details Gautier's view of criticism, his concept of what
makes an artist, and the nature of his critical practice.
Snell's main points: (1) Gautier appreciated that art which
could transport him out of the present and into "alternative
worlds"; at the same time he was attracted to an idealizing
art that aimed for the timelessly typical (thus his high
regard for both Delacroix and Ingres); (2) the great artist,
for Gautier, would be a unique individual creating new
realities from the ordinary stuff of the world; (3) Gautier
was essentially a conservative, finding most appealing in
modern art the grandeur, the sweep, and the nobility of
the classical and Renaissance traditions; (4) Gautier's
professed role as journalistic critic was to be a sympathetic
yet discriminating guide through the museum of contemporary
art; (5) if Gautier seemed indifferent in his later criticism, it was not that he had abandoned his ideals but rather
that recent works of art did not afford him that transport
he always sought.

Snell covers the same ground as does Michael C. Spencer
in *The Art Criticism of Théophile Gautier* (Geneva: Droz,
1969), but with more sympathy. Since he is in general
disagreement with Spencer as to the value of Gautier's criticism, Snell would have done well to challenge openly Spencer's often severe judgments. (A.B.S.)

Voyage en Espagne. Nouvelle ed. 70 photos en noir d'Olivier
Garros. Paris: La Palatine, 1982. Pp. 240. Fr. 145.00.

See also Lacassin, Luciani ("French 1. General"); Gimenez
("Spanish 2. General").

Reviews of books previously listed:

BERCHET, Jean-Claude, ed., *Voyage en Espagne* (see *RMB* for
1981, p. 199), rev. by Anne-Marie Christin in *RHL* 82 (1982):
930-31; by Arlette Michel in *IL* 34 (1982): 31 and in *Romantisme* 36 (1982): 108-09; BERTHIER, Patrick, ed., *Voyage en
Espagne* (see *RMB* for 1981, p. 199), rev. by Anne-Marie
Christin in *RHL* 82 (1982): 930-31; by Carlo Cordié in *SFr*
26 (1982): 165; by Arlette Michel in *IL* 34 (1982): 168 and
in *Romantisme* 36 (1982): 108-09; GAUDON, Jean, ed., *La
Morte amoureuse* (see *RMB* for 1981, p. 200), rev. by Carlo
Cordié in *SFr* 26 (1982): 165-66; GOTHOT-MERSCH, Claudine,
ed., *Emaux et camées* (see *RMB* for 1981, p. 201), brief
rev. in *BCLF* 438 (1982): 840; SENNINGER, Claude-Marie, ed.,
Honoré de Balzac (see *RMB* for 1980, p. 195), rev. by Annette
Rosa in *Romantisme* 36 (1982): 115-17; by Gilbert Sigaux in
QL 371 (May 16-31, 1982): 21-22; VOISIN, Marcel, *Le Soleil
et la nuit* (see *RMB* for 1981, pp. 202-03), rev. in *SFr* 26
(1982): 364.

GÉRICAULT

See Rosenthal ("French 1. General").

GIRODET

MacGregor, Neal. "Girodet's Poem *Le Peintre*." *Oxford Art
Journal* 4 (1981): 26-30.

On the analogy between the artist's didactic-descriptive
poem and his painterly style. Some stress is laid on his
relations with Romantic poets, notably Byron and Vigny.

GOBINEAU

Boissel, Jean. *Gobineau (1816-1882). Un Don Quichotte tragique.* Paris: Hachette, 1981. Pp. 377. Fr. 98.00.

Rev. by Michael D. Biddiss in *FS* 36 (1982): 341-42.

Rey, Pierre-Louis. *L'Univers romanesque de Gobineau.* Paris: Gallimard, 1981. Pp. 411. Fr. 120.00.

Rev. by Michael D. Biddiss in *FS* 36 (1982): 341-42.

See also Tilby ("Constant, A.-L.").

GUERIN, E. de

Duhamelet, Geneviève. "La formation littéraire d'Eugénie de Guérin." *AmG* 142 (1982): 147-53.

Peyrade, Jean. "La vie quotidienne au Cayla au temps d'Eugénie de Guérin." *AmG* 140 (1982): 5-17; 141 (1982): 57-65.

Continuation and conclusion of Peyrade's lecture at Le Cayla on June 19, 1981.

Review of book previously listed:

BARTHES, Mgr Emile, ed., *Journal* (see *ELN* 16, Supp., 101), rev. by C. Gély in *Romantisme* 24 (1979): 138.

GUERIN, M. de

Humphreys, Frank III. "La vision poétique de Maurice de Guérin." *AmG* 141 (1982): 71-83 (à suivre).

First installment is a chapter ("Le sentiment de la nature") from the author's dissertation.

Pujo, Maurice. "Maurice de Guérin." *AmG* 142 (1982): 141-46.

Roux, Albert. "Guérin et la nature." *AmG* 142 (1982): 156-58 (à suivre).

Vest, James. "Note sur 'Trois ans de rêve.'" *AmG* 142 (1982): 137-38.

Vest, James. "'La Prière du chevalier' de Maurice de Guérin."
   AmG 142 (1982): 134-36.

   A "texte retrouvé" based on the G.-S. Trébutien MS, "Les
   vers de Maurice de Guérin," in the Musée du Cayla.

Vest, James. "Les textes retrouvés: 'Les Rêves' et 'Trois ans
   de rêve' de Maurice de Guérin." AmG 140 (1982): 19-22; 141
   (1982): 87-92.

   Texts (with Vest's commentary) of two poems by Maurice
   de Guérin preserved in the G.-S. Trébutien MS, "Les vers
   de Maurice de Guérin," in the Musée du Cayla.

GUIZOT

Hay, Louis, and Michel Espagne. "Genèse du texte et études
   comparées. Histoire d'un article de Heine. Les moissons
   de François Guizot." RLC 55 (1981): 11-29.

Johnson, Douglas. "Guizot protestant." H-Histoire 7 (Jan.-
   Mar. 1981): 151-63.

Review of book previously listed:

   SOCIETE DE L'HISTOIRE DU PROTESTANTISME FRANÇAIS, Actes du
   Colloque François Guizot (see ELN 16, Supp., 101-02), rev.
   by Christine Franconnet in Bibliothèque de l'Ecole des
   Chartes 138 (1980): 328-30.

HERSART DE LA VILLEMARQUET

Laurent, D. "Le père de Louis Hémon et la chanson populaire
   bretonne." Etudes Canadiennes 10 (1981): 21-25.

HUGO, V.

Barrère, Jean-Bertrand. "Pour un dossier d''Eviradnus.'"
   RHL 82 (1982): 445-52.

Benanti, Rosa Maria. "La Préface de Cromwell vue par la
   critique." Francia, Jan.-Mar. 1981, pp. 23-39.

Bonjour, Alexandre, ed. Hernani: drame; avec ... une ...
   notice ... une analyse ... des notes. (Univers des lettres:
   Etude critique illustrée. Texte intégral; 229.) Paris:
   Bordas, 1979. Pp. 159. Fr. 9.50.

Brady-Papadopoulou, Valentini. "The Sun, the Moon and the
Sacred Marriage: An Alchemical Reading of *Notre-Dame de
Paris*." *ECr* 22 (1982): 11-17.

Brombert, Victor. "V.H.: l'auteur effacé ou le moi de l'infini."
Poétique 52 (1982): 417-29.

Carrera, Roselina de la. "History's Unconscious in Victor
Hugo's *Les Misérables*." *MLN* 96 (1981): 839-55.

Chatelain, Martine. "Ruy Blas ou le miroir aux alouettes."
SFr 24 (1981): 24-36.

Hugo's preface to the play is a *miroir aux alouettes*
urging the analysis of a "character" who is only "un personnage fictif, qui n'a d'autre existence que celle d'un
ensemble de signes." Thus *Ruy Blas* anticipates the modern
novel and the modern theatre, whose creatures "sans identité
et sans caractère sont affichés comme un pur effet de
langage."

Descotes, Maurice. "Du drame à l'opéra: les transpositions
lyriques du théâtre de Victor Hugo." *RHT* 34 (1982): 103-56.

Dormann, Geneviève. *Le Roman de Sophie Trébuchet*. Paris:
Albin Michel, 1982. Pp. 348. Fr. 69.00.

On the mother of Victor Hugo.

Eigeldinger, M., and G. Schaeffer, eds. *L'Homme qui rit*.
2 vols. (Garnier-Flammarion.) Paris: Garnier-Flammarion,
1982. Pp. 856.

Fairchild, Sharon L. "Les théories de Victor Hugo appliquées
à son théâtre." *RHT* 34 (1982): 157-68.

Gaillard, Pol. *"Les Contemplations" 1856, de Victor Hugo*.
(Profil d'une OEuvre, série: Littéraire, 76.) Paris: Hatier,
1982. Pp. 78. Fr. 12.25.

Greenberg, Wendy. "Structure and Function of Hugo's Condensed
Metaphor." *FR* 56 (1982-83): 257-66.

Drawing in part upon ideas of Henri Morier, Gérard
Genette, and Henri Meschonnic, author examines the 113
condensed metaphors she finds in *Les Contemplations* (1856)
and the 92 in *Les Châtiments* (1853) to isolate for discussion "three outstanding features of condensed metaphor"
with exemplifying tables for her discoveries in each: "1)

Condensed metaphor as 'restricted rhetoric'; 2) the role of
proper nouns in creating a system of condensed metaphor; and
3) condensed metaphors that appear in 'couples.'"

Grimaud, Michel. "Les mystères du ptyx: hypothèses sur la re-
motivation psycho-poétique à partir de Mallarmé et Hugo."
Pp. 96-162 in Floyd Gray, ed., *Poétiques: théories et
critique littéraires*. (Michigan Romance Studies, Vol. I.)
Dept. of Romance Languages, University of Michigan, 1980.
Pp. 207.

Grossman, Kathryn M. "Hugo's Romantic Sublime: Beyond Chaos
and the Conventions in *Les Misérables*." *PQ* 60 (1981): 471-
86.

An attempt "first to examine the cognitive-ethical universe
of *Les Misérables*, then to probe the relation of that universe to the poet's aesthetics." The study is focused on
Javert, Thénardier, and Jean Valjean on the assumption
that "the behavior and interaction of such characters ...
may yield an implicit commentary on Hugo's aesthetics as
well."

Guerlac, Suzanne. "Exorbitant Geometry in Hugo's *Quatrevingt-
treize*." *MLN* 96 (1981): 856-76.

Ionesco, Eugène. *Hugoliade*. Translated (from the Rumanian) by
Dragomir Costineanu. Paris: Gallimard, 1982. Pp. 160. Fr.
45.00.

Jauss, Hans Robert. *AEsthetic Experience and Literary Her-
meneutics*. (Theory and History of Literature, Vol. 3.)
University of Minnesota Press, 1982. Pp. xl+357. $29.50;
$12.95 paper.

"In closing, Jauss turns to a specific time and place to
show how three very different kinds of lyric poetry--that
of Hugo, Baudelaire, and several lesser poets--became part
of the aesthetic experience of French readers in the year
1857." (From advertising blurb.)

Joseph, Jean R. "'Galatea bifrons': étude structurale d'un
poème de Victor Hugo." *AJFS* 17 (1980): 241-61.

On "Elle était déchaussée, elle était décoiffée" (*Les
Contemplations* I, 21).

Menarini, Piero. "Eugenio de Ochoa e il teatro francese:
Antony, Hernani e alcuni nuovi dati." *Francofonia* 2 (Spring
1982): 131-42.

Mitchell, Robert L. "Poetry of Religion to Religion of Poetry: Hugo, Mallarmé, and the Problematics of 'Preservation.'" *FR* 55 (1981-82): 478-88.

Muray, Philippe. "Hugo nécromantique." *Tel Quel* 97 (1982): 5-34.

Mutigny, Dr. Jean de. *Victor Hugo et le spiritisme.* (Histoire et Documents.) Paris: Fernand Nathan, 1981. Pp. 126. Fr. 52.00.

Concerns Hugo's relations with the *tables parlantes* that Mme de Girardin introduced at Marine Terrace in 1853. Includes interesting photographs, and texts from the séances with the tables. Author concludes that "il n'y a plus de mystère des tables de Jersey. Il n'y a pas un coupable mais des coupables. Victor Hugo, atteint de paraphrénie fantastique dans son délire onirique, faisait dire à la table ce qu'il aurait voulu dire lui-même.

"Les autres étaient des complices inconscients qui prenaient le relai du maître quand celui-ci était absent ou fatigué. Et tout semblait concorder dans une ambiance faite de grandeur, de poésie, de mystère et d'au-delà." (A.G.E.)

Pouilliart, Raymond. "Jeux d'intertextualité chez Hugo. La 'Préface' des *Burgraves*." *LR* 35 (1981): 343-51.

Suggests as some of the sources for details and imaginative inspiration for Hugo's "Préface": Alexis Pierron's translation of Aeschylus with its revealing preface; Lucan's *Pharsalia*; Jean-Jacques Barthélemy's *Voyage du jeune Anacharsis en Grèce* (1788), especially for its "Atlas" of illustrative plates; and Pouqueville's *Voyage dans la Grèce* (1820-21).

Roos, Jacques. *Etudes de littérature générale et comparée.* Paris: Ophrys, 1979. Pp. 147.

Rev. by François Jost in *CLS* 19 (1982): 389-90. Contains three articles on Victor Hugo.

Rosa, Guy. "Entre 'Cromwell' et sa Préface: du grand homme au génie." *RHL* 81 (1981): 901-18.

Seebacher, Jacques. "Sur la datation du 'Dernier jour d'un condamné' de V. Hugo." *RHL* 82 (1982): 90-94.

On the political and biographical symbolism of the dates given in the manuscript.

Senart, Philippe. "La revue théâtrale--Victor Hugo: Marie
Tudor (Comédie Française)." *RDM*, June 1982, pp. 691-94.

On Jean-Luc Boutté's production introducing Hugo's play
at the Comédie Française after 150 years: "C'est une charge,
une caricature, une parodie burlesque du drame romantique";
but it has at least "le mérite ... d'avoir mis en évidence
par l'extravagance des situations, la richesse des costumes,
la profusion de tous les moyens matériels, la pauvreté du
texte hugolien."

See also Antoine, Biermann, Braun, Faletti, Farwell, Middleton
("French 1. General"); Murphy ("Ballanche"); Viard ("Leroux");
Etudes Nervaliennes et Romantiques 3 ("Nerval"); Ward ("Ger-
man 2. General").

Reviews of books previously listed:

ALBOUY, Pierre, ed., *Odes et ballades* (see *RMB* for 1981, p.
205), rev. by Carlo Cordié in *SFr* 25 (1981): 572; AREF,
Mahmoud, *La Pensée sociale et humaine de Victor Hugo dans
son oeuvre romanesque* (see *RMB* for 1979, p. 187), rev. by
C. Gély in *Romantisme* 25-26 (1979): 247; EIGELDINGER, Marc,
ed., *Les Travailleurs de la mer* (see *RMB* for 1980, p. 199),
rev. by Wendy Greenberg in *FR* 55 (1981-82): 683; GLAUSER,
Alfred, *La Poétique de Hugo* (see *RMB* for 1979, p. 188), rev.
by Reinhard Kuhn in *MLN* 95 (1980): 1087-91; GOHN, Yves,
ed., *Les Travailleurs de la mer* (see *RMB* for 1980, p. 199),
rev. by Wendy Greenberg in *FR* 55 (1981-82): 683; by W.J.S.
Kirton in *FS* 36 (1982): 482-83; GORILOVICS, Tivador, *La
Légende de Victor Hugo de Paul Lafargue* (see *RMB* for 1980,
p. 199), rev. by John Flower in *FS* 36 (1982): 212; JOURNET,
René, and Guy Robert, *Contribution aux études sur Victor
Hugo*, T. II (see *RMB* for 1980, p. 200), rev. by J.-P.
Jossua in *RSPT* 64 (1980): 164-65; JUIN, Hubert, *Victor Hugo*,
T. I (see *RMB* for 1981, p. 207), rev. by J.-P. Jossua in
RSPT 65 (1981): 518-19; PETREY, Sandy, *History in the Text*
(see *RMB* for 1981, p. 207), rev. by David Bellos in *MLR*
77 (1982): 212-13; by L.B. Cooper in *Romantisme* 36 (1982):
117-20; by Carlo Cordié in *SFr* 25 (1981): 572-73; by Michel
Grimaud in *FR* 56 (1982-83): 323-24; PETROVSKA, Marija,
Victor Hugo: l'écrivain engagé en Bohême (see *ELN* 16, Supp.,
104), rev. by Pierre L. Horn in *NCFS* 10 (1981-82): 374-75.

INGRES

See Rosenthal, Whitely ("French 1. General").

JANIN

Deburau. *Histoire du théâtre à quatre sous.* Préface d'Arsène Houssaye. (Les Introuvables.) Plan-de-la-Tour: Editions d'Aujourd'hui, 1982. Pp. 212. Fr. 65.00.

Reprints the text of the edition of Paris, 1881.

Williams, Gareth. "Pushkin and Jules Janin: A Contribution to the Literary Background of *The Queen of Spades.*" *Quinquereme* (July 1981): 206-24.

JOUBERT

See Anster ("French 1. General").

Reviews of book previously listed:

WARD, Patricia A., *Joseph Joubert and the Critical Tradition* (see *RMB* for 1980, p. 204), rev. by Carlo Cordié in *SFr* 25 (1981): 370-71; by Charles A. Porter in *FR* 56 (1982-83): 155-56; by Murray Sachs in *French Forum* 7 (1982): 82-84; by A.J. Steele in *MLR* 77 (1982): 960-61.

KRÜDENER

See Raoul ("French 1. General"); *Annales Benjamin Constant* 2 ("Constant, B.").

LACORDAIRE

Cabanis, José. *Lacordaire et quelques autres. Politique et religion.* Paris: Gallimard, 1982. Pp. 444. Fr. 98.00.

Rev. by John McManners in *TLS*, Dec. 3, 1982, p. 1342, as "a confusing and compelling book."
The "others" of the title are Montalembert and Dupanloup.

Duval, André, and Jean-Michel Hornus. "Madame de Vivens, Lacordaire, l'Ecole de Sorèze et les Protestants. (Documents inédits, 1854-1857)." *BSHPF* 128 (1982): 207-50.

On Lacordaire's relationship with Protestants, as seen in
the circumstances surrounding his take-over of the Ecole
de Sorèze and reflected in a correspondence with a Protestant
lady. The whole is heavily documented.

See also Carré ("Lamennais").

LAMARTINE

Birkett, Mary Ellen. *Lamartine and the Poetics of Landscape.*
(French Forum Monographs, 38.) Lexington, Ky.: French Forum,
1982. Pp. 105.

Lamartine's landscape artistry, often dismissed as merely
"vague," is here rehabilitated in a clear, straightforward
study, elegantly simple in style and form, subtle but not
obscure in its argumentation. Prof. Birkett shows how, despite
its Neo-Classic "allures," Lamartine's descriptive style
transcends and transforms the *Ut pictura poesis* tradition
of eighteenth-century descriptive poetry (Delille et al.)
and the esthetic doctrine (Port-Royal, Batteux) that under-
lay it. She brings delicate attention to bear on the new
poetics which Lamartine devised, "one that gives landscape
the power totally to purvey its meaning, and words the power
to transform the world." From the *Méditations* of 1820 to
the *Harmonies* of 1830, as revealed in this insightful
analysis of the landscapes in key poems (notably "L'isole-
ment," "Le lac," "Le vallon," "Milly," "Ischia," "La prière,"
"L'Occident," and "Novissima verba"), Lamartine's occasionally faltering progress is charted. We see the "méditation"
evolving into the "harmonie," and an esthetic of riches
being replaced by one of totality, which is, at the same
time, an esthetics of the fragmentary and the incomplete.
     The author concludes by projecting Lamartine's new view
of poetry forward into the twentieth century. His definition
of poetry, given in "Les destinées de la poésie" (1834),
is related to ideas of Valéry and Michaux, to the practice
of Rimbaud, Mallarmé, and Verlaine, and to Baudelaire's
"sorcellerie évocatoire." She might have cited Valéry's
famous words about modern poets' wresting of their *bien*
from music. (One small complaint: although this book needs
it less than most, an index would have been desirable
nevertheless.)
     All in all, exemplary and highly rewarding. (J.S.P.)

Hamlet-Metz, Mario. "Napoléon chez Lamartine: usurpateur et poète." Pp. 43-52 in *Historical Figures in French Literature*. (French Literature Series, Vol. VIII.) Dept. of Foreign Languages and Literatures, University of South Carolina, 1981. Pp. 146.

Winegarten, Renée. "In Quest of Lamartine: A Poet in Politics." *Encounter* 59 (Aug. 1982): 22-29.

See also Antoine, Raoul ("French 1. General"); *Friends of George Sand Newsletter* 5,i ("Sand"); Moreno Alonso ("Spanish 2. General").

Review of book previously listed:

GUYARD, Marius-François, ed., *Méditations poétiques. Nouvelles Méditations poétiques suivies de Poésies diverses* (see *RMB* for 1981, p. 210), briefly rev. by Danielle Moreau in *Europe* 640-41 (1982): 228.

LAMENNAIS

Cahiers mennaisiens 14-15 (1982).

This double issue is entirely devoted to a monograph by Louis Miard entitled *Un disciple de Lamennais, Michelet et Quinet en Amérique du Sud: Francisco Bilbao (Santiago du Chili 1823--Buenos Aires 1865)*. (See the article by Frank McDonald Spindler listed in *RMB* for 1981, p. 212.) This is a satisfying and solid piece of work and should remain the definitive treatment of the subject for a long time. (J.S.P.)

Carré, A.-M., O.P. "Lamennais et Lacordaire." *RDM*, Aug. 1982, pp. 287-94.

Nothing really new. (J.S.P.)

Hourdin, Georges. *Lamennais. Prophète et combattant de la liberté*. Paris: Librairie académique Perrin, 1982. Pp. 416. Fr. 90.00.

This is, for the most part, a straightforward account of Lamennais's life, occasionally marred by naïveté (some passages sound as if they were written while listening to the election returns in 1981). In any case, the book is a work of popularization, not of scholarship, and never rises above superficiality. As the title suggests, it is informed by a sympathy for Lamennais, that is, for the Lamennais who can be seen as a precursor of liberal trends within modern Catholicism and of French Socialism à la Mitterrand. (J.S.P.)

Kenec'hdu, Tanguy. *Lamennais, un prêtre en recherche.* (L'Auteur et son Message, 7.) Paris: Téqui, 1982. Pp. 259. Fr. 33.00. Like the preceding item, this biography adds nothing to the scholarship on Lamennais. Rather, it is the work of an ardent admirer, a Christian Democrat who sees in Lamennais an expression of "le libéralisme catholique" (rather than the usual "catholicisme libéral"); e.g., Kenec'hdu emphasizes Lamennais as an ancestor of the modern campaign for "local liberties" and "decentralization." A curious side-light is that he does not think of Lamennais as a Breton writer. Kenec'hdu finds an underlying unity in Lamennais's thought, unearthing democratic ideas in embryo in the *Essai sur l'indifférence.* But it is the Lamennais of the *L'Avenir* period (1830-31) whom he most admires. The post-rupture Lamennais is downgraded: he was only one of a number of militant opponents of the July Monarchy; even *Les Paroles d'un croyant* are dismissed as "du Chateaubriand revu par le vicomte d'Arlincourt." Along the way, Kenec'hdu debunks a few ingredients of the Lamennais myth (his "harsh" imprisonment, his alleged poverty). But the author's essential message is an identification of Lamennais as a precursor of Vatican II Catholicism and of "prêtres 'en recherche' ou 'en difficultés' ou 'réduits à l'état laïc.'" (J.S.P.)

Le Guillou, Louis, ed. *Correspondance générale.* T. VIII: *1841-1854.* T. IX: *Suppléments inédits.* 2 vols. Paris: Armand Colin, 1981. Fr. 320.00 (each vol.).

Rev. by Hugo Aubert in *RHE* 77 (1982): 157-64; by Peter Byrne in *Friends of George Sand Newsletter* 5,i (1982): 49-50; by A.R. Vidler in *FS* 36 (1982): 480-81.

Le Guillou, M.-J., and Louis Le Guillou, eds. *La Condamnation de Lamennais. Dossier inédit.* (Textes, Dossiers, Documents, 5.) Paris: Beauchesne, 1982. Pp. 740. Fr. 333.00.

See also L'Ecuyer Lacroix ("French 1. General"); Klinck ("Bonald").

Reviews of books previously listed:

L'Actualité de Lamennais (see *RMB* for 1981, p. 211), rev. by René Epp in *Revue des Sciences religieuses* 55 (1981):

276-77; by Pierre Petit in *Etudes théologiques et religieuses*
57 (1982): 136-37; LE GUILLOU, Louis, ed., *Correspondance
générale* (see *ELN* 11, Supp., 87; 12, Supp., 99; 13, Supp.,
97; *RMB* for 1979, p. 195), rev. by André Bourin in *RDM*,
June 1982, pp. 681-82; by Jacques Gadille in *RHEF* 67 (1981):
111-16; RUBAT DU MERAC, Anne-Marie, *Lamennais et l'Italie*
(see *ELN* 17, Supp., 141), rev. by Maryse Jeuland-Meknaud
in *REI* 27 (1981): 87-95; by Yvon Tranvouez in *ASSR* 53,ii
(1982): 352.

LATOUCHE

Borowitz, Helen O. "The Man Who Wrote to David." *The Bulletin
of the Cleveland Museum of Art*, Oct. 1980, pp. 256-74.

Mostly a discussion in art historical terms of Latouche's
Lettres à David sur le Salon de 1819. In passing, his "pre-
dilection for sensual beauty" is related to the eroticism
of his literary works, *Fragoletta* and *La Reine d'Espagne*.

Pelckmans, M. Paul. "Androgyne et mythes familiaux. Une lecture
de *Fragoletta* (1829) de Henri de Latouche." *OL* 36 (1981):
13-27.

LEQUIER

Turpin, Jean-Marie. "La Feuille de Charmille." Pp. 219-49 in
Dorian Tiffenau, ed., *La Narrativité*. (Centre régional de
Publication de Paris. Phénoménologie et Herméneutique.)
Paris: Editions du CNRS, 1980. Pp. 271. Fr. 70.00.

LERMINIER

Smith, Bonnie G. "The Rise and Fall of Eugène Lerminier."
FHS 12 (1981-82): 377-400.

A skillful and trenchant portrait of the legal scholar
and journalist (1803-1857), who seemed to incarnate Romantic
idealism in the years 1828-38. Smith points out Lerminier's
relations with the literary world (he was a mainstay of the
Revue des Deux Mondes) and suggests him as a model for Lucien
Chardon in *Illusions perdues*.

LEROUX

Boudard, René. "Pierre Leroux et son imprimerie creusoise de Boussac (1844-1850)." Pp. 131-37 in *1848. Les Utopistes sociaux. Utopie et action à la veille des journées de février.* (Société d'Histoire de la Révolution de 1848 et des Révolutions du XIXe Siècle.) Paris: C.D.U./SEDES, 1981. Pp. 290. Fr. 121.84.

La Puma, Leonardo. "Affinità e convergenze nella formazione ideale di Pierre Leroux e Giuseppe Mazzini (1827-1830)." *Quaderno filosofico* (Lecce) 4 (1980): 129-53.

Prontera, Angelo, and Fernando Fiorentino, trans. and eds. *Corso di frenologia.* Lecce: Milella, ca. 1980. Pp. 365.

Rev. by Jacques Viard in *RHL* 81 (1981): 1016-17.

Viallaneix, Paul. "Pierre Leroux, théologien socialiste (à propos de *La Grève de Samarez*)." *Romantisme* 32 (1981): 75-80.

Viard, Jacques. "Pierre Leroux et les romantiques." *Romantisme* 36 (1982): 27-50.

On Leroux's relations with Michelet, Hugo, and Quinet; in general, Viard vindicates Leroux.

Viard, Jacques. "Pierre Leroux, Proudhon, Marx et Jaurès." *RHMC* 29 (1982): 305-23.

On Marxist neglect of and disdain for Leroux (unlike Proudhon, Saint-Simon, and Fourier, he is not listed among the precursors on the obelisk in the Alexandrowski Garden in the Kremlin). A rehabilitation began ca. 1900, thanks to Jaurès and other Socialists. Along the way, Viard seeks to strip Proudhon of his prestigious place in the French revolutionary-socialist tradition.

See also Gregory ("French 1. General"); Tilby ("Constant, A.-L.").

Reviews of books previously listed:

GOBLOT, Jean-Jacques, *Aux origines du socialisme français* (see *ELN* 17, Supp., 142), rev. by Jean Albertini in *Europe* 643-44 (Nov.-Dec. 1982): 228-29; LACASSAGNE, Jean-Pierre, ed., *La Grève de Samarez* (see *RMB* for 1979, p. 196), rev. by Nadine Dormoy Savage in *NCFS* 9 (1981): 266-68; VIARD,

Jacques, *Pierre Leroux, George Sand, Mazzini, Péguy e noi* (see *RMB* for 1980, p. 208), rev. by Annarosa Poli in *SFr* 26 (1982): 163–64.

LITTRE

Battail, Jean-François. "Littré hors de son dictionnaire." *Moderna Språk* 75 (1981): 363–71.

An introduction to and overview of the lexicographer's literary and scholarly career. Usually labeled a Positivist-- in fact, "plus comtien que Comte"--but not an uncritical one, he was also a translator of Homer, Pliny, Dante, and Schiller, as well as of Strauss's *Life of Jesus*; he corresponded with A.W. Schlegel.

LOAISEL DE TREOGATE

Bowling, Townsend Whelen. *The Life, Works, and Literary Career of Loaisel de Tréogate*. (SVEC, 196.) Oxford: The Voltaire Foundation of the Taylor Institution, 1981. Pp. 254.

Listed last year without comment (*RMB* for 1981, p. 213), this solid monograph on the pre-Romantic author of *Dolbreuse* (1752–1812) provides, for the first time, a sure foundation in biographical and bibliographical fact for future work on him. There is no literary criticism of his works, but there are "descriptive summaries" of seven novels and ten plays. In his introduction, the author surveys the scholarship on Loaisel de Tréogate. The biography itself is rather brief, understandably in view of the paucity of information. The chapter on Loaisel's literary career is largely the story of the critical reaction to individual works. (J.S.P.)

MAINE DE BIRAN

Babini, Valeria Paola. "Maine de Biran e Antoine Athanase Royer-Collard. Il filosofo letto da un alienista contemporaneo." *Rivista di Filosofia*, June 1980, pp. 270–84.

Crippa, Romeo. "Presenza e assenza dell'anima bella nello spiritualismo francese del secondo Ottocento." *Giornale di Metafisica* 35 (1980): 95–116.

Tisserand, Pierre, ed. *OEuvres complètes.* Geneva: Slatkine
  Reprints, 1982. 14 vols. Sw.Fr. 1000.00.
  A reprint of the edition of Paris, 1920-49.

MAISTRE, J. de

Darcel, J.-L., and J. Boissel, eds. *Considérations sur la
  France.* (Publications du Centre d'Etudes franco-italien.
  Universités de Turin et de Savoie. Bibliothèque Franco
  Simone, 5.) Geneva: Slatkine, 1980. Pp. 212. Fr. 76.40.

Lebrun, Richard A. "Joseph de Maistre's 'Philosophic' View
  of War." Pp. 43-52 in *Proceedings of the Seventh Annual
  Meeting of the Western Society for French History. 1-3
  November 1979, Omaha, Nebraska.* Santa Barbara: Western
  Society for French History, 1981. Pp. 187.

  Lebrun tries to win a more favorable hearing for Maistre's
  position by arguing that he deliberately used exaggeration
  and paradox in his defense of Christian truths and developed
  a new kind of apologetics (see comments of W. Jay Reedy,
  pp. 53-56).

Pachet, Pierre. "Le Sang et l'action à distance selon Joseph
  de Maistre." *Romantisme* 31 (1981): 9-16.

Paulinich, Marina. "Joseph de Maistre e la relazione del
  giugno 1813 a Vittorio Emanuele di Savoia." *Pisa: Annali
  della Scuola Normale Superiore* (Classe di Lettere e Filosofia, serie III) 10 (1980): 451-82.

  See comment by Carlo Cordié in *SFr* 25 (1981): 566-67.

Petyx, Vincenza. "Stato e nazione nel pensiero contro-
  rivoluzionario di Maistre e Bonald." *Rivista di Filosofia*,
  Oct. 1980, pp. 416-53.

Reviews of book previously listed:

TULARD, Jean, ed., *Considérations sur la France* (see *RMB*
  for 1980, p. 210), rev. by Malcolm Cook in *JES* 12 (1982):
  230-31; by Françoise Gaillard in *Romantisme* 37 (1982): 122-24.

MAISTRE, X. *de*

Coelho, Alain, ed. *Voyage autour de ma chambre.* Post-face de
Sainte-Beuve. Nantes: Le Temps singulier, 1981. Fr. 38.50.

Fusero, Sergio. "Lettere inedite di Joseph e Xavier de Maistre,
parte II: lettere di Xavier." *Studi Piemontesi* 9,i (1980):
132-41.

See comment by Carlo Cordié in *SFr* 25 (1981): 370.

MERCIER

Kaplow, Jeffry, ed. *Le Tableau de Paris.* (Découverte-Poche,
10.) Paris: Maspero, 1979. Pp. 352. Fr. 30.00.

MERIMEE

Cogman, P.W.M. "The Brother and the Beast: Structure and Meaning of Mérimée's *La Jaquerie.*" *FS* 36 (1982): 26-36.

Crecelius, Kathryn J. "Fictional History in Mérimée's
Chronique du règne de Charles IX." Pp. 31-42 in *Historical
Figures in French Literature.* (French Literature Series,
vol. VIII.) Dept. of Foreign Languages and Literatures,
University of South Carolina, 1981. Pp. 146.

The conclusion seems to be that the historical figures
of the novel are not autonomous but exist in relation to
the fictional ones. The article would benefit from a sharper
focus. (E.F.G.)

Crecelius, Kathryn J. "French Historical Monuments Revisited."
Contemporary French Civilization 5 (1980-81): 235-45.

A sketchy survey of Mérimée's role in awakening concern
for France's deteriorating monuments.

Crecelius, Kathryn. "Mérimée's 'Federigo': From Folktale
to Short Story." *SSF* 19 (1982): 57-63.

In spite of Mérimée's disclaimer, the literary and
structural differences between "Federigo" and the known
versions of the folktale "The Smith and the Devil" make
of the former a true short story and not a mere transcription.

Freustié, Jean. *Prosper Mérimée (1803-1870). Le nerveux hautain.* Paris: Hachette-Littéraire, 1982. Pp. 287. Fr. 85.00.

Hamilton, James. "Pagan Ritual and Human Sacrifice in Mérimée's 'Mateo Falcone.'" *FR* 55 (1981-82): 52-59.

> Mérimée's story is seen within the framework of primitive myth (Fraser and Eliade). One would like to know the relationship of "Mateo Falcone" in this respect with other works by Mérimée. Well worth reading. (E.F.G.)

Kajino, Kichiro. *La Création chez Stendhal et chez Prosper Mérimée. Du romantisme à la première création romanesque.* Tokyo: Jiritsi-Shobo, 1980. Pp. 457.

> Rev. by V. Del Litto in *SC* 25 (1982-83): 86-87.

Porter, Laurence M. "The Subversion of the Narrator in Mérimée's *La Vénus d'Ille*." *NCFS* 10 (1981-82): 268-77.

> In this essentially Freudian interpretation, the author refuses to read Mérimée's story as a murder mystery, concentrating instead on the intertwined themes of sexuality and terror. The ostensibly neutral narrator is the key to this interpretation, which sheds important light on Mérimée's poetic imagination. Two misprints occur: p. 273, l. 14, read *to* instead of *of*; p. 276, l. 23, add *de* after *pas*. (E.F.G.)

Tilby, Michael. "The Rewriting of a Mérimée Short Story: 'La Double Méprise' and Bourget's 'Un Crime d'amour.'" *SFr* 26 (1982): 44-53.

> The author contends that Bourget, when writing his novel, had Mérimée's story in mind. The article thus focuses more on Bourget than on Mérimée.

"La Vénus d'Ille" et autres nouvelles. (G.-F., 368.) Paris: Garnier-Flammarion, 1982. Pp. 283. Fr. 19.84.

Williams, Elizabeth. "Mérimée et l'archéologie médiévale du Midi de la France en 1834." *Annales du Midi* 93 (1981): 293-312.

See also García Felguera ("French 1. General"); Gimenez, Soria ("Spanish 2. General").

Review of book previously listed:

THIELTGES, Gerd, Bürgerlicher Klassizismus (see ELN 15,
Supp., 118), rev. by Y. Chevrel in RBPH 59 (1981): 718-21.

MICHELET

Baruffi, Luisa, ed. Les Femmes de la Révolution (Le Donne
nella Rivoluzione). Milan: Bompiani, 1978. Pp. 216.

   Rev. by Néréma Zuffi in Quaderni di Lingue e Letterature
(Padua-Verona) 3-4 (1978-79): 461-62.

Borie, Jean. "Une gynécologie passionnée." In Jean Paul Aron,
ed., Misérable et glorieuse: la femme au XIXe siècle. Paris:
Fayard, 1980. Pp. 248. Fr. 53.95.

Douchin, Jacques-Louis. "Michelet inspirateur de Jules
Laforgue." RHL 81 (1981): 968-70.

La Femme. (Champs.) Paris: Flammarion, 1982. Pp. 369. Fr.
30.00.

Gallo, Max. "The Rediscovery of Michelet." Encounter, Mar.
1982, pp. 92-93.

   An enthusiastic welcome for the revived Michelet revealed
by the Journal and the OEuvres complètes.

Haac, Oscar A. Jules Michelet. (Twayne's World Author Series,
638.) Boston: Twayne Publishers (G.K. Hall), 1982. Pp. 199.

   The dean of American Michelet scholars has done a remarkable
job of compressing the vast and multifarious work and thought
of the great Romantic historian into the format of a Twayne
book. And, in so doing, he succeeds somewhat better than
Stephan A. Kippur did in his 1981 volume (see RMB for 1981,
p. 217) in telling clearly the story of Michelet's life,
and this despite his prefatory renunciation of any claim
to be writing a biography. Though obviously an admirer of
Michelet ("inspired spokesman for a new France"), Haac
summarizes the works with objectivity and, as one would
expect, with insight. He acknowledges some flaws of character or personality, e.g., Michelet's adhesion to the double
standard in sexual matters (true, Haac primarily blames
the inadequacy of scientific information in Michelet's time
as responsible for some of the historian's stranger ideas
in this field).

There is a sprinkling of dubious or erroneous statements,
e.g., Napoleon III "declared himself emperor" on Dec. 2,
1851; in 1854-55 Guizot was "in retirement in England";
Charles IX had the Duc de Guise assassinated at Blois;
Gustavus Adolphus died in 1732. But such slips are not crucial.
The picture of Michelet the man and the account of his ideas
emerge unscathed. Haac has written the best available
general introduction to Michelet in English. (J.S.P.)

Le Goff, Jacques. "Le Moyen Age de Michelet." Pp. 19-45 in
Jacques Le Goff, *Pour un autre Moyen Age. Temps, travail
et culture en Occident: 18 essais*. (Bibliothèque des
Histoires.) Paris: Gallimard, 1977. Pp. 424. Fr. 85.00.

Mettra, Claude, ed. *Histoire de France au XVIe siècle: Renaissance et Réforme*. (Bouquins.) Paris: Robert Laffont, 1982.
Pp. 820. Fr. 59.00.

  Rev. by René Elvin in *HT* 32 (Nov. 1982): 50-52.

Michelet, Madame Jules (Athénaïs-Marguerite Mialaret). *Les
Chats*. Ed. by Gabriel Monod. (Les Introuvables.) Plan-de-
la-Tour: Editions d'Aujourd'hui, 1978. Pp. 392. Fr. 91.00.

Mitzman, Arthur. "Rome Is to Carthage as Male Is to Female:
Michelet, Berlioz, Flaubert and the Myths of the Second
Empire (Abstract)." Pp. 378-80 in *Proceedings of the Eighth
Annual Meeting of the Western Society for French History.
October 23-25, 1980, Eugene, Oregon*. Las Cruces: Western
Society for French History, 1981. Pp. 597.

  A psychohistorical discussion of the theme of Rome vs.
Carthage as treated by Michelet (primarily in *La Bible de
l'humanité*), Berlioz (*Les Troyens*), and Flaubert (*Salammbô*)
(see comment by James G. Chastain, pp. 391-93).

Moreau, Thérèse. *Le Sang de l'histoire. Michelet, l'histoire
et l'idée de la femme au XIXe siècle*. (Nouvelle Bibliothèque scientifique.) Paris: Flammarion, 1982. Pp. 256.
Fr. 80.00.

Moreau, Thérèse. "Sang sur: Michelet et le sang féminin."
Romantisme 31 (1981): 151-65.

  Defines Michelet's rather odd form of male chauvinism,
taking his preoccupation with the menstrual cycle as
starting-point and focus.

L'Oiseau. (Demain et son Double.) Paris: Robert Laffont, 1982.
Pp. 424. Fr. 110.00.

Orr, Linda. "A Sort of History. Michelet's *La Sorcière.*" *YFS*
59 (1980): 119-36.

Paulinich, Marina. "Un itinerario della libertà: *La Sorcière.*"
Saggi 20 (1981): 93-125.

Pintacuda De Michelis, Fiorella. "Alle origini della 'histoire
totale': Jules Michelet." *Studi Storici* 21 (1980): 835-54.

Richard, Jean-Pierre. "Nappe, charnière, interstice, point."
Poétique 12 (1981): 293-302.

Trousson, Raymond. "Michelet lecteur de Rousseau." *Spicilegio
Moderno* (Pisa) 12 (1979): 35-48.

Viallaneix, Paul, and Bernard Leuilliot, eds. *OEuvres complètes.*
T. XXI: *Histoire du XIXe siècle (1872-1874).* Paris: Flammarion, 1982. Fr. 350.00.

See also Viallaneix ("French 1. General"); *Cahiers mennaisiens*
14-15 ("Lamennais"); Viard ("Leroux").

Reviews of books previously listed:

KIPPUR, Stephan A., *Jules Michelet: A Study of Mind and Sensibility* (see *RMB* for 1981, p. 217), rev. in *AR* 40 (1982):
12; by Stanley Mellon, negatively, in *JMH* 54 (1982): 328-
30; by Thérèse Moreau in *RHL* 82 (1982): 931-32; TIEDER,
Irène, *Michelet et Luther* (see *ELN* 16, Supp., 110-11), rev.
by Philippe Muret in *RBPH* 59 (1981): 1000-05.

MONNIER

See Wechsler ("French 1. General").

MONTALEMBERT

See Cabanis ("Lacordaire").

MUSSET

Allem, Maurice, and Paul Courant, eds. *OEuvres complètes en prose*. (Bibliothèque de la Pléiade.) Nouvelle éd. Paris: Gallimard, 1982. Pp. xiv+1326. Fr. 165.00.

Berteau, Roland. "Procédés de revivication des comparaisons traditionnelles de renforcement dans les *Premières Poésies* d'A. de Musset." Pp. 39-46 in Marc Dominicy and Marc Wilmet, eds., *Linguistique romane et linguistique française: hommages à Jacques Pohl*. (Université libre de Bruxelles: Faculté de Philosophie et Lettres, LXXII.) Editions de l'Université de Bruxelles, 1980. Pp. 285. Bel.Fr. 800.00.

Musset's rich talent is evident in the great variety of similes he uses, some traditional, but most transformations of trite comparisons "dans un souci de meilleure adaptation au contexte ou d'accroissement de l'expressivité" (p. 44).

Hoffmann, Léon François. "Five Documents Concerning Alfred de Musset from the Edward Bailey Meyer '21 Collection." *PULC* 42 (1981): 212-16.

Padgett, Graham. "Bad Faith in Alfred de Musset: A Problem of Interpretation." *Dalhousie French Studies* 3 (1981): 65-82.

The ambiguities evident in Musset's personal pronouncements and in his literary projections are examined from the standpoint of Existentialist thought. Conclusion: there *is* a strong odor of bad faith; but, to be fair, we must remember the historical context in which Musset grew up and sympathize with his feeling that he was the victim of an untimely birth.

Siegel, Patricia Joan, compiler. *Alfred de Musset: A Reference Guide*. (A Reference Guide to Literature.) Boston: G.K. Hall, 1982. Pp. 439.

A major contribution, this annotated bibliography covers Musset scholarship from 1828 to 1980. In addition to the main listing, it contains: an introduction, acknowledgments, a chronological list of Musset's principal works, a catalog of modern (since World War II) translations, a separate schedule of articles appearing in *L'Intermédiaire des Chercheurs et Curieux* (1865-1940), and an index.
Any negative criticism would represent carping, but two minor complaints are in order: occasional typographical errors which may pose problems for users, and the unexplained

significance of asterisks before certain items, which leaves the user puzzled. One recommendation: that Professor Siegel expand her introduction to include a review of the history of Musset criticism. (A.B.S.)

Thomas, Jean-Jacques. "Les maître-mots de Musset: peuple et pouvoir dans *Lorenzaccio*." Pp. 179-96 in Michel Glatigny and Jacques Guilhamou, eds., *Peuple et pouvoir: études de lexicologie politique*. Presses universitaires de Lille, 1981. Pp. 196.

The value of *Lorenzaccio* is not in its psychology or its moral lesson but in its concern with language. By what he does and has his characters do with words, Musset undermines the absolutist view of language as an instrument of referential clarity. *Lorenzaccio* is an early instance of the recognition that words are slippery, susceptible of purposeful misuse: manipulation of reader or hearer.

Reviews of books previously listed:

DOMENICO, Elio de, *Musset et l'Italie* (see *ELN* 16, Supp., 112), rev. by Jacques Landrin in *IL* 32 (1980): 36; LAINEY, Yves, *Musset ou la difficulté d'aimer* (see *RMB* for 1979, p. 208), rev. by Jacques Landrin in *IL* 32 (1980): 35-36.

NAPOLEON

Tulard, Jean, ed. *Lettres d'amour à Joséphine*. Paris: Fayard, 1981. Pp. 464. Fr. 64.00.

Rev. by John Eldred Howard in *TLS*, July 16, 1982, p. 762.

NECKER DE SAUSSURE

Montandon, Alain. "Albertine Necker de Saussure et Jean-Paul." *RLC* 55 (1981): 76-89.

NERVAL

Bony, Jacques. "Nerval et les aspects matériels du spectacle." *Romantisme* 38 (1982): 127-39.

Bony draws both on Nerval's own dramatic works and on his theatrical criticism in an effort to define his conception of the place of such material aspects of theater as costumes

and scenery. It appears that the poet-dramatist was not
entirely above being concerned with the "show-business"
side of things but, as we might expect, dreamed of an ideal
theater.

Buffetaud, Eric. *Gérard de Nerval*. Préface de Jacqueline
Sarment et Jean Richer. Paris: Maison de Balzac, 1981. Pp.
124.

    Catalogue of a show given at the Maison de Balzac, Dec.
18, 1981--Mar. 21, 1982. See *BduB* 1982-II, pp. 227-28.

Cahiers Gérard de Nerval 4 (1981): "*Dossier*: Le Paris de
Nerval." Pp. 82.

    A nostalgic issue devoted to "Le Paris de Nerval" and to
photographs and details related to his life, newly discovered
writings, and death. A major section ("Nerval piéton de
Paris. Nerval et Paris historique et anecdotique") includes
André Pieyre de Mandiargues, "Paris de Nerval" (3-4); Jean
Richer, "Le début du manuscrit de *Promenades et souvenirs*"
(variantes établies par Richer) (5-8), and "Autour des
Nuits d'octobre" (35-38); Alice Planche, "J'ai longtemps
habité Montmartre ..." (9-20); Pierre-André Touttain,
"Souvenirs d'un parisien en promenade à Montmartre" (21-24);
Lucien Richer, "Autour du quartier des Halles" (25-30);
Henri Bonnet, "Le Ventre de Paris dans les *Nuits d'octobre*"
(31-34); Jean Senelier, "Le lieu du Bal des Ardents dans le
Prince des Sots" (39-41), and "Un fait-divers parisien ou
l'enigme du *Diable vert*" (42-46). Among the illustrations
are those of the home of Dr. Blanche (Hôtel de Lamballe)
at Passy, Célestin Nanteuil's engraving of "La Rue de la
Vieille Lanterne," and Nerval's tomb in Père Lachaise.
Peter J. Edwards introduces two of four "textes retrouvés"
by or related to Nerval; and Louis Levionnois and Jean
Gaulmier have brief studies, in turn, on "Gérard de Nerval
était-il Franc-maçon?" (59-63) and "Autour du séjour de
Nerval à Liban" (64-68). Finally, there are a few pages
of general information (78-82): a notice of the "Exposition
Nerval à la Maison de Balzac," a list of new members of the
Société Gérard de Nerval which publishes the *Cahiers*,
material on Nerval in the theatre and on the Société
japonaise Gérard de Nerval, and a bibliography.

Etudes Nervaliennes et Romantiques 3 (1981). Pp. 151.

    Contents: Jean Ziegler, "Le voyage de Gérard de Nerval
à Londres en 1849" (9-13), "Alexandre de Cayrol (1814-1862),
ami de Stadler et de Nerval" (15-18), "Rigo 'Maître Jacques'"

(19-24), "Douët d'Arcq, 1808-1883" (105-07), "Adrien
Maître de Ballet" (109-11), "La servante du Dr Labrunie et
de son fils: Gabrielle Benard (1812-1853)" (113-14), and
"La Comtesse de Persigny" (115-16); Jean Céard, "Raoul
Spifame, Roi de Bicêtre. Recherches sur un récit de Nerval"
(25-50); Lieven D'Hulst, "Le voyage allemand de Nerval et
Dumas en 1838" (53-57); Claude Schopp, "Les excursions de
Dumas sur les bords du Rhin (1838). Restitution chronologique"
(59-71), and "Le Docteur Vallerand de La Fosse" (117-21);
Pierre Enckell, "Documents pour servir à l'histoire de
Crédeville et de Bouginier" (73-94), and "Autour d''El
Desdichado'" (123-29); Jacques Bony, "Nerval et la Société
des Gens de Lettres: une lettre inédite à Victor Hugo"
(95-103); Jean Guillaume, "A propos de 'G.G.'" (131-38);
Marina Mureşanu-Ionescu, "Hommage. Nicolas I. Popa et les
études sur Nerval" (141-51).

Études Nervaliennes et Romantiques 4: *Gérard de Nerval et la
Bibliothèque Nationale* (1982). Pp. 53.

A three-part corrective (with additional titles and dele-
tions) for Jean Richer's list of Nerval's supposed library
borrowings ("Nerval lecteur à la Bibliothèque royale puis
impériale" [*Cahiers de l'Herne* 37 (1980)]). In part I,
Jean Ziegler ("Gérard de Nerval à la Bibliothèque Nationale,"
pp. 11-18) notes that thirty-one of the titles in Richer's
list were, in fact, borrowed by Augustin Gérard (whose name
was confused with Nerval's library signature, "M. Gérard")
and a certain A. Morel. In part II ("Recherches dans les
registres de prêt du Département des Imprimés," pp. 19-31),
Huguette Brunet, a professional librarian, explains technical details in the cataloguing of books and the changing
practices in recording names of borrowers from the national
library, and demonstrates from detailed entries her method
of separating Gérard's actual borrowings from books borrowed
by others. In part III ("Livres prêtés à Gérard de Nerval,
à d'autres emprunteurs homonymes de Gérard et à des amis
de Gérard," pp. 33-53), Brunet lists the books clearly
borrowed from the national library by or for Nerval from
Apr. 5, 1830, to Oct. 4, 1854, with indication of their
location in the library at the time, their present location
and condition if they survive, and their availability or
replacement. Listed also (from Mar. 10, 1829) are the titles
of books shown to have been borrowed by homonymous individuals
who were confused with "M. Gérard" and by borrowers whose
identification with Nerval in Richer's list is in doubt.

Études Nervaliennes et Romantiques (Aux origines de "Pandora"
et d'"Aurélia") 5 (1982). Pp. 53.

Contains two separate, but related, studies by Jean Guillaume, S.J.: "Aux origines de Pandora" (9-27) and "Lueurs
sur Aurélia" (29-53). The first considers the complex
origins of Pandora, offers a theoretical history of the text
and elements for a tentative chronology, and concludes that
"la fin de Pandora porte en germe Aurélia, dans une tension
manichéenne qu'avouait déjà l'epigraphe." The second study
concerns complexities in the various elusive "layers" of
text in Aurélia and in the details of Nerval's life, and
concludes that Nerval's replacement of the phrase "cruelle
maladie" by "Vita nuova" in a surviving MS suggests that
the saint of Sylvie, Adrienne, "dans la forme 'Aurélie' ...
commence à revivre."

Furst, Lilian R. The Contours of European Romanticism. London:
Macmillan, 1979. Pp. xvi+158. £10.00.

Rev. by Richard Littlejohns in MLR 77 (1982): 156-57.
Contains an essay on Novalis and Nerval. (See RMB for
1980, p. 19.)

Geninasca, Jacques. "De la fête à l'anti-fête: reconnaissance
et construction de l'équivalence sémantique des chapitres
IV et VII de Sylvie de Gérard de Nerval." Versants (Lausanne)
1 (Autumn 1981): 93-108.

Author studies the semantic correlation of chapters IV
and VII of Sylvie and sees them as serving "to oppose two
apparently incompatible poetics" in the "Fête du Bouquet
provincial" and the "fête à Châalis," which in turn are
shown to reveal surprising parallels to the contrasting
"fêtes publiques" and "spectacles exclusifs" of Rousseau's
Lettre à Mr d'Alembert sur les spectacles.

Gordon, Rae Beth. "Dentelle: métaphore du texte dans Sylvie."
RR 73 (1982): 45-66.

An exquisitely subtle study of Sylvie as "la dentelle de
l'écriture," with a persuasive insistence on the logic of
her particular metaphor dentelle-texte (in which dentelle
is seen as a unique kind of tissu, especially in its "caractère aérien et fragile et l'importance des vides dans sa
composition et dans sa texture"). The paper shows numerous
intertextual developments of this particular metaphor in
Nerval's writings and its remarkable pertinence to the
structure and meaning of Sylvie.

Gordon, Rae Beth. "Eros et Thanatos dans *Sylvie*." *NCFS* X (1981-82): 278-90.

A Freudian analysis focused especially on Chapter VII of *Sylvie*: "C'est là qu'on verra la confrontation de l'Eros avec Thanatos."

Gundersen, Karin. *Textualité nervalienne. Remarques sur la Lettre de l'Illustre Brisacier.* Romansk Institutt, Universitet i Oslo, 1980. Pp. 191.

Rev. by Gabrielle Malandain in *Romantisme* 38 (1982): 165-66.

Jeanneret, Michel. "Sur le 'Voyage en Orient' de Nerval." *CREL* 4 (1980): 29-46.

Shows Nerval, in shaping finally his *Voyage en Orient*, as accomplishing as best he could a union of sorts between illusion and reality--between the dream and reason--and establishing the perspective that would dominate his later works.

Knapp, Bettina L. *Gérard de Nerval: The Mystic's Dilemma.* University of Alabama Press, 1980. Pp. viii+372. $21.50.

Rev. by Alice G. Tunks in *MLJ* 66 (1982): 90-91.

The Mystic's Dilemma, as conceived by the author, may well be a "livre infaisable." It sets the stage with a brief sketch of the French political, philosophical, and literary scene of early Romanticism, traces at length the life of Nerval, discusses his literary antecedents, examines in great detail his important writings, and above all seeks "to evaluate Nerval's dreams along philosophical, esthetic and psychological lines." This last entails the introduction of a vast mass of relatively undigested details that Nerval introduced from his exceedingly varied occult readings. Nerval's madness, for all its strange logic, only adds to the difficulty--and Professor Knapp's interpretations (at times persuasive, but often with no clear authorization from Nerval's text) frequently introduce further complications, as in the alchemical interpretation of *Le Marquis de Fayolle* in chapter 14. Some errors are undoubtedly typographical; but, for example, "El Desdichado" does not mean "The Disinherited," *ingénuité* (p. 215) is not "ingenuity," and Adoniram (in the symbolic "Masonic" murder in the *Histoire de la Reine du Matin et de Soliman Prince des Génies*) is struck down by hammer, chisel, and compass-point--not as described on pp. 149 and 152, where *ciseau*

is translated "scissors." And how can Nerval be described
as Christian (pp. 233, 234)? One comes from the book with
a sense that the author is justified in many of her very
subtle interpretations, but that she is attempting the
impossible and advancing with assurance where angels should
fear to tread. (A.G.E.)

Laszlo, Pierre. "El Desdichado--38." Romantisme 33 (1981):
    35-57.

    Author aims to "restituer la dynamique du poème, à le
remettre en marche" by reestablishing the fusion of Nerval's
rich classical, medieval, and personal allusions with their
plurality of meanings. His suggestions are richly poetic
and imaginative, but lead to the conclusion that the meaning
of the poem must remain ambiguous, full of echoes and directions that lead one back into its mystery.

Pastoureau, Michel. "Soleil noir et flammes de sable. Contri-
    bution à l'héraldique nervalienne: El Desdichado." BduB
    1982-III, pp. 321-38.

    Attempt to show influence on Nerval's sonnet of the famous
Codex Manesse heraldic manuscript painted around 1300-1312
and preserved in the Bibliothèque Nationale until 1888, when
it was taken to the university library at Heidelberg, where
it is today. But relation of the proffered illustrations
to the text seems remote.

Pozzato, Maria Pia. "La communicazione e l'autocomunicazione
    nell'opera narrativa. Note su Proust e Nerval." Francofonia
    1 (Autumn 1981): 51-64.

    Finds great differences in the nature of communication
between the personages of A la recherche du temps perdu
and Sylvie, and in the results of the autocommunication of
the two protagonists. "Marcel retrouve le sens de sa vie,
Gérard le perd."

Riegert, Guy. "Sources et ressources d'une île: Syra dans le
    'Voyage en Orient' de Gérard de Nerval." RHL 81 (1981):
    919-43.

Schärer, Kurt. Pour une poétique des "Chimères" de Nerval.
    (ALM 194, Archives nervaliennes, 13.) Paris: Minard (Lettres
    Modernes), 1981. Pp. 45.

Senelier, Jean. Bibliographie nervalienne. 1968-1980 et complé-
    ments antérieurs. Paris: A.-G. Nizet, 1982. Pp. 158. Fr.
    90.95.

See also Viallaneix ("French 1. General"); Schaeffer ("Sand").

Reviews of books previously listed:

FAIRLIE, Alison, Imagination and Language (see RMB for 1981,
p. 221), rev. by John Cruickshank in FS 36 (1982): 225-26;
FELMAN, Shoshana, La Folie et la chose littéraire (see RMB
for 1980, pp. 153, 220), rev. by Ann Demaitre in FR 55
(1981-82): 539-40; GILBERT, Claire, Nerval's Double: A
Structural Study (see RMB for 1981, p. 221), rev. by Susan
Noakes in SiR 21 (1982): 117-18; JEANNERET, Michel, La
Lettre perdue (see ELN 17, Supp., 147), rev. by J.-C. Fizaine
in Romantisme 27 (1980): 148-51; by Norma Rinsler in FS
36 (1982): 82-83; KNAPP, Bettina L., Gérard de Nerval: The
Mystic's Dilemma (see RMB for 1979, p. 210), rev. by Norma
Rinsler in FS 36 (1982): 213; by Alice G. Tunks in MLJ 66
(1982): 90-91; PORTER, Laurence M., The Literary Dream in
French Romanticism (see RMB for 1979, pp. 151-52), rev. by
Carlo Cordié in SFr 25 (1981): 171; by Brian Juden in MLR
77 (1982): 213-15; by Susan Noakes in SiR 21 (1982): 114-17.

NODIER

Blanchard, Gérard. "Charles Nodier, l'homme-livre ou l'Histoire
du roi de Bohême et de ses sept châteaux." Impressions 18
(Aug. 1981): 13-21.

Jeune, Simon. "Plus jeune qu'à sa naissance, Le Roi de Bohême
a cent cinquante ans." RFHL 49 (July-Sept. 1980): 499-513.

Knapp, Bettina L. "La Fée aux miettes: An Alchemical Hieros
Gamos." Pp. 15-23 in Robert L. Mitchell, ed., Pre-Text/Text/
Context: Essays on Nineteenth-Century French Literature.
Ohio State University Press, 1980. Pp. x+284.

An elaborate attempt to show that Nodier's story reveals
its truth via symbolism drawn from alchemy: "two cosmic
principles, the universal male and female forces as they
participate, symbolically, in a hieros gamos, the alchemical
formula for the sacred marriage of sun and moon." No evidence is offered as to where and how Nodier might have
acquired this alchemical lore.

Pearson, R.A.G. "Poetry or Psychology? The Representation of
Dream in Nodier's Smarra." FS 36 (1982): 410-26.

Claiming that "Smarra ... is the first work of literature
in the French language to take dream as its central subject,"

Pearson wishes to study this tale from the standpoint of
the Romantics themselves in hopes of dispelling "the critical ambivalence which *Smarra* has provoked since it was
first published." The tale's "concentric structure," the
transitions, "the tone of incantation," "the oneiric transformation," and the style are analyzed and related to Nodier's
theory of dreams. The major conclusion: "the dreams in
Smarra are not merely a factitious 'excuse' for fantastical
narrative and bizarre imagery.... Nodier was also a would-
be psychologist."

Ract-Madoux, Pascal. "Les reliures aux écussons de Charles
Nodier." *BduB* 1982-III, pp. 381-91.

Lists sixty-one such bindings; two are illustrated. Done
by Thouvenin, they date from 1830-33 and most are for books
by sixteenth-century French writers.

Rodgers, Brian. "Charles Nodier lecteur de Madame de Staël."
CS 29-30 (1981): 63-76.

Apropos of his articles on *De l'Allemagne*, *Delphine*, and
Corinne (1819). On this basis, the author situates Nodier
vis-à-vis Madame de Staël in the evolution toward Romanticism
(she appears bolder and more innovative than he). He takes
the occasion to point out general affinities between the
two writers (literature as the expression of society,
esthetic relativism, political liberalism).

Rogers, Brian. "Nodier lecteur de Chateaubriand. Chateaubriand
et le romantisme." *Société Chateaubriand: Bulletin* 23
(1980): 44-51.

Vaulchier, Henri de. "Nodier et Manzoni, positions sur le
problème de la langue." *REI* 27 (1981): 69-83.

Vaulchier, Henri de, et al., eds. *Morceaux choisis*. (Auteurs
comtois, 1.) Besançon: CRDP de Besançon, 1982. Pp. 68.
Fr. 40.00.

See also L'Ecuyer Lacroix, Raoul ("French 1. General").

Reviews of books previously listed:

PICAT-GUINOISEAU, Ginette, *Une Oeuvre méconnue de Charles
Nodier* (see *ELN* 16, Supp., 115-16), rev. by Robert Dumont
in *RLC* 56 (1982): 218-19; PORTER, Laurence M., *The Literary*

Dream in French Romanticism (see *RMB* for 1980, p. 226),
rev. by Brian Juden in *MLR* 77 (1982): 213-15; by Susan Noakes
in *SiR* 21 (1982): 114-17; SETBON, Raymond, *Libertés d'une
écriture* (see *RMB* for 1980, p. 227), rev. by Albert Kies
in *LR* 36 (1982): 168-69.

OZANAM

Review of book previously listed:

OZANAM, Didier, ed., *Lettres de Frédéric Ozanam*, T. III
(see *RMB* for 1979, p. 214), rev. by Jean-René Derré in *RHL*
82 (1982): 309-10.

PIXERECOURT

Denis, Andrée. "Guilbert de Pixérécourt et l'Allemagne." Pp.
15-33 in *La Littérature lieu de connaissance et d'amitié
entre les peuples: mélanges offerts à M. le professeur
André Monchoux*. (Annales ... de l'Université de Toulouse-
Le Mirail, N.S., 14.) Toulouse: Université de Toulouse-
Le Mirail, Service des Publications, 1979. Pp. xx+379.
Fr. 94.00.

POTOCKI

Review of book previously listed:

BEAUVAIS, Daniel, ed., *Voyages au Caucase et en Chine* (see
RMB for 1980, p. 229), rev. (very briefly) by Yan de
Kerorguen in *Esprit* 62 (Feb. 1982): 246.

PROUDHON

Bancal, Jean. "Proudhon. La liberté, l'individu, la propriété."
Cadmos 4 (Fall 1981): 42-58.

Besnier, Jean-Michel. "P.-J. Proudhon: la sociologie et le
droit." *Revue de Métaphysique et de Morale* 87 (1982): 267-
79.

Bouglé, C., and H. Moysset, eds. *OEuvres complètes*. 15 tomes
(in 19 vols.). Geneva: Slatkine Reprints, 1981. Sw.Fr. 1800.00.
Reprint of the editions of Paris, 1923-59.

Haubtmann, Pierre. *La Philosophie sociale de P.-J. Proudhon.* Presses universitaires de Grenoble, 1980. Pp. 294. Fr. 60.00.

Haubtmann, Pierre. *Pierre-Joseph Proudhon. Sa Vie et son oeuvre.* Paris: Beauchesne, 1982. Pp. 1104. Fr. 228.00.

Haubtmann, Pierre. *Proudhon, Marx et la pensée allemande.* Presses universitaires de Grenoble, 1981. Pp. 316. Fr. 60.00.
    Rev. by Fernand Rude in *QL* 361 (Dec. 16-31, 1981): 22, 24.

Michaud, Eric. "Proudhon et Courbet." *Avant-Guerre* 2 (1er trimestre 1981): 85-88.

Migalk, Harry. "Arbeiterklasse, lexisch-semantische Darstellung bei Proudhon." *Wissenschaftliche Zeitschrift der Humboldt-Universität in Berlin. Gesellschafts- und sprachwissenschaftliche Reihe* 29 (1980): 585-90.

See also Gregory ("French 1. General"); Viard ("Leroux").

Reviews of books previously listed:

MARAZZA, Camillo, *Il Linguaggio della libertà* (see *RMB* for 1980, p. 230), rev. by Nicole Allegra in *Micromégas* 6,xv-xvi (1979): 173-74; RUBIN, James Henry, *Realism and Social Vision in Courbet and Proudhon* (see *RMB* for 1981, p. 226), rev. by Neil McWilliam in *Art International* 25,i-ii (1982): 112-13; by Aaron Sheon in *Art Journal* 42 (1982): 69, 71, 73.

QUINET

Angrisani Guerrini, Isa. "La fortuna di Quinet in Italia." *Risorgimento* 1 (1980): 73-76.

Angrisani Guerrini, Isa. *Quinet e l'Italia.* Prefazione di Alessandro Galante Garrone. (Centre d'Etudes franco-italien. Universités de Turin et de Savoie. Textes d'Etudes. Domaine français, 4.) Geneva: Slatkine, 1981. Pp. xvi+232. Sw.Fr. 40.00.
    Rev. by Carlo Cordié in *SFr* 26 (1982): 360-61.
    Based on Quinet's early writings about Italy and especially on *Les Révolutions d'Italie*, this book analyzes his political opinions in the years around 1848, seen against the backdrop of events in France, then studies the Italian enthusiasm for that work. In addition to information about Quinet's

relationships with leading figures in the Italian Risorgimento, there is material about Quinet and Sismondi.

Crossley, Ceri. *"La Création* d'Edgar Quinet et le darwinisme
social." *Romantisme* 32 (1981): 65-73.

Though he seeks to incorporate Darwin's thought into his
own system, Quinet spiritualizes it, distinguishing man and
human societies from the rest of nature; man is, ultimately,
free and can evolve toward perfection.

Crossley, Ceri. *"La Création* d'Edgar Quinet: île, eau et
mouvement." *NCFS* 10 (1982): 215-27.

Quinet's picture of the evolutionary forces at work in
the creation of major topographical features (oceans and
mountains, notably) and even of human society is marked
by symbolic imagery: the horizontal, the vertical, the fluid.

Crossley, Ceri. *Edgar Quinet (1803-1875): A Study in Romantic
Thought*. (French Forum Monographs, 43.) Lexington, Ky.:
French Forum, 1982. $12.50.

Crossley, Ceri. "The Treatment of Architecture in the Works
of Edgar Quinet Published before 1851." Pp. 13-22 in
*Literature and Society: Studies in Nineteenth and Twentieth
Century French Literature Presented to R.J. North*. Birmingham: John Goodman & Sons, 1980. Pp. vii+247. £14.00.

Apparently influenced by German thought, Quinet saw the
history of architecture primarily in symbolic terms:
"Architecture becomes a tangible expression of the stages
through which the religious consciousness has evolved. The
pyramids of Egypt, the temples of Greece, the Gothic
cathedral are all visible milestones which mark stages along
the road of mankind's quest for the Absolute."

Fromentin, Eugène, and Paul Bataillard. *Etude sur l'Ahasvérus
d'Edgar Quinet*. (Textes littéraires français, 308.) Geneva:
Droz, 1982. Pp. 224. Fr. 150.00.

See also Viard ("Leroux"); Moreno Alonso, Soria ("Spanish
2. General").

REYBAUD

Jérôme Paturot. Paris: Art et Culture, 1979. Pp. 460. Fr.
138.00.

A facsimile reprint of the 1846 edition (with Grandville's illustrations).

SAINTE-BEUVE

Le Hir, Yves. "Le réseau nocturne dans *Volupté* de Sainte-Beuve." Pp. 399-407 in *Le Génie de la forme: mélanges de langue et littérature offerts à Jean Mourot*. Presses universitaires de Nancy, 1982. Pp. 651.

Complements studies on the themes of lake, sea, and abyss in *Volupté* with an analysis of nocturnal imagery. Evening and night are times associated with the presence of evil, moral distress, and temptation. Diurnal imagery, on the other hand, marks an "exorcism" of the night--and of the anguish characterizing Amaury's youth.

Pitwood, Michael. "Sainte-Beuve and Dante." *MLR* 77 (1982): 568-76.

"The range and interest of Sainte-Beuve's remarks on Dante are worthy of a far more detailed study than they have re-ceived so far; it is the aim of this article to remedy that deficiency" (p. 569).

Rigolot, François. "Les Ronsard de Sainte-Beuve." *O&C* 6,i (1981-82): 81-87.

See also Raoul ("French 1. General").

Review of book previously listed:

CHADBOURNE, Richard M., *Charles-Augustin Sainte-Beuve* (see *ELN* 17, Supp., 151), rev. by François Rigolot in *FR* 55 (1981-82): 552-53.

SAINT-MARTIN

Rioli, Luciana. "Saint-Martin di fronte alla Rivoluzione." Pp. 189-230 in *Saggi e Ricerche di Letteratura francese*, T. XX. Rome: Bulzoni, 1981. Pp. 230.

On his *Lettre à un ami sur la Révolution française* (1795), his first work from the Revolutionary period. It contains the germ of his Providential view of the great upheaval.

SAINT-SIMON

Bulciolu, Maria Teresa. "Documenti dell'utopia san-simoniana: scrittura maschile e scrittura femminile." *Istituto universitario orientale. Annali. Sezione romanza* 23 (July 1981): 385-407.

Goldstun, Leslie F. "Early Feminist Themes in French Utopian Socialism: The Saint-Simonians and Fourier." *JHI* 43 (1982): 91-108.

Hamm, Heinz. "Julirevolution, Saint-Simonismus und Goethes abschliessende Arbeit am 'Faust.'" *Weimarer Beiträge* 28,xi (1982): 70-91.

Moses, Claire G. "Saint-Simonian Men/Saint-Simonian Women: The Transformation of Feminist Thought in 1830s France." *JMH* 54 (1982): 240-67.

The Enfantin phase of Saint-Simonisme is presented briefly. Emphasis here is on "the experience of Saint-Simonian women": feminine participation in Saint-Simonian meetings; the integration of women into the hierarchy; the *maisons de famille* (communes); the creation of an autonomous feminist movement, with its own newspaper, *La Tribune des Femmes* (1832-34); women's experiments with sexual and economic independence (eventually, they gave up on radical sexual ideas). Well done. (J.S.P.)

See also Gregory, Viallaneix ("French 1. General").

Reviews of book previously listed:

BULCIOLU, Maria Teresa, *L'Ecole saint-simonienne et la femme* (see *RMB* for 1981, p. 229), rev. by Francine Daenens in *LR* 36 (1982): 169-71; by Leslie S. Herrmann in *NCFS* 10 (1982): 372-74; by Ivanna Rosi in *RLMC* 35 (1982): 78-80; by Helen C. Staples in *FR* 55 (1981-82): 697-98.

SAND

Baroli, Marc. *La Vie quotidienne en Berry au temps de George Sand (1830-1914).* (Vie quotidienne.) Paris: Hachette, 1982. Pp. 300. Fr. 65.00.

Rev. by Jean Courrier in *Présence de George Sand* 14 (1982): 55.

Berthier, Philippe, ed. *Contes d'une grand-mère*. Paris: L'Aurore, 1982. Pp. 320. Fr. 80.00.

> Rev. by R. Bourgeois in *Présence de George Sand* 14 (1982): 57.

Cecioni, Pier Luigi, trans. *Lettere*. Introduzione di Angela Bianchini. Bologna: Cappelli, 1979. Pp. 338.

> Rev. by Patrizia Lombardo in *Friends of George Sand Newsletter* 4,ii (1981): 63-64.

Colombo, Anna, trans. *George Sand* (by Joseph Barry). Milan: Dall'Oglio, 1981.

> Rev. by Italo Vanni in *Il Resto del Carlino*, June 5, 1981.

Courrier, Jean, and Jean-Hervé Donnard, eds. *Le Péché de Monsieur Antoine*. Paris: L'Aurore, 1982. Pp. 416. Fr. 160.00; Fr. 83.00 paper.

Courrier, Nicole, and Thierry Bodin, eds. *Horace*. Paris: L'Aurore, 1982. Pp. 398. Fr. 80.00.

> Rev. by R. Bourgeois in *Présence de George Sand* 14 (1982): 55-56.

Didier, Béatrice. *L'Ecriture-femme*. (Ecriture.) Paris: Presses universitaires de France, 1981. Pp. 288.

> Rev. by Claude Coustou in *NRF* 352 (May 1982): 135-36; by Diane de Margerie in *QL* 360 (Dec. 1-15, 1981): 15.

Espinosa, Maria, ed. and trans. *Lélia*. Foreword by Ellen Moers. Indiana University Press, 1982. $12.50; $5.95 paper.

Friends of George Sand Newsletter (Hofstra University) 4,ii (1981).

> Contents: Georges Lubin, "George Sand voyageuse" (3-9); Joseph Barry, "Marx, Freud and a Touch of Einstein: Or Writing George Sand's Biography" (10-13); Gérard Roubichou, "En relisant George Sand: notes sur *Adriani*" (14-15); Albert Sonnenfeld, "George Sand: Music and Sexualities" (16); Mireille Bossis, "La correspondance" (17-19); Dorothy Zimmerman, "George Sand and the Feminists of the 1830's and 1840's in France (Part I)" (20-24); Lucy M. Schwartz, "Feminism in George Sand's Early Novels (Part II)" (25); Pierrette Daly, "George Sand: écrire au féminin" (26-28); Alex Szogyi, "The Dramas of George Sand" (29-34); Marie-

Jacques Hoog, "Un art poétique sandien (Part I)" (35-37);
Isabelle Naginski, "George Sand's Poetics (Part II)" (38-
41); Thelma Jurgrau, "Translation of George Sand's Auto-
biography" (42-45); Sergine Dixon, "L'esthétique du roman
Les Maîtres Sonneurs" (46-48); Nancy Rogers, "Mauprat et
Jeanne, Prelude to the Pastoral Novel: Myth, Allusion and
Education" (49-51); Timberlake Wertenbaker, "Variations:
The Life of George Sand" (52-61); "Angelina Bianchini, Voce
Donna, Momenti strutturali dell'emancipazione femminile,
rev. by Antoinette Roubichou" (62); "George Sand, Lettere,
rev. by Patrizia Lombardo" (63-64); "Evelyne Sullerot,
Women on Love: Eight Centuries of Feminine Writing, rev.
by Marie M. Collins" (65-66); "Giorgio Albertazzi, George
Sand, rev. by Annarosa Poli" (67-68); "Miscellany" (69-78).
This issue, devoted to the George Sand workshops held at
the University of Tours, June 11-16, 1981, in addition to
many brief articles of varying importance presents an
original play about George Sand (Wertenbaker), summaries
of papers (Sonnenfeld, Schwartz), and a report on the re-
cruitment of translators for L'Histoire de ma vie (Jurgrau).
Among the major contributions are Lubin's chronology of
George Sand's many travels and his assessment of their
results in George Sand's personal and literary life, Roubichou's analysis of ambiguity as the link between form and
meaning in Adriani, Zimmerman's study of George Sand's
problematic stance vis-à-vis the politically active feminist
groups of her time, and Szogyi's descriptive overview of
George Sand's plays that sees each as a reflection of one
of her own personal myths. Other papers treat George Sand's
works on a theoretical level (Daly, Bossis), on a general
plane (Hoog, Naginski), or as individual texts (Dixon,
Rogers). (M.E.B.)

Friends of George Sand Newsletter (Hofstra University) 5,i
(1982).

Contents: Alex Szogyi, trans., "Excerpts from George
Sand's Lucrezia Floriani" (3-14); Francis Steegmuller,
"George Sand and Alexis de Tocqueville: A Meeting" (15-16);
George Sand, "Lettre sur Salammbô" (17-19); Louis Le
Guillou, "George Sand and Lamennais" (20-22); Louis Le
Guillou, "Brève chronologie des relations George Sand-
Lamennais" (23); Peter Byrne, "The Lamennais Bicentenary:
1782-1982" (24-26); Dominique Desanti, "Flora Tristan:
The Pioneer of French Feminism" (27-30); Nancy Rogers, "An
Interview with Gisela Spies-Schientz" (31-32); Livia Linden,
"'A Room of Charlotte Gusay's Own': An Interview" (33-34);
Alastair Maitland, "Letter from Paris: 'Plush Garter and

Bluestocking'" (35-36); Alex Szogyi, "The Sandistes in and
Around Tours--A Memoir" (37-40); Thelma Jurgrau, "Histoire
de ma vie: A Group Translation" (41-44); "Georges Lubin, ed.,
Correspondance, Vol. XV, rev. by Marie-Jacques Hoog" (45-46);
"Alphonse Jacobs, ed., Gustave Flaubert-George Sand,
Correspondance, rev. by Francis Steegmuller" (47-48);
"Louis Le Guillou, ed., Félicité de Lamennais, Correspon-
dance, rev. by Peter Byrne" (49-50); "James Smith Allen,
Popular French Romanticism, rev. by Peter Byrne" (51);
"Conférences, Conventions, Colloquia" (52-64).

The articles in this issue fall into three categories:
the publication or translation of documents relating to
George Sand (Szogyi, Steegmuller); descriptive papers tying
in to the Lamennais bicentenary (Le Guillou, Byrne); and
reports of cultural activities relevant to Sandistes
(Desanti, Rogers, Linden, Maitland, Szogyi, Jurgrau).

The George Sand Papers: Conference Proceedings, 1978.
(Hofstra University Center for Cultural and Intercultural
Studies, 2.) New York: AMS Press, 1982. Pp. ix+241. $27.50.

Contents: Germaine Brée, "Préface" (vii-ix); Helen Laird,
"George Sand: Social Historian and Poet" (3-11); Carol V.
Richards, "Structural Motifs and Limits of Feminism in
Indiana" (12-20); Marilyn Yalom, "Dédoublement in the Fiction
of George Sand" (21-31); Janis Glasgow, "The Use of Doubles
in George Sand's Jacques" (32-48); Michael Danahy, "Growing
Up Female: George Sand's View in La Petite Fadette" (49-58);
Tatiana Greene, "Women and Madness in the Works of George
Sand" (59-69); Lucy M. Schwartz, "Persuasion and Resistance:
Human Relations in George Sand's Novels" (70-76); Pierrette
Daly, "The Fantastic in Consuelo" (77-82); Marie-Jacques
Hoog, "George Sand: Etre/Paraître (To Be/To Appear)" (83-
92); Alex Szogyi, trans., "Preface to the Prologue of Les
Mississipiens" (93-121); Eve Sourian, "Madame de Staël and
George Sand" (122-29); Nancy E. Rogers, "George Sand and
Honoré de Balzac: Stylistic Similarities" (130-43); Nadia
Coiner, "National Chauvinism and Male Chauvinism: The
British Critics React to George Sand" (144-52); Thelma
Jurgrau, "George Sand's Attitude Towards the English" (153-
60); Robert Godwin-Jones, "George Sand, Charlotte Brontë
and the Industrial Novel" (161-70); Marie-Jeanne Pécile,
"George Sand et l'Amérique" (171-79); Carole Karp, "George
Sand in the Estimate of the Russian 'Men of the Forties'"
(180-88); Gaylord Brynolfson, "Works on George Sand, 1964-
80: A Bibliography" (189-234); "Index" (235-41).

The papers in this second volume from the George Sand
seminar at Hofstra University fall under two main headings:

those devoted to the psychology, style, and content of
George Sand's work, and those centered on the relationship
of her life and work to those of other French, English,
American, and Russian writers. Within these broad categories
a wide variety of approaches prevails. Some studies offer
a feminist slant on George Sand's writings (Richards, Danahy,
Greene); some explore her use of doubles or the fantastic
(Yalom, Glasgow, Daly); some analyze techniques of charac-
terization, narration, or description (Laird, Schwartz,
Hoog). Others give comparatist readings (Sourian, Rogers)
or belong to comparative literary history (Coiner, Jurgrau,
Godwin-Jones, Pécile, Karp). There is a translation (Szogyi)
and a bibliography of 485 additional works on George Sand
(Brynolfson). A collection of essays that is solid and
vigorous in its recognition of George Sand's importance.
(M.E.B.)

Giulietti, Maria Antonietta. "Difendo Chopin." *Il Resto del
Carlino*, June 21, 1981.

Polemical letter addressed to Italo Vanni and Vanni's
response defending his claim that Chopin suffered from
latent homosexuality.

Livingston, Beverly. "George Sand and Flora Tristan." *Topic*
35 (1981): 38-44.

Morgan, Natasha. *By George!*

A play. Rev. in *TLS*, Dec. 3, 1982, p. 1336.

OEuvres complètes. 35 vols. Geneva: Slatkine, 1982. Pp. 35,000.

La Petite Fadette. (Bibliothèque de Prestige.) Paris: Garnier,
1982. Fr. 124.80.

Piazza, Maria, and Paola Spazzali-Forti, trans. *Storia della
mia vita*. La Tartaruga, 1981.

Rev. by Maria Brunelli in *Il Giornale*, June 12, 1981;
by Leda Di Malta in *Grazia*, June 26, 1981.

Présence de George Sand 13 (1982).

Contents: Jean-Hervé Donnard, "S/B" (2-3); Thierry Bodin,
"George Sand and Balzac: Histoire d'une amitié" (4-21);
"Petite bibliographie balzaco-sandienne" (22); Arlette
Michel, "Musique et poésie: Hoffmann, Sand et Balzac"
(23-31); Pierre Citron, "Postérité de *Sarrasine* chez George

Sand?" (32-35); Georges Lubin, "De qui ce compte rendu d'*In-diana*?" (36-37); Jean-Hervé Donnard, "A propos du *Péché de M. Antoine*: Sand, Balzac et les marginaux" (38-42); Jo Vareille, "George Sand à la télévision" (43); Simone Czapek, "Le Téléfilm de *La Ville noire*" (44-45); Jean Courrier, "Impression sur *La Ville noire*" (46); Annarosa Poli, "George Sand à la télévision italienne" (47); "Nohant" (48); Jean Pons and Yves Prayer, "*Les Maîtres Sonneurs* au CES d'Echirolles" (50-53); "Georges Lubin répond" (54); "Les auteurs parlent de leur livre: *Histoire de la Châtre-en-Berry* par Jean Gaultier" (55); "Lu (Comptes rendus de Georges Lubin, René Bourgeois, Jean Courrier)" (56-59); V. Del Litto, "A travers les catalogues" (60-62); Mireille Parise, "Bibliographie" (63); Jean Courrier, "Informations" (64-65).

Relationships between George Sand and Balzac form the basis for the studies in this issue. Bodin details the highlights of this long-lived literary friendship; other Balzacians--contributors to the recent Pléiade edition of *La Comédie humaine*--join Lubin in examining some of the intellectual meeting grounds for the two authors, whose individuality emerges all the more forcefully for having undergone comparison on specific issues. (M.E.B.)

Présence de George Sand 14 (1982).

Contents: Jean Lavédrine, "De *La Ville noire* à *L'Auberge rouge*" (2-4); "*L'Auberge rouge* (L'Affiche)" (3); Thierry Bodin, "*L'Auberge rouge*: Présentation" (4-9); *L'Auberge rouge* (10-43); Marie-Louise Hermitte, "Les '*Auberge rouge*'" (44-45); Nadine Lemoine-Guéry, "La femme froide chez H. de Balzac et George Sand" (46-52); "Georges Lubin répond" (53-54); "Marc Baroli, *La Vie quotidienne en Berry au temps de George Sand*, rev. by Jean Courrier" (55); "Suzanne Sens, *Chopin*, rev. by Marie-Paul Rambeau" (55); "Nicole Courrier, ed., *Horace*, rev. by R. Bourgeois" (55-56); "Philippe Berthier, ed., *Contes d'une grand-mère*, rev. by R. Bourgeois" (57); Jo Vareille, "George Sand à la télévision" (58); V. Del Litto, "A travers les catalogues" (59); Jean Courrier, "Bibliographie" (61); Jean Courrier, "Informations" (62).

An issue centered on the text of George Sand's previously unpublished melodrama first enacted at Nohant in 1859. Bodin lists the play's sources, gives manuscript corrections, and recounts the play's representation; Hermitte gives a bibliography of works featuring "auberges rouges"; Lemoine-Guéry continues exploring the literary relationships between Balzac and George Sand by comparing the female protagonists of *La Peau de chagrin* and of the first version of *Lélia*; finally, Lubin replies briefly to several queries concerning George Sand's works.

Présence de George Sand 15 (1982).

Contents: René Bourgeois, "Correspondances" (2-3); La
Correspondance retrouvée: Georges Lubin, "Présentation"
(4); Georges Lubin, "Quarante-quatre lettres inédites"
(5-49); "Table des correspondants" (50); "Georges Lubin
répond" (52); Alex Szogyi, "Activités sandistes aux Etats-
Unis" (54); "Table des illustrations" (55); V. Del Litto,
"A travers les catalogues" (56-58); Jean Courrier, "Bibliographie" (59).

Forty-four previously unpublished letters written by
George Sand between 1820 and 1860, selected by Georges
Lubin for the wide range of their dates of composition,
for the variety of their themes (friendship, politics,
humor, literary ideas or influences), and for the diversity
of their recipients (Jane Bazouin, Eugène Delacroix, Eugène
Lambert, and more than thirty others).

Ronte, Liselotte, trans. *Sie und er*. Munich: Winkler, 1982.
Pp. 256. Fr. 29.80.

Schaeffer, Gérald. *Espace et temps chez George Sand*.
(Langages.) Neuchâtel: A la Baconnière, 1981. Pp. 148.
Fr. 70.00.

Contents: "Avant-dire de Marc Eigeldinger" (7-11);
"George Sand voyageuse" (13-32); "'Nature' chez George
Sand: une lecture de *Mauprat*" (33-49); "*Consuelo*, le temps
et l'espace, lieux symboliques et personnages" (51-73);
"*Laura, voyage dans un cristal*" (75-116); "Nerval et Gautier"
(117-40); "Nerval et Texier, ou de Pérégrinus à Olibrius"
(141-47); "Notice bibliographique" (148).

In this posthumous collection of previously published
essays, Schaeffer studies mythical structures and textual
strategies. He concludes, in "George Sand voyageuse," that
George Sand's imagery assimilates travel to the interior
journey toward the ideal world of childhood and toward
the source of imaginative powers. "Nature chez George
Sand" is a reading of the reticences and focalizations out
of which George Sand creates the rhetorical construct of
nature (both human and exterior) with which she explores
esthetically the relationship between liberty and fatality.
The essay on *Consuelo* sees the novel's complex architecture
as one of repetitions, reflections, and "emboîtements"
refusing to oversimplify the problem of how an individual
comes to be conscious of his own particular destiny. *Laura*
is also a voyage of initiation, one where the two heroes,
far from condemning what is fantastic, succeed in integrating

it into their daily lives; Schaeffer's analysis points up
the traditional aspects of Laura's romanticism and, at the
same time, underscores the originality of its structure.
(M.E.B.)

Siganos, André. "Sur Hoffmann et George Sand: L'Histoire du
véritable Gribouille et L'Enfant étranger." RLC 56 (1982):
92-95.

Numerous points of comparison between the two texts show
that both authors sought to be rigorous yet extravagant
in their use of the imagination.

Singer, Armand E., Mary W. Singer, and Janice S. Spleth, eds.
West Virginia George Sand Conference Papers. Department of
Foreign Languages, West Virginia University, 1981. Pp. 111.
$7.50.

Contents: Joseph Barry, "Sand, Héloïse, and Beauvoir: On
Children, Family, and the Couple" (1-10); Georges Lubin,
"George Sand and America" (11-21); Pierrette Daly, "The
Problem of Language in Sand's Indiana" (22-27); Sharon L.
Fairchild, "Political and Historical Events in George Sand's
Correspondance (1812-June 1835)" (28-36); Thelma Jurgrau,
"George Sand and Education: The Mythic Pattern in Three
Works" (37-44); Sylvie L.F. Richards, "A Psychoanalytic
Study of the Double in the Novels of George Sand" (45-53);
Pierre-Edmond Robert, "George Sand's Presence in Proust's
A la recherche du temps perdu" (54-60); Nancy Rogers,
"George Sand and Germaine de Staël: The Novel as Subversion"
(61-74); Enid M. Standring, "George Sand and the Romantic
Composers of France" (75-84); Erdmute Wenzel-White, "George
Sand: She Who Is Man & Woman Together" (85-95); Dora J.
Wilson, "George Sand's Musical Aesthetic" (96-104); Dorothy
Zimmerman, "George Sand and La Dame à la licorne Tapestries"
(105-11).

The two keynote papers of the conference are Barry's,
which examines against a historical background the ways
George Sand puts marriage into question without abandoning
maternalism, and Lubin's, which reviews George Sand's relations with the America she never visited. A number of papers
offer literary analyses spanning different approaches: Fairchild surveys instances in George Sand's early letters where
she demonstrates the liberal sympathies that later would
develop into republicanism and social utopianism; Jurgrau
studies the conversion from brutality to sensitivity of a
youth raised outside culture in three of George Sand's
works; Richards argues that the unifying structure of the

double allows George Sand to express her creative anxieties
in the quest for her own ideal "moi"; in addition to assess-
ing the place of *François le champi* in Proust's novel,
Robert sees George Sand's art as a forerunner of certain
Proustian techniques. Another set of papers gives a feminist
interpretation of George Sand: Daly analyzes the effects
had on the narrator and characters of *Indiana* by the convention that a novel's narrator must be male in order to claim
objectivity; Rogers formulates the thesis that in *Corinne*
and in *Indiana* a new value system grounded in love, peace,
and tranquility comes to take precedence over patriarchal
principles of wealth, power, and rank; Wenzel-White maintains that since George Sand made the traditional limitations
imposed on women work for her, she can be but a failed
feminist. A final group of essays links George Sand to music
and art: Standring seeks to determine from George Sand's
writings how she may have aided the French public's recognition of Berlioz and Meyerbeer; Wilson focuses on how George
Sand's works reflect certain aspects of her attraction to
music; Zimmerman examines George Sand's taste and judgment
in the visual arts as revealed in her writings on the Uni-
corn Tapestries from 1844 to 1871. On the whole, a lively
and diversified contribution to the study of George Sand.
(M.E.B.)

Wolfzettel, Friedrich. "Proletarier in bürgerlicher Perspektive: Zum Problem der Erzählhaltung im französischen Sozial-
roman des 19. Jahrhunderts." *GRM* 30 (1980): 73-92.

See also Biermann, Garavini, Jordan, Luciani, Mozet ("French
1. General").

Reviews of books previously listed:

ATWOOD, William G., *The Lioness and the Little One* (see
RMB for 1981, p. 230), rev. by L.J. Austin in *FS* (1982):
80-82; BALAYÉ, Simone, ed., *Journal intime* (see *RMB* for
1981, p. 230), rev. by Georges Lubin in *Présence de George
Sand* 13 (1982): 59; *The George Sand Papers: Conference
Proceedings, 1976* (see *RMB* for 1980, pp. 234-35), rev. by
L.J. Austin in *FS* 36 (1982): 80-82; JACOBS, Alphonse, ed.,
Gustave Flaubert, George Sand, Correspondance (see *RMB* for
1981, p. 233), rev. by René Bourgeois in *Présence de
George Sand* 13 (1982): 57; by Jacques Neefs in *Romantisme*
36 (1982): 109-11; by Francis Steegmuller in *Friends of
George Sand Newsletter* 5,i (1982): 47-48; LACCASAGNE,
Jean-Pierre, ed., *Mauprat* (see *RMB* for 1981, p. 233), rev.

by Jean Courrier in *Présence de George Sand* 13 (1982): 58-
59; LACASSIN, Francis, ed., *Le Chêne parlant* (see *RMB* for
1981, p. 233), rev. by Jean Courrier in *Présence de George
Sand* 13 (1982): 57; LUBIN, Georges, ed., *Correspondance*,
T. XIV (see *RMB* for 1980, p. 236), rev. by Jean Chalon, *Le
Figaro*, Apr. 2, 1982; LUBIN, Georges, ed., *Correspondance*,
T. XV (see *RMB* for 1981, p. 234), rev. by L.J. Austin in
FS 36 (1982): 80-82; by Marie-Jacques Hoog in *Friends of
George Sand Newsletter*, 5,i (1982): 45-46; by Annarosa
Poli in *SFr* 26 (1982): 163; MAILLON, Jean, and Pierre
Salomon, eds., *Les Maîtres Sonneurs* (see *RMB* for 1981, p.
234), rev. by René Bourgeois in *Présence de George Sand* 13
(1982): 58; RHEAULT, Raymond, ed., *Mademoiselle de Merquem*
(see *RMB* for 1981, p. 235), rev. by Georges Lubin in
Présence de George Sand 13 (1982): 56-57; SALOMON, Pierre,
and Jean Maillon, eds., *La Mare au diable; François le champi*
(see *RMB* for 1981, p. 236), rev. by René Bourgeois in
Présence de George Sand 13 (1982): 58; SALOMON, Pierre,
and Jean Maillon, eds., *La Petite Fadette* (see *RMB* for 1981,
p. 236), rev. by René Bourgeois in *Présence de George Sand*
13 (1982): 58.

SCHOELCHER

Adélaïde-Merlande, Jacques, ed. *Vie de Toussaint-Louverture*.
(Relire.) Paris: Karthala, 1982. Pp. 460. Fr. 75.00.

SCRIBE

Centre d'Etudes et de Recherches théâtrales et cinématographiques
Organon 82: Théâtres du XIXe siècle. *Scribe, Labiche, Dumas-
Sartre*. Université de Lyon II, 1982. Pp. 252. Fr. 50.00.

Relevant contents: Michel Corbin, "De Scribe à Sartre";
Eugène Scribe, "*Une Répétition générale*, pièce inédite";
Jean-Pierre Devoine, "*Une Répétition générale*, parodie
polémique"; Jean Gilardeau, "De Scribe à Labiche"; Michel
Pruner, "Sur le 'Kean' de Sartre, approche d'une théorie
de l'acteur selon Sartre."

Pendle, Karin. *Scribe and the French Opera of the Nineteenth
Century*. (Studies in Musicology, 6.) Ann Arbor: UMI Research
Press, 1979. Pp. vi+627.

Reviews of book previously listed:

KOON, Helene, and Richard Switzer, *Eugène Scribe* (see *RMB*
for 1981, p. 238), rev. by Fernande Bassan in *NCFS* 9 (1981):
278-79; by Maurice Descotes in *RHL* 82 (1982): 492-93; by
Louise Fiber Luce in *French Forum* 7 (1982): 80-81; by John
R. Williams in *FR* 56 (1982-83): 322-23.

SENANCOUR

Didier, Béatrice. "Senancour et la description romantique."
Poétique 51 (1982): 315-28.

Situates Senancour within modern theories of description
as well as within the framework of literary history, then
gives astute analyses of descriptive styles and themes in
Les Rêveries, Les Méditations, Obermann, and *Isabelle.*
(M.E.B.)

Walser, Jürg Peter. "Stapfer, Liszt und Senancour: Zwei Kon-
junktionen in Kunst und Politik." *SchM* 62 (1982): 41-52.

See also Raoul ("French 1. General").

SISMONDI

Laibier, Patrick de, ed. *Quatre Études sur la politique et
le développement économique.* Vevey: Delta; Paris: Masson,
1981. Pp. 106.

Sofia, Francesca. "Sul pensiero politico-costituzionale del
giovane Sismondi." *Rassegna Storica del Risorgimento* 68
(1981): 131-48.

See résumé by Carlo Cordié in *SFr* 26 (1982): 159.

Waeber, Paul. "A propos d'une réédition: la place du *Tableau
de l'agriculture toscane* dans l'oeuvre du jeune Sismondi."
Musées de Genève, Jan. 1981, pp. 7-12.

See also Antoine, Gregory, Lafont ("French 1. General");
Angrisani Guerrini ("Quinet"); *Cahiers staëliens* 29-30
("Staël").

Review of book previously listed:

STELLING-MICHAUD, Sven, ed., *Sismondi européen* (see *ELN* 15, Supp., 139), rev. by Kurt Kloocke in *O&C* 6,i (1981): 141-43.

STAEL

Cahiers Staëliens 29-30 (1981).

Contents: Victor de Pange, "Hommage à Pierre Cordey" (1); Simone Balayé, "Pierre Cordey: Le Constantien et le Staëlien" (2-4); Philippe Carton, "Sur les traces de Madame de Staël à Vienne, en Bohême et en Moravie" (5-10); Arnaud Tripet, "Madame de Staël et la rêverie italienne" (11-29); Nicolas Sombart, "De Madame de Staël à Charles Fourier" (31-62); Brian Rodgers, "Charles Nodier lecteur de Madame de Staël" (63-76); Benjamin Constant, "Lettres à Louis-Ferdinand et à Thérèse Huber, 1798-1806, p.p. Etienne Hofmann" (77-122); Madame de Staël, "Deux lettres inédites, p.p. John Rogister" (123-28); Marie-Claude Jequier, "A propos de F.-C. de La Harpe et de Madame de Staël" (129-36); Norman King, "Quelques lettres d'Auguste et d'Albertine de Staël à Sismondi" (137-54); Paul Delbouille, "Une edition d'*Adolphe* à Vienne en 1817" (155-57); "Madame de Staël, Une lettre inédite à Elisabeth Hervey, duchesse de Devonshire, p.p. Victor de Pange" (159-66); "Comptes rendus" (167-78).

Along with tributes to Pierre Cordey (Pange, Balayé), the report of a trip made by the Société (Carton), and the publication of several new documents concerning Mme de Staël (Hofmann, Rogister, Jequier, King, Delbouille, Pange), this rich issue contains three studies conducted from the point of view of literary history. Tripet examines the role of reverie in the interplay between love, eroticism, and feminism in *Corinne*. Taking as his point of departure a little-known letter from Mme de Staël to Charles Fourier, Sombart explores the possible connections between the two theorists of perfect society. Rodgers' reading of Nodier's articles on *De l'Allemagne* concludes that Nodier's ambivalent stance is but a reflection of the mixed reaction Mme de Staël's work continued to produce in the 1820s. (M.E.B.)

Cordié, Carlo. "L'abate Savereo Scrofani e i corrispondenti del *Viaggio in Grecia*: con alcune note su Madame de Staël e il *Paragone delle donne francesi con le italiane*." *La Rassegna della Letteratura Italiana* 1 (1981).

Corredor, Eva. "Madame de Staël: Romanticism and Femininity."
Papers in Romance (University of Washington, Seattle) 2
(1980): 105-10.

A feminist interpretation of how four powerful men—Necker,
Napoleon, J.-J. Rousseau, Benjamin Constant—influenced
Madame de Staël's destiny as a woman and a writer.

Denis, Andrée. "Poésie populaire, poésie nationale: deux
intercesseurs: Fauriel et Madame de Staël." Romantisme
35 (1982): 3-24.

Although De l'Allemagne contains no chapter on popular
poetry, Mme de Staël's book had an important role in the
nineteenth century's awakened interest in popular culture,
for it purveyed ideas of the German Romantics taken up and
developed by the historian of popular Provençal and Greek
poetry, Fauriel.

Goldberger, Avriel H. "Corinne Refuses Oswald, from Corinne,
by Madame de Staël." FAR 6 (1982): 31-51.

English translation of Book XIV, chapters 1-4, with brief
introduction.

Hartman, Elwood. "Madame de Staël, the Quarrel of the Ancients
and the Moderns, and the Idea of Progress." Research Studies
(Washington State University) 50 (1982): 33-45.

This description of Mme de Staël's ideas concludes that
she "serves as a bridge between two generations. She continues the philosophic outlook of the eighteenth century and
summarizes the basic concept of the pre-revolutionary parti-
sans of progress. She announces the Romantic point of view
in calling for liberty in the arts, the rejuvenation of
literature by the inclusion of new sources and the cessation
of imitation" (44).

Hofmann, Etienne, ed. Benjamin Constant, Madame de Staël et
le groupe de Coppet. Actes du deuxième congrès de Lausanne
et du troisième colloque de Coppet (15-18 juillet 1980).
Université de Lausanne, Institut Benjamin Constant, 1982.

Holý, Jiří. "Les opinions esthétiques de Madame de Staël et
les conceptions des premiers romantiques allemands."
Philologica Pragensia 25 (1982): 18-25.

A comparison of certain key ideas about art indicating
that the discovery of German Romanticism awoke French literature to consciousness of its own values.

Hrbata, Zdeněk. "'De la littérature' de Madame de Staël."
   Philologica Pragensia 25 (1982): 1-12.

   An exposition of the main tenets of Mme de Staël's treatise
   that concludes: "le système de théories et la valeur des
   notions adoptées--l'univers du raisonnement clair et consé-
   quent des Lumières--s'y voient toujours confrontés à l'authen-
   ticité du vécu qui rectifie souvent le système et le fait
   s'ouvrir à la réalité qui s'impose" (11).

Procházka, Martin. "Les opinions esthétiques des romantiques
   anglais et 'De la littérature.'" *Philologica Pragensia* 25
   (1982): 12-18.

   Highlights the differences between Mme de Staël's esthetics
   and those of Wordsworth, Hazlitt, and Shelley.

Rosso, C. "L'impossible féminisme de Madame de Staël." Pp.
   82-85 in *Mythe de l'égalité et rayonnement des Lumières*.
   Pisa: Editrice Libreria Goliardica, 1980.
   Rev. by Carlo Cordié in *SFr* 26 (1982): 158-59.

Tripet, Arnaud. "Madame de Staël et la rêverie italienne."
   Saggi 19 (1980): 293-319.

Vallois, Marie-Claire. "Les Voi(es) de la Sibylle: aphasie
   et discours féminin chez Madame de Staël." *SFR* 6,i (1982):
   35-48.

   The feminine subject becomes a constant object for censure,
   fragmentation, and alienation in the play of narrative
   voices in *Zulma* and *La Folle de la forêt de Sénart*. So marked
   by aphasia is the feminine voice that it must rely upon the
   presence of a male narrator; this dependence creates narrative strategies that, in *Corinne*, express woman's impossible
   autonomy in the face of society and its discourse.

Wais, Kurt. *Europäische Literatur im Vergleich*. Ed. Johannes
   Hösle, Wolfgang Theile, and Dieter Janik. Tübingen: Niemeyer, 1982.

   Includes a chapter on Madame de Staël.

See also Antoine ("French 1. General"); *Annales Benjamin
   Constant* 2 ("Constant, B."); *The George Sand Papers*,
   Singer ("Sand").

Reviews of books previously listed:

BALAYÉ, Simone, Madame de Staël: Lumières et liberté (see
RMB for 1979, p. 227), rev. by Jacques Godechot in AHRF
248 (1982): 307-11; by Etienne Hofmann in EdL ii (Apr.-
June 1982): 118-21; by Norman King in CahiersS 29-30
(1981): 169-78; by Kurt Kloocke in Annales Benjamin Constant
2 (1982): 123-28; D'ANDLAU, Béatrix, Madame de Staël, Don
Pedro de Souza, Correspondance (see RMB for 1980, p. 243),
rev. by Simone Balayé in CahiersS 29-30 (1981): 167; GUT-
WIRTH, Madelyn, Madame de Staël, Novelist (see RMB for
1979, p. 228), rev. by Norman King in CahiersS 29-30
(1981): 169-78; JASINSKI, Béatrice, ed., Correspondance
générale, T. IV, 1ère partie (see ELN 15, Supp., 130),
rev. by Jean Gaulmier in RHL 82 (1982): 668-70; JASINSKI,
Béatrice, ed., Correspondance générale, T. IV, 2e partie
(see RMB for 1979, p. 229), rev. by Norman King in CahiersS
29-30 (1981): 169-78; OMACINI, Lucia, ed., Des Circonstances
actuelles qui peuvent terminer la révolution (see RMB for
1979, p. 229), rev. by Jacques Godechot in AHRF 247 (Jan.-
Mar. 1982): 153-56; by Etienne Hofmann in EdL ii (Apr.-
June 1982): 118-21; by Norman King in CahiersS 29-30 (1981):
169-78; PANGE, Victor de, Le Plus Beau de toutes les fêtes
(see RMB for 1981, p. 241), rev. by Simone Balayé in CahiersS
29-30 (1981): 168-69; SOLOVIEFF, Georges, Madame de Staël:
choix de textes (see ELN 14, Supp., 100), rev. by Simone
Balayé in RHL 82 (1982): 126; TODD, Janet, Women's Friendship in Literature (see RMB for 1980, p. 244), rev. by
Douglas Brooks-Davies in MLR 77 (1982): 150-53; by Ruth
Perry in PQ 60 (1982): 424-25; by Susan Rava in FR 55
(1981-82): 896-97.

STENDHAL

Albert, Mechthild. "Le regard d'autrui: lecture ontologique
d'une obsession stendhalienne." SC 24 (1981-82): 344-55.

     Using Sartre's analysis of autrui, Albert comments per-
ceptively on the function of regard in Armance, "Les Cenci,"
and La Chartreuse de Parme. (E.J.T.)

Backus, David. "Opera Made to Order." Opera News 46,xv (Mar.)
13, 1982): 12-13, 38.

     On Stendhal's Vie de Rossini.

Backus, David. "Stendhal et Proust." SC 24 (1981-82): 258-
64.

This essay is divided in two parts: (1) Backus sees possible reminiscences of Stendhal in several passages in Proust, but the *rapprochement* is not altogether convincing; (2) Backus sees the painter Ernest Hébert, who had known Stendhal in Rome and who later knew Proust in Paris, as a possible link between the two novelists. (E.J.T.)

Baehr, Rudolph. "1809, l'année autrichienne de Stendhal." *SC* 24 (1981-82): 356-73.

Detailed chronology of Stendhal's year in Austria.

Baudoin, Henri. "Stendhal et Cie." *SC* 25 (1982-83): 1-12.

Discusses a few musical documents which have some pertinence to Stendhal's first visit to Milan. A second section discusses the passage of le comte de Chambord in the Papal States while Henri Beyle was consul at Civitavecchia.

Baudoin, Henri, and Albert Ledoux. "Deux lettres peu connues de Stendhal." *SC* 24 (1981-82): 233-38.

A letter to Durzy (1808) and another to General Michaud (1810).

Berthier, Philippe. "HB, Urbi et Orbi." *Recherches et travaux* (Grenoble) 21 (1981): 7-17.

Comments on the double lie with which Stendhal's *Vie de Henry Brulard* begins: the pretense that the author has just turned fifty and that he is in Rome. The claim to be fifty is explained by the symbolic force of the half-century number; the claim to be at San Pietro in Montorio in Rome becomes understandable when we realize that this spot has a panoramic view of ancient, medieval, and modern Rome and thereby imposes a meditation not only on the passage of time but also on the identity of the self. Raphaël's *Transfiguration*, which plays an important part in this passage, urges reflection on transcendance through art. A solid and intelligent essay. (E.J.T.)

Blueher, Karl Alfred. "L'amour tragique dans les premières nouvelles de Stendhal." *SC* 24 (1981-82): 374-87.

Argues that the four short stories that Stendhal wrote in 1829-30 contain similar sequential structures and thereby a single paradigm: an *amour passion* which releases enormous energy when it meets an obstacle but which leads finally to a tragic end.

Brooks, Peter. "The Novel and the Guillotine; or Fathers and Sons in *Le Rouge et le Noir*." *PMLA* 97 (1982): 348-62.

A perceptive and original essay on an old topic. Taking as his point of departure the fact that paternity is a dominant issue in the nineteenth-century novel, Brooks examines its problematics as it relates to history, politics, and the possibilities and limits of narration. (E.J.T.)

Bryant, David. "Stendhal, la *Vie de Henry Brulard* et les images du passé." *SC* 24 (1981-82): 265-76.

Argues that images in *Vie de Henry Brulard* are consciously structured by Stendhal as a way of evoking "mouvements de l'âme."

Buss, Robin. "Quick on the Draw? Stendhal's Lottery Ticket and Some Early Critics of *Le Rouge et le Noir*." *L&H* 8 (1982): 95-107.

Detailed analysis of an interesting, largely unknown review of *Le Rouge et le noir* written by Anselme Petetin in 1831. Petetin sees *Le Rouge* as a novel firmly integrated in its own time and as dramatizing its conflicting social and ideological currents. Buss sees contemporary criticism of Stendhal's work as a necessary background to our understanding. Solid. (E.J.T.)

Carnevale-Mauzan, Marino. "Stendhal au Pont du Var, ou la poste des occasions manqueés." *Recherches et travaux* (Grenoble) 21 (1981); 47-52.

In 1833 some letters and a package which Stendhal was bringing into Italy were seized by Sardinian officials. Carnevale-Mauzan explains the relevant postal regulations necessary for the understanding of this incident.

Chessex, Robert, and Guy Sheyven. "Les fautes de Clélia." *SC* 24 (1981-82): 291-301.

An exchange of views on Clélia, with Chessex seeing her in a more poetic light.

Chroniken und Novellen, ed. Kurt Wais. Berlin: Propyläen, 1980. Pp. 779.

Rev. by G.M. Moinet in *SC* 24 (1981-82): 481-84. Partially new German translation.

Claudon, Francis. *L'Idée et l'influence de la musique chez
quelques romantiques français et notamment Stendhal*. Atelier
de reproduction de thèses, Université de Lille III, 1979.
Pp. 662.

Rev. by J.M. Bailbé in *RHL* 82 (1982): 133-35; by P.
Berthier in *Romantisme* 35 (1982): 137-39.

Colesanti, Massimo, ed. *Passeggiate romane*. Rome: Edizione
speciale fuori commercio per la Casa di Risparmio di Roma,
1980. Pp. 308; 345.

A new Italian translation of *Promenades dans Rome*, with
introduction and notes.

Crouzet, Michel. "Ecriture et mal du siècle chez Stendhal:
de l'angélisme à l'esprit." Pp. 273-312 in Marc Fumaroli,
ed., *Le Statut de la littérature: mélanges offerts à Paul
Bénichou*. (Histoire des Idées et Critique littéraire, 200.)
Geneva: Droz, 1982. Pp. 372.

Perceptive commentary on a number of issues but particularly
on Stendhal's understanding of writing. The writer or poet
is seen first as an inspired seeker of the happiness of
humanity. Writing is thereby a social activity. It is in
opposition to vanity, money, and work, which are anti-
artistic. But there is also in Stendhal a recognition that
writing cannot be done during a state of passion and that
wit has a place in literature. (E.J.T.)

Crouzet, Michel. "Stendhal et la poétique du fragment." *SC*
24 (1981-82): 157-80.

An important discussion of Stendhal's penchant for brief,
aphoristic, and fragmentary writing. Crouzet points out
that Stendhal's principle of skipping "intermediate ideas"
is a radical departure from the teaching of Destutt de
Tracy and derives primarily from Montesquieu. Stendhal
was aware of the dangers and drawbacks of extreme concision
and did look for a middle ground between the aphorism and
the tirade. But, if he had to err, he preferred to err on
the side of concision. (E.J.T.)

Crouzet, Michel. *Stendhal et l'italianité: essai de mythologie
romantique*. Paris: José Corti, 1982. Pp. 415. Fr. 110.00.

Rev. by V. Del Litto in *SC* 25 (1982-83): 88-90; by G. Spi-
teri in *NL* 2833 (April 22-28, 1982): 50.

Del Bo, Dino. *Le Iscrizioni di Stendhal*. Milan: Vanni Schei-
willer, 1981. Pp. 190. L. 12,000.00.

Its title notwithstanding, this volume contains only one
brief article on Stendhal commenting on his reactions to
inscriptions on monuments, statues, and buildings in Italy.

Del Litto, V. "Bibliographie stendhalienne: année 1981."
SC 25 (1982-83): 102-18.

Del Litto, V. "Stendhal admirateur et disciple du président
de Brosses." Pp. 97-105 in Jean-Claude Garreta, ed., *Charles
de Brosses. 1777-1977. Actes du colloque organisé à Dijon
pour le deuxième centenaire de la mort du président de
Brosses*. (Bibliothèque du Voyage en Italie/Biblioteca del
Viaggio in Italia.) Geneva: Slatkine, 1981. Pp. 280. Sw.Fr.
40.00.

An excellent *mise au point* of Stendhal's debt to de Brosses.
Stendhal admired his *Lettres sur l'Italie* for their attention to mores, their aesthetic preferences, their style,
and their confidential tone. (E.J.T.)

Del Litto, V., ed. *Le Rose et le vert, Mina de Vanghel et
autres nouvelles*. (Folio, 1381.) Paris: Gallimard, 1982.
Pp. 557.

A solid edition, complete with marginalia, notes, and
introduction. (E.J.T.)

Denier, Renée. "Quelques inédits d'Edouard Mounier." *Recherches et Travaux* (Grenoble) 21 (1981): 53-74.

Some unpublished letters by Stendhal's friend relating
to the Russian campaign.

Devos, Willy. "Stendhal en néerlandais: bibliographie 1981."
SC 25 (1982-83): 101.

Works by Stendhal published in Dutch translation and
articles on Stendhal in Dutch.

Doyon, André. "Henri et Pauline Beyle: histoire de la 'cara
sorella' (d'après des documents inédits), III." *SC* 24
(1981-82): 181-99, 239-57.

The second and third chapters of Pauline's life, dealing
with her marriage to François Périer-Lagrange. Suggests
that Pauline may have had a lesbian relationship with
Sophie Gauthier and that her husband's death in 1816 was

a suicide. After this event, Pauline is left destitute and has to be assisted financially by her brother.

Doyon, André, "Henri et Pauline Beyle: histoire de la 'cara sorella' (d'après des documents inédits)." *SC* 25 (1982-83): 25-39.

Argues, convincingly, that Stendhal loved in his sister a female double of himself and proposes that his love for Pauline, as well as his love for Mme Daru, were transfers of affection for his mother. (E.J.T.)

Félix-Faure, Jacques. "Dans l'entourage de Stendhal: Mimi de Bézieux retrouvée (d'après des documents inédits)." *SC* 25 (1982-83): 13-24.

Letters from Joséphine de Bézieux, whom Stendhal briefly courted, to her husband.

Geninasca, Jacques. "L'invention du détail vrai." *SC* 24 (1981-82): 388-402.

An important discussion of the scene of the assassination attempt on Madame de Rênal. In striking the pillar and knocking off some of its plaster, Julien's bullet is metaphorically striking at the pillar of the religious structure of his time. (E.J.T.)

Goebler-Lingens, Hannelore. "Le chapeau de Clélia: à propos des rapports stendhalo-balzaciens." *SC* 24 (1981-82): 403-10.

A discussion of Stendhal's attempts to revise *La Chartreuse* along the lines suggested by Balzac. The addition of a hat in the description of Clélia shows, however, that Stendhal rejects the type of description Balzac had in mind, since for Stendhal the hat becomes not a sign of social status but rather a sentimental object.

Gruen, Ruth. "L'impuissance à parler: aspects du discours et du comportement non verbal dans *Armance*." *SC* 24 (1981-82): 411-23.

Argues that Octave's "impuissance à parler" is really an "impuissance à tout dire."

Guérin, Michel. *La Politique de Stendhal*. Préface de Régis Debray. (La Politique éclatée.) Paris: Presses Universitaires de France, 1982. Pp. 261. Fr. 75.00.

Rev. by V. Del Litto in *SC* 25 (1982-83): 87-88; by J. Garcin in *NL* 2833 (April 22-28, 1982): 51.

Imbert, Henri-François. "De Stendhal à Dostoevskij." *RLC* 55 (1981): 292-305.

Although there is no clear evidence that Dostoevskii ever read Stendhal, Imbert proposes several *rapprochements* between the two: both dealt with the question of self-interest and the need for an interior freedom; both emphasized the importance of the young man's entry into society; both saw the aristocracy as decadent and highlighted the tensions that befall a superior man (Julien and Raskolnikov, for example). While these parallels are not equally convincing, they are suggestive and intriguing. (E.J.T.)

Jansse, Lucien. "Stendhal et l'administration." *SC* 24 (1981-82): 277-82.

Comments on Stendhal as an administrator and presents his views on various French administrations.

Jones, Grahame C. "L'intrusion de l'auteur en particulier dans *Lucien Leuwen*." *SC* 25 (1982-83): 50-66.

Comments on Stendhal's intrusions in the first part of *Lucien Leuwen* and on his use of secondary characters as ironic observers of the activities of the hero.

Liprandi, Claude. "Sur un passage du *Touriste*: du portrait de Madame de Grignace à celui de la 'Marquise de Ganges.'" *SC* 24 (1981-82): 200-06.

Erudite details on the pages in *Mémoires d'un touriste* dealing with Avignon.

Macquet, Albert. "Leopardi et Stendhal." *SC* 25 (1982-83): 79-83.

A reaction to Jean-Michel Gardair's introduction to a French edition of Leopardi's poetry which Macquet considers unfair in its treatment of Stendhal.

Merler, Grazia. "Modalités du discours commentatif dans *La Chartreuse de Parme*." *SC* 24 (1982-83): 283-90.

Stylistic analysis of two descriptive passages in *La Chartreuse*.

Moelk, Ulrich. "Stendhal, die Liebe und das Mittelalter: Bemerkungen zu *De l'Amour*." *SC* 24 (1981-82): 424-34.

On the medieval sources of *De l'Amour*. (See article by Robert Lafont listed in "General" section.)

Moinet, Gisela M. "Sur le théâtre de Stendhal." *SC* 25 (1982-83): 83-85.

Proposes that theater is an important contributing factor to Stendhal's novelistic techniques and reports that her work in progress will show Stendhal's play *Letellier* to be a primary source of *Le Rouge et le noir*.

Pizzorusso, Arnaldo. "Le due stesure di *Lamiel*." *Saggi* 20 (1981): 129-56.

A wide-ranging discussion of the two versions of *Lamiel* with pertinent comments on clothes, education, fantasy, love, and the characters of Lamiel and Sansfin. (E.J.T.)

Rannaud, Gérald. "*Seraphiana*, ou la promenade aux Granges." *Recherches et Travaux* (Grenoble) 21 (1981): 19-45.

Proposes that Stendhal's admission in *Vie de Henry Brulard* of his incestuous love for his mother masks an incestuous desire for his aunt Séraphie. Admitting the oedipal complex regarding his mother is a way of hiding from the reader and from his own conscience another oedipal complex which is repressed because it is intolerable. Rannaud's serious analysis of various texts in *Brulard* lend credence to this hypothesis. An original and provocative essay. (E.J.T.)

Riehn, Christa. "Stendhal en Allemagne: bibliographie 1977-1981." *SC* 24 (1981-82): 459-76.

Ringger, Kurt. "Aspects de l'audience stendhalienne auprès du public germanophone." *SC* 24 (1981-82): 339-43.

An overview of Stendhal's reception in Germanic countries, from Goethe to the present.

Ringger, Kurt. "Le délai fatal: à propos d'une situation stendhalienne dans *La Peau de chagrin*." *SC* 24 (1981-82): 209-11.

Sees Raphael's decision to speak to Foedora within three minutes or else kill himself as a possible influence from *Le Rouge et le noir*.

Rom, Neapel und Florenz im Jahre 1817, ed. Bernhard Frank, and *Racine und Shakespeare*, ed. Carsten Peter Thiede. Berlin: Propyläen, 1980. Pp. 360.

Rev. by G.M. Moinet in *SC* 24 (1981-82): 481-84.
Partially new German translations.

Rosa, George M. "Byronism and 'Babilanism' in *Armance*." *MLR* 77 (1982): 797-814.

An important discussion of the presence of Byron and Byronism in *Armance*. Rosa proposes that the initial reason why Stendhal obscured the real situation of his protagonist is that Octave is cast in the mold of Byronic heroes whose secrets are almost never revealed. Moreover, Octave's contempt for human passion and his vows never to fall in love are commonplace characteristics of the Byronic hero. "Once the Olivier scandal gave him the root idea of the book," Rosa contends, "the themes and style of Byron's Romantic poetry provided a ready-made vehicle for describing how a man might behave if burdened by Octave's secret affliction." (E.J.T.)

Russell, Lois Ann. "Les jeux de l'écriture dans la *Chartreuse de Parme*." *SC* 25 (1982-83): 67-77.

A survey of the instances of written communication in *La Chartreuse*. Russell's conclusion that the novel can be placed in the tradition of epistolary novels appears to be exaggerated, however. (E.J.T.)

Saraydar, Alma. *Proust disciple de Stendhal: les avant-textes d'"Un Amour de Swann" dans "Jean Santeuil."* (Archives des Lettres Modernes, 191.) Paris: Minard (Lettres Modernes), 1980. Pp. 88.

Rev. by D. Backus in *NCFS* 10 (1981-82): 368-39; by V. Del Litto in *SC* 24 (1981-82): 322-23.

Schellekens, Oscar. "En marge de *Lucien Leuwen*: l'origine lorraine du nom 'Chasteler.'" *SC* 24 (1981-82): 304-08.

Historical information on the Chasteler family into which Stendhal chose to place the heroine of *Lucien Leuwen*.

Seylaz, Jean-Luc. "L'effet Cimarosa dans les romans stendhaliens." *SC* 25 (1982-83): 40-49.

Discusses several passages in *Le Rouge* and *La Chartreuse* which manifest what Seylaz calls a "Cimarosa effect," that is, a mix of comedy and tenderness.

Stivale, Charles J. "Ordre et duration: la structuration temporelle d'*Armance*." *SC* 24 (1981-82): 141-56.

Detailed study of the temporal structure of Stendhal's first novel, with particular attention to Stendhal's use of analepsis.

272   French / 2. Studies of Authors

Uchida, Yoshitako. "Le vocabulaire du cheval." *SC* 24 (1981-82): 126-40.

Statistical study of *cheval* and related words in Stendhal's work. Stendhal used the word most frequently in the period 1799-1814, but in general the frequency of his usage is considerably above average for the entire period of his writing.

Wais, Kurt. "Stendhal zwischen Novelle und Roman: Mina de Vanghel und ihre Schwestern." *SC* 24 (1981-82): 435-49.

Stendhal realized his ideal of feminine heroism in his short fiction.

Weiand, Christof. "En marge de *Lucien Leuwen*: 'L'Orange de Malte:' titre ou énigme." *SC* 24 (1981-82): 450-58.

Wieland suggests that Stendhal first chose *L'Orange de Malte* as the title of his third novel because he was aware that the expression sometimes refers to money, which plays an important role in this novel. Stendhal's readings of Galiani probably suggested the use of the expression in this way.

See also Miller ("General 3. Criticism"); L'Accademia delle Scienze di Torino, Curtis, Lafont, Luciani, Mozet, Wald Lasowski ("French 1. General").

Reviews of books previously listed:

ALTER, Robert, *A Lion for Love* (see *RMB* for 1979, p. 230), rev. by G.M. Rosa in *FR* 55 (1981-82): 412; ATTUEL, Josiane, *Le Style de Stendhal* (see *RMB* for 1981, p. 242), rev. by L. Le Guillou in *Romantisme* 36 (1982): 107-08; CROUZET, Michel, *Stendhal et le langage* (see *RMB* for 1981, p. 244), rev. by E. Constans in *SC* 24 (1981-82): 487-90; by V. Del Litto in *SC* 25 (1982-83): 88-90; by G. Strickland in *MLR* 77 (1982): 454-55; JAMESON, Storm, *Speaking of Stendhal* (see *RMB* for 1979, p. 234), rev. by V. Del Litto in *SC* 24 (1981-82): 216; KAJINO, Kijiro, *La Création chez Stendhal et chez Prosper Mérimée* (see *RMB* for 1980, p. 249), rev. by V. Del Litto in *SC* 25 (1982-83): 86; MOUTOTE, Daniel, *Egotisme français moderne* (see *RMB* for 1981, p. 249), rev. by I.M. Frandon in *RHL* 82 (1982): 135-37; PEYTARD, Jean, *Voix et traces narratives chez Stendhal* (see *RMB* for 1981, p. 249), rev. by E. Constans in *SC* 24 (1981-82): 484-86; by J.M. Gleize in *RHL* 82 (1982): 484-86; PIZZORUSSO, Arnaldo, *Prospettive seconde* (see *RMB* for 1980, p. 251),

rev. by J. Chupeau in *DSS* 33 (1981): 110-11; SCHELLEKENS,
O., ed., *Stendhal, le saint-simonisme et les industriels*
(see *RMB* 1980, p. 253), rev. by F.W. Saunders in *FS* 36
1982): 481-82; SIMONS, Madeleine, *Sémiotisme de Stendhal*
(see *RMB* for 1981, p. 251), rev. by P. Berthier in *RHL* 82
(1982): 482-84; by G. Strickland in *MLR* 76 (1981): 970-71;
TALBOT, Emile, ed., *La Critique stendhalienne de Balzac à
Zola* (see *RMB* for 1979, p. 237), rev. by J.T. Day in *FR* 55
(1981-82): 553-54; by D. Hoeges in *RF* 94 (1982): 344-46.

SUE

Eco, Umberto. "Rhetoric and Ideology in Sue's *Les Mystères
de Paris*." Pp. 125-43 in Umberto Eco, *The Role of the
Reader. Explorations in the Semiotics of Texts.* (Advances
in Semiotics.) Indiana University Press, 1979. Pp. viii+273.

Europe 643-644 (Nov.-Dec. 1982). Special Issue on Eugène Sue.

Contents: Roger Ripoll, "Eugène Sue" (3-5); René Guide,
"Les débuts littéraires d'Eugène Sue" (6-16); Emilien
Carassus, "Le miriflore, le romancier et le socialiste:
le dandysme d'Eugène Sue" (17-30); John S. Wood, "Situations
des *Mystères de Paris*" (31-36); Anne-Marie Thiesse, "Ecri-
vains/public(s): les mystères de la communication littéraire" (36-46); Yves Olivier-Martin, "Structures de la
fiction policière" (47-55); Brynja Svane, "Divertir et
politiser: le jeu du double discours dans *Le Juif errant*"
(55-66); Patrick Maurus, "Eugène Sue, ou l'écriture référen-
tielle" (67-77); Roger Bellet, "Le saltimbanque et l'insti-
tuteur dans *Les Misères des enfants trouvés*" (78-91); Jean-
Paul Colin, "La marquise n'est pas sortie ou: l'écriture
de la paresse chez Eugène Sue" (92-101); Roger Bozzetto,
"Eugène Sue et le fantastique" (101-10); Jean-Claude
Vareille, "'Il était une fois' ou l'héritage impossible"
(111-19); Michel Nathan, "Socialisme cosmique et métaphysique du feuilleton" (120-25); Pierre Michel, "Sex-pol
Sue ou femme et révolution dans *Les Mystères du peuple*"
(127-37); Jean-Pierre Leduc-Adine, "A propos de *Jean-Louis
le journalier* d'Eugène Sue, ou 'les sauvages de la civilisation'" (137-48); Roger Ripoll, "Du roman feuilleton au
théâtre" (148-56); Pierre Orrecchione, "Eugène Sue: mesure
d'un succès" (157-66); René Guise, "Bibliographie chronologique d'Eugène Sue" (167-80).

Guise provides an *état présent* on the somewhat murky
phase of Sue's literary career before *Plik et Plok* (1831).
Carassus takes an indulgent view of Sue's notorious dandyism

and wishes to find in Sue's work a permanent "volonté
d'être contre." Wood, like Jean-Louis Bory in his groundbreaking 1962 book, takes Sue seriously as a socialist
novelist in Les Mystères de Paris. Thiesse throws light on
Sue's mysterious "conversion" to socialism by studying the
letters his readers addressed to him during the publication
of the Mystères. Olivier-Martin studies the relationship
between Sue and the detective story, using both structuralist
and historical approaches. Svane finds that "l'idéologie de
Sue change considérablement dans Le Juif errant and que ce
change a des conséquences pour le discours didactique aussi
bien que pour les structures des intrigues." Maurus studies
Sue's manner of naming and portraying characters in Le Juif
errant--"recherche de la justification, de la preuve ...
tendance à la systématisation de la référence externe."
Bellet brings out the "message" of Martin ou les enfants
trouvés--a criticism of the exploitation of children--through
analysis of the theme of identity or appearance and reality.
Colin examines the vocabulary of La Paresse (from the series
Les Sept Péchés capitaux), in the process revealing Sue's
"socialisme humanitaire." Bozzetto defines a special form
of the fantastic--"le fantastique social"--exemplified in
Les Mystères de Paris: "cette tentative de donner à saisir,
dans et par les failles d'un système de représentation codé,
le refoulé social." Vareille finds in Sue's three major
works of his socialistic phase a common structure: history
replaces the fabulous treasure of Utopian (i.e., childish)
dreams. Nathan reveals the "national (i.e., Druidic) religion"
expounded in Les Mystères du peuple, linking it to Sue's
1848-style socialism. Leduc-Adine finds Sue's socialism,
as expressed in Jean-Louis le journalier, far from revolutionary in its application to the rural proletariat. Ripoll
examines the stage adaptations of Les Mystères de Paris,
Le Juif errant, and Martin; each adaptation exhibits the
"compromise instable entre des nécessités contraires"
imposed by the difficulty of fitting the huge, disparate
contents of each novel to the requirements of the stage;
in the last analysis, these adaptations are unsuccessful.
Orrecchione attempts, by statistical means, to "déterminer
l'étendue et la composition de son [Sue's] public"; admittedly, the results are somewhat inconclusive: e.g., Sue's
readership was not crushingly superior in numbers to that
of other "popular" novelists (Kock, etc.); his original
public was generally from the advantaged sectors of society--
only after his death did he reach "the people" in large
numbers.

Guise, René. "Les Mystères de Paris. Histoire d'un texte:
légende et vérité." BduB 1982-III, pp. 358-74.

Latréaumont. (Classiques populaires reliés.) Paris: Garnier,
1982. Fr. 48.00.

Les Mystères de Paris. 6 vols. La Seyne-sur-mer: A. de Vesgre,
1980. Fr. 99.80 each vol.
Facsimile of the 1843 edition.

Tannenbaum, Edward R. "The Beginnings of Bleeding-Heart
Liberalism: Eugène Sue's Les Mystères de Paris." Comparative
Studies in Society and History 23 (1981): 491-507.

Aside from the use of the tendentious term "bleeding-
heart," the article is an honest attempt at showing how
Sue's novel illustrates the middle-class ideology of the
1840s. (E.F.G.)

See also Farwell ("French 1. General").

THIERRY

Delort, Robert. Récits des temps mérovingiens. (L'Arbre
double.) Paris: Les Presses d'Aujourd'hui, 1982. Pp. 300.
Fr. 52.00.

Rev. by André Bourin in RDM, June 1981, pp. 686-91.

See also Moreno Alonso ("Spanish 2. General").

TOUSSENEL

Lehouck, Emile. "Utopie et antisémitisme: le cas d'Alphonse
Toussenel." Pp. 151-60 in 1848. Les Utopismes sociaux.
Utopie et action à la veille des journées de février.
Préface de Maurice Agulhon. (Société d'Histoire de la
Révolution de 1848 et des Révolutions du XIXe Siècle.)
Paris: C.D.U./SEDES, 1981. Pp. 290. Fr. 121.84.

TRISTAN

Adler, Laure. "Flora, Pauline et les autres." In Jean-Paul
Aron, ed., Misérable et glorieuse: la femme au XIXe siècle.
Paris: Fayard, 1980. Pp. 248. Fr. 53.95.

Michaud, Stéphane. "Flora Tristan, les *Promenades dans Londres*."
Pp. 139-50 in *1848. Les Utopismes sociaux. Utopie et action
à la veille des journées de février*. Préface de Maurice
Agulhon. (Société d'Histoire de la Révolution de 1848 et
des Révolutions du XIXe Siècle.) Paris: C.D.U./SEDES, 1981.
Pp. 290. Fr. 121.84.

Palmer, Dennis, and Giselle Pincetl, trans. "The Necessity of
Assuring a Proper Welcome for Foreign Women." *FAR* 6 (1982):
116-35.
  A translation of Tristan's first published work (Paris,
1835), with a brief introduction.

See also *Friends of George Sand Newsletter* 5,i, Livingston
("Sand").

Reviews of book previously listed:

MICHAUD, Stéphane, ed., *Lettres* (see *RMB* for 1980, p. 258).
rev. by Petre Ciureanu in *SFr* 26 (1982): 162-63; by Diana
Cooper-Richet in *Esprit*, May 1981, pp. 173-74; by Jean
Gaulmier in *RHL* 82 (1982): 307-09; by Nicole Mozet in
Romantisme 32 (1981): 121-22.

VEUILLOT

Review of book previously listed:

FOUCART, Claude, *L'Aspect méconnu d'un grand lutteur* (see
RMB for 1981, p. 259), rev. by Claude Savart in *RHEF* 68
(1982): 150-51.

VIGNY

Association des Amis d'Alfred de Vigny. Bulletin No. 12:
1982-83. Pp. 88.

  Contents: S. Pirard, "Vie de l'Association" (3-6); "Ex-
trait de l'éloge de Pierre Emmanuel par Madame la Duchesse
de la Rochefoucauld" (7-8); "Remerciement de Mademoiselle
Yolande Legrand à M. le Maire de Paris" (9); "Soutenance
de thèse" (10); Paul Viallaneix, "M. de Vigny, homme
d'honneur et poète" (11-18); Christiane Lefranc, "La frégate,
le malheur, la prison ..." (19-46); C. Dietschy-Picard,
"Essai de généologie de la famille Baraudin: autour d'un

document inédit" (47-52); Michel Cambien, "Une entrée en
littérature: les 'Poëmes' de 1822" (53-66); Yolande Legrand,
"Poème politique ou poème personnel: les 'Oracles' d'Alfred
de Vigny" (67-87); "Bibliographie" (88).

Viallaneix's study represents a clear, incisive thematic
approach to Vigny's audacious personal definition of honor
and to its force as an article of faith in Vigny's works.
Lefranc's essay augments her article in *RHL* (1964) concerning the imprisonment of Vigny's paternal uncle in 1782.
The discovery of a marriage deed in Blois permits Dietschy-
Picard to call into question some traditionally-held assumptions about Vigny's maternal ancestry. Cambien's reading of
the poems in Vigny's early anthology emphasizes each as a
narrative text. Legrand's psychoanalytic interpretation
finds Vigny's poem to document its author's unresolved guilt
complex. (M.E.B.)

Brabant, Roger. "Alfred de Vignys Reflexion über die Literatur."
OL 37 (1982): 302-26.

Cooper, Barbara T. "Exploitation of the Body in Vigny's
Chatterton: The Economy of Drama and the Drama of Economics."
Theatre Journal 34 (1982): 20-26.

Jarry, André, ed. *Poèmes antiques et modernes. Les Destinées.*
2nd ed. (Poésie, 99.) Paris: Gallimard, 1980. Pp. 315.

Rev. by Carlo Cordié in *SFr* 26 (1982): 161.

Picot, Jean-Pierre. "Variations philosophiques autour d'un
grain de sable: nature et société dans *Les Destinées* d'Alfred
de Vigny." *Romantisme* 33 (1982): 17-34.

Interprets the architecture of *Les Destinées* as the coherent
itinerary formed by two symmetrical, centrifugal movements
away from the core formed by "La mort du loup" and "La
maison du berger" toward the opposing values of nature in
the anthology's opening text, "Les destinées," and of
society in its closing poem, "L'esprit pur." The philosophy
of Vigny's anthology leaves behind belief in oppressive,
immutable nature and comes to articulate faith in the per-
fectibility of society through the transcendent powers of
the human spirit.

Wren, Keith. "A Suitable Case for Treatment: Ideological Confusion in Vigny's *Cinq-Mars*." *FMLS* 8 (1982): 335-50.

Although Vigny intended to demonstrate Montesquieu's thesis
that monarchy degenerates into despotism when it oppresses

the nobility, he signally fails to do so in *Cinq-Mars*; it is the Napoleonic myth that is responsible for the novel's ideological confusion.

See also Braun, Festa-McCormick, Kluck ("French 1. General"); MacGregor ("Girodet").

Reviews of books previously listed:

Relire "Les Destinées" d'Alfred de Vigny (see *RMB* for 1980, p. 263), rev. by Jean-Pierre Picot in *RHL* 82 (1982): 305-07; SAINT-GÉRAND, Jacques-Philippe, *Les Destinées d'un style* (see *RMB* for 1980, p. 264), rev. by André Jarry in *RHL* 82 (1982): 303-05.

VILLEMAIN

See Moreno Alonso ("Spanish 2. General").

VILLENEUVE DE BARGEMONT

Voyage dans la vallée de Barcelonnette. Marseille: Jeanne Laffitte Reprints, 1980. Pp. 165. Fr. 88.79.

Reprint of the edition of Agen, 1815.

VITET

Cooper, Barbara T. "Ludovic Vitet: An Historical Dramatist at the Turning Point." *Topic* 35 (1981): 20-25.

On Vitet's theatrical esthetic as cautiously expressed in the prefaces to his "Scènes historiques." For Vitet, the playwright was an educator rather than an inventor. His views stem from eighteenth-century liberal thought.

VOLNEY

Raskolnikoff, Mouza. "Volney et les Idéologues: le refus de Rome." *RH* 542 (Apr.-June 1982): 357-73.

Volney's attack on the cult of antiquity in his *Leçons d'histoire* (1795) is studied as a moment in the evolution of historiography: "Privée ainsi de sa dimension normative,

l'histoire romaine est alors en mesure de devenir un objet
d'étude." Fustel de Coulanges looms on the horizon.

See also Gillet ("Chateaubriand").

Reviews of book previously listed:

GAULMIER, Jean, ed., La Loi naturelle; Leçons d'histoire
(see RMB for 1981, p. 256), rev. by Malcolm Cook in JES 12
(1982): 230; by Françoise Gaillard in Romantisme 37 (1982):
122-24.

WEILL

Reviews of book previously listed:

FRIEDEMANN, Joë, Alexandre Weill écrivain contestataire
et historien engagé, 1811-1899 (see RMB for 1980, p. 265),
rev. by Jean-Claude Fizaine in Romantisme 36 (1982): 105-
07; by Bettina L. Knapp in NCFS 10 (1982): 380-81; by Freddy
Raphael in ASSR 52,ii (1981): 225-26.

WEISS

Lepin, Suzanne. "Une vie d'homme au service d'une province:
Charles Weiss et la Franche-Comté." Académie des Sciences,
Belles-Lettres et Arts de Besançon. Procès-verbaux et
Mémoires (1978-79): 333-47.

GERMAN

(Compiled by Konstanze Bäumer, Syracuse University;
John F. Fetzer, University of California, Davis; Wulf
Koepke, Texas A & M University; Robert Mollenauer,
University of Texas, Austin; Jeffrey L. Sammons, Yale
University; Stephen P. Scher, Dartmouth College;
Leonard Schulze, University of Texas, Austin)

1. BIBLIOGRAPHY

Allen, Robert R., ed. *The Eighteenth Century: A Current
Bibliography.* N.S. 4, for 1978. New York: AMS Press, 1981.
Pp. 526. Eds. for German: John A. McCarthy (University of
Pennsylvania) and Barbara Becker-Cantarino (University of
Texas, Austin).

"Annotierte Auswahlbibliographie germanistischer Disserta-
tionsschriften." *ZG* (Leipzig) 1 (1980): 250-54, 379-82,
504-07; 2 (1981): 384.

*Deutsche Bücher: Referatenorgan germanistischer, belletris-
tischer und deutschkundlicher Neuerscheinungen* (vorm. *Het
Duitse Boek*) 12 (1982). Amsterdam: Editions Rodopi N.V.

This review journal offers broad but apparently selective
coverage of recent critical works. Each number of Vol. 12
begins with an interview of a contemporary new writer.
Survey reviews in the concluding "Kurz Berichtet."

"Doctoral Dissertations 1980-81 [U.S. and Canada]." *Monatshefte* 74 (1982): 298-300.

Lists only dissertations completed in German departments
(not in comparative literature departments).

*Germanistik: Internationales Referatenorgan mit bibliographis-
chen Hinweisen.* Jahrgang 23. 4 Hefte: Jan., Apr., July,
and Oct. Tübingen: Niemeyer, 1982.

For Romanticism see "II. Allgemeines"; "XVII. Allgemeines
zur Literaturwissenschaft"; "XVIII. Vergleichende Literaturwissenschaft"; "XXI. Deutsche Literaturgeschichte, Allgemeines"; "XXIX. Goethezeit (1770-1830)"; "XXX. Von der
Spätromantik bis zum Realismus (1830-1880)." Books but not
articles are reviewed. Articles and independent chapters
within *Sammelwerke* are cross-listed by epoch and author.
Heft 4 includes the annual index of authors and topics.

Hartke, Werner, ed. *Deutsche Literaturzeitung für Kritik der
internationalen Wissenschaft: Herausgegeben im Auftrage
der Akademie der Wissenschaften der DDR* (= *DLZ*). Vol. 104,
1983. Berlin: Akademie-Verlag, 1983.

The monthly installments include a small section for
Germanistik.

Hohnholz, J., ed. *Literature--Music--Fine Arts: A Review of
German-Language Research Contributions on Literature, Music,
and Fine Arts* (= *LMFA*). (German Studies, Section III, edited
by the Institute for Scientific Co-Operation.) Vol. 16,
Nos. 1 and 2, 1983.

English-language reviews of German-language studies in
the three named fields, each section accompanied by a
"Selected Bibliography." Editor's note: "The original German
titles appear in brackets and in quotation marks. The English
translation of titles does not imply that the books and
articles have actually been translated into English."

Lederer, Herbert. "American Doctoral Dissertations on Austrian
Authors." *Modern Austrian Literature* 13,4 (1980): 226-28.

Zeller, Otto and Wolfram. *Internationale Bibliographie der
Rezensionen wissenschaftlicher Literatur (IBR)*. Vol. 12
(Pars 1 and 2, each in 3 vols.), 1982. Osnabruck: Felix
Dietrich, 1981.

Review listings for each half-year are arranged in three
volumes: A. Index of periodicals consulted (Periodica);
B. Classified subject index of book reviews (Index rerum);
C. Index of book reviews by reviewed authors (Index autorum);
D. Index of book reviews by reviewing authors (Index recen-
sorum); and E. Systematic index of key words (Index systematicus).

Zeller, Otto and Wolfram. *Internationale Bibliographie der
Zeitschriftenliteratur aus allen Gebieten des Wissens (IBZ)*.
Vol. 18 (Pars 1 and 2, each in 6 vols.), 1982. Osnabruck:
Felix Dietrich, 1982.

The article listings for each half-year are arranged in:
A. Index of periodicals consulted (Periodica); B. Classified
subject index of articles (Index rerum); C. Index of articles
arranged by the names of authors (Index autorum); and D.
Systematic index of key words (Index systematicus).

See also Kanzog ("German 3. Hoffmann").

Review article:

Hester, Goldia. "Databases in the Study of German Romanticism."

Databases in this article may be defined as computer-readable
files of bibliographic information open to public use, usually for a fee. In the United States most academic libraries
provide database searching for their clientele; those
libraries that do not provide this service can refer the
interested to the nearest agency doing searching. At present
the scholar usually works with a librarian who is trained
in the techniques of computer searching.

Since most of the humanities databases have print equiva-
lents, why does one choose to pay money to search a database rather than leisurely peruse the printed index? The
three major advantages of database searching are the combination of several search steps into one statement, the access
to information not indexed in the printed form, such as
titles and abstracts, and the possibility of printing out
large numbers of citations in an arrangement chosen by the
scholar.

The *MLA International Bibliography* (*MLA*) now has available
the years 1970-1980, about 570,000 citations, for searching
by computer. For the first time one may search the titles
of articles and books listed in the *MLA*. The capacity to
search titles provides a means of identifying materials about
themes, motifs, and schools. An advantage to the scholar
of Romanticism in a computer search of this database is the
fact that a computer search covers all the parts of *MLA* at
one time. In the print form those working on the relationship of English and German Romanticism find it necessary
to consult both volume one and volume two each year.

Philosophers' Index, which has 80,000 citations and covers
1940 to the present, and *ATLA Religion Database*, which has
100,000 citations and covers journal articles from 1945
to the present and multi-authored books from 1960 to the
present, should be considered by scholars dealing with
philosophical or religious aspects of Romanticism or with
individuals such as Schleiermacher or Fichte. While these
databases are produced in the United States, both cover

major European journals in their areas and provide abstracts for many of the citations.

Scholars concerned with the place of music and art in Romanticism or with individuals such as Beethoven, Schubert, or Richter have the possibility of searching two fine arts databases. *Artbibliographies Modern*, 52,000 citations on nineteenth- and twentieth-century art, and *RILM Abstracts*, 27,000 citations on music, are both international in coverage and contain abstracts.

Historical Abstracts, 100,000 citations published since 1973, abstracts and indexes journal articles on world history since 1450. Its coverage of intellectual and social history is probably of the greatest interest to the student of Romanticism.

Expected shortly is the ability to search with the computer the *Arts and Humanities Citation Index* (*AHCI*) which indexes selected books and 1100 journals in the humanities and the fine arts. While *AHCI* lacks traditional subject headings, it, like *MLA*, will provide the ability to search words in titles as well as the unique ability to search for works cited. While citation indexing is well established in the sciences, several modifications of the system, including provision for implicit citations, were necessary to adapt to the pattern of humanities usage. Citation searching makes it possible, for example, to identify all the authors in 1981 who cited *Des Knaben Wunderhorn*, or, for those seeking tenure, to identify all those who have cited their work in a given year. (G.H., Librarian, Reference Services Department, The General Libraries, The University of Texas at Austin.)

2. GENERAL

Abbé, Derek van. "Zweifel an der 'deutschen Klassik.'" Vol. 8, Nr. 3, pp. 326-33 in Heinz Rupp and Hans-Gert Roloff, eds., *Akten des VI. Internationalen Germanisten-Kongresses Basel 1980*. (Jahrbuch für Internationale Germanistik. Reihe A.) Bern, Frankfurt, and Las Vegas: Lang, 1980.

Ashwin, Clive. "Peter Schmid and *Das Naturzeichnen*: An Experiment in the Teaching of Drawing." *Art History* 5 (1982): 154-65; 10 illus.

    The German painter and teacher (1769-1853) used "purpose-built geometric solids."

Barnouw, Jeffrey. "The Morality of the Sublime: Kant and
Schiller." *SiR* 19 (1980): 497-514.

Barnouw convincingly discusses the major differences
between the aesthetic theories of Kant and Schiller in
order to prove that the continuity of the Enlightenment
and Romanticism is based on the recurrence of unsolved
problems. He points out the affinities between Schiller's
rational-empirical-ethical conception of the aesthetic
experience and John Dennis' critical theory and argues
that Schiller's comprehensive theory of the aesthetic
condition makes Schiller, together with Blake, Goethe,
and Wordsworth, a member of the first generation of European Romanticism. By means of a detailed analysis of the
dissimilarities of Schiller's and Kant's conceptions of
the morality of the sublime, Barnouw attempts to show the
plausibility of the claim that the empirical psychology
of Schiller's *On the Aesthetic Education of Man* undercuts
the presupposed faculty psychology of Kant's critical
philosophy by consistently attempting to reintegrate the
Kantian dualities. (R.M.)

Beaufils, Marcel. *Le Lied romantique allemand.* (Les Essais.)
Paris: Gallimard, 1982. Pp. 352. Fr. 78.00.

Behler, Ernst. "The Impact of Classical Antiquity on the
Formation of the Romantic Literary Theory of the Schlegel
Brothers." *Proceedings ICLA* (Innsbruck, 1979) 9,1 (1981):
139-43.

Behler, Ernst. "The Reception of Calderón among the German
Romantics." *SiR* 20 (1981): 437-60.

Romantic thought about drama, less than the products
of Romanticists for the theater, was critical to the ideas
that shaped the whole of Romantic art theory. Professor
Behler has demonstrated admirably how "during the process
of discovering Calderón, something essential happened to
Calderón as well as to the German romantics" (437). Relating
in his concluding remarks to Fr. Schlegel and the problem
of reconciling poetry with Christian faith, Behler reminds
us of another catholicity of the *Frühromantik* when he
shows that Dante was the model for the allegorical approach
and Calderón for the symbolizing way of poetry. This is
reception scholarship at its best. (R.M.)

Bennett, Benjamin. "The Classical, the Romantic, and the Tragic
in Part Two of Goethe's *Faust*." *SiR* 19 (1980): 529-50.

Bennett presents an intriguing argument for the synthesis of Classical and Romantic elements in *Faust*, especially in light of his discussion of Goethe's idea of the ironic factor inherent in ancient myth. He contends that the tragic vision in *Faust*, which is represented metaphorically by the cycles in the "Classical Walpurgis Night," is a manifestation of philosophical hypochondria and is thus essentially Romantic in character. Bennett's uncontested equating of the Romantic with hypochondria and the negative, although based on Goethe's sense of the word as "sickness," is a shopworn thesis. (R.M.)

Bennett, Benjamin. *Modern Drama and German Classicism: Renaissance from Lessing to Brecht.* Cornell University Press, 1979. Pp. 359. $17.50.

Rev. by Vicki Williams Hill in *Monatshefte* 74 (1982): 202; by James F. Hyde, Jr., in *GQ* 54 (1981): 380-81; by Ladislaus Löb in *MLR* 77 (1982): 202.

A blockbuster of a book that challenges received ideas about the import of Classical German drama (1) by imbedding it more firmly in the social-aesthetic philosophy of the time, and (2) by arguing that it is the basis not only of modern German drama, but also of modern theater in general. The strength of this book is twofold: it is not afraid to re-ask the monumentally simple questions that plagued (and informed) the dramaturgy of Lessing and his immediate successors, and it asks these questions with sensitivity and erudition. Bennett asks, along with Lessing: why should there be drama, why theater, at all? What is the ethical value associated with this genre that is unavailable to narrative or to lyric? The "answer," in drastically simple terms, is that drama confronts us with a ritualized version of the unresolvable dilemma of our own self-consciousness as both our human condition (i.e., as determined) and as the locus of our freedom. It would seem that Bennett overstates the case when he argues that the very *palpability* of the stage, along with the spectators' collective *distance* from it, constitute an irreducible encounter with Otherness which other genres cannot provide because the scene in which they are actualized is already interiorized, already appropriated by the imagination. Do we not experience an analogous hermeneutic resistance in textuality as such, in the oscillations of identification and alienation involved in the experience of fiction? Despite this theoretical quibble, one must admire Bennett's achievement, for he brings new life to a constellation of Classical texts and theoretical issues, thereby demonstrating the vitality of a beleaguered

"canon." And he provides us exciting ways to think about
modern drama as well, as in this nugget: "And the lesson
inherent in the very form of German Classical drama, that
we can meet the problem of self-consciousness by intensify-
ing it, but not by circumventing it, corresponds to Brecht's
implied teaching ... that our rational remaking of the
world confronts us eventually with the necessity of carrying out an irrational and highly questionable self-conscious
operation on ourselves by the use of art" (331). The book
is a model of energetic criticism that integrates speculative insight and scholarly rigor. (L.S.)

Bennholdt-Thomsen, Anke, and Alfredo Guzzoni. *Der "Asoziale"*
in der Literatur um 1800. Königstein/Ts.: Athenäum, 1979.
Pp. 336.

Many new ideas are to be gained from this provocative
sociological study of non-conformity and criminality in
German literature around 1800. Kleist's *Kohlhaas*, Bonaventura's *Nachtwachen*, Tieck's *Lovell*, and Jean Paul's *Titan*
are discussed briefly, but the insights brought to bear
generally on Romantic problems such as nihilism vs. idealism,
the outsider or outcast vs. the bourgeois conformist, a
personal vs. the state's sense of justice, are refreshingly
modern. Students of Gothic and of detective literature should
find their concerns rewarded; traditionalists will be
encouraged to broaden theirs. (R.M.)

Boie, Bernhild. *L'Homme et ses simulacres: essai sur le*
romantisme allemand. Paris: José Corti, 1980. Pp. 360.
Fr. 90.00.

   Rev. by M. Milner in *Romantisme* 30 (1980): 116-18.

Brown, Marshall. "The Logic of Realism: A Hegelian Approach."
PMLA 96 (1981): 224-41.

After concisely surveying the major positions in the
realism debate, Brown shows that the Romantic Age was the
only period in which realism was approved of as a standard
of value. According to Brown, realism emerged as a major
issue in the middle of the nineteenth century because it
had become increasingly problematic in the preceding age.
Brown argues that the discordant positions of the realism
issue can be systematized by reformulating them according
to the pattern of the dialectic of reality in Hegel's
Science of Logic. (R.M.)

Brummack, Jürgen. *Satirische Dichtung: Studien zu Friedrich Schlegel, Tieck, Jean Paul und Heine.* (Theorie und Geschichte der Literatur und der schönen Künste. Texte und Abhandlungen, Bd. 53.) Munich: Fink, 1979. Pp. 239.

See also Brummack ("German 3. Tieck").

Rev. by M. Espagne in *EG* 141 (1981): 89-91; by Bruno Hannemann in *Monatshefte* 74 (1982): 206-07; by Jeffrey L. Sammons ("German 3. Heine") in *RMB* for 1980, p. 297.

Brummack carries out a creditable bit of housecleaning to sweep the cobwebs away from some discrediting ideas about Romantic satire on the one hand and to refurbish the major examples (1789-1848) of Romantic satire on the other. The study features Fr. Schlegel (*Komödientheorien und Satirebegriff*), Tieck (*Modell der politischen Satire*), Jean Paul (*Das Kleinstädtische und das Gottestädtische*), and Heine (*Politisierung und Krise der satirischen Dichtung*). One misses E.T.A. Hoffmann here. (R.M.)

Dmitriew, Aleksandr Sergeevič. "Zu den Romantikkapiteln der 'Geschichte der deutschen Literatur,' Band 7." *WB* 27 (1981-82): 142-47.

Frank, Manfred. *Das individuelle Allgemeine: Textstrukturierung und -interpretation nach Schleiermacher.* Frankfurt: Suhrkamp, 1977. Pp. 382. DM 32.00.

Rev. by Ulrich Knoop in *Germanistik* 22 (1981): 5.

Gerndt, Siegmar. *Idealisierte Natur: die literarische Kontroverse um den Landschaftsgarten des 18. und frühen 19. Jahrhunderts in Deutschland.* Stuttgart: Metzler, 1981. Pp. 204; 79 illus.

Rev. by Alain Montandon in *Romantisme* 35 (1982): 140-41.
"Garten bedeutet immer gestaltete Sehnsucht, ist immer ein Aufbruch nach Utopia." With this pleasing insight the author opens his richly illustrated study of the concepts and the historical developments in literature and life that led to the aesthetic choices made when deciding between French landscaping style (Künstlichkeit: *feudal, höfisch, aristokratisch, absolutistisch*) which had to be overcome and the progressive English model that had become the ideal (Natürlichkeit: *demokratisch, bürgerlich, freiheitlich*). The advantage of this over previous studies by literary scholars (e.g., Blume, Lovejoy, Sengle, Thalmann) is that the author brings so much more technical, plastic information--conceptually as well as visually--to bear on his aesthetic evaluation. Perhaps too much attention is paid

to Goethe (and Schiller), but the concluding chapter makes up for that with a pleasing "Die romantische 'Synthese' der Gartenstile."--A.W. Schlegel, Tieck, Jacobi, Hegel, and F. Th. Vischer. (R.M.)

Gillespie, Gerald. "Romantic Oedipus." Pp. 331-45 in Gerhart Hoffmeister, ed., *Goethezeit: Studien zur Erkenntnis und Rezeption Goethes und seiner Zeitgenossen*. Festschrift für Stuart Atkins. Bern and Munich: Francke, 1981. Pp. 392. DM 165.00.

Glaser, Hermann, ed. *The German Mind of the 19th Century: A Literary and Historical Anthology*. New York: Continuum, 1981. Pp. 389. $19.50. (Trans. of *Soviel Anfang war nie: Deutscher Geist im 19. Jahrhundert*. Munich: Hanser, 1981.)

Rev. by Donna L. Hoffmeister in *MLJ* 66 (1982): 425.

Gockel, Heinz. *Mythos und Poesie: zum Mythosbegriff in Aufklärung und Frühromantik*. (Das Abendland, N.F., 12.) Frankfurt: Klostermann, 1981. Pp. x+358. DM 74.00; 62.00 paper.

Rev. by Gerhart von Graevenitz in *Germanistik* 22 (1981): 81.

Gruber, Edith Maria. "The Early Translations of the *Bhagavadgita* in Germany." *Proceedings ICLA* (Innsbruck, 1979) 9,2 (1980): 265-70.

Guthke, Karl S. "The Fortunes of Chatterton in Germany." Pp. 90-101 in Lee B. Jennings and George Schulz-Behrend, eds., *Vistas and Vectors: Essays Honoring the Memory of Helmut Rehder*. University of Texas Press, 1979. Pp. 214.

Guthke's examination of the pre-history--or pre-Romanticism--of the "latter-day [20th-century] cult of the forgergenius" (90) provides new information, especially regarding the German appreciation of this "Mozart der Dichtkunst." (R.M.)

Heinrich, Helmut T. "Auf frischer Tat." Pp. 45-56 in Hess and Liebers, eds., *Arbeiten mit der Romantik heute* (see below).

Heise, Wolfgang. "Zur Diskussion über die 'Romantik.'" Pp. 18-21 in Hess and Liebers, eds., *Arbeiten mit der Romantik heute* (see below).

Hess, Heide, and Peter Liebers, eds., *Arbeiten mit der*
Romantik heute. (Arbeitsheft, 26.) Berlin: Akademie der
Künste der Deutschen Demokratischen Republik, 1978. Pp.
165. M. 10.00.

(The various articles from this book which are reviewed
in this section will be cited under "Hess and Liebers, eds.,
Arbeiten mit der Romantik heute.")

Heyse, Eva. "Auswahlbibliographie der in der DDR erschienen
Romantik-Ausgaben." Pp. 154-60 in Hess and Liebers, eds.,
Arbeiten mit der Romantik heute (see above).

Higonnet, Margaret R. "Bachelard and the Romantic Imagination."
CL 33 (1981): 18-37.

Because of the "central ontological function assigned to
the imagination" (22), the aesthetic theories of Gaston
Bachelard are clearly traceable to Romantic idealism.
Margaret R. Higonnet has demonstrated with wit, insight,
and compelling range of vision the indebtedness of those
theories to English and especially German Romanticism.
Blake, Shelley, Wordsworth, and Coleridge are discussed on
the one side; Novalis, Fr. Schlegel, Jean Paul, Solger, and
E.T.A. Hoffmann predominate on the other, plus Jung for the
connection with alchemy (Novalis). Higonnet's study provides
on its own a rich assessment of European Romanticism (her
theory models: Korff, Wellek, Abrams, and Nivelle). (R.M.)

Hoffmeister, Gerhart. *Deutsche und europäische Romantik.*
(Sammlung Metzler, Bd. 170.) Stuttgart: J.B. Metzler/Carl
Ernst Poeschl, 1978. Pp. 209.

Rev. by Gerald Gillespie in *SN* 54 (1982): 332-33; by
Heinrich Henel in *SiR* 19 (1980): 554-58; by Alain Montandon
in *Romantisme* 24 (1979): 137; as rev. art. (together with
Sötér, I., and I. Neupokoyeva, eds., and É. Rona, trans.,
European Romanticism--see *RMB* for 1981, p. 270) by Rüdiger
von Tiedemann in *Arcadia* 16 (1980): 90-97.
The value especially of the Tiedemann review is that a
comparison between the Moscow (-Hungarian) and a German
synoptic, comparatist approach is made. Hoffmeister's work
is mind-boggling for the interplay across history and cultures
that are made in such a tight format. One could also
question the validity of viewing European history from a
German perspective, yet the supra-nationalist concern is to
be praised. Still, it is a shotgun approach that too often
dazzles where it should attempt to lead one through a convincing overview. (R.M.)

Holst, Günther J. "Karl Immermann and the Romantic Fairy Tale:
Between Two Literary Poles." Pp. 152-56 in Lee B. Jennings
and George Schulz-Behrend, eds., *Vistas and Vectors: Essays
Honoring the Memory of Helmut Rehder*. University of Texas
Press, 1979. Pp. 214.

Immermann's use of the fairy tale to reject Romanticism
and espouse a realistic world view is recounted simplistically
and in an awkward style. A pity that Friedrich Gundolf's
views were not considered. (R.M.)

Hörisch, Jochen. "Herrscherwort, Geld und geltende Sätze:
Adornos Aktualisierung der Frühromantik und ihre Affinität
zur poststrukturalistischen Kritik des Subjekts." Pp. 397-
414 in Burkhardt Lindner and W. Martin Lüdke, eds., *Materialien zur ästhetischen Theorie Theodor W. Adornos: Kon-
struktion der Moderne*. (suhrkamp taschenbuch wissenschaft,
122.) Frankfurt: Suhrkamp, 1980. Pp. 555.

Rev. by Horst Günther in *Germanistik* 21 (1980): 538-39.

Huyssen, Andreas. *Drama des Sturm und Drang: Kommentar zu
einer Epoche*. Munich: Winkler Verlag, 1980. Pp. 262. DM 28.80.

Rev. by Mark O. Kistler in *JEGP* 81 (1982): 86-87.

Koopmann, Helmut, ed. *Mythos und Mythologie in der Literatur
des 19. Jahrhunderts*. (Studien zur Philosophie und Literatur
des 19. Jh., Bd. 36.) Frankfurt: Klostermann, 1979. Pp.
385. DM 80.00; 72.00 paper.

Listed previously for "Heine"; see *RMB* for 1980, p. 302.
Rev. by Eric W. Herd in *Germanistik* 22 (1981): 272.
Chapters focusing on Heine, Kleist, and Eichendorff in
addition to general topics.

Krenzlin, Norbert. "Zur Dialektik von Sprachcharakter und
Unmittelbarkeit der Kunst." Pp. 66-75 in Hess and Liebers,
eds., *Arbeiten mit der Romantik heute* (see above).

Kurella, Alfred. "Deutsche Romantik." Pp. 141-47 in Hess and
Liebers, eds., *Arbeiten mit der Romantik heute* (see above).

Lang, Helmut W. "Die Zeitschriften in Österreich zwischen
1740 und 1815." Pp. 203-27 in Herbert Zeman, ed., *Die
österreichische Literatur: ihr Profil an der Wende vom 18.
zum 19. Jahrhundert (1750-1830)*. T. 1. 2. (Die österreichische Literatur. Eine Dokumentation ihrer literarischen
Entwicklung.) Graz: Akademische Druck- und Verlagsanstalt,
1979. Pp. x+969. ÖS 1180.00; DM 169.00.

Rev. by Joachim Müller in *Germanistik* 21 (1980): 137-
38.

Lauth, Ruth. "La position spéculative de Hegel dans son écrit
  'Differenz des Fichte'schen und Schelling'schen System der
  Philosophie' à la lumière de la Theorie de la Science."
  Archives de Philosophie 46 (1983): 59-103.

  From the author's summary: "The article considers not
  the criticism of the *Wissenschaftslehre* by Hegel but whether
  his own philosophical point of view can hold facing the requirements of the *WL*. Hegel's Idealism, slightly different
  from the Idealism of Schelling, his ally in 1801, lacks
  any scientific foundation and indulges in assumptions which
  lack any epistemological support. Therefore Hegel was unable
  to refute the *WL*."

Lillyman, William J. "Monasticism, *Tableau Vivant*, and Romanticism: Ottilie in Goethe's *Die Wahlverwandtschaften*." *JEGP*
  81 (1982): 347-66.

Lukács, Georg. "Die Romantik als Wendung in der deutschen
  Literatur." Pp. 136-41 in Hess and Liebers, eds., *Arbeiten
  mit der Romantik heute* (see above).

Malsch, Wilfried. "Klassizismus, Klassik und Romantik der
  Goethezeit." Pp. 381-408 in Karl Otto Conrady, ed., *Deutsche
  Literatur zur Zeit der Klassik*. Stuttgart: Philipp Reclam
  jun., 1977. Pp. 460.

  See also Struc below.
  A smoothly presented, comprehensive overview of all the
  important orientations of that Romantic age which we grudg-
  ingly concede as having also offered something called Classicism, and which we then misname as *Goethezeit*. The balance
  and judgment here is so impressive, hopefully, as to justify this tardy review. Not only are the distinctions and
  non-distinctions within the German movement clarified (including the scholarship of the subject), but attention is
  also drawn to a contrast of European Romanticism and German
  Goethezeit. Students and teachers will find this a rewarding summary. (R.M.)

Melzwig, Brigitte. "Zur Bibliographie der germanistischen
  Literaturgeschichte in der DDR." *WB* 27 (1981): 65-82.

Menhennet, Alan. *Literary History of Germany*. Part 6: *The
  Romantic Movement*. London: Croom Helm, 1981. Pp. 276.
  £15.95.

Rev. by Horst S. Daemmrich in *GQ* 54 (1981): 494-95;
by Michael Hofmann in *TLS*, Dec. 18, 1981, p. 1474.

Menninghaus, Winfried. *Walter Benjamins Theorie der Sprachmagie.*
Frankfurt: Suhrkamp, 1980. Pp. 282. DM 26.00.

Rev. by Michael Rumpf in *Germanistik* 22 (1981): 16.
Benjamin, Romanticists like Fr. Schlegel and Novalis, and
kindred mystics like Böhme, Hamann, Humboldt, and Scholem,
Benjamin's contemporary, have all cherished the *Kabbala* and
evoked the special Romantic magic of *Sprachreflexion.*
Menninghaus repeats himself too often, yet he elucidates
nicely a central concern of Romantic transcendent aesthetics--
Sprachmagie--while at the same time clarifying where Benjamin was dependent on either the historical cabala or on
the assimilation (*Aneignung*) of it by German "Romantic"
thinkers. In a compact little book characterizing Benjamin's
essays on language (including translation, tragedy, pornog-
raphy, magic, and *Sprachmystik*) these revealing references
to Romanticism come in the last forty pages--Chap. 3. (R.M.)

Meyer-Krentler, Eckhardt. "Romantik als Verirrung: zur Abwehr
romantischen Lebensgefühls in der 'bürgerlichen' Literatur
um 1800." Pp. 131-52 in Gerd Michels, ed., *Festschrift für
Friedrich Kienecker zum 60. Geburtstag.* Heidelberg: Julius
Gross, 1980. Pp. 295.

It is helpful to view Romanticism occasionally from the
other side. Meyer-Krentler proceeds from a review of a contemporary attack on Tieck, where Tieck is apparently cari-
catured as a "windiger Literat," to a sobering analysis
of an anonymous anti-Romantic novel of 1801: *Die beiden
Freunde, oder Beispiele von Verirrungen des menschlichen
Herzens.* In this touching triangle-love-novel erring
persons are able to find their way back to reason and
morality. The buzzwords--"Genielosigkeit," "Tugendempfind-
samkeit," etc.--are fun. (R.M.)

Mitchell, Timothy. "From *Vedute* to Vision: The Importance of
Popular Imagery in Friedrich's Development of Romantic
Landscape Painting." *ArtB* 64 (1982): 414-23.

Mittenzwei, Werner. "Zur Diskussion." Pp. 39-40 in Hess and
Liebers, eds., *Arbeiten mit der Romantik heute* (see above).

Mounier, Jacques. *La Fortune des écrits de Jean-Jacques
Rousseau dans les pays de langue allemande de 1782 à 1813.*
(Publications de la Sorbonne, série: N.S. Recherches, n°
38.) Paris: Presses universitaires de France, 1980. Pp. 344.
Fr. 150.00.

Nejgebauer, Aleksandr. "Romantička i neoromantička ironija."
Filološki Pregled [Revue de philologie] 16 (1978): 1-20.
English summary (Romantic and Neo-Romantic irony).

Pfaffenberger, Wolfgang. *Blutezeiten und nationale Literatur-
geschichtsschreibung: eine wissenschaftsgeschichtliche
Betrachtung*. (Europäische Hochschulschriften, Reihe 1, Bd.
353.) Frankfurt am Main, Bern, and Cirencester/UK: Peter D.
Lang, 1981. Pp. 506.

This ambitious work cannot hide its dissertation paternity.
About 40% of its information consists of notes, bibliography,
and index. But the thesis is all the more satisfying for the
exhaustive scholarship behind it as well as for its conclusion that periodization based on *Blüte- und Verfallszeiten*
is no longer tenable. The author's overview of the national,
cultural, ethnic, and linguistic forms that were at work
in the process of literary canonization is impressive ("Die
Kanonisierung der Klassik als normatives 'Blütezeit' der
deutschen Literaturgeschichte," title of Chap. II,2). The
connections between such historians as Winckelmann, Herder,
Humboldt, Gervinus, Hettner, and Scherer and those who made
German cultural history are brought into sharp focus. One
could argue that Hegel and Lukács, or the literary histories
of Eichendorff and Heine, should figure larger, but the
overall problems and the mistakes to which the writing of
national literary history is prone are amply demonstrated
here. 1830 was a critical juncture in such historicizing
as well as being Romanticism's swan song: "Solange man, von
Vico bis zur Romantik, den Menschen als Teil der Natur ansah
und auf seine Vergesellschaftung nicht das Augenmerk richtete,
konnte die Analogie von Natur und Kultur wenigstens system-
intern überzeugen. Das 19. Jahrhundert aber führte die
moderne Massengesellschaft herauf, revolutionierte die
Produktion und schuf den Antagonismus von Lohnarbeit und
Kapital; warf den Menschen also in eine entfremdete Natur,
die er nicht mehr als ihm 'wesensidentisch' anerkennen
konnte" (311). Pfaffenberger concludes with the refreshing
suggestion that a "Wissenschaftsgeschichte der Germanistik"
be written—but by an international research team. (R.M.)

Pöggeler, Otto, intro., and Christoph Jamme, ed. "Werner
Kirchner: *Johannes von Müller über den Fürstenbund* (aus
dem Nachlaß)." *DVLG* 55 (1981): 419-56.

Werner Kirchner was a student of Friedrich Gundolf, and
both of them were concerned that a biography be written of
Johannes von Müller, the *Goethezeit* contemporary whose un-

completed history of the age remains a challenge to modern
Romantic historiography. Pöggeler's lucidly written introduction is a positive step in that direction, and it highlights von Müller's intentions as well as those of the genial
Kirchner. The text edited by Jamme relates to the year 1784
when Müller was in accordance with Prussian "Fürstenbund-
publizistik." (R.M.)

Rathke, Ursula. *Preussische Burgromantik am Rhein: Studien
zum Wiederaufbau von Rheinstein, Stolzenfels und Sooneck
(1823-1860)*. (Studien zur Kunst des 19. Jahrhunderts, Bd.
42.) Munich: Prestel-Verlag, 1979. Pp. 280.

Schmid, Christoph. *Die Mittelalterrezeption des 18. Jahr-
hunderts zwischen Aufklärung und Romantik*. (Europäische
Hochschulschriften, Reihe 1, Bd. 278.) Frankfurt, Bern, and
Las Vegas: Peter Lang, 1979. Pp. 431. Sfr. 57.00.

   Rev. by Klaus Düwel in *Germanistik* 22 (1981): 16-17; by
Otfrid Ehrismann in *GRM* 32 (1982): 479-82.

Schmitz, Victor A., and Fritz Martini, eds. *Friedrich Gundolf:
Beiträge zur Literatur- und Geistesgeschichte*. Mit einer
Abbildung, fünf Faksimiles und einer Beilage. (Veröffent-
lichung der Deutschen Akademie für Sprache und Dichtung.
Darmstadt. Nr. 54.) Heidelberg: Lambert Schneider, 1980.
Pp. 463.

   Victor A. Schmitz justifies his selectiveness regarding
the essays that were chosen for this collection in an
afterword (445-51) that focuses poignantly on Gundolf's
special interest in German Romanticism: "... wie in
seinem Buch über die Romantiker spiegelt sich Gundolfs
eigentümliche und zwiespältige Einschätzung der Romantik,
die ihn als eine Gegenströmung zur Klassik faszinierte und
die er doch zugleich bekämpfte als eine Neigung in ihm
selbst, eine Gefahr in seiner eigenen Natur. Er fürchtete,
daß die Romantik in ihrer Vergeistigung, ihrer Musikalität
die Einheit des Lebens aus Geist und Sinnen auflöse, und
stellte ihr die Klassik als höheres Ideal gegenüber, das
er auch im Werk Georges wiederfand" (447). Of particular
interest will be the chapters "Jean Paul (1900)," "Über
die romantische Schule (1907)," and "Henrik Steffens:
Lebenserinnerungen aus dem Kreise der Romantik (1908)."
(R.M.)

Schwarz, Egon, ed. *Bernhard Blume: Existenz und Dichtung.
Essays und Aufsätze*. Frankfurt/M.: Insel, 1980. Pp. 319.

This volume consists of essays published previously which
center about either Rilke or the image of water. The chapters
which concern us more or less directly are: "Die Insel als
Symbol in der deutschen Dichtung" (1949), pp.
167-79; "Sein und Scheitern: Zur Geschichte einer Metaphor" (1959),
pp. 180-94; and "Das Bild des Schiffbruchs in der Romantik"
(1958), pp. 237-57.

Segeberg, Harro. "Deutsche Literatur und Französische Revolu-
tion: Zum Verhältnis von Weimarer Klassik, Frühromantik und
Spätaufklärung." Pp. 243-66 in Karl Otto Conrady, ed.,
Deutsche Literatur zur Zeit der Klassik. Stuttgart: Philipp
Reclam jun., 1977. Pp. 460.

The style as well as the structuring of the subject is
overly dense. It would seem that the author is straining
to find a new position on old issues: the late Enlightenment, more than Weimar Classicism or Early Romanticism,
found a way to be meaningfully engaged, to combine thought
and action. Special attention is given to Fr. Schlegel,
Novalis, Hölderlin, and Jean Paul. (R.M.)

Struc, Roman. "Some Remarks on the Concepts of Romanticism
and Realism in German and Slavic Literatures." *Proceedings
ICLA* (Montreal, 1973) 7,2 (1979): 157-59.

This 2-1/2 page article is a jawbreaker. It reads like a
brilliant outline, fleshed out here with connecting words
and punctuation, but it will become *the* book on the two
possible, competing movements in modern European literature:
Romanticism and Realism. It should be read as a friendly
counterpoise to the Malsch article, cited above. Struc:
(a) acclaims periodization and refutes the nominalism of
Croce and the New Critics, (b) defends *Geistesgeschichte*
and its offspring the *Zeitgeist* as essential "realism," and
(c) counsels an enhanced respect for the distinctions between history of ideas (*Problemgeschichte*) and social or
political history exemplified in literature. Both Strich
(*Deutsch Klassik und Romantik*) and Auerbach (*Mimesis*) are
chastised for failing to approach their subjects methodologically as periods. Notably, the Strich title is the
only mention in Struc's essay of the concept "classic."
Then (horrors!), Struc concludes his first page with the
heretical advice: "German scholarship would be well advised
to listen to voices from abroad and, instead of relying
exclusively on the theoretical writings of such men as
Friedrich Schlegel, learn from East-European scholars who
find the zenith of German Romanticism in works of literature
through which they attempt to establish a more balanced

and comprehensive view of the entire period" (157-58). The
next 1-1/4 pages sum up that Slavic situation (Romanticism
supposedly progressing to Realism) equally succinctly and
chide *Germanistik* one last time for allowing a crisis situation to develop that perhaps only Lukács and the tradition
of the Frankfurt school will correct. And it will all photo-
copy on three pages! (R.M.)

Szegedy-Maszák, Mihály. "The Concept of the Tragic from the
Enlightenment to Romanticism." *Proceedings ICLA* (Budapest,
1976) 8,2 (1980): 649-55.

Szegedy-Maszák shows how Romanticism increased the complexity of the essentially homogeneous eighteenth-century
concept of the tragic by combining the tragic with irony,
the grotesque, and the tragicomic. According to Szegedy-
Maszák the two dominant concepts of the tragic in the
eighteenth century were (a) the Positivist denial of the
tragic and (b) the traditional cathartic view espoused by
Aristotle in the *Poetics* and the *Nicomachean Ethics*. He
argues that the non-cathartic view of the tragic did not
gain wide acceptance until the Romantic period; however,
this brief article does not contain sufficient evidence to
justify this claim. (R.M.)

Talgeri, Pramod. "Zur Frage Wertung und Umwertung der Romantik
in der Tradition der hegelianischen Romantikkritik: einige
Thesen." Pp. 353-57, Vol. 8, Nr. 3, in Heinz Rupp and Hans-
Gert Roloff, eds., *Akten des VI. Internationalen Germanisten-
Kongresses Basel 1980*. (Jahrbuch für Internationale German-
istik, Reihe A.) Bern, Frankfurt, and Las Vegas: Lang, 1980.

Tatar, Maria M. "The Houses of Fiction: Toward a Definition
of the Uncanny." *CL* 33 (1981): 167-82.

Vaughan, William. *German Romantic Painting*. Second printing.
Yale University Press, 1982. Pp. 260; 32 color pls., 163
black and white illus. $16.95 paper.

Rev. by John Gage in *BM* 124 (Aug. 1982): 514-15; by Marsha
Morton in *AJ* 42 (1982): 163-65.
Listed as "not seen" in *RMB* for 1980, p. 272. For reviews
of first (cloth) edition, see *RMB* for 1981, p. 272.
The favorable reception of this study when it was first
issued is well justified by the author's wide knowledge
and his skillful handling of his subject matter, which
ranges from the "classicism and expression" of Fuseli, through
landscape painting (led by Caspar David Friedrich) and the

archaizing revivalism of the Nazarenes, to the folk-tale
illustration and didactic history painting of the mid-nine-
teenth century. Of the individual artists discussed the best
known are Friedrich, to whom Vaughan devotes most attention,
and Philipp Otto Runge. The many others who are here introduced to a new audience include such interesting figures as
Asmus Jakob Carstens, Carl Blechen, Adolph von Menzel, and
Alfred Rethel.
Vaughan's perceptive comments on the pictures are aided
by excellently reproduced plates. (I.H.C.)

Vaughan, William. "Landscape and the 'Irony of Nature.'"
Art History 2 (1979): 457-73.

Vieillard-Baron, Jean-Louis. Platon et l'idéalisme allemand
(1770-1830). (Bibliothèque des Archives de Philosophie,
28.) Paris: Beauchesne, 1979.

Rev. by Alain Montandon in Romantisme 28-29 (1980): 319-
20.

Ward, Patricia A. "Medievalism in the Romantic Novel." Proceedings ICLA (Innsbruck, 1979) 9,4 (1982): 35-39.

Ward reformulates Morse Peckham's distinction between
positive and negative Romanticism and uses the descriptive
categories of positive medievalism and negative medievalism
as ideal constructs in this superficial discussion of the
historical attitudes toward the Middle Ages in Romantic
fiction. Ward claims that the treatment of the Middle Ages
in eighteenth-century fiction is significantly different
from the historical attitudes manifest in Romantic literature.
However, her attempt to show that Novalis' Heinrich von
Ofterdingen, Scott's Quentin Durward, and Hugo's Notre-
Dame de Paris exemplify Romantic medievalism is too vague
to establish the validity of this claim. (R.M.)

Wiese, Benno von. Eduard Mörike: ein romantischer Dichter.
(Heyne-Biographien, 61.) Munich: Heyne, 1979. Pp. 334.
DM 7.80.

Willson, A. Leslie. "Sakuntula: Indic Heroine, German Ideal."
Pp. 120-28 in Lee B. Jennings and George Schulz-Behrend,
eds., Vistas and Vectors: Essays Honoring the Memory of
Helmut Rehder. University of Texas Press, 1979. Pp. 214.

Charmingly associative but undiscriminating in the extension of a Sakuntula to Romantic and post-Romantic heroines
as disparate as Schiller's schöne Seele, Kleist's Käthchen,

Hölderlin's Diotima, and even Hebbel's Agnes Bernauer.
(R.M.)

Zeman, Herbert. *Die österreichische Literatur: ihr Profil an
der Wende vom 18. zum 19. Jahrhundert.* (Die österreichische
Literatur. Eine Dokumentation ihrer literarhistorischen
Entwicklung.) Graz: Akad. Druck und Verlagsanstalt, 1979.
Pp. 969. DM 169.00.
Rev. by Joachim Müller in *Germanistik* 21 (1980): 137-38.

See also Potts, Samuel and Jones ("General 2. Environment");
McFarland ("English 3. Criticism").

Reviews of books previously listed:

BRINKMANN, Richard, ed., *Romantik in Deutschland: Ein
interdisziplinäres Symposion* (see *RMB* for 1979, pp. 248-
50), rev. by Alain Montandon in *Romantisme* 24 (1979): 137-
38; BROWN, Marshall, *The Shape of German Romanticism* (see
RMB for 1980, pp. 271-72), rev. by John Fetzer in *Monatshefte* 74 (1982): 356-58; CONRADY, Karl Otto, ed., *Deutsche
Literatur zur Zeit der Klassik* (see *ELN* 17, Supp., 173),
rev. by Günther Mahal in *LMFA* 13 (1980): 7-8; DISCHNER,
Gisela, and Richard Faber, eds., *Romantische Utopie--
utopische Romantik* (see *RMB* for 1981, p. 261), rev. by
Heinz Härtl in *DLZ* 102 (1981): 438-40; HUGHES, Glyn Tegai,
Romantic German Literature (see *RMB* for 1980, p. 272), rev.
by Marshall Brown in *CLS* 19 (1982): 89-91; by Raymond
Immerwahr in *CG* 13 (1980): 378-79; by D.G. Little in *MLR*
76 (1981): 508-09; MENHENNET, Alan, *The Romantic Movement*
(see *RMB* for 1981, p. 266), rev. by Alan P. Cottrell in
JEGP 81 (1982): 291-92; SENGLE, Friedrich, *Biedermeierzeit:
Deutsche Literatur im Spannungsfeld zwischen Restauration
und Revolution 1815-1848* (Vol. 1, see *ELN* 10, Supp., 133;
Vol. 2, see *ELN* 12, Supp., 126), rev. of Vols. 1-3 by
Virgil Nemoianu in *SiR* 20 (1981): 532-39; of Vol. 2 by
Jeffrey L. Sammons in *GQ* 54 (1981): 359-63; SÖTÉR, I., and
I. Neupokoyeva, eds., and É. Rona, trans., *European
Romanticism* (see *RMB* for 1981, p. 270), rev. art. by
Rüdiger von Tiedemann in *Arcadia* 16 (1981): 90-97 (see
also Hoffmeister above); SWALES, Martin, *The German Novelle*
(see *RMB* for 1981, p. 270), rev. by Ehrhard Bahr in *GQ*
54 (1981): 395-96; THALMANN, Marianne, *Romantik in kritischer
Perspektive* (see *ELN* 15, Supp., 147), rev. by Karl W. Maurer
in *LMFA* 12 (1979): 68-70; ZIOLKOWSKI, Theodore, *The Classical German Elegy* (see *RMB* for 1981, p. 271), rev. by Beth

Bjorklund in *GQ* 54 (1981): 389-90; ZIPES, Jack, *Breaking the Magic Spell: Radical Theories of Folk and Fairy Tales* (see *RMB* for 1980, pp. 272-73), rev. by Gerhild Scholz Williams in *SiR* 19 (1980): 561-63.

3. STUDIES OF AUTHORS

(Due to unforeseen personnel and scheduling problems only the following authors are covered: Bettina von Arnim, Bonaventura, Brentano, Büchner, Heine, Hoffmann, Jean Paul, Kant, Kleist, Mozart, Wm. Müller, and Tieck. Accordingly, cross-listing has been sacrificed. The omissions will be attended to in the succeeding volume.)

ARNIM, BETTINA VON

Drewitz, Ingeborg. *Bettina von Arnim*. Trad. de l'allemand par Brigitte Gyr. Paris: Denoël, 1982. Pp. 310.

   Rev. by J.L. Pinard-Legry in *QL* 368 (Apr. 1-15, 1982): 17-18.

Hoocke-Demarle, Marie-Claire. *Bettina von Arnim: romantisme et révolution*. [Paris:] Syros éd., 1981. Pp. 174.

   Rev. by J.L. Pinard-Legry in *QL* 368 (Apr. 1-15, 1982): 17-18.

Meyer-Gosau, Frauke. "'Liebe Freundin, es ist nicht weit her mit all den wirren Worten': ein vertraulicher Brief der Caroline Schlegel-Schelling an Bettina von Arnim." *Alternative* 143/144 (1982): 82-88.

   Witty and ironic criticism of Gisela Dischner's recent publications on Bettina von Arnim (1971) and Caroline Schlegel-Schelling (1979). Possibly influenced by Christa Wolf's article about von Arnim, Meyer-Gosau imitates the Romantic epistolary style. The skillfully generated old fashioned language is intentionally contrasted with quotations strewn in from both of Dischner's books, thus exposing the latter's somewhat carelessly worded and "trendy" jargon. Meyer-Gosau's main criticism is directed against Dischner's off-hand manner of "discovering" modern points of view in Romantic thought and life. (K.B.)

Püschel, Ursula. "Weibliches und Unweibliches der Bettina von
Arnim." Pp. 48-82 in Püschel, *Mit allen Sinnen: Frauen in
der Literatur.* Halle-Leipzig: Mitteldeutscher Verlag, 1980.

Püschel's article is a revised and biographically oriented
offspring of her unpublished dissertation about Bettina von
Arnim (1965). In pursuit of balancing out von Arnim's dubious image as "Romantic hobgoblin" GDR researchers have always been strongly concerned with her neglected sociopolitical writings and her often misinterpreted role as political
activist. Püschel traces the history of the fact that von
Arnim's image has been distorted and falsified due to
patriarchal and conservative attitudes. She points out that
von Arnim's sociopolitical involvement has been viewed
opposingly as being "unfeminine" at one time and as an expression of "specifically female compassion" at another.
(K.B.)

Tekinay, Alev. "Zum Orient-Bild Bettina von Arnims und der
jüngeren Romantik." *Arcadia* 16 (1981): 47-49.

This very brief and sketchy article is based on Tekinay's
Munich MA thesis (1976) about Oriental influences in Romanticism. While Friedrich Schlegel, Novalis, and Karoline
von Günderode perceived the Orient as a "Poetisch-romantische
Urheimat," the Oriental influences in Bettina von Arnim's
late publications seem to be mere decorative elements.
Nevertheless, Tekinay argues that von Arnim intended "to
fuse the Oriental with the European on a political and religious level." (K.B.)

Wolf, Christa. "Bettina von Arnim (1785-1859)." Pp. 48-59 in
Hans Jürgen Schultz, ed., *Frauen: Porträts aus zwei Jahr-
hunderten.* Stuttgart and Berlin: Krenz-Verlag, 1981.

An abbreviated version--for broadcast by the Süddeutscher
Rundfunk--of the article immediately following. Wolf has
succeeded in publishing this same article four times, with
only minor changes. (K.B.)

Wolf, Christa. "Nun ja! Das nächste Leben geht aber heute an.
Ein Brief über die Bettine." *SuF* 32 (1980): 392-418.

Wolf's illuminating and carefully worded article is in
itself more a piece of literature than a piece of literary
criticism. Fusing sociopolitical, cultural, and psychological aspects it was originally drafted as an epilogue for
her 1980 edition of Bettina von Arnim's epistolary novel
Die Günderode. Wolf deliberately chose the art form of a

letter to a fictitious female friend in order to gain a
personal closeness to her subject. Bettina von Arnim's
avid refusal to adhere to the traditional set of aesthetic
rules for literary production as opposed to Karoline von
Günderode's compliance with them is in the center of interest.
Wolf wants the Günderode novel to be understood as an ex-
perimental dialogue between two female writers about the
ambivalent relationship between author and literary product
and the integration of personal artistic subjectivity in
it. While von Arnim has the strength and courage to defend
her freedom of expression von Günderode succumbs to socio-
cultural pressure in a patriarchal society. In linking
present and past Wolf recommends reading *Die Günderode* for
two major reasons: as an enlightening historical document
relating to social restrictions of present-day Germany
(both East and West in a sense) and as an encouraging
example for overcoming destructive forms of alienation by
holding on to personal convictions. (K.B.)

Wülfing, Wulf. "Zur Mythisierung der Frau im Jungen Deutschland." *ZDP* 99 (1980): 559-81.

Wordy and commonplace article about the formation of myths
surrounding Rahel Varnhagen, Bettina von Arnim, and
Charlotte Stieglitz. Wülfing is merely descriptive in his
approach and fails to critically analyze the subject of
discussion. In his section about von Arnim, Wülfing focuses
on three mythological elements: closeness to nature, the
demonic, and the childlike. He links the myth of the "child
Bettina" with von Arnim's literary self-portrayal as well
as the mythological concept of the hermaphrodite. While
failing to discuss von Arnim's well-known symbolic identification with Mignon, Wülfing concludes unconvincingly
that a comparison of the "real" to the "ideal" Bettina by
the "Jungdeutschen" ultimately led to the destruction of
the child myth surrounding her. (K.B.)

Review of book previously listed:

DISCHNER, Gisela, *Bettina von Arnim: eine weibliche Sozial-
biographie aus dem 19. Jahrhundert* (see *ELN*, Supp., 185-
86), rev. by Heinz Härtl in *DLZ* 102 (1981): 438-40.

BONAVENTURA

Hunter-Lougheed, Rosemarie. "Der 'Prolog des Hanswurstes':
Zur Entstehungsgeschichte und Datierung der *Nachtwachen*."
Seminar 8 (1982): 27-43.

With some interesting detective work, Hunter-Lougheed argues persuasively that when the "Prolog" was published in the *Zeitung für die elegante Welt* in July 1804, the *Nachtwachen* still had no publisher and may not even have been written; she makes plausible that the publisher Dienemann, who was always behindhand in his promises to his subscribers, solicited the announced novel, which was then written and printed quickly late in 1804. She shows that the "Prolog" was provoked by an attack on Erasmus Darwin's evolutionary theory the preceding March, and that it contains so many of the themes of the *Nachtwachen* that it may well have been the initial core of the whole work. The article demonstrates that perspicuous research can still hope to shed light on some of the mysteries surrounding the *Nachtwachen*. (J.L.S.)

Hunter-Lougheed, Rosemarie. "*Des Teufels Taschenbuch* von 'Bonaventura'?" *Neophilologus* 65 (1981): 589-93.

An advertisement in a St. Petersburg journal owned by the *Nachtwachen* publisher Dienemann reinforces the assumption that the promised *Teufels Taschenbuch*, which never appeared, was a continuation of the *Nachtwachen* by the same author. (J.L.S.)

Perez, Hertha. "Betrachtungen zu den 'Nachtwachen' von Bonaventura." Pp. 365-81, 446 in *Ansichten der deutschen Klassik*, ed. Helmut Brandt and Manfred Beyer. Berlin and Weimar: Aufbau-Verlag, 1981. Pp. 456. DM 17.00.

Reviews the authorship problem, re-orders the text and paraphrases it. Historical comparisons with Novalis and Kafka are suggested. Perez takes but passing and partial notice of *Nachtwachen* criticism and reduces the meaning of the text to social satire; on the whole she makes no significant advances. (J.L.S.)

BRENTANO

Behrens, Jürgen, et al., eds. *Clemens Brentano: Sämtliche Werke und Briefe*. Vol. XXVIII, Teil 1: *Materialien zu nicht ausgeführten religiösen Werken. Anna Katharina Emmerick*. Ed. Jürg Mathes. Stuttgart: Kohlhammer, 1981. Pp. 584. DM 188.00.

Rev. by Alfred Rieman in *Aurora* 42 (1982): 246-48.
Sketches and other raw materials for religious works which were planned but never executed provide the contents

of this volume. Included are data for the projected
biography of Anna Katharina Emmerick (Schmoeger, using
Brentano's notes, compiled his own version of the life of
the stigmatized nun) including fantasized visions (often
with gruesome subject matter), the description of experiments with sacred relics, and dream-journeys to sacred
places. The commentary for the biographical sketches and
the annotations will most likely appear in the next volume,
and thus much of the writing here is replete with cryptic
allusions and obscure references. (J.F.F.)

Bellmann, Werner. "'Bedlam' und 'Kasperle' auf dem literarischen Schützenplatz in Jena. Anmerkungen zu Brentanos
satirischem Frühwerk." *Aurora* 42 (1982): 166-77.

The satiric barbs against Kotzebue's *Gustav Wasa* are
shown to be only one level of satire in Brentano's multi-
layered work, another echelon of which is uncovered in the
Bedlam allusions. The literary Bedlamites such as Dante and
Cervantes are staunchly defended against the Kasperle fac-
tion, represented by the editors of the *Jena Allgemeine
Literaturzeitung* (Schütz and Hufeland). Subtly encoded
word plays on the name Schütz are extended even to the
*Schütz*engesellschaft in the *BOGS* satire some seven years
later. This is convincing detective work, through which
Bellmann rivals another sleuth of Romanticism, Heinz Rölleke.
(J.F.F.)

Frühwald, Wolfgang. "Anmerkungen Luise Hensels zu den *Gesammel-
ten Schriften* Brentanos." *Aurora* 42 (1982): 178-87.

The notations which Luise Hensel made in her copy of the
lyric poems in the 1852 edition constitute fascinating
marginalia (literally) for the Brentano scholar. Above all,
Hensel was interested in Brentano's poems to her from the
years 1816-1821, but it is interesting to note how she
spontaneously applied to herself numerous lyrics written by
the poet to Emilie Linder after 1833, only to eliminate
these misconceptions through erasures and angrily scribbled
corrections once she perused Brentano's posthumous papers
in 1855. Frühwald has once again made accessible to us a
gold mine of information which will eliminate much traditional misinformation. (J.F.F.)

Gajek, Bernhard. "Heidelberg--Regensburg--München: Stationen
Brentanos." *Euphorion* 76 (1982): 58-81.

A very eye-opening analysis of the destructive and constructive effects on Brentano of his reading (at age 8!) of

Tasso's *Gerusalemme liberata*. Not only do all "stations"
on the poet's existential odyssey bear traces of the clash
between "res fictae" and "res factae," of fantasy and reality,
but even his first major work--the novel *Godwi*--reflects
in form and content the powerful influence which Tasso, as
a creative poet and as a poetic creation (Goethe), was to
exert on the receptive mind of Brentano. Very revealing is
the Arminda-Loreley kinship. (J.F.F.)

Gersdorff, Dagmar von. *Lebe der Liebe und liebe das Leben.*
Der Briefwechsel von Clemens Brentano und Sophie Mereau.
Frankfurt am Main: Insel, 1981.

Rev. by Konrad Feilchenfeldt in *ZDP* 101 (1982): 596-603.
This is the third publication of the Brentano-Sophie
Mereau correspondence (1908, 1939, 1981) and the occasion
is the 175th commemoration of the death of Sophie in child-
birth. What is unique about this edition, however, is that
Gersdorff has used the materials in the Varnhagen archive
in the Biblioteka Jagiellonska in Cracow, a collection previously housed in the Prussian National Library in Berlin
and then believed lost after the war. Brentano's correspondence suffered considerably from Varnhagen's high-handed
censorship, for the latter deleted, either with scissors
or by other distorting tactics, those passages concerning
Rahel or the Jewish salons which proved offensive to him.
Gersdorff is a convinced advocate of the feminist cause,
and in her introduction she makes Brentano play second fiddle
to Sophie, who is characterized as the first professional
woman writer in the history of female authors. But even
given Brentano's acknowledged submissiveness to certain
strong women, he would hardly qualify as a champion of the
women's rights amendment. (J.F.F.)

Kirsch, Hans-Christian. "Achim von Arnim/Clemens Brentano:
Des Knaben Wunderhorn." Pp. 69-105 in Hans-Christian Kirsch,
ed., *Klassiker heute*. Frankfurt am Main: Fischer, 1980.
Pp. 349.

This essay, like most of the material in the volume, is
directed at the potentially interested reader who may have
been frightened off by the traditional study of literature
as practiced by dyed-in-the-wool Germanists. Consequently
it is eminently readable, free of jargon, and factually
straightforward. The writer has no axe to grind when it comes
to the standard debates between folk song versus art song
or to the nature and extent of the collaborators' emendations.
Printing selected *Wunderhorn* texts next to their originals

throws into clearer perspective the process of editorial
"improvements" and the attempt to present both the pros
and cons of critical resonance (Goethe versus Voss) is
nicely balanced. (J.F.F.)

Des Knaben Wunderhorn: Alte deutsche Lieder. Gesammelt von
Ludwig Achim von Arnim und Clemens Brentano. Studienausgabe
in neun Bänden. Ed. Heinz Rölleke. Stuttgart: Kohlhammer,
1979.
       Rev. by Alfred Rieman in Aurora 42 (1982): 249-50.

Maley, Uta. "Clemens Brentano: 'Frühlingsschrei eines Knechtes
aus der Tiefe.' Dokument einer religiösen Lyriktradition
oder Zeugnis der 'poetischen Existenz?' Versuch einer
Neuinterpretation." Pp. 309-21 in Werner M. Bauer, et al.,
eds., Tradition und Entwicklung. Festschrift Eugen Thurnher
zum 60. Geburtstag. (Innsbrucker Beiträge zur Kulturwissenschaft. Germanistische Reihe, Bd. 14.) Innsbruck: Institut
für Germanistik der Universität Innsbruck, 1982. Aus.
Schillings 576.00.

Martin, G.D.C. "The Principality of Liechtenstein in German
Fiction: Fantasy and Reality." Pp. 156-73 in Derek Attwood,
Alan Best, and Rex Last, eds., For Lionel Thomas: A Collec-
tion of Essays Presented in His Memory. Department of
German, University of Hull, 1980. Pp. 181.

       A factually informative--but critically uninspiring--
account devoted primarily to Brentano's Gockel which begins
with the incorrect assertion that this work is a "Rhein-
märchen" and concludes with the rather pedestrian observation that the poet's Vaduz is "a web of bizarre fiction
woven around a few grains of well-concealed fact." (J.F.F.)

Matthias, Ursula. Kontextprobleme der Lyrik Clemens Brentanos:
eine Studie über die Verseinlagen im "Godwi." (Europäische
Hochschulschriften, Reihe I: Deutsche Sprache und Literatur,
Bd. 432.) Frankfurt am Main: Lang, 1981. Pp. 284.

       The basic premise of this consistently argued publication
is that critics have been dead wrong to interpret Brentano's
Godwi lyrics "out of context," as it were, without reference
to the immediate prose surroundings or to even more remote
contexts in the novel. Careful differentiations are made
between the poems of Part I--the prime example being "Sprich
aus der Ferne"--and altered states of interpretive analysis
due to relativizing factors which blunt the edges of an
ostensibly wholehearted affirmation of blissful harmony,

and those of Part II, where the role of the individual lyric in a cycle may preclude a monodimensional interpretation in favor of dimensions of ambi- or polyvalence. The major problem with this basically sound approach is the delineation of the parameters of "context," which, if extended to drag in everything including the kitchen sink, make any "Kontextinterpretation" as suspect as another critical fallacy, quoting "out of context." (J.F.F.)

Watanabe, Hiroko. "Über Clemens Brentanos Frühlingskranz von Bettine von Arnim." Forschungsberichte zur Germanistik 23 (1981): 61-80. (Japanese with German summary.)

Reviews of books previously listed:

DENNERLE, Dieter, Kunst als Kommunikationsprozeß (see ELN 16, Supp., 143-44), rev. by Volkmar Stein in Aurora 42 (1982): 260-61; SEIDLIN, Oskar, Von erwachendem Bewußtsein und vom Sündenfall (see RMB for 1981, pp. 280-81), rev. by Volkmar Stein in Aurora 42 (1982): 252-54.

BÜCHNER

Schings, Hans-Jurgen. Der mitleidigste Mensch ist der beste Mensch: Poetik des Mitleids von Lessing bis Büchner. Munchen: Verlag C.H. Beck, 1980. Pp. 116. DM 19.80.

Rev. by Benjamin Bennett in JEGP 81 (1982): 537-38. Not seen.

HEINE

Betz, Albrecht. "Der 'Poet der neuesten Zeit' als Journalist." Pp. 127-36 in Arbeiterbewegung--Erwachsenenbildung--Presse: Festschrift für Walter Fabian zum 75. Geburtstag, ed. Anne-Marie Fabian. Cologne and Frankfurt am Main: Europäische Verlagsanstalt, 1977. Pp. 240.

An uncritical and rather superficial review of Heine's career as a political and social writer. (J.L.S.)

Draper, Hal. The Complete Poems of Heinrich Heine: A Modern English Version. Boston: Suhrkamp/Insel, 1982. Pp. xviii+ 1032. $29.95.

Rev. by John T. Brewer in MLJ 66 (1982): 423; by Rika Lesser in New York Times Book Review, Aug. 8, 1982, pp. 11,

17; by S.S. Prawer in *TLS*, July 9, 1982, p. 738; by Henry
J. Schmidt in *NGC*, No. 23 (1981): 171-77; by Gerhard Schulz
in *Frankfurter Allgemeine Zeitung*, Aug. 7, 1982, section
Bilder und Zeiten, p. [5]; by J.P. Stern in *The Sunday Times*
(London), June 6, 1982, p. 40.
Normally translations are not listed in this bibliography,
but this is too remarkable a publication to pass without
notice. It is an extraordinary and unprecedented feat: the
translation, in original rhyme schemes and meters, of *all*
of Heine's poetic works, including the verse dramas, the
mock-epics, and all variants and paralipomena. Draper's
translations are uncommonly resourceful, reproducing
Heine's tone, ingenuity, and play with language while re-
maining faithful to his literal meaning. The achievement
places all previous translations of Heine's poetry in the
shade and renders them obsolete. The volume contains 146 pp.
of notes, and indexes of first lines and titles in English
and German, and of proper names. (J.L.S.)

Engelsing, Rolf. "Heinrich Heines ursprüngliche Wirkung auf
die deutsche und europäische Gesellschaft." *Francia* 7
(1979): 271-84.

The well-known student of German reading habits in the
nineteenth century (chief example: Bremen) argues that
Heine was the only politically conscious writer of his time
who made a real impression on the public; like the young
Goethe in his time, he was enthusiastically received by a
discontented public of young intellectual officials, offi-
cers, employees, etc., while the spokesmen of good society
rejected him. After 1848 this form of his popularity declined
considerably. (J.L.S.)

Galley, Eberhard, and Alfred Estermann, eds. *Heinrich Heines
Werk im Urteil seiner Zeitgenossen*. Vol. I: *Rezensionen
und Notizen zu Heines Werken von 1821 bis 1831*. (Heine-
Studien, ed. Joseph A. Kruse.) Düsseldorf: Hoffmann und
Campe, Heinrich Heine Verlag, 1981. 2 parts: pp. 596, 111.
DM 124.00.

    Rev. by Gerhard Schulz in *Frankfurter Allgemeine Zeitung*,
Nov. 16, 1982, p. L6.
    The reviews of Heine's publications in the first years of
his career show the extraordinary promptness and rapidity
with which this obscure Rhenish-Jewish outsider rose to
public visibility and, within a decade, to something
approaching fame. The lively response is owing partly, but
only partly, to Heine's own vigorous public-relations ini-

tiatives; he really did at once impress the literary public
with his originality and provocation. Every one of his
publications was reviewed; seventy separate reviewers with
a total of 214 items are represented in this volume. Furthermore, the reviews show that the notion of uniform
public hostility to Heine is a legend; they contain much
positive judgment, along with, naturally, many reservations
and criticisms. Not until the 1830s, with the sharpening
of his political and religious challenges, did public resistance increase. This volume will be followed by two
others carrying the reception to the end of Heine's life,
and two more containing foreign-language reviews. It is
sensibly introduced and edited; the annotation is mainly
informational, and much effort has been expended on identifying the often anonymous reviewers.

The value of this material for the student of Heine and
his times is undeniable. Still, one may feel some concern
at the thoroughness of the project. The publication is very
expensive as well as bulky; the volume became so fat that
the commentary had to be bound separately (even so, the
binding will probably not stand much wear). And these are
only the first stirrings of the reception; can the rest
of the German material actually be fit into two more
volumes? Must all of the documents of the past be reproduced
verbatim in modern print? Can our library budgets and
shelves stand it? (J.L.S.)

Grawe, Christian. "Crampas' Lieblingsdichter Heine und einige
damit verbundene Motive in Fontanes 'Effi Briest.'" *Jahrbuch
der Raabe-Gesellschaft 1982*, pp. 148-70.

A finely crafted interpretation shows how the Heine poems
indirectly and slightly misleadingly cited by Crampas not
only meet Effi's stifled longings for love and romance,
contributing to her seduction, but also contain ominous
elements closely integrated into Fontane's chain of motifs.
(J.L.S.)

Grésillon, Almuth, and Jean-Louis Lebrave. "Manuscrits,
linguistique et informatique." Pp. 263-86 in *Communications
du Colloque International de Textologie à Mátrafüred
(Hongrie), 13-16 octobre 1978*. Budapest: Magyar Tudományos
Akadémia Könyvtára; Paris: Centre Nationale de la Recherche
Scientifique, n.d.

For the problem of producing a total and intelligible
variant apparatus for *Lutezia*, the authors turn to linguistics and information theory, and propose an "automatic
edition" that will make the process of "enunciation" visible,

in particular Heine's incessant "alternation between a
pseudo-historical narrative and a discourse clearly marked
by subjectivity." (J.L.S.)

Grubačić, Slobodan. "Heinrich Heine und Ivo Andrić. Auffassung
von Geschichte als déjà vu." Pp. 151-56 in *Akten des VI.
Internationalen Germanisten-Kongresses Basel 1980*, Pt. 3,
ed. Heinz Rupp and Hans-Gert Roloff (*JIG*, Series A, Vol.
8). Bern, Frankfurt am Main, and Las Vegas: Peter Lang,
1980. Pp. 519.

    Parallels of the imagery of historical recurrence in the
two writers. (J.L.S.)

Grumbach, Detlef. "Heines 'Atta Troll'--Die 'Unveräußerlichen
Rechte des Geistes.'" *Kürbiskern* No. 3 (June 1981): 54-72.

    A dull and fuzzy effort to rescue *Atta Troll* for Marxism.
(J.L.S.)

Habermann, Willy, and Erhard Jöst. "Harry Heinrich Heine
heute. Ein polemisch Flugblattduo im Lehrerzimmer." *DD* 12
(1981): 283-301.

    A rather farcical exchange of open letters by two teachers
in the same school over a public reading of the *Wintermärchen*,
in which one (Habermann) tried to set a more differentiated
view of Heine against Jöst's employment of him for Leftist
propaganda purposes. For his part, Jöst, the author of the
article, tells how his inclusion of a couple of anti-cleri-
cal lines from the *Wintermärchen* in his wedding announcement caused a storm of protest and a campaign to get him
fired. (J.L.S.)

Hannach, Richard W. "The Broken Heart and the Accusing Flame:
The Tension of Imagery and the Ambivalence of Political
Commitment in Heine's 'Deutschland ein Wintermärchen.'"
CG 14 (1981): 289-312.

    An observant analysis of the image of the conflicted
heart in the *Wintermärchen*, showing the ambivalences between
Heine's patriotic attachment to the real Germany and his
revolutionary hopes for an ideal Germany, between his
claims of the power of the prophetic word and the fear of
its impotence. (J.L.S.)

Heinemann, Gerd. "Heine-Manuskripte in der Sekundarstufe II:
Textkritik als eine Möglichkeit des historischen Verstehens."
WW 32 (1982): 20-30.

Using as an example the passage about fear of Communism in the *Geständnisse*, Heinemann tries to show how the genetic variants of a manuscript have pedagogical value in exhibiting the historical meaning of a text. He also unwittingly shows that the most detailed philological work can be used to color Heine's meaning ideologically. (J.L.S.)

Heinrich-Heine-Institut, ed. *Heine-Jahrbuch 1982* (= *HeineJ 1982*). Hamburg: Hoffmann und Campe, 1982. Pp. 307; 8 pls.

Rev. by Gerhard Schulz in *Frankfurter Allgemeine Zeitung*, Nov. 16, 1982, p. L6.

Gisela Benda shows that Heine's criticisms of Germany are similar to common French views, and rightly points out that they often run parallel to those of Mme. de Staël despite his opposition to her. She stresses less that he also shared many German stereotypes of France. The discussion remains on the surface, uncritically reproducing Heine's assertions, and is occasionally insecure in scholarly judgment. Ignace Feuerlicht provides a long, somewhat idiosyncratic interpretation of "Auf Flügeln des Gesanges." Hans-Joachim Helmich expands the commentary to "Verkehrte Welt," with a little insouciance in regard to facts, and offers Marx's employment of variants of the topos of the topsy-turvy world as evidence of the Heine-Marx convergence in 1844. Eberhard Scheiffele, in a rather naive essay, originally published in Japanese, argues conventionally that, while Kraus and Adorno were right to disparage *Buch der Lieder*, the political verse was the true beginning of a new, modern tradition. In a brief but interesting analysis of *Atta Troll*, Brendan Donnellan distinguishes a narrator commenting on the poem, identical with the author, from a rational narrator of the frame and a Romantic narrator of the hunt. In an effort to recover the reception of the silent common reader, Günter Häntzschel examines anthologies, albums, singing groups, etc., and concludes that women, by reason of education, leisure, and sex-role differentiation, were the major audience for poetry, and he makes the female audience largely responsible for the censoriously selective, re-Romanticized trivialization of Heine's poetry in the later nineteenth century. Jürg Mathes follows the publication of a letter to Heine by August Meyer (see *ELN* 17, Supp., 205-06), a Hanoverian legal official devoted to combatting liberal reforms, with an extended account of Meyer's youthful literary connections and picture postcard collection. Meyer was a tangential figure in Heine's life, but the article gives a detailed picture of personal relations among late Romantics. Peter Hasubek and Marianne

Kreutzer present a detailed account of their edition of Karl Immermann's letters and the planned commentary volume, with examples of the apparatus, including a previously unpublished letter to Felix Mendelssohn.
Among smaller items, Margaret A. Rose suggests a source for "Belsatzar" in a Gothic poem of Justinus Kerner about the banker Fugger. Gerhard Weiss discusses the impact of weather conditions on Heine's works, dating the Hamburg passage of *Schnabelewopski* in the fierce winter of 1829/ 30. Michael Werner shows that a passage in *Lutezia* on re- publicanism was originally intended for *Börne*, then excised. The volume concludes with Martin Walser's intelligent, elegant, and in places debatable address upon receiving the Heine Plaquette, and Marcel Reich-Ranicki's introduc- tion of Walser. Book reviews, annual bibliography (17 pp. of small print!), and chronicle of Heine events as usual. (J.L.S.)

Hermand, Jost. "Heine und Brecht: Über die Vergleichbarkeit des Unvergleichlichen." *Monatshefte* 73 (1981): 429-41.

Although there are no linkages of influence between Heine and Brecht, they are comparable on numerous grounds: both interconnected literature with morality, philosophy, and politics; both refunctioned materials from literary tra- dition; both stressed the artistic dimension; both pursued concreteness in politics, betrayed their own social class, fixed their vision on progress and the future; both were consistent materialists, opposed to wishful thinking; both were in favor of play and pleasure, etc. (J.L.S.)

Holub, Robert C. "Heine's Sexual Assaults: Towards a Theory of the Total Polemic." *Monatshefte* 73 (1981): 415-28.

Holub places Heine's sexual polemics against A.W. Schlegel, Platen, and Börne in the larger thematic context of his ideas, in order to show that they were "ideologically consistent." No reasonably observant reader can doubt this, but since the coherence lies entirely in Heine's metonymical imagination, and in all three cases the polemics are of little relevance to their real-world objects, they do not support but detract from the effort "to carry the critique into all spheres of human activity." It might as plausibly be argued that Heine used these devices to mobilize prejudices and unenlightened affects in the reader. In the matter of Platen, Hans Mayer took a more mature view some years ago (see *ELN* 13, 148). Holub's argument is a further example of the insistence that we should suspend our normal civilized and ethical responses for the sake of an uncritical apotheosis of Heine. (J.L.S.)

Holub, Robert C. *Heinrich Heine's Reception of German Greco-philia: The Function and Application of the Hellenic Tradition in the First Half of the Nineteenth Century.* (Reihe Siegen, 27.) Heidelberg: Carl Winter, 1981. Pp. 248.

Rev. by Gerhard Weiss in *HeineJ 1982*, pp. 250-52.

Heine had little direct relationship to Classical antiquity; in all probability he knew no Greek, and the only Greek authors to whom he pays much attention are Homer and Aristophanes. Nevertheless, "Hellenism" is a central component in his pattern of thought and political activism. Holub sees clearly that his "Hellenism" is mediated by and is a reaction to the Grecophilia of Schiller, the Romantics, and Hegel, and that it consistently involves Heine's complex assessment of Goethe. He analyzes this context, the polemic against Platen, the Young German movement and Saint-Simonianism, the polemic against Börne, Heine's allegiance to Aristophanes, and the repudiations in the last years of the "mattress-grave." The argument oscillates between a refreshing independence of outlook with intelligent, precise formulations and more or less conventional apologetics concerning Heine's political and philosophical position. Some parts, especially the careful location of Heine's nuanced antinomies within the Grecophilic context, are very good; others, such as the treatment of Platen and Börne, are less persuasive. Overall the study is thoughtful and extremely well written; it improves substantially on all previous examinations of the topic, and makes a valuable contribution to contemporary Heine studies. (J.L.S.)

Jens, Walter. "'Der Teufel lebt nicht mehr, mein Herr.' Ein Totengespräch zwischen Heine und Lessing." *Die Horen* 25,3 (Fall 1980): 53-64.

An imagined dialogue of the dead, in which it appears that Lessing is a knowledgeable and appreciative critic of Heine's works. (J.L.S.)

Kaufmann, Hans. "Gesang aus dem Grab." *NDL* 29,5 (May 1981): 121-31.

A historical explication of "Im Oktober 1849" in the hope that a better understanding of the poem will help to make it relevant to the present. (J.L.S.)

Kolb, Jocelyne. "Heine's Amusical Muse." *Monatshefte* 73 (1981): 392-404.

A persuasive demonstration that Heine, who knew little about music and perhaps did not even like it very much, in his commentaries transforms musical experience into poetic image and dramatic narrative. Berlioz was the most perceptive observer of Heine's irrelevance as a music critic; Heine's interests lay, as usual, not in the musical object but in poetry and politics. (J.L.S.)

Kruse, Joseph A. "Ein Abkömmling jener Märtyrer.... Heinrich Heine, die Juden und das Judentum." *Emuna* no. 3 (1977): 33-35; no. 4 (1977): 21-30.

A summary popular essay on Heine's Jewishness, superior to most exercises of this kind not only by reason of its eloquence and refinement, but also because, unlike many others on this subject, it is grounded in genuine and thorough knowledge. (J.L.S.)

Laveau, Paul. "Un cas limite de traduction: l'autotraduction (exemple: les traductions autorisées des oeuvres de Henri Heine)." Pp. 260-83 in *La Traduction: un art, une technique. Actes du 11º Congrès de l'Association des Germanistes de l'Enseignement Supérieur (A.G.E.S.) Nancy 28-30 Avril 1978.* Nancy: n. pub., 1979.

In contrast to the views of Claude Porcell (see below, Werner, *Cahier*), Laveau argues that Heine had excellent facility in French, despite his faults, that he can be assigned the "paternity" of the French versions of his works, and that the French versions enjoyed an independent and successful reception in France. Laveau may take this view, which is hedged in some of the details, because he is associated with the East German edition, which has chosen to treat the French texts as independent works rather than as variants. (J.L.S.)

Lübbe, Hermann. "Heinrich Heine und die Religion nach der Aufklärung." *Merkur* 35 (1981): 1024-33.

Reviews Heine's religious thought to show that his late "piety" was consistent with Enlightenment principles and presuppositions of religious freedom, and that it was a rational insight into the contingency of mortal life. (J.L.S.)

Mende, Fritz. "Prüfstein und Gegenbild. Heinrich Heines Auseinandersetzung mit Victor Hugo." *WB* 27,11 (Nov. 1981): 114-29.

Argues that Heine's changing, ultimately annihilating opinion of Hugo was consistent with his changing aesthetic and political views, developing toward an allegiance to the Classical "plasticity" of Goethe, whose dismissive view of *Notre Dame de Paris* Heine is likely to have known. (J.L.S.)

Opitz, Alfred, and Ernst-Ullrich Pinkert. *Heine und das neue Geschlecht (I.). Von der POESIE DER LÜGE zur POLITISCHEN SATIRE: die Rezeption von Heines Lyrik in der Literaturkritik der Junghegelianer.* (Serie om fremmedsprog, No. 17.) Aalborg: Universitetsforlag, 1981. Pp. 262.

A differentiated though unfriendly analysis of the Young Hegelians' criticism of Heine's poetry, showing their resistance to the positions and strategies of his first Parisian phase. The Young Hegelian views are grounded in an optimistic philosophy of history that Heine regarded skeptically, and are measured unfavorably against a "Socialist" tradition of Marx, Engels, Moses Hess, and Georg Weerth; Heine himself is said to have transcended contemporary positions and achieved an allegiance to Socialism. The view of Heine is very abstract; there is no examination of the texts that aroused such resistance in his public, so that his critics appear entirely in the wrong, and there is some bending of the evidence to make Heine a proto-Socialist partisan. A second volume, examining the Young Hegelian reception of Heine's prose writings, is promised. On the whole the enterprise, despite some impressive research, seems conventional and of limited insight. (J.L.S.)

Pollak, Felix. "Mehr Praktisches als Profundes: Marginalien zum Übersetzen von Heines Lyrik." *Monatshefte* 73 (1981): 379-82.

Complaint about the quality of English Heine translations, with some examples of how to do it better. (J.L.S.)

Rose, Margaret A. "The Politicization of Art Criticism: Heine's 1831 Portrayal of Delacroix's *Liberté* and Its Aftermath." *Monatshefte* 73 (1981): 405-14.

In an unacknowledged different version of her presentation of the same issue in *HeineJ 1979* (see *RMB* for 1979, pp. 281-82), Rose argues that Heine's description of Delacroix's revolutionary allegory combines Saint-Simonian with (Left-)

Hegelian ideas, and therefore he had discovered the
progressive "secret" of Hegel's philosophy as early as
1831. To me the argument remains unpersuasive, mainly
because it loads too much intellectual and cultural baggage
on Heine's brief passage of quips and *double-entendres*, and
her effort at an "esoteric" reading looks more like free
association, stretching tenuously to Peter Weiss and Picasso.
(J.L.S.)

Rosenthal, Ludwig. *Heinrich Heines Erbschaftsstreit: Hinter-
gründe, Verlauf, Folgen.* (Abhandlungen zur Kunst-, Musik-
und Literaturwissenschaft, Vol. 323.) Bonn: Bouvier, 1982.
Pp. 115. DM 16.80.

The Judaic historian Ludwig Rosenthal, who has made a
major contribution with his studies of Heine's great-uncle,
the "Chevalier" van Geldern (*RMB* for 1980, p. 308), and a
more uneven one with a book on Heine as a Jew (*ELN* 13, Supp.,
149-50), here sets out the inheritance feud in detail.
Virtually all the correspondence with Salomon, Carl, and
Cécile Heine and most of the materials relating to the feud
are set out verbatim, accompanied by detailed and sometimes
tedious commentary. On the whole, the account is just, although one can hardly say that in the outcome Heine suffered
a "total defeat"; he got what he wanted, though at a high
cost. Rosenthal rightly disposes of Hirth's invention of
a sexual relationship between Heine and Carl's fiancée
Cécile, though he perpetuates another of Hirth's erotic
legends, the supposed liaison with the actress Caroline
Olivier. As for the motivation of Uncle Salomon's testamentary
arrangement, Rosenthal recapitulates my interpretation of
it without acknowledgment. There is nothing new in the study,
either in information or assessment. As is sometimes the
case with Rosenthal, scholarship and accuracy are not quite
up to the mark. The correspondence is quoted mostly from
the old Hirth edition and Eisner's articles, rather than
from the new East German edition, where some of Salomon's
clumsy letters that Rosenthal found partly indecipherable
have been decoded. (For some unexplained reason, the umlauts
are expanded in all the quoted material.) From his earlier
book he continues a serious and misleading error: Heine
certainly did not yield to Campe the honoraria for all his
future works for eleven years in his contract of 1837, nor
was this contract "disadvantageous" to Heine. Rosenthal
does not make use of Harry Steinhauer's study of Heine's
relationship with Cécile and her family (*ELN* 14, Supp.,
127), nor of Gerd Heinemann's re-examination of the fate
of Heine's memoirs (*ELN* 17, Supp., 202). Although the family

history is recapitulated in detail, there is no mention of
the researches into Uncle Salomon's role in the bankruptcy
of Heine's father. There are a number of other doubtful
details, misprints, and bibliographical errors. The book
may be of some interest to one or another general reader;
as a scholarly contribution it is superfluous. (J.L.S.)

Rubini, U. H. *Heine a Parigi 1831-1856*. Bari: Cacci Editore,
1979. Pp. 166.

> Rev. by Pier Raimondo Baldini in *GSR* 5 (1982): 121-22.
> Not seen.

Sammons, Jeffrey L. *Heinrich Heine: A Selected Critical
Bibliography of Secondary Literature 1956-1980*. (Garland
Reference Library of the Humanities, Vol. 302.) New York
and London: Garland, 1982. Pp. xviii+194. $30.00.

> Rev. by [La Vern J. Rippley] in *Choice* 19 (1981-82): 1384;
> by Olga B. Wise in *LJ* 107 (1982): 801.

> A bibliography of secondary sources on Heine, striving
> for completeness on the significant scholarly and intellec-
> tual work of twenty-five years, with brief evaluative com-
> ments, thoroughly indexed. The coverage reaches to items
> that were actually available at the end of 1980, so that
> the latest imprints may not be complete up until that date.

Sammons, Jeffrey L. "Problems of Heine Reception: Some
Considerations." *Monatshefte* 73 (1981): 383-91.

> Points out that much reception study is pursued to buttress
> a preconceived view and has left important gaps, especially
> in Wilhelminian scholarship, Jewish reception, and East
> German propagation.

Schnierle, Herbert, and Christoph Wetzel, with Reinhold Erz
and Roland Otterbreit. *Heinrich Heine*. (Die großen Klassiker:
Literatur der Welt in Bildern, Texten, Daten, Vol. 11.)
Salzburg: Andreas & Andreas, 1980. Pp. 304. DM 46.00.

> This is certainly the best-looking book on Heine to have
> appeared in a long time: it is generously printed in a bright
> and cheerful format, and contains a year-by-year chronicle
> of Heine's life, extended to some of the high and low points
> of his reputation; essays on his lyrical development, his
> philosophical views, and metaphor in his Paris journalism;
> and texts with marginal annotation. The commentary is fairly
> elementary--the layout suggests a school textbook--and in
> places naive, especially in matters of politics. The best
> of the essays, on metaphor, is oddly anonymous; unfortunately

it concludes with a serious misrepresentation of Heine's view of Louis-Philippe. But the level of accuracy, on the whole, is not bad by the standard of general books on Heine. Its real value, however, lies in its 131 illustrations, inventively selected to show salient features of Heine's life and cultural environment; the book is recommendable for pedagogical show-and-tell. Unless I misremember, it is also the first book on Heine in the modern era to have appeared in Austria. (J.L.S.)

Spencer, Hanna. *Heinrich Heine.* (Twayne's World Authors Series, 669.) Boston: Twayne, 1982. Pp. 173. $13.95.

The Canadian scholar, who has contributed a number of worthwhile essays (see especially *ELN* 17, Supp., 208), has now produced a thoughtful and sympathetic compact introduction to Heine's life and works. There are many judicious formulations, and the exemplary local interpretations, especially of the poetry, are managed with a sure hand. Unfortunately there are a rather large number of errors and factual blurs, some of which may be partly owing to the notorious indifference of Twayne's grimly commercial enterprise to production quality. This is regrettable, because most of the flaws might have been easily relieved; nevertheless, there is a good deal of sound judgment, and the book will be of value to the reader who wants to learn something about Heine for the first time. (J.L.S.)

Voigt, Jürgen. *Ritter, Harlekin und Henker: der junge Heine als romantischer Patriot und als Jude. Ein Versuch.* (Europäische Hochschulschriften, Series 1, Vol. 454.) Frankfurt am Main and Bern: Peter Lang, 1982. Pp. 488. DM 89.00.

In a long, ingenious, and often obsessive monograph, Voigt argues that Heine's Jewishness was a ubiquitous if sometimes underground force, penetrating into all details of his life, shaping his view of society and politics, permeating his poetry and prose, and accounting for his notorious reticence about himself and for the distance he put between himself and others. Heine attempts to mask and evade his Jewishness with the Romantic nationalist persona of the knight, becomes a clown as he is made aware of the hopelessness of social integration, and an executioner in his rage at the denial of the Munich professorship and the anti-Semitic attacks of Platen and Massmann. Poetry and prose, psychology and politics, personal relations and career misfortunes, are all related to the burden of Jewishness and the hostility of the environment, with relentless

allegorizations of texts and sometimes arbitrary treatment
of evidence. Heine's isolation and the importance of his
Jewishness for the setbacks in his life are exaggerated,
while some of his Jewish interests and concerns are neglected.
Voigt regularly speaks disparagingly of Jewish traditions,
about which he knows little. The argument essentially ends
with the *Wintermärchen*, so that the whole issue of Heine's
"Return" is barely alluded to. Still, Voigt has worked hard
and knows Heine's texts well, and in the midst of this sometimes exasperating dissertation there are not a few perspicacious arguments and worthwhile observations, suggesting
a genuinely subtle and capable critical talent that might
have been employed to better advantage with better guidance.
(J.L.S.)

Walsh, James E. "Contributions to the Bibliography of Heinrich
Heine." *Philobiblon* 25 (1981): 181-83.

The Keeper of Printed Books of the Houghton Library at
Harvard provides evidence that the Voigt printings of *Roman-
zero* and *Faust* are the first ones and the Hotop printings
reprints, instead of vice versa, as has been assumed. Such
useful corrections turn up all the time, but Walsh exaggerates
when he claims that, of nineteenth-century writers, Heine
is "one of the most poorly served by bibliographers." (J.L.S.)

Weil, Hans. "'Eine neue Zeit mit einem neuen Prinzipe.'
Grundzüge der Poetologie der Ideen- und Formenwelt in Heines
'Reisebildern.'" *WB* 27,11 (Nov. 1981): 78-113.

Despite the assertion of a need for a new view of the whole
sequence of *Reisebilder*, the essay addresses only the *Harz-
reise* and subjects it to a conventionally orthodox reading.
Of some interest, however, is the admission of Heine's
Romantic origins and his view of himself at the end of his
life as primarily a poet; here Weil is explicitly following
the lead of Soviet critics, who exhibit less of a phobia
toward Romanticism than German Marxists. (J.L.S.)

Werner, Michael, ed. *Cahier Heine 2: écriture et genèse*.
Paris: Editions du Centre National de la Recherche Scientifique, 1981. Pp. 132. Fr. 48.00.

Rev. by Bernd Kortländer in *HeineJ 1982*, pp. 242-44.
Like its predecessor (see *ELN* 15, Supp., 166-67), the
second *Cahier Heine* contains sober, philologically-based
work by the Heine research team in Paris. Claude Porcell
attacks a number of myths concerning Heine's French texts,
pointing out that they were not much read by the public and

for the most part were not well translated, and that Heine
spoke and wrote French badly, sometimes irritating his
translators with his interventions. He argues quite rightly
that, despite some variants and additions, the texts are
adaptations and translations, not independent French works
of Heine, which may be an indirect reproach to the East
German edition, which has printed them as such. Michael
Werner re-examines the MS. fragment of the *Memoiren*, concluding, like Gerd Heinemann before him, that the missing
segments were excised by Heine himself, primarily for the
Geständnisse, not mutilated by brother Maximilian in the
family interest, and he goes on to make a persuasive if
not quite air-tight case that a larger text of memoirs never
existed, for all that Heine talked of one. Michel Espagne,
examining a MS. draft of *Religion und Philosophie*, follows
the genesis of Heine's thinking, especially the movement
away from Saint-Simonianism and toward a pantheism of
Spinozist and German origin, away from Voltaire and toward
the revolutionary sequence from Luther to Kant. Jean-Pierre
Lefebvre, drawing one more time from his 1970 dissertation
on Heine and Hegel, argues correctly, I believe, that Heine
developed a revived interest in Hegel in the 1840s, by
reference to the marginal markings in Heine's copy of Hegel's
Philosophie der Geschichte and other works in his library
about Hegel, but he draws no conclusions from them here,
and he still has not proved what he wants to prove about an
intimacy with Hegel's philosophy. Marianne Bockelkamp compares two unpublished MS. drafts, one a dream passage excised from Chapter VII of *Reise von München nach Genua*,
the other in connection with the French version of the
Geständnisse, both concerned with the Anabaptist Jan van
Leyden. All of this useful work is helping to clarify
Heine problems. (J.L.S.)

Werner, Michael. "Frères d'armes ou frères ennemis? Heine et
Boerne à Paris (1830-1840)." *Francia* 7 (1979): 251-70.

Observing correctly that in recent times Börne has come
to be seen largely in Heine's perspective, Werner re-examines
their relationship by stressing, in the first instance,
their large areas of congruence, against the background of
which he works out the development of their personal and
political differences, pointing out also the peculiar paradoxes and contradictions in the attitudes of each to the
other. To this often conventionally and inattentively
treated topic Werner brings some thoughtful new ideas, not
all of which are immediately convincing, but all are certainly discussible. (J.L.S.)

Werner, Michael. "Heine und die französischen Frühsozialisten."
IASL 7 (1982): 88-108.

In a worthwhile and instructive article, Werner examines
Heine's views on the French proto-socialists, particularly
Louis Blanc and Pierre Leroux, showing that Kreutzer's
influential argument that Heine's use of "communism" applied
only to the Neobabouvists (see *ELN* 10, Supp., 151-52) is
not wholly accurate. Werner demonstrates that Heine never
concerned himself with the details of socialist doctrines
or with factional disputes and did not differentiate
socialists from communists, as some other observers did
at the time. He took a long view of universal history,
keyed to his concepts of sensualism and the end of Christianity, and to his awareness of the challenge to property
relations. Marx had no influence on either the continuity
or the internal dilemmas and contradictions of Heine's
views. A persuasive step forward in a more accurate understanding of Heine's perceptions of his French environment.
(J.L.S.)

Wulf, Kurt, and Karl-Ewald Tietz. "Eine interessante Heine-
Wiederholung in Klasse 8: Einsatz des Songs 'Ansichtskarte
aus Düsseldorf' von Dieter Süverkrüp." *DU* (East) 35 (1982):
15-19.

Shows how a West German satirical song about contemporary
Düsseldorf's relationship to Heine can be used for the
propagandistic treatment of Heine in the eighth grade in
East Germany. (J.L.S.)

Zagari, Luciano, ed. "Heinrich Heine: il poeta, l'intellettuale e la molteplicità dei linguaggi." *AION-SG* 23 (1980):
5-201.

The papers of a Naples conference of 1978, by Durzak,
Chiarini, Destro, Sauerland, Secci, Montinari, Preisendanz,
and Zagari, appeared in German in Luciano Zagari and Paolo
Chiarini, eds., *Zu Heinrich Heine* (see *RMB* for 1981, pp.
302-04). (J.L.S.)

See also Hay and Espagne ("French 2. Guizot").

Reviews of books previously listed:

BEHAL, Michael, et al., *Heinrich Heines Epoche--Werk--
Wirkung* (see *RMB* for 1980, pp. 296-97), rev. by Richard C.
Figge in *JEGP* 81 (1982): 294-96; by Fritz Mende in *DLZ* 103

(1982): cols. 34-36; by Manfred Windfuhr in *HeineJ 1982*,
pp. 239-42; BRUMMACK, Jürgen, *Satirische Dichtung* (see *RMB*
for 1980, p. 297), rev. by M. Espagne in *EG* 141 (1981): 89-
91; by Bruno Hannemann in *Monatshefte* 74 (1982): 206-07;
FENDRI, Mounir, *Halbmond, Kreuz und Schibboleth* (see *RMB*
for 1980, pp. 290-91), rev. by Peter Heine in *HeineJ 1982*,
pp. 245-46; by Rudiger Scholz in *Germanistik* 22 (1981): 782;
HEINRICH-HEINE-INSTITUT, ed., *Heine-Jahrbuch 1979* (see *RMB*
for 1979, pp. 281-82), rev. by D.P. Meier-Lenz in *Die Horen*
25,3 (Fall 1980): 110-11; KLINKENBERG, Ralf H., *Die Reisebilder Heinrich Heines* (see *RMB* for 1981, p. 295), rev. by
Larry D. Wells in *GQ* 55 (1982): 598-600; MAYSER, Erich,
H. Heines 'Buch der Lieder' im 19. Jahrhundert (see *RMB* for
1980, p. 305), rev. by Hartmut Kircher in *Germanistik* 23
(1982): 134-35; NETTER, Lucienne, *Heine et la peinture de
la civilisation parisienne 1840-1848* (see *RMB* for 1980, p.
306), rev. by Fritz Mende in *DLZ* 103 (1982): cols. 117-19;
RADDATZ, Fritz J., *Heine: ein deutsches Märchen* (see *ELN*
16, Supp., 163), rev. by D.P. Meier-Lenz in *Die Horen* 25,3
(Fall 1980): 109; SAMMONS, Jeffrey L., *Heinrich Heine: A
Modern Biography* (see *RMB* for 1979, p. 288), rev. by John
M. Ellis in *GQ* 55 (1982): 255-59; by Felix Gilbert in *JMH*
54 (1982): 166-68; by Lucienne Netter in *RLC* 224 (1982):
521-23; by Michael Perraudin in *JES* 11 (1981): 141-42;
by John Winkelman[n] in *GR* 57 (1982): 85-87; UEDING, Gert,
Hoffmann und Campe (see *RMB* for 1981, p. 300), rev. by
Jeffrey L. Sammons, *GQ* 55 (1982): 472-74; WERNER, Michael,
Genius und Geldsack (see *RMB* for 1979, pp. 290-91), rev.
by D.P. Meier-Lenz in *Die Horen* 25,3 (Fall 1980): 111-12;
WINDFUHR, Manfred, ed., *Heinrich Heine: historisch-kritische
Gesamtausgabe der Werke*, Vol. XI (see *ELN* 17, Supp., 209),
rev. by Walter Grab in *GRM* n.s. 32 (1982): 114-17; ZAGARI,
Luciano, and Paolo Chiarini, eds., *Zu Heinrich Heine* (see
RMB for 1981, pp. 302-04), rev. by Jeffrey L. Sammons in
GQ 55 (1982): 260-62; ZLOTKOWSKI, Edward A., *Heinrich Heine's
Reisebilder* (see *RMB* for 1980, p. 312), rev. by Warren R.
Maurer in *GQ* 55 (1982): 259-60; by Karl Pörnbacher in
Germanistik 22 (1981): 783-84.

HOFFMANN, E.T.A.

Brantly, Susan. "A Thermographic Reading of E.T.A. Hoffmann's
 'Der Sandmann.'" *GQ* 55 (1982): 324-35.

    Brantly's thermographic reading reveals Hoffmann as a
"temperature-conscious author." Her carefree and often
original analysis of Hoffmann's language of temperature

succeeds in illuminating "some of the more baffling
aspects of the tale" (324). She concludes that the images
of heat and flame connect Nathanael's father, Nathanael,
and the narrator, whose "heated poetic temperaments ...
are threatened by the cold, prosaic reason of friends and
lovers" (333). (S.P.S.)

Castein, Hanne. "Zum Naturverständnis E.T.A. Hoffmanns. Am
Beispiel einer exemplarischen Stelle in den *Elixieren des
Teufels*." *MHG* 27 (1981): 16-21.

Castein convincingly illustrates that for Hoffmann nature
was no mere backdrop but an integral constituent of his
fiction. (S.P.S.)

Daemmrich, Horst S. "E.T.A. Hoffmann: *Kater Murr* (1820/22)."
Pp. 73-93 in *Romane und Erzählungen zwischen Romantik und
Realismus. Neue Interpretationen*, ed. Paul M. Lützeler.
Stuttgart: Reclam, 1983.

Circumspect and comprehensive, this latest critical
treatment of *Kater Murr* assumes intimate familiarity with
the novel and is thus of limited value for the non-specialist.
Daemmrich's up-to-date assessment of *Kater Murr* scholarship
is exemplary. The interpretive sections focus on five
salient aspects: "Struktureigenheiten," "Erzählperspektive,"
"Künstlerthematik," "Gesellschaftskritik," and "Werke der
Zeitwende." Hoffmann's all-pervasive humor and irony receive
less prominent consideration. (S.P.S.)

Elardo, Ronald J. "The Maw as Infernal Medium in 'Ritter
Gluck' and *Die Bergwerke zu Falun*." *NGS* 9 (1981): 29-49.

Though promising in its initial premise and fascinating
local insights, Elardo's reading of the two novellas suffers
from curiously forced misreadings that render his conclusions
ineffective. (S.P.S.)

Gorski, Gisela. "*Das Fräulein von Scuderi* als Detektivges-
chichte." *MHG* 27 (1981): 1-15.

Whether or not *Scuderi* may be defined specifically as a
detective story rather than (or as well as) a crime story
is a topic that deserves more discriminating treatment
than Gorski's pedestrian and open-ended exercise. (S.P.S.)

Holtus, Günter. "Die Rezeption E.T.A. Hoffmanns in Frankreich.
Untersuchungen zu den Übersetzungen von A.-F. Loève-Veimars."
MHG 27 (1981): 28-54.

A thorough and philosophically exacting comparative
analysis of Adolphe-François Loève-Veimars' early (1829)
French translations of *Ritter Gluck* and *Der Artushof* yields
the astonishing conclusion "dass es sich hier weniger um
das Werk E.T.A. Hoffmanns als um das des Übersetzers A.-F.
Loève-Veimars handelt.... Inhalt und Gestaltung der Erzählungen sind ... derartig von der Person des Übersetzers
beeinflusst und in bisweilen willkürlicher Weise umgestaltet,
dass man Original und Übersetzung grundsätzlich nicht mehr
gleichsetzen kann und darf" (53). (S.P.S.)

Jennings, Lee B. "Kater Murr und Kätzchen Spiegel: Hoffmann's
and Keller's Uses of Felinity." *CollG* 15 (1982): 66-72.

Jennings persuasively demonstrates that for both authors
the "choice of the cat as a mirror for humans seems similarly
motivated" (70). He suggests that "an experiential pragmatism
of outlook found largely in the English prose of the period
and often missed in its German counterpart" (71) is inherent
in both works. (S.P.S.)

Jennings, Lee B. "The Role of Alcohol in Hoffmann's Mythic
Tales." Pp. 182-94 in *Fairy Tales as Ways of Knowing:
Essays on Märchen in Psychology, Society and Literature*,
ed. Michael Metzger and Katharina Mommsen. Bern, Frankfurt,
and Las Vegas: Lang, 1981.

Jennings discusses pertinent passages from *Kater Murr,
Der goldne Topf, Elixiere, Die Abenteuer der Silvester-
Nacht, Irrungen, Die Brautwahl, Die Bergwerke zu Falun*, and
Meister Floh and concludes: "Hoffmann's alcohol is a mind-
expanding drug. It may be the key to ethereal bliss; it may
animate and then befuddle; it may yield glimpses of heaven
or hell. It does nothing, however, that the mind may not do
alone" (190). (S.P.S.)

Kanzog, Klaus. "Zehn Jahre E.T.A. Hoffmann-Forschung: E.T.A.
Hoffmann-Literatur von 1970-1980. Eine Bibliographie." *MHG*
27 (1981): 55-103.

This is the fourth of Kanzog's bibliographies for *MHG*:
(1) 1945-61: *MHG* 9 (1962), 1-30; (2) 1962-65: *MHG* 12 (1966),
33-38; (3) 1966-69: *MHG* 16 (1970), 28-40. Hoffmann literature has become so voluminous that Kanzog admits to provid-
ing primarily an "Orientierungshilfe." Editions of single
works are not included. Still, this bibliography is the
most complete that exists to date. (S.P.S.)

Köhn, Lothar. "E.T.A. Hoffmann." Pp. 159-71 and 576-77 in
Handbuch der deutschen Erzählung, ed. Karl K. Polheim.
Düsseldorf: Bagel, 1981.

This is an exemplary critical assessment of the story-
teller Hoffmann, admirably concise yet astonishingly comprehensive. Köhn's narratologically informed portrait of Hoffmann's complex poetics of prose fiction treats the diverse
stories and tales in a plausible typological framework and
includes brief comparative interpretations of Scuderi, Rat
Krespel, and Die Abenteuer einer Silvester-Nacht. (S.P.S.)

Kovach, Thomas A. "Mythic Structure in E.T.A. Hoffmann's
Das Fräulein von Scuderi: A Case Study in 'Romantic Realism.'"
Pp. 121-27 in Sprache und Literatur: Festschrift für Arval
Streadbeck zum 65. Geburtstag. Eds. Gerhard P. Knapp and
Wolff A. von Schmidt. Bern, Frankfurt, and Las Vegas: Lang,
1981.

Kovach makes a persuasive case for viewing Scuderi as an
early example of what Donald Fanger termed "Romantic realism"
and applied to Dickens, Balzac, and Dostoyevsky. (S.P.S.)

Kross, Siegfried. "Brahms and E.T.A. Hoffmann." 19th Century
Music 5 (1981-82): 193-200.

Attributing the numerous documented instances of Brahms's
identification with the figure of Kapellmeister Kreisler
to the composer's intimate familiarity with and admiration
for Hoffmann's fictional universe, particularly with Kater
Murr and the Kreisleriana pieces in the Fantasiestücke,
Kross convincingly demonstrates that "the process of identification with Kreisler was complete before Brahms entered
the Schumann circle" (194) and lasted until 1854. (S.P.S.)

McGlathery, James M. "E.T.A. Hoffmann and the Liebesmärchen."
Pp. 168-77 in Fairy Tales as Ways of Knowing: Essays on
Märchen in Psychology, Society and Literature, ed. Michael
Metzger and Katharina Mommsen. Bern, Frankfurt, and Las
Vegas: Lang, 1981.

McGlathery stresses the importance of the psychology of
desire for the interpretation of Hoffmann's magical love
stories and sees "unadmitted male sexual panic" (176) as
the "ultimate object of portrayal" (170) in six of the
seven Märchen: Der goldne Topf, Nußknacker, Klein Zaches,
Die Königsbraut, Prinzessin Brambilla, and Meister Floh.
The exception is Das fremde Kind. (S.P.S.)

Mitteilungen der E.T.A. Hoffmann-Gesellschaft. Sitz in Bamberg.
27. Heft 1981. Bamberg: E.T.A. Hoffmann-Gesellschaft e.V.,
1981 [= *MHG*].

In addition to the articles listed by author in this
section, the 1981 volume contains pictures, portraits,
facsimiles, reports on commemorative celebrations, announce-
ments, and other miscellany of interest to Hoffmann scholars.
The separate review section, expertly edited by Wulf Segebrecht, continues to bring extensive reviews of recent Hoffmann editions, criticism, and selected dissertations. An
additional review section by Franz Loquai offers concise
commentary on selected recent articles and other bibliographical items not reviewed in detail. (S.P.S.)

Mornin, Edward. *"Der goldne Topf* und *Das Marmorbild*: A
Comparison." *UP* 1 (1978): 32-38.

Apart from its pedagogical value, Mornin's contrastive
approach yields illuminating--though hardly novel--inter-
pretive insights. (S.P.S.)

Nehring, Wolfgang. "E.T.A. Hoffmann: *Die Elixiere des Teufels*
(1815/16)." Pp. 325-50 in *Romane und Erzählungen der deutschen
Romantik*, ed. Paul Lützeler. Stuttgart: Reclam, 1981.

A must for serious Hoffmann-scholars, Nehring's essay is
exemplary in every respect. His circumspect and informative
critical summary of nineteenth- and twentieth-century Hoffmann reception in general serves as the appropriate framework for his cogent and text-oriented analysis of *Elixiere*
in particular. Nehring interprets the novel as both "Schauer-
gemälde" and "Seelengemälde" and concludes: "Der Roman ist
eines der seltenen Beispiele in der deutschen Literatur, in
denen sich die Konventionen der populären Unterhaltungs-
literatur mit literarischen Ansprüchen zu einer tragfähigen
Synthese vereinigen" (347). (S.P.S.)

Pavlyshyn, Marko. "Interpretations of Word as Act: The Debate
on E.T.A. Hoffmann's *Meister Floh.*" *Seminar* 17 (1981): 196-
204.

Pavlyshyn's cogent critical account of the political circumstances surrounding the suppression of the Knarrpanti
episode makes it clear that "Hoffmann's announcement of his
satirical design is the declaration of an intention to
treat art as a public medium" (201). His "personal act of
defiance" (204) resulted in the publication of "an officially
mutilated work of art" (204). Pavlyshyn convincingly demon-

strates that *Meister Floh* is "an early and successful exercise in literary activism" (204). (S.P.S.)

Schmidt, Jochen. "Die Krise der romantischen Subjektivität: E.T.A. Hoffmanns Künstlernovelle 'Der Sandmann' in historischer Perspektive." Pp. 348-70 in *Literaturwissenschaft und Geistesgeschichte: Festschrift für Richard Brinkmann*, ed. Jürgen Brummack et al. Tübingen: Niemeyer, 1981.

The primary value of this insightful but by no means original analysis of *Sandmann* is Schmidt's genre-oriented historical framework which ranges from Wackenroder's Berglinger to Kafka's hunger artist. Schmidt portrays Nathanael as an early model for the artist as "krisenhafte Ausnahmefigur" (348). (S.P.S.)

Schneider, Peter. "Das Funktionieren von Literatur. Eine Skizze zu zwei Erzählungen E.T.A. Hoffmanns." *MHG* 27 (1981): 22-27.

Drawing on Michael Balint's theory of "primary love" and "basic fault," Schneider offers plausible hints for a psychological reading of *Die Abenteuer der Sylvester-Nacht* and *Der Elementargeist*. He regards "illusionäre Grenzverwischung als literarisches Verfahren" (24) as Hoffmann's fundamental narrative strategy. (S.P.S.)

Siganos, André. "Sur Hoffmann et George Sand: *l'histoire du véritable Gribouille* et *l'enfant étranger*." *RLC* 56 (1982): 92-95.

Steinwender, Ernst-Dieter. "Odysseus in der 'Mid-Life Crisis' oder Der Gang zu den Müttern: Zu 'Die Abenteuer in der Sylvesternacht.'" *Bargfelder Bote*, No. 54 (1981): 3-15.

This interpretation of Arno Schmidt's story makes only passing mention of the similar psychological motifs underlying both Schmidt's and Hoffmann's narratives of the same title. (S.P.S.)

Vietta, Silvio. "Romantikparodie und Realitätsbegriff im Erzählwerk E.T.A. Hoffmanns." *ZDP* 100 (1981): 575-91.

Vietta offers a promising, new theoretical construct for reading Hoffmann. As reflected in his analysis of *Der Sandmann*, Vietta views Hoffmann's concept of perspective as a historically oriented, temporal rather than spatial, category (577) and interprets the well-known contrast between two worlds or realities as a "Perspektivenkonflikt" (576 and 590). Through Nathanael's narcissistic solipsism,

for example, Hoffmann parodies early Romantic poetic
theories. (S.P.S.)

Weiner, Marc A. "Richard Wagner's Use of E.T.A. Hoffmann's
'The Mines of Falun.'" *19th Century Music* 5 (1981-82): 201-
14.

Weiner's article constitutes an important contribution
toward substantiating fundamental points of tangency between
Hoffmann and Wagner. Only a rough prose sketch of Wagner's
abandoned opera project is extant (here published for the
first time in English in Weiner's translation, 210-14).
Yet Weiner's informed comparative analysis clearly shows that
in addition to the obvious Hoffmann-Wagner parallel "thematic
echoes from the great Wagnerian music dramas can be discerned,
in nuce, in this early text" (209). (S.P.S.)

See also Jackson ("English 4. Coleridge"); Picot ("French
2. Gautier"); *Présence de George Sand* 13 ("French 2. Sand").

Reviews of books previously listed:

BOURKE, Thomas, *Stilbruch als Stilmittel: Studien zur
Literatur der Spät- und Nachromantik* (see *RMB* for 1981,
pp. 312-13), rev. by Friedhelm Auhuber in *MHG* 27 (1981):
119-21; ETTELT, Wilhelm, *E.T.A. Hoffmann: Der Künstler und
Mensch* (see *RMB* for 1981, p. 315), rev. by Wulf Segebrecht
in *MHG* 27 (1981): 112-13; GORSKI, Gisela, *E.T.A. Hoffmann
"Das Fräulein von Scuderi"* (see *RMB* for 1981, p. 317),
rev. by Hans-Ulrich Lindken in *MHG* 27 (1981): 121-23;
NAHREBECKY, Roman, *Wackenroder, Tieck, E.T.A. Hoffmann,
Bettina von Arnim: Ihre Beziehungen zur Musik und zum
musikalischen Erlebnis* (see *RMB* for 1981, p. 322), rev. by
Steven P. Scher in *MHG* 27 (1981): 125-26; SCHNAPP, Friedrich, ed., *E.T.A. Hoffmann: Nachlese. Dichtungen, Schriften,
Aufzeichnungen und Fragmente* (see *RMB* for 1981, p. 325),
rev. by Alfred Kalletat in *Germanistik* 22 (1981): 755-56;
TRAUTWEIN, Wolfgang, *Erlesene Angst: Schauerliteratur im
18. und 19. Jahrhundert* (see *RMB* for 1981, p. 327), rev.
by Lothar Pikulik in *MHG* 27 (1981): 113-16.

JEAN PAUL

Davies, Martin L. "Notes on Esthetic and Moral Integrity in
Jean Paul." *Neophilologus* 66 (1982): 235-45.

Espagne, Geneviève. "Die blaue Blume im Ton-Töpfchen: Selbst-
parodie der Idylle und literarische Satire im 'Leben Fibels.'"
JJPG 17 (1982): 31-45.

Fertig, Ludwig. "Jean Paul und die Pädagogik: I. Jean Paul und
die zeitgenössischen Erziehungsschriftsteller. II. Jean Paul
in der pädagogischen Geschichtsschreibung." *JJPG* 17 (1982):
47-69.

The first of the two studies describes Jean Paul's personal
relations with and opinions of educators during his lifetime.
The second study shows how little attention has been given
to Jean Paul's *Levana* and his ideas on education in general
both by literary critics and writers on education, and offers
reasons for this neglect. (W.K.)

Jahrbuch der Jean-Paul-Gesellschaft (= *JJPG*). Im Auftrag der
Jean-Paul-Gesellschaft, Sitz Bayreuth, ed. Kurt Wölfel, 17.
Jg. Munich: C.H. Beck, 1982. Pp. 159.

Maurer, Peter. *Wunsch und Maske: eine Untersuchung der Bild-
und Motivstruktur von Jean Pauls Flegeljahren.* (Palaestra,
Vol. 273.) Göttingen: Vandenhoeck & Ruprecht, 1981. Pp. 172.

An investigation of the masque motif in *Flegeljahre* which
is indeed one of the central complexes of the work. The motif
of the masque is placed in the context of poetry and the
existence of the poet as well as the psychological structures
of desire. New dimensions of the text emerge in spite of some
shortcuts in the interpretations. (W.K.)

Müller, Götz. "Der verborgene Prinz: Variationen einer Fabel
zwischen 1768 und 1820." *JJPG* 17 (1982): 71-89.

Discusses the influence of Louis Sebastien Mercier's story
of the prince who comes into a future age on Wieland, Jean
Paul, and Schiller, and the variations of the story of the
prince who is brought up far from the court ignorant of his
position, from Wieland's *Goldener Spiegel* to Jean Paul's
Hesperus, Titan, and *Komet,* and Schiller's *Demetrius.* (W.K.)

Naumann, Ursula. "Eine Korrektur. Zum Aufsatz: Urania in
Ketten. Jean Pauls 'Titaniden' (mit einem Anhang: fünf
Briefe der Charlotte von Kalb) im Jahrbuch 1980." *JJPG*
17 (1982): 145.

The last letter published in *JJPG* 15 (1980) was to Bernhard
Rudolf Abeken instead of Karl Ludwig von Knebel. (W.K.)

Pietzcker, Carl. "Narziβtisches Glück und Todesphantasie
in Jean Pauls *Leben des vergnügten Schulmeisterlein Maria
Wutz in Auenthal.*" Pp. 30-53 in Klaus Bohnen, Sven-Aage
Jørgensen, and Friedrich Schmöe, eds., *Literatur und Psycho-
analyse.* Vorträge des Kopenhagener Kolloquiums am 6. und 7.
Oktober 1980. (Text und Kontext, Sonderreihe Bd. 10.)
Copenhagen and Munich: Wilhelm Fink, 1981. Pp. 232.

Schulmeisterlein Wutz, the first of Jean Paul's humoristic
writings after his period of satires, is analyzed from a
psychoanalytical point of view. Pietzcker finds similar
structures of narcissism in the protagonist Wutz, the narrator, and the author Jean Paul. He draws the connections between this attitude and the psychological and social conditions under which the young Jean Paul grew up and began to
write. Implicit in this analysis is a general interpretation
of Jean Paul's writings. (W.K.)

Sprengel, Peter. "Zur Wirkungsgeschichte von Jean Pauls
'Titan.'" *JJPG* 17 (1982): 11-30.

The study analyzes some of the first reactions to Jean
Paul's most important novel, *Titan*; it also treats the two
reception problems of Jean Paul as an alternative to Goethe,
and Roquairol as a "modern" character, both in the reception
during the earlier nineteenth and the twentieth centuries.
(W.K.)

Verschulen, Harry. *Jean Pauls "Hesperus" und das zeitgenössische
Lesepublikum.* Assen: Van Gorcum, 1980. Pp. 152.

Rev. by J. Campe in *Archiv* 218, 133. Jg. (1981): 405-08.

Zeller, Bernhard. "Das Jean-Paul-Museum in Bayreuth." *JJPG*
17 (1982): 7-10.

See also Montandon ("French 2. Necker de Saussure"); Brummack
("German 2. General"); Brummack ("Tieck").

Reviews of books previously listed:

OEHLENSCHLÄGER, Eckart, *Närrische Phantasie: zum metaphorischen Prozeβ bei Jean Paul* (see *RMB* for 1981, pp. 332-33),
rev. by Wulf Koepke in *GQ* 55 (1982): 422-23; PAULER, Klaus,
ed., *Jean Paul: Die unsichtbare Loge. Text der Erstausgabe
von 1793 mit den Varianten des Ausgabe von 1826* (see *RMB*
for 1981, p. 333), rev. by Engelhard Weigl in *JJPG* 17
(1982): 147-59; SPRENGEL, Peter, *Jean Paul im Urteil seiner*

Kritiker: Dokumente zur Wirkungsgeschichte Jean Pauls in Deutschland (see *RMB* for 1980, pp. 324-25), rev. by J. Campe in *Archiv* 218, 133 Jg. (1981): 405-08.

Composite review:

Higonnet, Margaret R. *JEGP* 81 (1982): 87-93.

Review of Sprengel, Peter, heraus., *Jean Paul im Urteil seiner Kritiker: Dokumente zur Wirkungsgeschichte Jean Pauls in Deutschland* (see *RMB* for 1980, pp. 324-25); Wiethölter, Waltraud, *Witzige Illumination: Studien zur Aesthetik Jean Pauls* (see *RMB* for 1979, p. 299); and Oehlenschläger, Eckart, *Närrische Phantasie: zum metaphorischen Prozeß bei Jean Paul* (see *RMB* for 1981, pp. 332-33).

KANT

Rogerson, Kenneth F. "The Meaning of Universal Validity in Kant's Aesthetics." *JAAC* 40 (1982): 301-08.

Shell, Susan Meld. *The Rights of Reason: A Study of Kant's Philosophy and Politics*. University of Toronto Press, 1980. Pp. xii+205. $13.50.

Rev. by Jack Iwanicki in *QQ* 89 (1982): 213-15. Not seen.

KLEIST

Angress, Ruth. "Kleist's Nation of Amazons." Pp. 99-134 in Susan L. Cocalis and Kay Goodman, eds., *Beyond the Eternal Feminine. Critical Essays on Women and German Literature.* (Stuttgarter Arbeiten zur Germanistik, Nr. 98.) Stuttgart: Heinz, 1982. Pp. 439.

Bennholdt-Thomsen, Anke. "Die Tradierung einer unbewiesenen Behauptung in der Kleist-Forschung." *Euphorion* 76 (1982): 169-73.

In a letter dated 13 Sept. 1800, Kleist wrote to his fiancée of four mental patients he had observed in the Julius-Hospital in Würzburg. But it has been widely believed that the fourth patient, an eighteen-year-old boy suffering the alleged ravages of onanism, was invented by Kleist, for his description of the boy is far more engaged and intense than that of the other three (a monk, a professor, and a

businessman). This epistolary case-study would thus be the
first recorded example of Kleist's fiction, and would be
of further interest to those who pursue a certain reading
of the relationship between Kleist's psyche and his writing.
But it is all bosh, Bennholdt-Thomsen argues, because there
exists no real evidence that the boy did *not* exist. In fact,
she has discovered a doctor's report which documents that
just such a boy was in the institution from 1798 to 1801.
(L.S.)

Bogdal, Klaus-Michael. *Heinrich von Kleist: Michael Kohlhaas.*
(Text und Geschichte, Nr. 9; Uni-Taschenbücher, Nr. 1027.)
Munich: Fink, 1981. Pp. 125. DM 9.80.

   Rev. by Thomas Rothschild in *Germanistik* 23 (1982): 411-12.

Clausen, Bettina, and Harro Segeberg. "Technik und Natur-
beherrschung im Konflikt. Zur Entzerrung einiger Bilder
auch über Kleist und Goethe." *Text und Kontext* 10 (1982):
47-63.

Gallas, Helga. "Das Begehren des *Michael Kohlhaas.* Eine struk-
tural-psychoanalytische Interpretation der Novelle von
Heinrich von Kleist." Pp. 112-32 in Klaus Bohnen, Sven-
Aage Jørgensen, and Friedrich Schmöe, eds., *Literatur und
Psychoanalyse, Vorträge des Kolloquiums am 6. und 7. Oktober
1980.* (Kopenhagener Kolloquien zur deutschen Literatur, Nr.
3.) Copenhagen and Munich: Wilhelm Fink, 1981.

   See next entry. This essay is a shorter version of Gallas's
book on the same topic. (L.S.)

Gallas, Helga. *Das Textbegehren des "Michael Kohlhaas." Die
Sprache des Unbewußten und der Sinn der Literatur.* Reinbek:
Rowohlt, 1981. Pp. 127. DM 10.00.

   A fascinating treatment of patterns of substitution and
desire in Kohlhaas. Gallas is obviously an astute student
of Lacanian psychoanalysis and its implications for literary
study, especially as informed by the categories of structural linguistics (in particular, Jakobson's descriptions
of the metaphoric-paradigmatic and metonymic-syntagmatic
axes). She identifies four major "transformations" or substitutions in the narrative, whose "logic" has troubled
readers: (1) the emphasis on the restitution of Kohlhaas'
horses is supplanted by the emphasis on the capsule containing the gypsy's prophecy; (2) the Kurfürst of Sachsen
replaces the Junker Wenzel von Tronka as the object of
Kohlhaas' revenge; (3) Kohlhaas' desire for justice is re-

placed by a desire to torture; and (4) there is a series
of transformations in which hope and disappointment displace
each other. These substitutions suggest the "meaning" of the
story in that the only thing the elements have in common
is their desirability, their status as objects of desire.
They are significant because they are all *signifiants* of
an unreachable *signifié* which informs all desire: absolute
self-identity in which all contradictions are subsumed,
in which authority and primacy are assured. The oedipal
structure of Kohlhaas' confrontation with the father-figures
in the text, as well as his relationship to the women in
the text (the gypsy woman resembles his dead wife, and he
calls her "Mütterchen"), is described with force. *Michael
Kohlhaas* thus emerges as the story of desire-as-such, and,
as such, is representative of the role of writing in Kleist's
Prussian-military life. This slim volume suggests provocative new directions in Kleist studies. (L.S.)

Gelus, Marjorie. "Displacement of Meaning in Kleist's *Der
Findling*." *GQ* 55 (1982): 541-53.

Helbling, Robert. "*Kohlhaas*-Metamorphosen." Pp. 65-74 in
Gerhard P. Knapp and Wolff A. von Schmidt, eds., *Sprache
und Literatur*. *Festschrift für Arval L. Streadbeck zum 65.
Geburtstag*. (Utah Studies in Literature and Linguistics,
Nr. 20.) Bern, Frankfurt, and Las Vegas: Lang, 1981. Pp.
207. Sw.Fr. 48.00.

A brief analysis of two modern adaptations of Kleist's
material, and of their relation to Kleist's style: E.L.
Doctorow's *Ragtime* and Elisabeth Plessen's *Kohlhaas*. There
is also a side-look at the GDR journalist Kurt Neheimer's
1979 "historischer Bericht," *Der Mann, der Michael Kohlhaas
wurde*. Helbling links the resurgence of interest in Kohlhaas with modern social issues, including, predictably
enough, bureaucracy and terrorism. He concludes, though:
"... trotz aller Virtuosität und Sprachfertigkeit stehen
die modernen Variationen sehr im Schatten des klassischen
Modells, dessen dramatische Wucht unübertroffen bleibt"
(74). (L.S.)

Hettche, Walter. "Heinrich von Kleists Gedicht 'Das letzte
Lied' in einer Kopie Charlotte von Steins." Pp. 251-61 in
Jahrbuch des Freien Deutschen Hochstifts, 1982.

Hoff-Purviance, Linda. "The Form of Kleist's *Penthesilea* and
the *Iliad*." *GQ* 55 (1982): 39-48.

Huff, Steven R. "Kleist and Expectant Virgins: The Meaning of
the 'O' in *Die Marquise von O*." *JEGP* 81 (1982): 367-75.

Has found the long-sought source in the Marian cult of
"La Madonna de la O" (in English, Our Lady of Expectation,
but not in Dickens's sense). One wonders if there is any
further connection with the Grove Press's "The Story of O."
(B.C.H.)

Jauß, Hans Robert. "Poetik und Problematik von Identität und
Rolle in der Geschichte des Amphitryon." Pp. 213-53 in Odo
Marquand and Karlheinz Stierle, eds., *Identität*. (Poetik und
Hermeneutik, Nr. 8.) Munich: Fink, 1979. Pp. 765. DM 36.00.

A long essay (almost a monograph) on the social and
philosophical implications of historical variations in the
treatment and development of the Amphitryon-Alcmene-Jupiter
myth. Jauß appeals to Lévi-Strauss's notion of *bricolage* in
his attempt to explicate the recombinatory force of the
material. He suggests that Kleist's *Amphitryon* simply
abandons the possibility of human identity and happiness,
whereas Giraudoux's *Amphitryon 38* suggests an existentialist
possibility of finding identity by the very affirmation of
one's own alienation. As usual, Jauß's contentions are worthy
of reflection, if only because of the wide range of allusions
to modern critical thought. (L.S.)

Kunz, Josef. "Die Tragik im dichterischen Werk Kleists." *Revue
d'Allemagne* 14 (1982): 229-44.

Labhardt, Robert. *Metapher und Geschichte: Kleists dramatische
Metaphorik bis zur "Penthesilea" als Wiederspiegelung seiner
geschichtlichen Position*. Kronberg/Ts: Scriptor, 1976.
Pp. 340.

Rev. by Jörg Villwock in *GRM* N.F. 32 (1982): 240-42.
Originally a Basel dissertation, this book is an attempt
to build a hermeneutic bridge between formalist and historical criticism via a theory of metaphor as the structural
principle constitutive both of literature and of a response
to the incommensurabilities of historical experience. Labhardt restricts his analysis to the early dramas because
they are the most challenging to his theory of the relation
between poetry and history: if even the early "pure" art
of Kleist can be shown to exist in this relation, then the
relation holds ipso facto for the later, avowedly political,
writings. Essentially, the claim concerning the social origins of metaphoric language in Kleist consists in this
quasi-Marxian commonplace: "Zwischen der französischen

Revolution und dem Zusammenbruch des alten Preussen und des
deutschen Reichs steht Kleist als ein widerwilliger Ent-
decker der gesellschaftlichen Eigengesetzlichkeit, welche
die bürgerliche Epoche anzeigt und den alten Glauben an die
Integration des Menschen in eine ewige Naturwahrheit un-
lösbaren Paradoxien ausliefert" (300-01). Kleist's alogical
style is said to reflect these paradoxes. While the book
is an admirable attempt to do something constructive with
the perennially troublesome political dimensions of Kleist's
work, its ultimate reductiveness fails to take into account
the nettlesome issue of (political and linguistic) representation *as such* in both Kleist's essays and his fictions. There
is a way in which the problem of language *precedes* the
problem of politics, a precedence the French Enlightenment
(with which Kleist was intimately familiar) pondered in a
much less monolithic manner than Labhardt suggests. The book
is frustrating not so much because it is wrong, but because
it takes on themes that transcend its methodology. (L.S.)

Loukopoulos, Wassili. *Heinrich von Kleist: Der Zweikampf:
eine Strukturanalyse unter dem Aspekt des Subjektgebrauchs*.
(Hochschulsammlung Philosophie. Literaturwissenschaft, Nr.
2.) Stuttgart: Hochschulverlag, 1978. Pp. 182. Dm 25.00.

Rev. by Theo Bungarten in *Germanistik* 23 (1982): 817-18.
    An attempt to address the peculiar density of Kleist's
style, a density that seems to carry special semiotic import,
in that it not only represents, but enacts, what it signi-
fies. While Loukopoulos has here identified a promising
topic, he does very little of genuine interest with it.
He promises a syntactical analysis which is "äusserst
subtil," but he in fact limits himself to nominal construc-
tions and their displacement. Furthermore, he has completely
avoided the central question: *if* Kleist's language is so
concrete, so seamlessly and essentially united with its
signified, why is it that the treacherousness of all signs
is the most constant *thematic* dimension of Kleist's texts?
At the very least, we would hope for a dialectical account
of this peculiar *Sprachproblematik*; but we hope in vain.
The author is simply not up to the task he has set himself.
(L.S.)

Lützeler, Paul Michael. "Heinrich von Kleist: *Michael Kohlhaas*
(1810)." Pp. 213-39 in Paul Michael Lützeler, ed., *Romane
und Erzählungen der deutschen Romantik: Neue Interpretationen*.
Stuttgart: Reclam, 1981. Pp. 389. DM 34.80.

Müller, Joachim. "Zufall und Vorfall: Geschehenswelt und Erzählstruktur in Heinrich von Kleists Novelle *Der Findling*." *Zeitschrift für Germanistik* (Leipzig) 3 (1982): 427-38.

Müller-Michaels, Harro. "Insubordination als Autonomie: Heinrich von Kleists *Prinz Friedrich von Homburg*." Pp. 128-44 in Vol. 1, Harro Müller-Michaels, ed., *Deutsche Dramen. Interpretationen zu Werken von der Aufklärung bis zur Gegenwart*. Königstein/Ts: Athenäum, 1981. Pp. 2162. DM 48.00.

Pott, Hans-Georg. "Fröhlicher Ich-Verlust. Die Gestalt des Sosias in Kleists *Amphitryon*." *Literatur für Leser* (1981): 129-44.

Riedel, Volker. "*Amphitryon* bei Kleist und Hacks: Traditionsbeziehungen in Peter Hacks' Komödie *Amphitryon*." *Impulse* 3 (1981): 153-76.

Samuel, Richard H., and Hilda M. Brown. *Kleist's Lost Year and the Quest for "Robert Guiskard*." Leamington Spa: Hall, 1981. Pp. ix+126. £5.95.

Rev. by Ruth K. Angress in *Germanistik* 23 (1982): 818.
A well-crafted little book that reports the fruits of much labor, this volume sets itself the task of filling in one of those frustrating biographical voids in Kleist's life: the entire year between July 1803 and June 1804. Surmising that we may have so little information about this period because Kleist's family was anxious to destroy evidence of his activities (perhaps out of fear that the family reputation would be still further tarnished by its black sheep), Samuel and Brown pursue the clues to reconstruct the period as best they can. They come up with new evaluations of Kleist's activity and relationships, particularly with Christoph Wilhelm von Werdeck (and his wife, Adolphine) and with the multifarious Dr. Georg Christian Wedekind of Mainz. Thoroughness in pursuing the evidence and judiciousness in interpreting it are evident throughout. (L.S.)

Schaefer, Margret. "Kleists 'Über das Marionettentheater' und der Narzissmus des Künstlers." Pp. 265-92 in Claire Kahane, ed., *Psychoanalyse und das Unheimliche: Essays aus der amerikanischen Literaturkritik*. Bonn: Bouvier, 1981. Pp. 300. DM 58.00.

Schlawe, Fritz. "Kleists 'Schmerz.'" *ZDP* 101 (1982): 495-506.

Scholz, Ingeborg. "Zur Problematik von Traum und Tod in
Kleists *Prinz Friedrich von Homburg.*" *Literatur für Leser*
(1980): 148-56.

Sembdner, Helmut. "Schauspieler interpretieren Kleists *Prinz
Friedrich von Homburg.*" Pp. 246-63 in Joachim Krause et al.,
eds., *Sammeln und Sichten: Festschrift für Oscar Fambach
zum 80. Geburtstag.* (Mitteilungen zur Theatergeschichte der
Goethezeit, Nr. 4.) Bonn: Bouvier, 1982. Pp. 344. DM 79.00.

Sembdner, Helmut. "Wilhelm Grimms Kleist-Rezensionen: Zu
Sibylle Obendaus' Methodenproblem." *Schillerjahrbuch* 26
(1982): 31-39.

Stierle, Karlheinz. "Amphitryon--Ein dialektisches Märchen
der Identität." Pp. 734-39 in Odo Marquand and Karlheinz
Stierle, eds., *Identität.* (Poetik und Hermeneutik, Nr. 8.)
Munich: Fink, 1979. Pp. 765. DM 36.00.

Argues that Kleist's version of the Amphitryon-*Stoff* is by
far the most sophisticated, indeed, that it is the first
version to relate all the components of the myth "in einer
wirklich umgreifenden Sinnkonfiguration." Contends that
the myth's repetition in literature mirrors the historical
increase in a sense of mankind's alienation from the divine.
But the essay is far too sketchy and merely assertive in
tone to support such grand contentions. It really doesn't
tell us anything we don't already know about *Amphitryon*,
and is best thought of as a footnote to Jauß' more systematic
treatment (see above). (L.S.)

Sträßner, Matthias. *Analytisches Drama.* Munich: Fink, 1980.
Pp. 272. DM 48.00.

Rev. by Klaus Harro Hilzinger in *Germanistik* 22 (1981):
88-89.
A Stuttgart dissertation, taking its cue from Schiller's
letter to Goethe of 2 Oct. 1797, in which he discusses a
form of drama in which the "Handlung ja schon geschehen
ist und mithin ganz jenseits der Tragödie fällt" (9).
Sträßner seeks to extend the definition, as well as the
commonly accepted notion that only two plays--Sophocles'
Oedipus and Kleist's *Der zerbrochne Krug*--completely fulfill
its terms. After a seventy-page section in which he attempts
to elucidate a (somewhat fanciful) typology of the characteristics of analytical drama, Sträßner proceeds to "Einzel-
studien" of plays by Schiller, Lessing, Kleist, and Ibsen.
Kleist is represented by a twelve-page essay on *Käthchen*

von Heilbronn. But Sträßner is so concerned to document
the existence of his "typical characteristics" that he tells
us hardly anything new or interesting about the play. The
entire exercise seems rather mechanical and uninspired,
especially in the light of the sophistication of drama theory
in German classicism. (L.S.)

Swales, Erika. "Configurations of Irony: Kleist's *Prinz Friedrich von Homburg.*" *DVJS* 56 (1982): 407-30.
    A remarkable essay which argues that "the play ... forces
the reader and critic to experience its riddling structure"
(419). Swales shows that the drama "generates harmony and
disharmony in equal measure" (420). She is sensitive not
only to the generative difficulties of Kleist's syntax, but
to their political, religious, and philosophical implications.
The parodistic import of Kleist's citations and revisions of
Schiller and Goethe is seen correctly as part of a larger
problematic of *Nachahmung*: representation is suspended between legitimacy and illegitimacy. One can only hope that
she herself will do the "more work [that] will have to be
done on Kleist's use of traditions" (427). Must reading.
(L.S.)

Träger, Christine. "Heinrich von Kleists Weg zur Novelle.
Geschichtlicher Prozess und Gattungsentscheidung." *Impulse*
3 (1981): 132-52.

Ugrinsky, Alex, ed. *Heinrich von Kleist-Studien.* Berlin: Erich
Schmidt, 1981. Also issued as *Heinrich von Kleist Studies.*
(Hofstra University Cultural and Intercultural Studies,
Nr. 3.) New York: AMS Press, 1980.
    Rev. by John Grandin in *JEGP* 81 (1982): 388-89.
    The volume is a collection of papers based on a bicentennial
Kleist conference held at Hofstra University in 1977. After
an appreciative and energetic introductory essay by Ilse
Graham ("Homage to a Misfit"), it is divided into six sec-
tions, each containing from three to seven "essays." Perhaps
due to their original status as conference papers, however,
many of the essays deliver less than they promise. Barbara
Meck's treatment of "Unglück und Verwirrung: Bemerkungen zu
Kleists Erzählungen," for example, takes up a mere three
pages of text, and consists of nothing more than a series
of clichés. However, a number of widely respected Germanists
and Kleist scholars are represented (e.g., Laurence Ryan,
Jeffrey Sammons, Lilian Hoverland, Robert Helbling, Herminio
Schmidt), and some of the essays do represent new insights

and promising suggestions. Under "Dramas," only *Die Hermanns-schlacht*, *Prinz Friedrich*, and *Der zerbrochne Krug* are dealt with; under "Novellas," "Der Zweikampf" and "Der Findling." In the section "Marionettes," Sydna Stern Weiss's "Kleist and Mathematics: The Non-Euclidean Idea in the Conclusion of the *Marionettentheater* Essay" is by far the most substantive contribution. And Hal H. Rennert's essay (in the "Comparative Studies" section) on affinities between Keats and Kleist is fascinating. The last two sections, "Education, Linguistics, and Science" and "New Perspectives" seem to be makeshift categories for essays that don't fit elsewhere. Also included is the catalogue of the Kleist exhibition which ran simultaneously with the conference. There is an (accurate and complete) index, but no bibliography. All in all, the volume breaks no new ground, but it does offer a reasonably accurate picture of contemporary concerns about Kleist. (L.S.)

Weiss, Hermann F. "Heinrich von Kleists *Was gilt es in diesem Kriege?* Eine Interpretation." *ZDP* 101 (1982): 161-72.

A brief account of the style and rhetoric of this 1809 essay, the probable sources of some of its themes, and the socio-political context in which it was written. Weiss, who discovered a manuscript version of the essay in 1981, claims that it may be understood as an example of the spate of nationalistic pamphleteering evoked by the Napoleonic threat. In particular, it represents a more popular, journalistic appeal to Prussian chauvinism than scholarly treatises aimed at an intellectual elite (e.g., Kant, Fichte, Adam Müller). Its hortatory mode accounts for the use of a range of rhetorical devices (e.g., amplification, antithesis), stylistic turns (e.g., alliteration), and narrative features (e.g., peroratio); its multiplicity of strategies and techniques, argues Weiss, is a function of its goal: to mobilize wide resistance against French domination. The essay does not fall into mere glorification of things Prussian or German; it argues that true cosmopolitanism demands respect for individual *Gemeinschaften*. Yet it is easy to see how Kleist could be appropriated by the Nazis. (L.S.)

Weiss, Hermann F. "Zu Heinrich von Kleists letzten Wochen in Dresden." *Archiv* 219 (1982): 34-43.

A biographical note, relying heavily on archival material in Stuttgart, Vienna, Munich, and Dresden, which reconstructs the movements and associations of Kleist during the period immediately before and after the outbreak of war between

Austria and France (9 Apr. 1809). Weiss claims the archival
material shows that the Austrian delegation to Saxony
(which declared war on Austria on 24 Apr.) departed from
Dresden on 26 Apr., instead of on 9 Apr., as had heretofore
been thought. Kleist, who was with the delegation, remained
an additional three days in order, Weiss speculates, to
look after the family of one of the departed diplomats.
(L.S.)

Wiegel, Alexander. "König, Polizist, Kasperle ... und Kleist.
Auch ein Kapitel deutscher Theatergeschichte, nach bisher
unbekannten Akten." *Impulse* 4 (1982): 253-77.

Wijsen, Louk M.P.T. "Intrinsic and Extrinsic Psychological
Conflicts in Literature: Manifest in Kleist's *Michael Kohl-
haas* and Hofmannsthal's 'Chandos-Brief.'" Pp. 87-124 in
Bernd Urban and Winfried Kudszus, eds., *Psychoanalytische
und psychopathologische Literaturinterpretation*. (Ars
Interpretandi, Nr. 10.) Darmstadt: Wissenschaftliche
Buchgesellschaft, 1981. Pp. vi+485. DM 54.00.

Wittkowski, Wolfgang. "Hölderlin, Kleist und die deutsche
Klassik." Pp. 319-36 in Karl Otto Conrady, ed., *Deutsche
Literatur zur Zeit der Klassik*. Stuttgart: Reclam, 1977.

Taking his cue from recent German *Bildungspolitik* and
Universitätsreform, Wittkowski seeks to redeem the central
ethical concerns of German classicism, especially Schiller's
attempts in the 1790s to articulate a vision of the concrete social role of aesthetic education, and Goethe's pro-
to-phenomenological approach to the natural sciences. This
classicism, Wittkowski suggests, is wary of overdetermina-
tion by rationalist schemes, of repressive control from
above, and thus evinces many of the very values in whose
name it has been condemned by impatient youth. Both Hölderlin and Kleist shared classicism's distrust of repressive
ideologies, but they depart from the translucence that is
the stylistic and epistemological goal of classicism.
Hölderlin's sense of universals, his fear of sullying the
holy by articulating it too directly, allegedly leads him
into a "priesterliche Mystik" foreign to the supposedly
popular themes and diction of Schiller and Goethe. Kleist,
although closer to the greats than Hölderlin, departs
from them by taking his language *too* literally. With Hölderlin, symbols evanesce into indistinction; with Kleist,
they become reality. Both ultimately fall prey to different
kinds of absolutism which, each in its way, betray classicism's "konkrete Wertethik der allgemeinmenschlichen Ein-

zelsituation und des Verhaltens in ihr." A provocative,
wide-ranging essay; yet, despite its nuggets of insight,
unsatisfying because of its unexamined allegiance to a
still-enthroned high classicism. Most of the article,
despite the title, is devoted to Hölderlin. (L.S.)

Wittkowski, Wolfgang. "Schrieb Kleist regierungsfreundliche
Artikel? Über den Umgang mit politischen Texten." *Literaturwissenschaftliches Jahrbuch* 23 (1982): 95-116.

Zweig, Stefan. *Der Kampf mit dem Dämon: Holderlin--Kleist--
Nietzsche.* (Fischer Taschenbücher, Nr. 2282.) Frankfurt:
Fischer Taschenbuch Verlag, 1981. Pp. 229. DM 8.80.

One of a series of reprints issued in 1981 to commemorate
the centennial of Zweig's birth. Even if one makes judicious
(and necessary) allowances for the social and intellectual
milieu of the 1920s, and for the particular brand of existential heroism promulgated by Zweig, these essays still
recommend themselves. They are not scholarship, but they
might yet have something to teach contemporary scholars in
their attempts to master the phenomenon of Kleist (as well
as Hölderlin and Nietzsche). Even if one rejects the psycho-
drama of a "struggle with the demonic," the contours of such
an agon find themselves reformulated in contemporary criticism's terminology: the limits of representation, the
deconstruction of centered discourse, the duplicity and
intensity of irony, the incommensurability of ratio and
emotion, the peril of self-assertion amid structures and
epistemes. Zweig's paean, if read sensitively, might save
us from an overdomesticated appropriation of Kleist as
artist and as person. (L.S.)

Reviews of books previously listed:

ELLIS, John, *Heinrich von Kleist: Studies in the Character
and Meaning of His writings* (see *RMB* for 1979, pp. 301-02),
rev. by Robert E. Helbling in *MLQ* 40 (1979): 418-20; HORN,
Peter, *Kleist-Chronik* (see *RMB* for 1981, p. 338), rev. by
R. Masson in *EG* 143 (1981): 341; HOVERLAND, Lilian, *Heinrich von Kleist und das Prinzip der Gestaltung* (see *RMB*
for 1981, p. 338), rev. by Hartmut Binder in *Germanistik*
23 (1982): 412-13; KANZOG, Klaus, *Edition und Engagement:
150 Jahre Editionsgeschichte der Werke und Briefe Heinrich
von Kleists. Band 1: Darstellung* (see *RMB* for 1981, p. 338),
rev. by Marjorie Gelus in *GQ* 54 (1981): 350-51; KRAFT,
Helga, *Erhörtes und Unerhörtes: Die Welt des Klanges bei
Heinrich von Kleist* (see *ELN* 17, Supp., 229), rev. by Hilda

M. Brown in *Germanistik* 23 (1982): 817; SEMBDNER, Helmut, ed., *Heinrich von Kleists Lebensspuren: Dokumente und Berichte der Zeitgenossen* (see *ELN* 17, Supp., 232), rev. by Ernst Fedor Hoffmann in *LFMA* 13 (1980): 36-37; SIEBERT, Eberhard, *Heinrich von Kleist: Leben und Werk in Bild* (see *RMB* for 1981, p. 340), rev. by Klaus Kanzog in *Archiv* 218 (1981): 403-05; by R. Masson in *EG* 143 (1981): 341.

MOZART

Hildesheimer, Wolfgang. *Mozart*. Trans. Marion Faber. New York: Farrar, Straus & Giroux, 1982. Pp. 408. $22.50.

> Rev. by Alan Tyson ("Amadevious") in *NYRB*, Nov. 18, 1982, pp. 3-7.

MÜLLER, WM.

Baumann, Cecilia C. *Wilhelm Müller. The Poet of the Schubert Song Cycles: His Life and Works*. Pennsylvania State University Press, 1981. Pp. xv+191. $17.50.

> Rev. by Barbara Turchinin in *GR* 47 (1982): 46.

As an initial orientation to Müller, whose life and works are characterized by question marks and questionable merit respectively, this monograph adequately serves the English-speaking audience. What it lacks is an interpretive probing in depth, a critical spark which could ignite the smoldering curiosity of the reader and enable him to perceive--rather than merely ponder due to unsubstantiated assertions--what constitutes "dubious literary worth" or "superficial poetry." Is it a necessary aesthetic corollary that great musical settings are engendered by somewhat less than great poetry? If so, why is this the case? Or why are genuine lyricists like Heine or stylists like Mann fascinated by certain aspects of Müller's artifact (or is it his artificiality?)? While it is interesting to learn about Müller's forays into the novella genre, the plot summaries we are given tend to confirm, rather than counteract, the prevalent image of the writer as a shallow craftsman. We certainly gain insight into the breadth of this man's many-sided literary endeavors, but what we do not gain is inspiration. Müller remains a hermetically sealed, sterile show-case anomaly, the curious phenomenon of a second-rate writer who nevertheless inspired a first-rate composer to some of his most immortal musical settings. (J.F.F.)

TIECK

Askedal, John Ole. "Henrik Ibsens *Peer Gynt* og Ludwig Tiecks *Franz Sternbalds Wanderungen*: En komparativ studie i norsk og tysk romantisk diktning." Pp. 189-204 in *Diktning og idé*. Festskrift til Ole Koppang. (Osloer Beiträge zur Germanistik, Bd. 41.) Oslo: Univ. Germanistik Institut, 1981. Pp. 333.

Baumgärtner, Alfred Clemens. "Ludwig Tieck: Des Lebens Überfluß." Pp. 125-39 in Jakob Lehmann, ed., *Deutsche Novellen von Goethe bis Walser*, Bd. I. Königstein: Scriptor, 1980. Pp. 155.

The strong prejudices against the youthful Tieck as the appropriator of Romantic emotions and against the aging epigone and avowed anti-Romantic beginning in the 1820s are here relativized by examining the thematic substance and artistic structure of a tale from 1839. Very effective is the focus on the process of growing isolation, the insular existence of the protagonists in both spatial and temporal terms, as well as in the existential dimension. The analyses of Tieck's preference for gentle, twilight emotions over harsh outbursts of passion, of his anti-revolutionary dream visions and of his utilization of circular techniques of narration and image constellations, are quite revealing. As is the case with all interpretations in this volume, the critic concludes with some practical hints about presenting the text in the classroom, to which end the comparison with *Taugenichts* and *Kleider machen Leute* proves particularly well-suited. (J.F.F.)

Benay, Jeanne. "Le théâtre de Ludwig Tieck: tradition et révolution." *Revue d'Allemagne* 12 (1980): 547-66.

Birrell, Gordon. "Between 'Waldeinsamkeit' and Community: Time in the *Märchen* of Tieck. *Der blonde Eckbert*, *Der Runenberg*." Pp. 90-115 in Birrell, *The Boundless Present: Space and Time in the Literary Fairy Tales of Novalis and Tieck*. (University of North Carolina Studies in the Germanic Languages and Literatures, Nr. 95.) University of North Carolina Press, 1979. Pp. 160.

Rev. by Ralph W. Ewton, Jr., in *JEGP* 79 (1980): 417-18; by Gonthier-Louis Fink in *Germanistik* 23 (1982): 417; by Valentine Hubbs in *MGS* 6 (1980): 278-79; by Dennis F. Mahoney in *Aurora* 42 (1982): 254-55.

The spatial foci of *Eckbert*--the old woman's hut and the titular hero's castle--have corresponding modes of temporal

experience, which might be described as living in perfect
timelessness and "killing time." Whereas the former is a
rather monotonous even though pristine state, the latter is
psychologically provocative, since it reflects our all-too-
human condition, the fatal disjunction of time and timelessness in *Eckbert*, and an absolute rift in *Runenberg*. The
elements of negative theodicy found in the ostensibly
idyllic *Waldeinsamkeit* and the analysis of the three test
situations to which the protagonist is subjected with an increasing sense of acceleration are quite revealing. Sometimes the most penetrating insights are found on the periphery
of the central thesis. The "way homeward" for Tieck was
indeed considerably more problematic than it was for Novalis.
(J.F.F.)

Birrell, Gordon. "Split Terrain: Space in the *Märchen* of
Tieck: *Der blonde Eckbert, Der Runenberg*." Pp. 39-62 in
Birrell, *The Boundless Present: Space and Time in the
Literary Fairy Tales of Novalis and Tieck*. (University of
North Carolina Studies in the Germanic Languages and Litera-
tures, Nr. 95.) University of North Carolina Press, 1979.
Pp. 160.

Rev. by Ralph W. Ewton, Jr., in *JEGP* 79 (1980): 417-18;
by Gonthier-Louis Fink in *Germanistik* 23 (1982): 417; by
Valentine Hubbs in *MGS* 6 (1980): 278-79; by Dennis F.
Mahoney in *Aurora* 42 (1982): 254-55.

By split terrain in *Eckbert* the writer differentiates
the world of the old woman, which exhibits elements of
"spacelessness" indicative of a unified existence, from
the castle of Eckbert with its confined space in which
rational control attempts--unsuccessfully as we see--to
suppress the untidy memories of the past beneath a veneer
of order and organization. The narrative reveals a systematic
unmasking of the protagonist's defense mechanisms and guilt
repression. The close of the story is a far cry from the
splendid synthesis which characterizes Novalis' fairy tales.
Runenberg likewise concludes on a note of uneasy coexistence
between life in the plains or in the enchanted sphere of
the mysterious mountain with its allure of gold and love.
Somewhat less than convincing is the attempted correlation
of the mountain region with early, the plains with late
Romantic ideals respectively. (J.F.F.)

Brinker-Gabler, Gisela. *Poetisch-wissenschaftliche Mittelalter-
Rezeption: Ludwig Tiecks Erneuerung altdeutscher Literatur*.
(Göppinger Arbeiten zur Germanistik, Bd. 309.) Göppingen:
Kümmerle, 1980. Pp. 299.

Rev. by Otto F. Best in *GQ* 55 (1982): 420-22; by Rüdiger
Krohn in *Germanistik* 22 (1981): 420; by Roger Paulin in *MLR*
77 (1982): 759-62.
   Not only Tieck's reception of medieval literature, but
also the receptivity of his own age for the fruits of his
restorative labors (*Minnelieder* and *Frauendienst*) are analyzed
cogently and argued persuasively in this recently published
Cologne dissertation of 1973. A fine synoptic overview traces
the reception of older German literature from the period of
Humanism to the Romantic Age, and this is followed by the
raison d'être for Tieck's interest: restoration of medieval
splendor to justify the poetic principles of his own age.
Interesting from the standpoint of *Rezeptionsgeschichte* is
the fact that whereas the *Minnelieder* struck a responsive
chord in the literary avant-garde, the *Frauendienst* appealed
to a much broader reading public. (J.F.F.)

Brummack, Jürgen. "Ludwig Tieck." Pp. 46-81 in Brummack,
   *Satirische Dichtung: Studien zu Friedrich Schlegel, Tieck,
   Jean Paul und Heine.* (Theorie und Geschichte der Literatur
   und der schönen Künste, Bd. 53.) Munich: Fink, 1979. Pp. 239.

   See also Brummack ("German 2. General").
   Rev. by M. Espagne in *EG* 141 (1981): 89-91: by Bruno Hannemann in *Monatshefte* 74 (1982): 206-07; by Jeffrey L. Sammons
(for "Heine") in *RMB* for 1980, p. 297.
   In keeping with his central thesis that the Romantics did not
neglect satire, but rather rejected the eighteenth-century,
Enlightenment mode of satiric writing (with its normative,
moral-didactic aims) in favor of an autonomous satire which
sought neither to ameliorate nor demolish, but rather hinted
subliminally at a poeticized world view, Brummack focuses
on Tieck's *Kater* as a model for this new perspective in two
dimensions: the poetic and the political. Brummack argues
plausibly that the satiric barbs are directed not at specific
flaws, but rather at general attitudes and conceptions--be
these manifested in the aesthetic, social, or political sphere.
Somewhat less satisfying is the excursion into the *Briefe
über Shakespeare,* even though the view that by 1800 Tieck
had run the gamut of his satirical talents certainly hits
the mark. (J.F.F.)

Favier, Georges. "L'âge de raison: note sur un conte de Tieck:
   Die Elfen." Pp. 47-91 in G. Brunet, ed., *Études allemandes:
   Recueil dédié à Jean-Jacques Anstett.* University of Lyon,
   1979. Pp. vii+276.

Fickert, Kurt J. "The Relevance of the Incest Motif in *Der
   blonde Eckbert.*" *GN* 13 (1982): 33-35.

The revelation of an incestuous relationship at the end
of the fairy tale has been chided as melodramatic, as an
afterthought, or as a contrived embellishment. Yet Fickert
does show that this "turn of the screw" is not only forecast
by other dire warnings and presentiments throughout the tale,
but can be traced to the *Volksmärchen*. Specifically, in
Hänsel und Gretel the sibling ties are "disconcertingly
close" and incest is "subliminally present." Whereas such
Freudian-Jungian claims that the oven constitutes a womb
symbol may strike one as forced, the conclusion that the
motif of incest should not be considered an "explanation"
but rather "a heightened symbolic expression of human falli-
bility" does ring true. (J.F.F.)

Fischer, Jens Malte. "'Selbst die schönste Gegend hat Gespens-
ter.' Entwicklung und Konstanz des Phantastischen bei Ludwig
Tieck." Pp. 131-49 in Christian W. Thomsen and Jens Malte
Fischer, eds., *Phantastik in Literatur und Kunst*. Darmstadt:
Wissenschaftliche Buchgesellschaft, 1980. Pp. 563. DM 55.00.

As the subtitle indicates, the fantastic was a constant
in Tieck's oeuvre, and this thesis is demonstrated here with
reference to the late novella *Das alte Buch und die Reise
ins Blaue hinein*, with its often precise description of
paranormal phenomena, and to the much earlier tale *Der blonde
Eckbert*. Very challenging is the contention that at least
one of Todorov's categories of the fantastic in literature
was already anticipated in Tieck by his frequent perception
of an effect without a cause. This results in a high degree
of uncertainty on the part of the reader. A good case is
made to account for Tieck's rejection of E.T.A. Hoffmann's
form of the "rohen Mantschen" with its irreconcilable dualism
of commonplace environment and poetic inner realm, since
Tieck sought to abrogate the conflict between the ordinary
and the marvelous. (J.F.F.)

Fritz-Grandjean, Sonia. *Das Frauenbild im Jugendwerk von Ludwig
Tieck als Mosaikstein zu seiner Weltanschauung*. (Europäische
Hochschulschriften, Reihe 1, Vol. 320.) Berne: Peter Lang,
1980. Pp. 208.

Rev. by Margarete Arndt in *Aurora* 42 (1982): 261-62; by
Manfred Frank in *Germanistik* 22 (1981): 174-75.

As laudable and as up to date as the aims of this book
might be, certain persistent methodological features tend
to pall on the reader: an inclination to pontificate via
ex cathedra pronouncements, a plethora of hypothetical
questions posed but seldom answered, simplistic formulations

and meaningless statements such as the following: "Symbolik
ist ein empfindliches und schwieriges Kunstmittel" (35);
"In der Romantik verschmelzen Poesie, Prosa und Ironie zu
einer Melodie, die das Bild der Zeit wiedergeben soll" (21).
To rely heavily on Kluckhohn's sixty-year-old study on love
is questionable since current feminist literature has made
giant strides beyond the findings of 1922, but to cite
Frenzel's *Daten deutscher Dichtung* in scholarly contexts
is highly suspect. There is, finally, a heavy dependence
on the work-life correspondences, undergirded by such unin-
formative assertions as: "Ohne Zweifel dürfen wir eine
gewisse Identifizierung des Dichters mit seinem Helden
erwähnen" (185). In sum, not an inspired or inspiring work
in spite of its spirited topic. (J.F.F.)

Gish, Theodore. "*Vorspiele auf dem Theater*: Dramatic and
Theatrical Elements in Ludwig Tieck's *Straußfedern*." Pp.
51-58 in Edward R. Haymes, ed., *Theatrum mundi: Essays on
German Drama and German Literature. Dedicated to Harold
Lenz on his 70th Birthday, September 11, 1978.* (Houston
German Studies, Vol. 2.) Munich: Fink, 1980. Pp. 230. DM
38.00.

Theatrical elements and stage devices in Tieck's rather
trite and banal prose contributions to *Die Straußfedern*
(1795-1798) are underscored in order to show the true
significance of this collection for the writer's aesthetic
development as a Romantic dramatist. The role of irony,
especially of Romantic irony, in both the prose pieces and
their theatrical counterparts is highlighted by the observation that the same words do not necessarily connote the
same thing when used by two different artists or, for that
matter, in two different media by the same artist. (J.F.F.)

Klussmann, Paul Gerhard. "Ludwig Tieck." Pp. 130-44 in Karl
Konrad Polheim, ed., *Handbuch der deutschen Erzählung*.
Düsseldorf: Bagel, 1981. Pp. 653.

By distilling certain constants of theme and technique
in Tieck's tales, fairy tales, novels, and novellas from
1790 to 1838, the critic supplies even the non-initiate
with an interpretive tool with which to cope with the
writer's seemingly amorphous and unwieldy fictional arsenal.
Very enlightening are the correspondences which Klussmann
uncovers in Tieck's persistent structural ambivalence, in
the juxtaposition of the realistic and fantastic as a basis
of comedy and humor, in the devices of Romantic irony and
the Tieckian *Wendepunkt*, and in narrative polyperspectivism

heightened through dialogue and conversation. The essay is
refreshingly clear in style, especially when it comes to
the role of the erstwhile Romantic in the Biedermeier age
or to the didactic function of the novella genre in laying
bare the abuses of society. (J.F.F.)

Knight, Victor. "The Perceptive Non-Artist: A Study of Tieck's
Der Runenberg." NGS 10 (1982): 21-31.

A sober and sobering assessment of Christian torn between
the desire for erotic freedom and limitless wealth on the
one hand, and familial responsibility and the societal
ethic on the other, with the ultimate balance tipping in
favor of the latter. The ranking of the protagonist with
Tieck's "arrogant hermits, unproductive pseudo-artists and
predatory aristocracy" seems like a harsh verdict. (J.F.F.)

König der Romantik: Das Leben des Dichters Ludwig Tieck in
Briefen, Selbstzeugnissen und Berichten. Vorgestellt von
Klaus Günzel. Tübingen: Wunderlich, 1981. Pp. 561. DM 38.00.

Rev. by Manfred Frank in Germanistik 23 (1982): 424-25.

This mosaic of chronologically arranged excerpts from the
correspondence to and from Tieck is divided into chapter
units, each of which is preceded by an informative introduction. Certainly a cornerstone to future Tieck studies.
(J.F.F.)

Mazur, Gertrud S. "Ein Stiefkind der deutschen Literaturkritik: Ludwig Tieck." Selecta, Nr. 2 (1981): 55-58.

Mecklenburg, Norbert. "'Die Gesellschaft der verwilderten
Steine.' Interpretationsprobleme von Ludwig Tiecks Erzählung
Der Runenberg." Der Deutschunterricht 34, Heft 6 (1982):
62-76.

This interpretation, punctuated by handy graphic charts,
not only points out the fundamental ambivalences in each
of the components in the prime polarity--village/plains
versus nature/mysterious mountain, but also tries to solve
the enigma of the ending. Whereas one can readily grasp
the commercialization and monetarizaton of the erotic
which befalls Christian, it is somewhat more difficult to
equate the mountain-mineral realm with the labyrinthine
city--hence the title of the essay--because of such factors
as discontinuity, the prismatic diffusion of human personality, and the displacement of organic nature and a vegetarian
metaphysics by the "fleurs du mal" of an artificial paradise. (J.F.F.)

Meves, Uwe. "Zu Ludwig Tiecks poetologischem Konzept bei
der Erneuerung mittelhochdeutscher Dichtungen." Pp. 107-
26 in Jürgen Kühnel, ed., *Mittelalter-Rezeption*. (Göppinger
Arbeiten zur Germanistik, Bd. 286.) Göppingen: Kümmerle,
1979. Pp. 631.

Although Tieck, in some quarters, is regarded as a
monetarily oriented writer who treats the products of his
pen as wares for commercial profit, the critic here contends
that Tieck actually resented the fact that the aesthetic
artifact had become a means to an end, rather than an end
in itself. Edifying is the contrast drawn between Nürnberg,
the city of poetry and art, as opposed to its modern, prosaic
counterpart, Fürth, whereby exposure to the mechanical
sterility of the latter instills a longing for the medieval
splendor of the former; this process is then equated with
Tieck's modernized renewal of the literature of the Middle
Ages (aside from the *Minnelieder*, *Frauendienst*, and the
Nibelungen editions, Tieck began a collection of epics for
a *Heldenbuch*) in the hope that the reader would be inspired
to return to the original. (J.F.F.)

Nahrebecky, Roman. "Ludwig Tieck." Pp. 37-86 in Nahrebecky,
*Wackenroder, Tieck, E.T.A. Hoffmann, Bettina von Arnim:
ihre Beziehungen zur Musik und zum musikalischen Erlebnis*.
(Studien zur Germanistik, Anglistik und Komparatistik, Bd.
86.) Bonn: Bouvier, 1979. Pp. 262.

Rev. by Steven P. Scher in *MHG* 27 (1981): 125-26.

A somewhat plodding, pedestrian, and quotation-laden jaunt
through Tieck's musical contributions to the *Phantasien über
die Kunst* together with his perceptions of the opera. In
most cases, what we get is a dry, descriptive paraphrase
of Tieck's views rather than interpretive insights which
elucidate the text. (J.F.F.)

Oettinger, Klaus. "'Was ist ein Leben ohne Freiheit?' Jakobin-
ertendenzen beim frühen Tieck." *AKG* 57 (1975): 412-25.

In the wake of the interest spawned by Peter Weiss's
Hölderlin drama and Pierre Berteaux' research into German
Jacobin trends, this essay traces the political dimensions
of several of Tieck's early tales such as that of the
"noble brigand" Mathias Klostermeyer. Since the issue of
hunting privileges flared up in 1790 to become a *cause
célèbre* of the Jacobins, Klostermeyer represents, to some
extent, a revolutionary. But Tieck was clever enough to
treat his protagonist with enough aesthetic distance to
avoid the wrath of the censor, and to handle the subject

so circumspectly that it remains a literary artifact
rather than a political manifesto--thus weakening considerably any case for Jacobinism. (J.F.F.)

Paulin, Roger. "Ludwig Tiecks Essayistik." *JIG* 14, Heft 1
(1982): 126-56.

This is a valiant attempt at a systematic overview of
Tieck's eclectic, improvisatory, and highly readable (in
contrast to the esoteric style of the *Athenäum*) expository
prose writings, ranging from introductions to editions,
postscripts, book and theatrical reviews, etc. Thumbnail
sketches of the basic thrust of each work make it possible
for the reader to establish some kind of ordering principle
for Tieck's essentially rambling productivity. After this
initial impetus, almost a prolegomenon to a critical edition, one can only hope that a qualified critic will under-
take such a venture. Whereas the claim that Tieck ranks
with a Coleridge or an A.W. Schlegel may surprise some and
shock others, one cannot deny to his aperçus about Shakespeare certain keen insights, and his discovery of Kleist
or his role as the "guardian of Hardenberg's grail" opened
vistas previously closed or veiled in a mystical blur.
Very astute is the discussion on the use of the conversation format as a means of maintaining ambivalent neutrality
to the subject, since the views of both participants are
expressed in point-counterpoint fashion. (J.F.F.)

Poggi, Tamara Baikova. "Ludwig Tieck, un anello di congiunzione
tra Nikolaj Evreinov e Luigi Pirandello." Pp. 132-48 in
Adam J. Bisanz and Raymond Trousson, eds., *Elemente der
Literatur: Beiträge zur Stoff-, Motif- und Themenforschung.
Elisabeth Frenzel zum 65. Geburtstag.* Vol. II. Stuttgart:
Kröner, 1980. Pp. 177. DM 25.00.

Ribbat, Ernst. "Ungleichzeitig-gleichzeitig: Goethe und Tieck."
Pp. 339-43 in *Akten des 6. internationalen Germanisten-
kongresses*, Part 3. Berne: Lang, 1980.

Sartori, Gemma. "Spunti per un Ludwig Tieck 'realista':
Reisegedichte eines Kranken." *Annali. Instituto universitario di lingue moderne. Feltre* 4 (1975-76): 229-48.

Sellner, Timothy F. "Jungian Psychology and the Romantic Fairy
Tale: A New Look at Tieck's *Der blonde Eckbert*." *GR* 55
(1980): 89-97.

A sensible, non-dogmatic, but doggedly psychoanalytic
investigation which seeks, with some success, to explain

those irritating residues of doubt which have plagued Tieck
critics for too long: the levels of reality, the name
Strohmian, the nature of Bertha's "sin," and the enigmatic
incest theme. What emerges, somewhat predictably, is a
story fusing archetypes and images from the collective unconscious with those shaped and colored by the writer's
creative imagination. The ultimate tragedy is ascribed to
the premature disregard of the Self for the stages of the
individuation process; Bertha's premature departure from
the forest idyll impinges on her journey to consciousness,
hence she founders in the stagnation of primitive, narcissistic self-love. A neatly tied package, with only a
few loose ends. (J.F.F.)

Szafarz, Jolanta. "Die Rezeption mittelalterlicher Volksbuch-
motive in Ludwig Tiecks Dramen." Pp. 127-40 in Jürgen Kühnel,
ed., Mittelalter-Rezeption. (Göppinger Arbeiten zur Germanistik, Bd. 286.) Göppingen: Kümmerle, 1979. Pp. 631.

After opening with a barrage of generalized cliches about
Romanticism, this loose, running commentary focuses on three
stage adaptations of chapbook materials: Genoveva, Oktavi-
anus, and Fortunatus. This piece provides evidence of why
a lecture, when published, may be as dull as a paper for
publication which is read aloud to an audience. (J.F.F.)

Trainer, James. "Sophie an Ludwig Tieck: neu identifizierte
Briefe." JDSG 24 (1980): 162-81.

The problematic and enigmatic relationship of Tieck to
his sister, Sophie, ranging in the perspective of critics
from an almost incestuous affair during the early years to
a growing estrangement, resentment, eventual hostility
and final indifference, is ready for a reassessment with
the publication of these letters. Of the five letters
printed here from Sophie to Ludwig, the last--from 1830
after a long period of silence--is particularly interesting
from the standpoint of its suppressed criticism. (J.F.F.)

Wheeler, Kathleen. "Coleridge's Friendship with Ludwig Tieck."
Pp. 96-112 in Donald Sultana, ed., New Approaches to Coleridge: Bibliographical and Critical Essays. London: Vision,
1981. Pp. 264.

Two actual encounters--1806 in Rome and 1817 in England--
took place between Tieck and Coleridge, and these writers
shared certain literary interests (Shakespeare, Faust) as
well as non-literary concerns (animal magnetism). In spite
of Coleridge's generally favorable assessment of Tieck's

creative output, he did not care for *Sternbald* very much, finding it imitative and derivative. Given the fruitful exchange of ideas suggested by this article, one can only share the writer's frustration that the conversations of the two were never recorded for posterity. (J.F.F.)

Wuthenow, Ralph-Rainer. "Ludwig Tieck und seine Mär vom alten Buch." Pp. 123-25 in Wuthenow, *Im Buch der Bücher oder der Held als Leser*. Frankfurt am Main: Europäische Verlagsanstalt, 1980.

Rev. by Jürgen C. Jacobs in *Arcadia* 17 (1982): 85-87. This mini-essay deals with the late "fairy tale novella" entitled *Das alte Buch und die Reise ins Blaue hinein* of 1835, a work which initially evokes the image of an anti-Romantic who then proves to be an arch-Romanticist. Somewhat abruptly the story is summarily dispatched by the critic as a retelling of a faded myth in which Romanticism and poetry are equated and in which the origins of yet older books and their strong fascination over people are debunked as a trivialized or prettified abbreviation of *Heinrich von Ofterdingen*. (J.F.F.)

Reviews of books previously listed:

KERN, Johannes P., *Ludwig Tieck: Dichter einer Krise* (see *ELN* 16, Supp., 187), rev. by Gerhard Kluge in *LMFA* 12 (1979): 181-83; LILLYMAN, William J., *Reality's Dark Dream* (see *RMB* for 1979, pp. 315-16), rev. by Patrizio Collini in *RLMC* 35 (1982): 72-77; by Hans-Dietrich Dahnke in *DLZ* 101 (1980): 570-73; by Valentine C. Hubbs in *MGS* 6 (1980): 279-81: by George F. Peters in *Monatshefte* 74 (1982): 205-06; by James Trainer in *MLR* 76 (1981): 991-92.

ITALIAN

(Compiled by Augustus Pallotta, Syracuse University;
Daniela Bini, University of Texas, Austin)

1. GENERAL

Ambrose, Mary. "Walter Scott, Italian Opera and Romantic Stage-
Settings." *IS* 36 (1981): 58-78.

Whether to foster patriotism or to suit public interest
in dramatic situations, Italian opera composers and librettists turned to Scott's novels with systematic frequency
from 1820 to the late 1840s. For, as Ambrose indicates,
"The human dramas incorporated by Scott into narratives
were the very stuff of Romantic opera, appealing to the
emotions and sensibilities of the audience" (62). Unfortunately such useful insights are stifled by the author's overriding concern with technical matters. From a cultural
perspective, what could have been an instructive assessment
of popular and critical response to Scott's work takes the
form of a tedious, if technically rigorous, description
of stage-settings. (A.P.)

Friggieri, Oliver. "Gan Anton Vassallo. L'introduzione dell'
eredità romantica nella poesia maltese." *CL* 9 (1981): 717-44.

Offers a wide-ranging study of the Maltese poet G.A.
Vassallo, who was instrumental in introducing Italian
Romanticism to the island. A patriot and faithful adherent
to the program of *Il Conciliatore*, Vassallo viewed literature and the use of his native language as the most important
means to promote Malta's cultural identity. His verse, marked
by a deeply pessimistic existential outlook and a recurrent
yearning for lost innocence, reflects a fully assimilated
appreciation of Foscolo and Leopardi. Focused on a significant ramification of Italian Romanticism, Friggieri's
study opens new avenues of research. (A.P.)

Martini, Alessandro. *La letteratura negata*. Saggio sulla
critica di parte cattolica nel secondo Ottocento italiano
attraverso le riviste. Friburgo: Edizioni Universitarie,
1981. Pp. 304.

> Rev. by Claudio Toscani in *ON* 6 (1982): 314, who states
> that Martini's work "ci porta alle origini o quanto meno
> a un punto focale e altamente casuale, di un problema--
> l'incontro-scontro (e, per la verità, qui si accentua il
> carattere del secondo termine) tra la militanza cattolica
> ed emergenza politico-ideologica della seconda metà del
> secolo scorso." The three chapters of the book are devoted
> to Manzoni's "sfortuna critica," to Leopardi, and De
> Sanctis.
> Not seen. (A.P.)

Timpanaro, Sebastiano. *Aspetti e figure della cultura ottocentesca*. Pisa: Nistri-Lischi, 1980. Pp. 471.

> Rev. by Robert S. Dombroski in *MLN* 97,1 (1982): 214-16.

See also Churchill, Kenneth ("English 3. Criticism").

2. STUDIES OF AUTHORS

D'AZEGLIO

Di Benedetto, Arnaldo. "Massimo D'Azeglio: gente di Marino."
CL 9 (1981): 668-80.

> Examines eight short stories by D'Azeglio inspired by
> his sojourn in Marino, a small town in the Roman country-
> side. Published in the weekly review, *Il cronista*, of Turin
> in 1856-57, the stories are regarded as stylized sketches
> of country life betraying a marked affinity for folklore
> and visual representation (D'Azeglio was also a gifted
> painter). "Da buon romantico," writes Di Benedetto, "D'Aze-
> glio vagheggiò il primitivo e il caratteristico, ma ha
> proprio l'aria di divertirsi allo spettacolo di quei gesti
> vigorosi e bizzarri" (672). In view of the writer's per-
> ceived lack of interest in the peasant class, Di Benedetto
> proceeds to rectify a study by Pompeati in which the stories
> mentioned are linked to Verga's "Cavalleria rusticana."
> (A.P.)

DE SANCTIS

La Sala, Raffaele. "Una biografia 'popolare' di Francesco
De Sanctis." *CL* 9 (1981): 777-800.

Publishes a biographical sketch of De Sanctis by Raffaele
Valagara. The text, consisting of a few pages, appeared
initially in three separate publications in 1885 and 1917.
Equally noteworthy is La Sala's careful reconstruction of
cultural life in Avellino based on disparate bibliographical
sources which are not easily accessible. (A.P.)

DI BREME

Ferraris, Angiola. *Ludovico di Breme. Le avventure dell'utopia.*
Firenze: Olschki, 1981. Pp. 224.

Rev. by Maria Grazia Pensa in *LI* 34 (1982): 435-38.

FOSCOLO

Cambon, Glauco. *Ugo Foscolo, Poet of Exile.* Princeton University Press, 1980. Pp. x+356. $21.50.

Listed in *RMB* for 1981, p. 350, but not reviewed.
Rev. by J.H. Whitfield in *SiR* 21 (1982): 260-65.

Overshadowed by Leopardi, Foscolo has received scant
attention in English-speaking countries, especially the
United States. If a learned study has the desired effect
of educating and reorienting the taste of cultured readers,
one can state with confidence that Cambon's brilliant work
will prove instrumental in rescuing Foscolo from undeserving
neglect. In Cambon's words, Foscolo "demands to be placed
in a European perspective if only because of the enduring
enrichment he has brought to poetry and of the tireless
experimentation that marked his intense career" (54). Moreover, if contemporary interest in Leopardi stems from our
precarious existential condition, in Foscolo, who led a
troubled and restless life, we discover, as Cambon puts
it, that "the vicissitudes of mankind are themselves a sort
of perennial exile, a perpetual loss of the *ubi consistam*"
(17).

With Foscolo's experience as a point of reference, Cambon
begins precisely on this note--the "condition of exile" in
Western culture, from the Old Testament Jews and Ovid's
banishment to the Black Sea to Dante and such modern poets
as James, Eliot, and Joyce. This comparative perspective,

rich in insights and analytical breadth, forms the cornerstone of Cambon's criticism. A second feature of the book
consists of acknowledging but not treating important questions studied by other critics, for Cambon seeks to break
fresh ground in his assessment of Foscolo's art. Thus his
analysis of *Jacopo Ortis* focuses on the theme of suicide
through a fruitful Foscolo-Goethe analogy that points to
a "suicide by proxy" "consummated on the white page"--an
act which, extended to Pavese's "self-sacrifice consummated
in the flesh" (63), is perceived as an ideological sign of
two distinct moments in the history of Western culture.
The wide-ranging study of *I Sepolcri* and *Le Grazie* (each
absorbing a full chapter) is marked by an impressive mastery
of all aspects of prosody coupled, consistently, with a
pervasive sensitivity to the phonic and semantic values
of poetic diction. For example, commenting on the opening
line of *I Sepolcri* ("All'ombra dei cipressi e dentro
l'urne"), Cambon writes: "The consonantal quality of words
like *ombra* and *cipressi* suggests a sigh, not a shout; the
enjambments work against the limits imposed by metric
strictness, as so often happens in Foscolo, and we then hear
a basso continuo lilt, loosely flowing, over and beyond
the blank verse measure" (158-59). The analysis of *Le Grazie*
offers a genetic reconstruction of the poem based on the
Florence and Leghorn manuscripts whose variants and salient
features are used to underline, often graphically, the evo-
lutions in Foscolo's continual striving for superior
artistic achievement. "To pursue a close analysis of *Le
Grazie*," remarks Cambon, "is to enter the workshop of
poetry" (206). One has to point out that Cambon is no mere
observer in Foscolo's "workshop"; he proves to be a cultured,
highly sensitive, and skilled craftsman in deciphering,
interpreting, and enlightening for us the creative process
and, with it, the many riches of Foscolo's poetry. In short,
this study stands out as a remarkable and enduring contribution to Foscolo studies. (A.P.)

Gibellini, Pietro, ed. *Foscolo e la cultura bresciana del
   primo Ottocento*. Brescia: Ed. Grifo, 1979. Pp. XIII+315.

   Rev. in *GSLI* 159 (1982): 314.

Gibellini, Pietro. "Gadda e Foscolo." *GSLI* 159 (1982): 26-63.

   In his effort to document Gadda's visceral antipathy
toward Foscolo, Gibellini leaves no stone unturned. Every
shred of evidence contained in Gadda's writings is examined
with commendable thoroughness. Even so, the study fails to

resolve a crucial question—the complex motivational forces
that compelled Gadda to lash out at Foscolo with such
virulence. In this respect, Gibellini's undertaking is at
best tentative; he merely alludes to Gadda's perception of
Foscolo's verses as "insensati, vacui, o retorici, o menzo-
gneri" (62). More penetrating is the explanation offered by
Oreste Macrí in his study on Foscolo (reviewed below):
"Sarebbe stolto risolvere [this matter] in termini d'invidia
e di desiderio, quasiché Carlo Emilio abbia dipinto se
stesso, consolandi gratia, il che è però possibile" (11).
And, "Gadda, acciccato, sembra scorgere (in Foscolo) la
propria desiderata—odiata controfigura" (26). (A.P.)

Jonard, N. "Le temps dans l'oeuvre de Foscolo." REI 27 (1981):
40-68.

In this polemical study, time is treated existentially as
a biographical-artistic experience that qualifies the main
thematic coordinates in Foscolo's work: love, beauty, death,
and glory. Proceeding in chronological order, Jonard under-
lines Foscolo's agnosticism and his sensationist views of
existence which in his youthful poetry find corresponding
expression in hedonistic pursuits and "la recherche de la
gloire." To this point, one can accept Jonard's analysis.
What proves highly debatable is the characterization of
Foscolo's subsequent work as little more than an engrossing
exercise in narcissistic indulgence—characterization which
is obtusely indifferent to Foscolo's concern with humanistic
and transcendental values. Thus I Sepolcri, Jacopo Ortis,
and the sonnets are placed on the same plane: "Il n'est
pas une seule de ses oeuvres qui ne soit sous-tendue par
un narcissisme esthétique qui le [Foscolo] conduit à dessiner
une image idéale de lui-même" (61). Not surprisingly, in
describing the main existential problem of I Sepolcri, this
critic moves from a valid premise ("par quels moyens l'homme
peut échapper à sa contingence et à sa temporalité," (61)
to a reductivist assessment: "Ce nouvel Homère est intime-
ment persuadé qu'en immortalisant les grands dans sa poésie
c'est lui-même qu'il immortalise" (62). No doubt Gadda would
have looked with favor upon Jonard's study. (A.P.)

Lindon, John. "Foscolo, Daru e la storia di Venezia." REI 27
(1981): 8-39.

Foscolo's writings on the history of Venice, "virtually
ignored" by historians and literary critics, are examined
here with extraordinary competence by a scholar who has no
reservations about Foscolo's contribution to historiography.

Actually the first of the two articles in question, the
Memoirs of Casanova, is dismissed as "giornalismo frettoloso"
devoid of "particolari pregi letterari.... e di valore critico"
(11). Moreover, Lindon points out that the arguments used by
Foscolo to disprove the authenticity of Casanova's memoirs
as historical document were refuted conclusively by R. Fulin
(1877) and E. Mola (1881). Much more important, "anche come
storiografia" is the *History of the Democratical Constitution
of Venice*, "documento di notevole interesse per la biografia
intellettuale del poeta" (13). Establishing "[un] rapporto
fra testo foscoliano e contesto britannico," Lindon remarks
that the work was motivated by contemporary British interest
in Venice (Samuel Rogers and Byron, among others), by the
favorable reception of P. Daru's seven-volume *Histoire de
la République de Venise* (1819), and by Foscolo's consequent
effort to rectify the mythic perceptions of the *Serenissima*
popularized by British Romantics. Foscolo, who regarded Daru's
work as "opera piena di pregi sommi e di sommi difetti in
tutte le sue parti" (23), sought to correct such aspects
of Daru's history as the establishment of the State Inquisi-
tion and the duration of democratic government in Venice.
Refuting Daru's assertion that "Venise fut une véritable
démocratie, depuis sa fondation, vers 420, jusqu'aux dernièrs
années du septième siècle" (26), Foscolo argued that "la
democrazia originaria era rimasta sostanzialmente intatta"
(27) to the end of the twelfth century. Lindon regards
Foscolo's insistence on this matter as a reflection of his
desire to offer the British audience a vigorous image of
Venice, "la Venezia libera e forte della maturità, modello
di vigore economico e di sapienza politica" (36). (A.P.)

Lindon, John. "Ugo Foscolo e la 'vera' Caroline Russell."
    GSLI 159 (1982): 74-81.

    Basing his conclusions on fresh research, Lindon points
out that the "real" Caroline Russell was not, as most
scholars would have us believe, a young girl. She is said
to have been in her late twenties when Foscolo fell in love
with her. Her refusal to marry the poet was based, according to Lindon, not on their age difference but on other con-
tingent factors: his religion, nationality, and precarious
financial situation. (A.P.)

Macrí, Oreste. *Il Foscolo negli scrittori italiani del
    Novecento*. Ravenna: Longo, 1980. Pp. 204.

    Among the merits of this work, one can single out Macrí's
successful effort to redress the imbalance between Foscolo
and Leopardi with regard to their presence in modern Italian

poetry--imbalance created by the propensity of many critics
to underline the relevance of Leopardi's existential outlook
to our time. Macrì does not underrate Leopardi; he points
instead to Foscolo as a concomitant presence which is not
readily discernible but equally pervasive. Not everyone,
however, will appreciate Macrì's critical treatment, especially his penchant for systematic, statistical accumulation
of supportive material without any sense of discrimination
as to what is peripheral, fortuitous, insignificant, and
what is truly important. To Macrì, *everything* relating to
Foscolo in some form or other is significant to understanding the poet's participation in twentieth-century poetry.
In this vein, he surveys a full spectrum of Novecento
poets underlining, in a terse and frequently cryptic fashion,
resonances (Saba, Quasimodo, Betocchi), critical testimonies
(Cecchi, De Robertis), iconoclastic acts (Gadda), reflexive
influence (Rebora), mediations (Homer through Foscolo in
Ungaretti), superpositions ("Leopardi foscoliano"), as well
as tangible influence (Cardarelli, Luzi, and Gatto, among
others). Two examples of Macrì's critical idiom. On Alfonso
Gatto: "Anche qui la lessematica foscoliana si riattualizza
originalmente tra spostamenti zonali e sinonimie, surcres-
cendo specifici moduli gattiani" (122). And Tommaso Landolfi
is defined "tardo prodotto postromantico o neodecadente o
semplicemente paraclassico acrono" (126).
      Nò doubt some readers will find this work difficult to
digest partly because a good share of its contents is presented as raw material awaiting further elaboration. However, those who finish the book will gain extraordinary insights into the sinewy and subterranean processes of poetic
assimilation. Included in the Appendix is the second part
of Macrì's "metodo comparatistico." Part I appeared as an
introduction to his *Varia fortuna del Manzoni in terre
iberiche* (Ravenna: Longo, 1976). (A.P.)

Pecoraro, Elisanna. "La seconda ode saffica nell'interpretazione
      del Verri e del Foscolo." *CL* 9 (1981): 538-47.

      Sappho's ode, translated first by Catullus ("Ille mi par
esse deo videtur") and highly regarded by Longinus as an
example of the sublime, was rendered in Italian by Alessandro
Verri (1872) and twice by Foscolo (1794, 1821). Verri's free
version ("sviluppa liberamente con immagini e modi espressi-
vi piuttosto languidi e accorati," 542) is juxtaposed to
the second (and best) translation by Foscolo, which combines
"l'eleganza formale alla fedeltà del testo" (547). Excellent
bibliography. (A.P.)

Toschi, Luca. "Foscolo lettore di Sterne e altri 'sentimental travellers.'" *MLN* 97,1 (1982): 19-40.

Toschi examines "il momento cosidetto sterniano" in Foscolo as an incisive intellectual experience occasioned by, but not limited to, the translation of *Sentimental Journey*. Reading Sterne, Foscolo is said to have acquired new insights as to the effectiveness of humor and polemical discourse. The second part of the essay is devoted to several Italian authors of travel literature who also heeded "la lezione sterniana." The author views travel literature as a cross-cultural activity with precise ideological connotations. Yet his tendency to shun textual exemplification and to intellectualize every facet of the subject matter results in abstruse and often arid excursions of questionable value. (A.P.)

Turchi, Roberta. *Ugo Foscolo e la "Patria infelice."* Padova: Liviana, 1981. Pp. 163.

Whitfield, J.H. "But Which Foscolo Do You Admire?" *IS* 37 (1982): 67-71.

Contains some afterthoughts on E.R. Vincent's *Ugo Foscolo, an Italian in Regency England* (1953), its limitations as a biography with an implicitly unflattering view of the poet. Whitfield also touches on the changing perception of Foscolo (shifting interest from his life to his work) reflected in the groundbreaking 1927 essay by Mario Fubini. (A.P.)

LEOPARDI

Barberi-Squarotti, Giorgio. "Leopardi: le allegorie della poesia." *Italianistica*, IX,1 (Jan.-Apr. 1980): 27-39.

The simile, sparrow-poet, in "Il passero solitario" has, in the past, been thought to reflect Leopardi's perception of the similarity of their lives--solitary and joyless. For Barberi-Squarotti, instead, Leopardi's simile is based on the sameness of their activity. The singing of the sparrow coincides with the poet's creative process. For both the price is solitude. In order to "sing" or to make poetry, the poet must renounce life. The end of the poem attests, in Squarotti's view, to the poet's admission that before death, even the myth of poetry collapses. To prove this point, he examines "Alla primavera" and "La sera del dì di festa" and points out that "there is constantly in

Leopardi's poetry the sense of the death of poetry" (31). All
Leopardi's poems, Squarotti continues, represent the contra-
dictory nature of poetry in the modern age. This statement,
however, is too drastic. Squarotti could have described
Leopardi's poetry as negative, but not dead. Leopardi, in
fact, continued to write it in an ironical vein ("Palinodia,"
"Nuovi credenti," *Paralipomeni*--for which the another shows
a clear antipathy) or in the renewed form of *canti*, as in his
last masterpieces. The metaphor poetry--*ginestra* (both bound
to die)--does not hold. The poem does not prove that Leopardi
shared Hegel's belief that philosophy spelled the end of
poetry. It proves, instead, its supreme power, for it is born
out of the negative reality which philosophy created. (D.B.)

Biasin, Gian Paolo. "Nel primordio della sera." *Paragone* 360-
62 (Feb.-Apr. 1980): 70-94.

Biasin applies pictorial criticism, in particular Arcangeli's concept of "Lo spazio romantico," to Leopardi's
sonnet "L'infinito" as a "necessary development" from Foscolo's
sonnet "Alla sera." The non-anthropocentric perspective of
Turner's paintings implies for Arcangeli a new relationship,
"coscienza-universo," as the essence of Romanticism. Biasin
confirms this view with a phonological, rhythmical, and syn-
tactic analysis of the two sonnets disclosing their thematic
novelty as the polarity of consciousness/universe or of
"objective" time and space versus an unreachable beyond.
Finding a precise correspondence of content and form--for
instance the new, untraditional use of the hendecasyllable--
Biasin sees the two sonnets as emblematic of a new epoch
of literary history. (D.B.)

Binni, Walter. "La poesia di Leopardi negli anni napoletani."
RLI 84, n.s. VII,3 (Sept.-Dec. 1980): 427-57.

Binni's thesis, Leopardi's heroism and social involvement,
is restated and his complete disagreement with the reactionary
interpretation of Leopardi (N. Jonard, V. Carpi, F.P. Botti)
clearly spelled out. Leopardi's hatred was not of politics
as a whole, Binni says, but only of the politics of his times.
His democratic spirit is visible in his compulsive effort to
bring truth to all men (as in his *Paralipomeni*, where the
most violent attack is against the Austrian "crabs"). If
there is no element of class struggle in Leopardi, Binni
continues, we must remember that he focused on the relationship between the intellectuals, carriers of truth, and "il
vulgo," to whom truth is owed (437). Leopardi is the great
intellectual poet who, after examining contemporary history,

finds it unacceptable, demystifies it, and prepares a new
notion of politics based on the preliminary acceptance of
a materialistic and atheistic truth and on acceptance of
the limitations of mankind. Binni concludes with an interesting parallel between Jacques Monod's *Le Hazard et la nécessité*
and Leopardi's convictions that the alliance between nature
and man is over and that there is no providential design in
life. (D.B.)

Blasucci, Luigi. "Una fonte linguistica (e un modello psicolo-
gico) per i *Canti*: la versione del secondo libro dell'*Eneide*."
RLI 85, n.s. VII,1-2 (Jan.-Aug. 1981): 157-69.

Leopardi's translation of Book Two of the *Aeneid* was influential in the development of his own poetical language,
as earlier studies have shown (Bigi, Stefani, De Robertis,
Shell, Fubini). Here Blasucci seeks to complete the list of
textual comparisons, which include single verbal elements,
syntagma, whole sentences, syntactical structures, lexical
elements, characteristic expressions in enjambment, coinci-
dence of lexicon as well as of images. Furthermore, he points
out that this infiltration of Virgilian elements in Leopardi's
poetry (*Canzoni* and "Bruto Minore") through the medium of
his translation denotes a strong similarity of feelings and
needs. The Aeneas of Book Two is the defeated hero, aware
of "the vanity of a cause which the gods have abandoned"
(168), a character destined to come alive again in Leopardi's
"All' Italia" and "Bruto Minore." (D.B.)

Brioschi, Franco. *La poesia senza nome. Saggio su Leopardi*.
Milano: Il Saggiatore, 1980. Pp. 303.

Contains four essays which, as the author says, maintain
their character as individual studies, although they aim at
a comprehensive interpretation of Leopardi's thought. The
first and the third essays, "Ovidio tra i barbari" and "Ars
amandi, ars moriendi," here revised, appeared respectively
in *Comunità* 178 (1977) and in *MLN* XLI (1976). In the second
chapter, "La poesia senza nome" (a quotation from the
Zibaldone), Brioschi's stylistic analysis of the "Coro dei
morti" and the *Operette morali* focuses on Leopardi's cosmic
pessimism, examined in the light of French materialism
(Cabanis, d'Holbach, La Mettrie, Dupuis, Volney). This
comparative study points out the similarities between the
two works as well as specific characteristics of Leopardi's
pessimism. His rigorous criticism of society, life, and art
is reflected both in his philosophy and in his poetry. He
will eventually abandon classicism and propose a "poesia
senza nome," without *genres*, rules, or schemata, whose form

needs to be reinvented each time and which lives only "nella soggettività umana" (171). In the analysis of Leopardi's late literary production, mainly *I pensieri* and *Paralipomeni* (chapter 4: "Al di là del principio del piacere"), Brioschi emphasizes the antisocial message present in them, and accepts it together with the heroic appeal to mankind in "La ginestra." Binni's interpretation remains intact, but next to it Brioschi places the portrait of a Leopardi "alle soglie del nichilismo" (279). The contradiction must be accepted, the author seems to say, for contradiction and paradox, as Leopardi teaches, rule the world. (D.B.)

Burchi, Elisabetta. *Il progetto leopardiano: "I pensieri."* Roma: Bulzoni, 1981. Pp. 217.

The book begins with the history of the very few and super- ficial critical studies of *I pensieri*, and accepts the dating by Moroncini. Examining Ranieri's and Moroncini's testimony, Burchi concludes that Leopardi wrote and revised each "pen- siero," making it an autonomous composition, and then or- ganized the material through the numbering which Ranieri completed. Through the analysis of the various drafts of the work, Burchi concludes that they were the result of a long and constant process of rewriting and re-elaboration.

The errors in past interpretations of *I pensieri* were caused, Burchi affirms, by the fact they were examined in isolation, without taking into account the entire poetics of the last Leopardian phase which prepared them. This is probably why almost half of the book is spent in reexamining and summarizing Binni's interpretation of Leopardi's heroism and social commitment in "Palinodia," *Paralipomeni*, "Nuovi Credenti," and "La ginestra." Here Burchi, following Binni, sees not only the negative philosophy of a materialist, in his attack against progress and the optimism of his times, but also the positive criticism of the artist who, allocating his own work space, is fully engaged on the social level. "La ginestra," in fact, offers a new model of the civic and social man. The contact Leopardi had with the cultural life in Florence and Naples, whose aim was mainly social and political, stimulated him, in a critical way, to reflect more on the nature of man as a social animal. It was in order to defend man from Nature that he developed, at the end, this interest in society seen as the coalition of men against Nature. Leopardi's social engagement refused the hegemonic tendency of his times. He did not believe in Tuscan and Neapolitan liberalism, idealism, or spiritualism. His approach was moralistic rather than political, for he assumed the highest value was man and he was concerned with his sur- vival.

Burchi examines also the relation *Zibaldone-Pensieri*, seeing
the former as reflections bound to specific moments and subjective experiences, and the latter, instead, as universally and
objectively valid statements on man in general. This development from a subjective to an objective phase is also seen
by Burchi as a democratic step taken by Leopardi to break
out of the privileged and isolated position of the intellectual, manifest in the *Zibaldone*. Burchi mentions the literary
antecedents to Leopardi's aphorisms (Isocrates, Epictetus,
Marcus Aurelius, La Rochefoucauld, La Bruyère, Pascal,
Guicciardini) and explains Leopardi's choice of the genre
also with his admiration and respect for the wisdom of
classical tradition and for its essential, rigorous form of
expression. Furthermore, Burchi adds, the "disconnection"
and fragmentation of this literary form reflects, in Leopardi,
the crisis of a systematic view of the world; the paradox
of the universe. (D.B.)

Carannante, Antonio. "Il pensiero linguistico di Giacomo
    Leopardi." *RLI* 84, n.s. VII, 1-2 (Jan.-Aug. 1980): 179-98.

Seven hundred are the pages of the *Zibaldone* in which
Leopardi deals with linguistic problems; yet the *Zibaldone*
must be read as a cohesive effort because there is no compart-
mentalization in Leopardi's mind. This is the premise and
the conclusion of Carannante's essay. Leopardi's great interest in the study of language and his aim to improve and
to modernize Italian are not to be seen as the sign of mere
formalism, but must be considered in relation to his philosophical and poetical thought. What Carannante finds is no
great discovery, yet the essay is useful, for it examines
in detail previous studies on this subject. Moreover,
Carannante connects missing links, surveys the linguistic
thought of the time (Cesarotti, Algarotti, Muratori,
Baretti, Giordani) and is able to show the very personal
and autonomous position taken by Leopardi, who benefited
from many thinkers, but was never completely dependent on
any of them. (D.B.)

Carsaniga, Giovanni. "Was Leopardi a Scientist?" Pp. 61-78
    in *Altro Polo, a Volume of Italian Studies*, ed. Silvio
    Trambaiolo and Nerida Newbigin. University of Sidney, 1978.

"Was Leopardi a scientist? My reply would be that he was.
He had a better understanding of science, its aims and
methods, its consequences for the so-called progress of
mankind, than most professional scientists of his generation. He would not have been such a penetrating thinker if
his poetic sensitivity had not warned him of the limitations

of science. But he would not have been such a great poet,
had his poetry not been the natural emotional outlet of his
profound philosophical meditations, the natural and inevitable culmination of his unusual scientific culture"
(75-76).

Casale, Ottavio Mark. *A Leopardi Reader*. University of Illinois
Press, 1981. Pp. 271.

Casale's book is a welcome English anthology of Leopardi's
writings addressed to "the general reader of world, comparative or romantic literature" and it will certainly broaden
the circle of Leopardi's admirers. The introduction gives
the reader some biographical data as well as a basic sketch
of Leopardian criticism from Leopardi's death to the present.
Casale, further, summarizes the development of Leopardi's
philosophical and poetical thought to enable the reader to
follow his selection of prose and poetry. Leopardi's texts
are presented chronologically; clear and brief prefaces
introduce the four major sections of the book. Short comments
often accompany the material chosen in order to clarify certain points or to fill in gaps. A very positive feature is
the ample use of Leopardi's prose for, as Casale says, "he
expressed himself more often" and "perhaps more revealingly
in prose." The prose is at times propaedeutic to the poetry
that follows; at times it is a commentary or a discussion
of the poetry that precedes. The reader can pass from poetry
to prose and vice versa without perceiving any abrupt logical or stylistic break. Accordingly, the book can be read
as an enlightening "autobiography" of Leopardi. Casale
translates sixteen *Canti*, eight *Operette* and parts from two
others, thirty-one *Pensieri*, many pages of the *Zibaldone*,
thirty-seven letters, and a few miscellaneous writings (but
none of Leopardi's late satirical poems). The prose is better
translated than the poetry (an almost impossible task in
my opinion) where Casale has problems in recreating the
rhythm and where the choice of words is often unfortunate.
There are some minor errors in the translation and a few
serious ones: in Pensiero X, p. 190, "cannot acquire" instead of "cannot be acquired"; in "Copernicus," p. 152,
"some listening to one minister, some to another" to translate Leopardi's "attendessero chi ad un ministero e chi a
un altro"; on p. 153, "and this will make them feel better
and save me from criticism" to translate Leopardi's "e a
me questi loro giudizi non daranno un dispiacere al mondo";
the end of the stanza before the last one in "Alla sua
donna," p. 243, has been misunderstood, as has the end of
"A se stesso" where Casale repeats Whithfield's error of

taking "Nature" as a vocative, thus misinterpreting Leopardi's idea of Nature, which he does, in fact, also in his brief introduction to the poem. A minor rectification: Leopardi did not invent the word "Hypermephelus," but Lucian from Samosata did. Yet credit must be given to a very courageous effort. Casale's translation offers a readable English, and it is often poetical, which was rarely the case with previous translations. His selection brings out well what he calls Leopardi's "integrity," his "constant concern for verbal and ethical rightness" (23) which makes him such a positive force still. But why does he say that "the moral dimension [in Leopardi] is undeniably and crucially present *despite* [his] materialism"? Why should materialism and morality be seen as opposites? Is not this attitude the residue of a biased concept of materialism? (D.B.)

Casale, Ottavio M., and Allan C. Dooley. "Leopardi, Arnold and the Victorian Sensibility." *CLS* XVII,1 (Mar. 1980): 44-65.

This is a worthwhile survey of Leopardi's fame in England. The authors "wish to discern and analyze significant moments in the Victorian response from the important early essays to the comments of Arnold" (45). They point out that in their criticism of Leopardi, the Victorians reveal as much about themselves as about Leopardi. After having considered Sainte-Beuve's study on Leopardi (1844), which shaped the later English studies, the authors begin to examine the essays by G.H. Lewes and W.E. Gladstone written in 1848 and 1850 respectively. The former praised Leopardi's genuine sentimentality, thus his true romantic spirit; the latter, his poetical skill and knowledge. Yet Lewes, a true positivist, dismisses the *Operette morali*; Gladstone, a strong believer in Christianity, censored them altogether. They established two images of Leopardi which persisted through the years: Leopardi the doomed, suffering Romantic artist (Lewes); Leopardi the apostate genius (Gladstone). Together with these, a new image of Leopardi, spokesman for pessimism, was emerging toward the latter decades of the century. Casale and Dooley examine some of the essays of that period up to the first article in 1880 by R. Garnett, which refused to speculate on the relationship between Leopardi's art and his life and which, also for the first time, showed an appreciation of previously ignored poems like "Canto notturno" and "La ginestra." Arnold was, of course, the most perspicacious of Leopardi's critics and the essay claims that he was so, precisely because his sensibility was very close to Leopardi's. Arnold's ambiguity in his judgment of Leopardi, whom he places, in many respects, above Wordsworth and Byron, but to whom he finally gives third place, can be explained with his own internal contradictions. Although he was akin to thought and belief to Leopardi, good poetry, for Arnold, had not only to "add to the knowledge of men," but also "to their happiness" (62). Arnold was incapable of either but he praised those abler than himself. (D.B.)

Ceragioli, Fiorenza. *I Canti fiorentini di Giacomo Leopardi*. Firenze: Olschi, 1981. Pp. 208.

The author's linguistic analysis focuses on these four "Canti" ("Il pensiero dominante," "Amore e Morte," "A se stesso," "Consalvo"), written between May 1830 and Sept. 1833. Ceragioli works with words which constitute the thematic structure of the poems and which tie them to Leopardi's philosophy. She brings out interesting connections between these poems and certain passages in the *Zibaldone* and the *Operette morali*. Her aim is to show that the first three poems ("Consalvo" receives a new and accurate critical edition in a separate chapter) are a unit in Leopardi's literary production, and represent the poet's unique cultural and linguistic experience in Florence. Their genesis points to the same experience of love (for Fanny Targioni Tozzetti), but the stamp of this uniqueness is the constant presence of the Love-Death theme. Love is here intellectualized and universalized and strictly bound to Death which is given the same treatment and is seen for the first time as a positive force, as a value. Love and Death are siblings for they alone can give to man the only possible happiness. Furthermore they exchange their original characteristics. Love becomes a painful and destructive power and Death loses its cruelty in order to participate in Love's conquest. Ceragioli, in fact, makes an interesting comparison between the prose and the poetry of this period. Love does not appear in the former, but only in the latter, and Death, which instead appears in the *Zibaldone* and in the *Operette* ("Tristano"), must acquire some of Love's characteristics in order for poetry to come into existence. Love, thus, is the true lyric force. The author sees this opposition and dualism as peculiar to the Florentine phase, yet she does not prove her statement with thematic and stylistic comparisons with Leopardi's earlier or his later poetry. Further, she offers no explanation for this phenomenon. The linguistic analysis is very precise, as befits a pupil of Peruzzi, but the essay is fragmentary and lacks a clear structure. (D.B.)

De Liguori, Girolamo. "Leopardi e i Gesuiti (1878-1898).
Appunti per la storia della censura leopardiana." *RLI* 85,
n.s. VII,1-2 (Jan.-Aug. 1981): 170-89.

A very interesting attempt to demonstrate that the long-
lasting separation between Leopardi the poet and Leopardi
the philosopher, the "miraculous" artist and the dangerous
thinker, had its foundation in the hegemony of Catholic
thought between 1800 and 1900, in particular the influence
of the Jesuits. This hegemony was made possible by the
crisis of scientific positivism and its progressive fading
into neo-idealism.

De Liguori examines the position of the Jesuits toward
Leopardi between the years 1878 and 1898, and uses many
quotations from various articles in *Civiltà Cattolica*.
Leopardi's moral philosophy was condemned, thus his *Operette
morali* were banned. The Jesuits, De Liguori states, much
more acutely than many of our twentieth-century critics,
immediately understood the revolutionary force of Leopardi's
philosophy and the dangerous impact it could have on youth.
The scholar shows the critical evolution of their position
toward Leopardi, which moved from a global condemnation
to a milder rejection of only the harmful aspects of his
thought and to the acceptance of his poetry and classicism.
The aim of the Jesuits, says De Liguori, was to play a
major role in the history of Italian culture, and to appear
as defenders of literary as well as moral values. Their
late defense of classicism was a clear reaction against
the dangers of Romanticism and an attempt to reevaluate
the past against the uncertainty of the present. Thus
Leopardi's classicism could be defended for his profound
respect for and knowledge of the classics and for his poetry
"che ci fa tosto accorti come lo spirito del Cristianesimo
le informi, senza che l'incredulo poeta se ne accorga"
(188). This manipulation of Leopardi represents one of the
many ways in which the Catholic Church opposed the modern
world. It well understood that in order to have an impact
over minds it had to work within the cultural world. (D.B.)

Gensini, Stefano. "Dinamiche linguistico-culturali e spazio
del letterato nelle discussioni del primo Ottocento."
Lavoro critico 23 (July-Sept. 1981): 75-112.

Gensini follows the development of the "querelle" about
language in Italy examining the position of his major
speakers (Cesarotti, Monti, Baretti, Foscolo, Giordani).
After the Cinquecento the split between literary and spoken
language (mainly dialects) grew stronger, with the result

that both literature and language, so separated from the
people, decayed and became incapable of expressing the
new thoughts and needs of society. Language, then, is viewed
as a metaphor for cultural development. This is what
Leopardi believes; language, culture, and thought are
strictly connected and Gensini well sees in this belief
the development from Locke's, Condillac's, and Leibniz's
theories of language.

He examines Leopardi's position in the debate on language
through the pages of the *Zibaldone*, pointing out his twofold
approach to the issue: Italy lacks a modern language because it lacks a modern national literature, and it lacks
such literature because it lacks besides social and national
leadership--a dialogue between the people and the literary
scholars. Yet this very negative condition becomes in
Leopardi's eyes a positive basis for the formation of a
new poetical language. If, in fact, a national language
would seem to need homogeneity and precision (like the
French language), a poetical language--which is what he
mainly aims at--requires the opposite: the vague, the indefinite, the uncommon, the rare. In a country, says
Gensini, marked by the separation between literary and
spoken language, Leopardi would find a possibility of renewal, paradoxically, in the "common" and familiar words.
In the high literary Italian context, it was precisely
the common word which could sound rare and "peregrina."
(D.B.)

Lattanzi, Liliana. "Leopardi e l'Italia." *Testo* II,1 (Jan.-
June 1981): 73-133.

A well-structured essay which aims to prove Leopardi's
constant involvement in and concern with his country.
Through a chronological analysis of his literary production,
the author distinguishes three "moments" in Leopardi's
political interest. The first moment, represented by the
patriotic "Canzoni," corresponds to the enthusiasm of the
first revolutionary attempts by Italian liberals. The
second movement, represented by the *Operette*, corresponds
to a reflective and negative phase, after the revolutionary
explosion of 1821. The third movement, represented by
Paralipomeni, expresses the doubts and perplexities about
the failure of Italian patriots.
Lattanzi stresses that Leopardi's patriotism must be
seen as a continuum of which the three movements are
necessary and connected phases. Leopardi's political commitment, Lattanza says, must be understood as a pedagogical
and moral reflection in view of his personal, literary--

not political—intervention. He was always aware of his
peculiar role as a poet. What comes out of this analysis
is Leopardi's acute diagnosis of Italian society in a
moment of crisis, that is, in its passage from the values
of nature, on which the ancient civilizations were founded,
to those of reason, typical of modern societies. Leopardi,
says Lattanzi, is modern, for he, better than anyone else
in his times, understood the necessity and irreversibility
of reason's progress. Yet he is ancient, because he is
nostalgic for a past filled with illusions. Lattanzi sees
his literary intervention as taking place on three levels
also: the lyrical, with the reproposal of illusions and
imaginative poetry; the philosophical, with the *Operette
morali*, and the satirical, with *Paralipomeni*. She admits,
however, the three levels cannot always be clearly distinguished.

The literary program (examined in the second part of the
essay) which Leopardi conceives as the answer to the
political situation of the time reproposes modes of nature
as well as modes of reason, revealing, with such planned
duality, a will of intervention which is at the same time
literary, political, and ethical. (D.B.)

Leopardi, Giacomo. *Pensieri.* Trans. by W.S. Di Piero.
Louisiana State University Press, 1981. Pp. 172.

This very elegantly printed bilingual edition of
Leopardi's *Pensieri* is yet another positive sign of renewed
interest in Leopardi. For students of Leopardi who need
or wish to learn clearly and rapidly about his philosophy,
this book of aphorisms is undoubtedly a better choice than
the impervious jungle of his *Zibaldone*. Di Piero's introductory essay helps the novice to place this work within
Leopardi's large production; bibliographical notes contribute to making the text more approachable. Di Piero
gives the right emphasis to Leopardi's "speculative intelligence" and his compulsive need for truth, felt as
man's main moral duty. Di Piero's words about Leopardi's
modernity and existential, almost Sartrian radicalism
kindle interest. His Appendix with references to the
Zibaldone helps the reader to find the sources of so many
Pensieri and to follow Leopardi in his often laborious
mental processes. Unfortunately the translation is marred
by errors. A few were clearly caused by textual difficulties (P. XLVI, where the irony of Leopardi's remark
"Tanta stima ..." was missed; P. XLIX, "loro estimazione"
translated as "self-esteem" instead of "their belief";
the following sentence was also misunderstood [p. 94],
likewise P. LI, pp. 97, 99; P. LXXIII at the end of p. 119,

P. LXXVII at the beginning, p. 123; P. LXXIX in the middle,
p. 127; P. XCV, p. 145). Others depend on lexical confu-
sions: in P. VII "Havvi" was misunderstood; in P. L
"i più simili" translated as "those closest." In P. LXXVII,
p. 123, "l'ultimo bene" translated as "the ultimate good";
"sulle porte di Livorno, Pisa ..." translated as "at
the seaport up at Pisan Leghorn...." In P. LXXXVIII
"crescendo nell'opinione di se medesimi" translated as
"they grow in other people's esteem" instead of "in their
own esteem"; in P. XCII "al mele" peculiar form of "miele"
translated as "to apples," p. 141; in P. C "il reo" translated as "the king," p. 151, "umanità," p. 153, translated
as mankind whereas its textual meaning is "humanity."
  The price of this volume somehow defies its purpose--
to make Leopardi accessible to a large audience of students.
Two suggestions to the author: a revision of the text and
a new paperback edition. (D.B.)

Martinotti, Sergio. "La concezione della musica in Leopardi."
Italianistica IX,1 (Jan.-Apr. 1980): 115-22.

  This highly original essay maintains that Italian nineteenth-century literary culture had little affinity for
classical music, in contrast to the rest of Europe. Leopardi
did not have a profound knowledge of it either. He went
rarely to the Opera and showed enthusiasm only for Rossini
(in particular for *La donna del lago*). Martinotti lists
all the operas Leopardi saw. He was totally ignorant of the
non-Italian musical events. Yet music, as theoretical reflection, long occupied his mind, as the *Zibaldone* bears
witness. Although Leopardi was well aware of the scarce
dramatic quality of the librettos, he saw the opera as
the only serious music of the time and the one art which
bridged the gap between the intelligentsia and the people.
Thus his praise of Rossini's popular success.
  Ignorant of the progress made at the time by the Germans,
he could not appreciate the importance of instrumental
music. Yet Leopardi's intuition about the expressive
possibilities of music parallelled those of the German
Romantics. Music could, in his eyes, express the "vague"
and the "indefinite" elements of life for it is the art
of the ideal, the immaterial, and of the infinite "par
excellence." These intuitions foreshadow Wagnerian and
Nietzschian conceptions. Leopardi wrote with insight on
the nature of music. Free from the imitation of nature,
he theorized, it must pose itself as an autonomous linguistic event, creating its own rules. (D.B.)

Piroué, Georges. "Leopardi, mon ami." *NRF* 352 (May 1982): 61-68.

A personal "letter" to Leopardi which is at once a moving lyrical tribute to the poet and a remarkable statement of self-revelation: "Je ne te connais que par l'illusion que je nourris de te rassembler un peu ... Je suis entré dans tes vues, je me suis identifié à toi" (64). Piroué's spiritual kinship with Leopardi is muted and restrained, his prose a model of subjectivity tempered by critical perception: "Ton romantisme est un immense révolu repassé au feu de la vie, un immense mémoire revivifiée" (63). (A.P.)

Sing, G. "Leopardi e Matthew Arnold: i miti e le delusioni dell'eredità romantica." *Italianistica* IX,1 (Jan.-Apr. 1980): 40-56.

Arnold had an ambiguous attitude toward Leopardi. Although he considered him one of the greatest nineteenth-century poets, in certain respects greater than Wordsworth and Byron, he nevertheless assigns English poets a greater importance in cultural history. Arnold's reason, as Sing makes clear, was not their poetry, but their personality. Arnold, like other Victorians, criticized Leopardi's pessimism on moral rather than artistic grounds. He shared the pessimism and knew it, as his refusal to publish "Empedocles on Etna" shows. Sing examines the poem and compares it to Leopardi's "Bruto Minore," pointing out the great similarity in their philosophy of nature and of man. They both "translate an ethical-philosophical datum into a poetical image" which, although personal and subjective, transcends its subjectivity and becomes "impersonal and universal" (40): Arnold cannot accept Leopardi's pessimism, according to Sing, because he cannot distinguish the material object of poetry from the conscious art form. (D.B.)

See also Macquet ("French 2. Stendhal").

MANZONI

Colombo, Giovanni. "Il cardinale Federico nella immortale trasfigurazione manzoniana." *ON* VI,1 (1982): 65-85.

Apologetic remarks extolling the morally edifying figure of Cardinal Borromeo in Manzoni's novel.

Comin, Antonio. "Fanfani v. Manzoni. A Tuscan Solution to the *Questione della lingua*." Pp. 45-60 in *Altro Polo, a Volume of Italian Studies*, ed. Silvio Trambaiolo and Nerida Newbigin. University of Sidney, 1978.

To Pietro Fanfani, "the existence of a grammatical structure common to all regions of Italy" (49) was evidence that, despite lexical variations, the country had a common language. This position contrasted with Manzoni's choice of Florentine as the national language, a choice based on the premise that usage determines the legitimacy of a language. To lend credence to his arguments, Fanfani published a series of illustrative works, among them the short story "La Paolina" (1868) and the historical novel *Cecco d'Ascoli* (1869). But, as Comin points out, Fanfani's thesis was based on "paradoxical premises" which "were destined to failure from the start" (58). In fact, sensing the discrepancy between his purist ideas (language as a literary medium) and the practical requirements of Italian unification, in time Fanfani recognized the merits inherent in Manzoni's position. (A.P.)

De Rienzo, Giorgio. *Lucia nel labirinto dei "Promessi sposi."* Torino: Giappichelli, 1981. Pp. 175.

Destri, Giovanni. "Il monologo interiore nei *Promessi sposi.*" *ON* VI,2 (1982): 5-46.

Despite its unevenness in argumentation, marred as well by frequent redundancies, this study contributes, in some ways significantly, to a broader appreciation of Manzoni's narrative strategies. Moving from self-evident considerations—the monologue as a device of psychological revelation, as ironical mode, and as a complement to the "gusto scenico-visivo" (apparent, for example, in the Ferrer/ Vicario episode)—Destri points to a less evident function of the interior monologue aimed at "ironicamente lievitare e nel contempo oggettivare il comportamento dei personaggi" (11). Accordingly, the measure of freedom and autonomy Don Abbondio displays in his monologues affords the highest degree of objective character revelation. "Don Abbondio è veramente Don Abbondio quando parla tra sé" (20). Destri notes further that the monologue, prevalent among fictional characters, is virtually nonexistent among historical figures. In other words, and this is noteworthy, Manzoni treated the monologue as a fictive device; as such, it was excluded (at least in the novel) from historical characterization. (A.P.)

De Vaulchier, H. "Nodier et Manzoni: positions sur le problème de la langue." *REI* 27 (1981): 69-83.

A comparative study on Nodier and Manzoni, their affinities in literary interests and differing concerns as regards the function of language in social and cultural activities. Useful as an introductory study, the article restates what is common knowledge among students of Manzoni. (A.P.)

Dombroski, Robert S. "The Ideological Question in Manzoni." *SR* 20 (1981): 497-524.

Closely allied to the ideological mainstream of Marxist criticism of Manzoni, Dombroski's essay differs significantly from similar studies in its purposeful rejection of simplistic arguments and a probing effort to strike a balance between militant and traditional analyses of Manzoni's work. Dombroski acknowledges "the misrepresentation of Manzoni's position in recent debates on the left" (499) and goes on to affirm that a focal point of such debates--the question of the lower classes--"must be viewed historically lest we conclude by incriminating Manzoni for not having written *I Promessi Sposi* according to the political sensibilities and the legal codes of our time" (506). Moreover, especially on pp. 512-13, he makes qualitative remarks that would easily satisfy a conservative critic of Manzoni. He states, for instance, that through Renzo and Lucia, Manzoni "seeks to define a universally valid moral code which cuts across all distinctions of class and station to ensure the free existence of every man" (513).

On the other hand, if Dombroski's analysis is more judicious and even-handed than that of Bollati, Moravia, and Simonini, among others, his conclusions are nearly identical. Essentially, Dombroski points out that Manzoni's moderate liberalism--his vision of a non-oppressive society receptive to "democratic sensibilities"--is heavily conditioned by two forces: (a) his faith in a coherent, rational order nurtured by his religious beliefs; (b) Manzoni's identification with his social class ("the wealthy Lombard landowners") and its ultimate interest in "keeping the populace under control, [in] protecting the status quo by defending [it] against insurgence from below" (501). Dombroski reaffirms that Manzoni's attitude toward the lower classes is one of "beneficent condescension." However, unlike Moravia, he dissociates Renzo and Lucia from the "undifferentiated masses"; Renzo is regarded, rather questionably, as "a prudent administrator, economical and careful in the handling of his resources" (511) who undergoes a process of *embourgeoisement* in the course of the novel. In the second part

of his study, Dombroski devotes several pages to the analysis
of the plague as "a sign of ideology, the ideology of death,"
prefiguring the advent of a social order marked, through
the "resurgent power of the Church," by the "rise of a new
entrepreneurial class and the consolidation of bourgeois
hegemony along moderate political and economic lines" (524).
However, Dombroski remarks earlier that such a vision,
fashioned to thwart the course of secular liberalism, proves
utopian because it ignores the forces of historical determinism.

Not unlike Moravia and Simonini, Dombroski judges Manzoni's
work through a series of ideological conjunctions (such
as M. and his social class; M. and Catholicism) based on
reductivist arguments. This approach leads to the insistence
on the conditioning force of religion in Manzoni's ideology
and to a compelling need to translate moral and religious
values into political ideology (i.e., faith = religious
authority = Catholicism = the Church as a conservative
socio-political institution allied with the economic interest
of the ruling class). Dombroski notes, for instance, that
"in opposing the certainty of Catholic morality to the
contingencies of utilitarian action, Manzoni reinforces
the political and cultural hegemony of the dominant class"
(506). A second conjunction (Church/religious faith/God's
will) is used to characterize Renzo's existential outlook:
"Renzo's experience will caution him ... to understand that
what is instituted on earth [i.e., capitalism] has been
determined by God's will" (512); "If in becoming bourgeois
Renzo remains Christian, it is through the influence and
cooperation of the Church" (512). Other debatable points
in this essay include the attempt to dissociate (on the
socio-economic plane) Renzo from the masses, which is not
supported by the thread of the narrative, and, more important,
the fact that Manzoni's waning faith in the progressivism
of the Enlightenment stems much less from a class-conscious
political ideology than from a firm conviction that social
progress cannot claim to foster the betterment of the human
condition unless it strives simultaneously for the much
more difficult progress in ethical and spiritual orientation. (A.P.)

Fauriel, Claude, trans. *Adelghis. Lettre à M. C +++ sur les
unités de temps et de lieu dans la tragédie.* Ed. Simone
Carpentari. (Saint-Etienne, Centre d'Etudes foréziennes,
Inventaires et Documents, 6.) Saint-Etienne: Centre d'Etudes
foréziennes, 1979. Pp. 366.

Manzoni, Alessandro. *I promessi sposi.* A cura di Giorgio De
Rienzo. Torino: S.E.I., 1981. Pp. 734.
Rev. by Claudio Toscani in *ON* VI,2 (1982): 397.

Manzoni, Alessandro. *Poesie e tragedie.* A cura di Alberto
Frattini. Brescia: La Scuola, 1981. Pp. 854.
Rev. by Laura Granatella in *ON* VI,2 (1982): 397-98.
Includes an Introduction and comprehensive bibliography
as well as critical excerpts on Manzoni by, among others,
Bigongiari, Negri, Ungaretti, and Vigorelli.

PRANDI

Misan, Jacques. "Un panorama culturel de l'Italie à Londres
et à Paris en 1837." *RLMC* 34 (1981): 286-98.

Examines an essay by Fortunato Prandi, the Italian patriot
who lived in London and befriended Foscolo. The essay,
"Movimento attuale della letteratura italiana," was published first in the *London and Westminster Review* in 1837
and, the same year, in the *Revue Britannique* of Paris.
Pointing to signs of moral and political awakening in
Italian life, Prandi offers a broad view of major Italian
writers of his day. (A.P.)

VARESE

Chandler, S.B. "Una curiosità ottocentesca." *EL* VIII,2
(1982): 28-30.

A bibliographical note on the English versions of two
historical novels by Carlo Varese, *Sibilla Odaleta, an
Historical Romance,* and *Folchetto Malaspina, or the Siege
of Tortona,* published in London in 1852 and 1860 respectively.
The second work did not go unnoticed; a review in *The
Athenaeum* of 1860 called Varese a faithful follower of
Scott lacking the humor and imagination of his model. (A.P.)

SPANISH

(Compiled by Brian J. Dendle, University of Kentucky)

1. BIBLIOGRAPHY

Conte Oliveros, Jesús. *Personajes y escritores de Huesca y provincia*. Zaragoza: Editorial Librería General, 1981. Pp. 206.

2. GENERAL

Allegra, Giovanni. *La viña y los surcos. Las ideas literarias en España del XVIII al XIX*. Universidad de Sevilla, 1980. Pp. 367.

Allegra surveys the traditionalist current in Spanish literature: the Gallophobia of the early years of the century, Bohl von Faber and the Calderonian polemic, Ferdinand Eckstein's vision of Spain (1836), *El Europeo*, Durán, Piferrer, Fernán Caballero, Gil y Carrasco, archetypal themes in Bécquer's *leyendas*.

Alvarez Pantoja, María José. "La Sevilla realista (1814-20). Restauración del Antiguo Régimen." *ArH* 61 (1978): 1-58.

Barceló Jiménez, Juan. *Historia del teatro en Murcia*. Murcia: Academia Alfonso X el Sabio, 1980. Pp. 292.

This revised second edition of a work originally published in 1958 now includes chapters on the eighteenth, nineteenth, and twentieth centuries. It includes numerous, if brief, details on Murcian and Cartagenan actors and dramatists of the nineteenth century.

Caballero, Fermín. *Fomento de la población rural*. Barcelona: Ediciones El Albir, 1980. Pp. 282; illus.

Facsimile of the third edition (1864).

Calvo, Juan Jacob, and Mercedes Jorda Olives. "La Iglesia
catalana en los inicios del régimen liberal (1832-1835).
Aportación a su estudio." *Hispania* (Madrid) 41 (1981): 589-
620.

Castro, Concepción de. *La Revolución Liberal y los municipios
españoles (1812-1868)*. Madrid: Alianza Editorial, 1979.
Pp. 236.

Cuenca Toribio, José Manuel. *Sociedad y clero en la España
del XIX*. Córdoba: Publicaciones del Monte de Piedad y Caja
de Ahorros de Córdoba, 1980. Pp. 416.

Activities of various nineteenth-century Spanish bishops.

Dérozier, Albert. "Argüelles y la cuestión de América ante
las Cortes de Cádiz de 1810-1814." Pp. 159-64 in Gil Novales,
Alberto, ed., *Homenaje a Noël Salomon*. Barcelona: Universidad Autónoma, 1979.

Escobar, José, and Anthony Percival. "Spanish Romanticism:
Literature and Ideology." *Scripta Mediterranea* 3 (1982):
135-51.

An overly succinct presentation of Spanish Romanticism,
seen in historical context. Curiously, no mention of the
Renaixença.

Fontanella, Lee. "The Fashion and Styles of Spain's *costumbrismo*." *RCEH* 6 (1982): 175-89.

Fontanella relates traditional *costumbrismo* to the new
illustrated periodical.

García Villarrubia, Fernando. *Aproximación al carlismo andaluz
en la guerra de los siete años (1833-1840)*. Madrid: Ediciones EASA, 1979. Pp. 283.

Clear exposition of the risings, repression, and dreadful
social conditions. Numerous documents.

Gil Novales, Alberto. *Las sociedades patrióticas (1820-1823)*.
2 vols. Madrid: Editorial Tecnos, 1975.

Volume I presents a highly detailed study of liberal
societies in Madrid and the provinces. Volume II lists
members (with biographies) of the societies, defines terms
of the contemporary political-social vocabulary, lists
and describes 680 periodicals of the period, and discusses
El Zurriago and *La Tercerola*. Bibliography. Detailed index.
A most informative study.

Gil Novales, Alberto. *William Maclure: Socialismo Utópico
en España (1808-1840)*. Barcelona: Universidad Autónoma,
1979. Pp. 155; illus.

Maclure (1763-1840) was a Scottish traveler, Benthamite,
and enthusiastic supporter of the French Revolution. He
observed Spanish manners in 1808. Settling in Spain between
1820 and 1824, he attempted to exploit property near Orihuela
according to rational principles and to establish a Lancastri-
an school. Index.

Giménez, Antonio. "El mito romántico del bandolero andaluz."
CA 383 (May 1982): 272-96.

Foreign travellers' observations of Spanish life were
simplistic, subjective, and escapist. Their accounts of
Spanish banditry owe more to legend than to reality. Travel-
lers mentioned are, among others, Ford, Mérimée, Custine,
Gautier, and Dumas. José María el Tempranillo and Juan
Caballero exemplify "Romantic" brigands.

González Muñiz, Miguel Angel. *Constituciones, Cortes y
Elecciones españolas. Historia y anécdota (1810-1936)*.
Gijón: Ediciones Júcar, 1978. Pp. 315.

Texts of Spanish constitutions (including those still-
born); listing of Spanish cabinets. Useful.

Hernández Serna, Joaquín. *Murcia en el "Semanario Pintoresco
Español." 1836-1857*. Murcia: Academia Alfonso X el Sabio,
1979. Pp. 392; illus.

In this labor of love, Hernández Serna lists, and for the
most part reproduces, articles and illustrations in the
Semanario Pintoresco Español either dealing with Murcian
topics or written by Murcians. He reproduces poems by:
Julián Romea, Fernando Garrido, Guillén Buzarán, Antonio
Arnao, Selgas, and Barrantes; and articles by Ivo de la
Cortina, Barrantes, Ponzoa, Cueto, Eguilaz, Bea, José de
la Revilla, Roca de Togores, Vicente de la Fuente, Nicolás
Magan, Valladares Saavedra, De la Corte, and Cayetano
Rossel. Biographical details of the authors. Indexed.

Jiménez, María Rosa. *El municipio de Zaragoza durante la
regencia de María Cristina de Nápoles (1833-1840)*. Zaragoza:
Institución Fernando el Católico, 1979. Pp. 317; illus.

Divers sectors of Zaragozan life: demography, economy,
administration, army, Church, education, political distur-
bances. Bibliography.

Longares Alonso, Jesús. *La ideología religiosa del liberalismo español (1808-1843).* Córdoba: Real Academia de Córdoba, 1979. Pp. 298.

An intelligent discussion of the philosophical underpinnings of liberal (and, in passing, Romantic) religious ideology, liberal religious legislation, and anticlericalism. Texts of numerous contemporary editorials on the religious question.

Marichal, Carlos. *La revolución liberal y los primeros partidos políticos en España: 1834-1844.* Madrid: Ediciones Cátedra, 1980. Pp. 334.

A Spanish translation, with minor revisions, of *Spain (1834-1844): A New Society.* (See *ELN* 17, supp., 260.)

Martín, Gregorio C. "*El Parnasillo*: Origen y circunstancias." Pp. 209-18 of *La Chispa '81.* (Selected Proceedings of the Second Louisiana Conference on Hispanic Languages and Literatures.) New Orleans: Tulane University, 1981.

Financial circumstances of the establishment of the Café del Príncipe in 1816. Lista's students met there as early as 1827 or 1828.

Moreno Alonso, Manuel. *La revolución francesa en la historiografía española del siglo XIX.* Prólogo de Jacques Godechot. Universidad de Sevilla, 1979. Pp. 292.

Spanish historians were influenced by Thierry, Barante, Lamartine, Guizot, Thiers, Mignet, Villemain, Carné, Bouchez y Roux, and Quinet (but not by Michelet or Tocqueville). Conservative treatments of the French Revolution are found in Koska Vayo, Balmes, and Donoso Cortés; a liberal approach is found in Flórez Estrada, Martínez de la Rosa, Alcalá Galiano, Llorente, Quintana, Lista, Modesto Lafuente, Fernando Garrido, and Pi y Margall. Index.

Núñez Ruiz, Diego. "Panteísmo y liberalismo en el siglo XIX español." *CHA* 379 (Jan. 1982): 11-36.

The search for harmony in Spanish liberal philosophers. "... casi podríamos decir que el krausismo español hubiera existido sin Krause."

Pecellin Lancharro, Manuel. *Literatura en Extremadura. Tomo II. Escritores: Siglos XIX y XX (Hasta 1939).* Badajoz: Universitas Editorial, 1981. Pp. 284.

Brief introductory essays, bibliographies, and representative texts of Gallardo (pp. 11-27), Espronceda (pp. 29-42), Donoso Cortés (pp. 43-55), and Carolina Coronado (pp. 57-71).

Reyes, Antonio de los. *Julián Romea. El actor y su contorno (1813-1868)*. (Biografías Populares de Murcianos Ilustres, VIII.) Murcia: Academia Alfonso X el Sabio, 1977. Pp. 239; illus.

Although based in large part on previous studies, nevertheless a useful biography of one of the leading actors of the Romantic period. Bibliography.

Roura i Aulinas, Lluís. "La relació entre il·lustrats i liberals a Mallorca." Pp. 103-11 in Gil Novales, Alberto, ed., *Homenaje a Noël Salomon*. Barcelona: Universidad Autónoma, 1979.

Ruiz, David, et al. *Asturias contemporánea, 1808-1975*. Madrid: Siglo XXI, 1981.

Includes: David Ruiz, "La crisis del Antiguo Régimen (1808-1833)" (7-29); Carmen García, "Liberalismo y democracia (1833-1874)" (31-74); and documents concerning agriculture, mining, and social attitudes in the early nineteenth century.

Sanchis Guarner, Manuel. *Els inicis del teatre valencià modern 1845-1874*. University of Valencia, 1980. Pp. 202.

Details of the dramatists and dramatic works of the Valencian *Renaixença*. Sanchis Guarner notes the lack of contact with the more advanced vernacular theater of Catalonia, the heavy emphasis on *costumbrismo* in the Valencian plays, and the preference for *sainetes*. Texts of extracts from the *sainetes*.

Saurín de la Iglesia, María Rosa. "Poder económico y represión ideológica en Galicia (1827-1841)." *Hispania* (Madrid) 41 (1981): 5-15.

Soria, Andrés. "De la Granada romántica y de la Alhambra (Páginas de album)." Pp. 111-42 in Andrés Soria, *De Lope a Lorca y otros ensayos*. Universidad de Granada, 1980.

The Granada of Chateaubriand, English travelers, Irving, Mérimée, Gautier, Quinet, Mesonero Romanos, Zorrilla.

Stoudemire, Sterling A. "Ramón Carnicer Aids Rossini, Donizetti and Bellini." Pp. 293-301 in Joseph Gulsoy and Josep M. Sola-Solé, eds., *Catalan Studies. (Estudis sobre el Català).* (Volume in Memory of Josephine de Boer.) Barcelona: HISPAM, 1977.

Lists performances, under Carnicer's direction, of Italian opera in Barcelona (1815-27) and Madrid (1827-43).

Sullivan, Henry. "Calderón's Reception in Spain During the Romantic Era." *OHis* 4 (1982): 27-54.

A critical summary of the activities of Böhl, Mora, Vargas Ponce, Cavaleri, and Alcalá Galiano in the Calderonian Quarrel. Later, Durán, Milá y Fontanals, Escosura, and Pedroso revealed an interest in Calderón. The influence of Calderón is also apparent in the dramas of Rivas, García Gutiérrez, and Zorrilla. The association of Calderón with reaction explains his limited popularity in nineteenth-century Spain.

Villacorta Baños, Francisco. *Burguesía y cultura. Los intelectuales españoles en la sociedad liberal, 1808-1931.* Madrid: Siglo XXI, 1980. Pp. 313.

Brief mentions of the *Ateneo* and *Liceo Artístico*.

3. STUDIES OF AUTHORS

ALCALA GALIANO

See Moreno Alonso, Sullivan ("Spanish 2. General").

AMADOR DE LOS RIOS

Amador de los Ríos, José. *Sevilla pintoresca.* Barcelona: Ediciones El Albir, 1979. Pp. 512; illus.

Facsimile of the first edition (1844).

Amador de los Ríos, José. *Toledo pintoresca.* Barcelona: Ediciones El Albir, 1976. Pp. 344; illus.

Facsimile of the first edition (1845).

AVELLANEDA

Suárez-Galbán, Eugenio. "La angustia de una mujer indiana,
o el epistolario autobiográfico de Gertrudis Gómez de
Avellaneda." Pp. 281-96 in L'Autobiographie dans le Monde
Hispanique. (Actes du Colloque International de la Baume-
les-Aix, 11-13 May, 1979.) Université de Provence, 1980.
In nine autobiographical letters written in 1839 to Ignacio
de Cepeda, la Avellaneda reveals sincerity, Romantic maso-
chism, psychological contradictions, and the "angustia de
ser mujer." Well argued.

BARRANTES

See Hernández Serna ("Spanish 2. General").

BECQUER

González, Angel, and Tomás Ruiz-Fábrega. "Presencia de
Espronceda en la Rima LXXII de Bécquer." RomN 22 (1981):
146-50.
Brief and futile indication of parallels between El diablo
mundo and Rima LXXII.

Prieto, Antonio. "Poética, Bécquer, Unamuno." Pp. 252-95 in
Antonio Prieto, Coherencia y relevancia textual (De Berceo
a Baroja). Madrid: Editorial Alhambra, 1980.
An attempt to understand the tú of Bécquer's poetry: the
woman is a creation of the mind of Bécquer, who needed
tension; it is therefore pointless to seek to identify her
in the external world. Intelligent.

See also Allegra ("Spanish 2. General").

BOHL VON FABER

See Allegra, Sullivan ("Spanish 2. General").

CADALSO

Schurlknight, Donald E. "En busca de los orígenes del romanticismo en España (Cadalso, Young, y las *Conjectures*):
hipótesis y analogía." *BBMP* 58 (1982): 237-61.

Cadalso used a French translation of Young's *Conjectures
on Original Composition* as the source for the *Noches lúgubres*.

CASTRO

Castro, Rosalía de. *Ruinas. El primer loco.* Santiago de
Compostela: Librería y Editorial "Galí," 1980. Pp. 175.

Miller, Martha LaFollette. "Aspects of Perspective in Rosalía
de Castro's *En las orillas del Sar.*" *KRQ* 29 (1982): 273-82.

Lengthy discussion of perspective in "Era apacible el
día"; briefer mentions of "En los ecos del órgano o en el
rumor del viento" and *Los tristes*.

CORONADO

See Pecellin Lancharro ("Spanish 2. General").

CUETO

See Hernández Serna ("Spanish 2. General").

DONOSO CORTES

See Pecillin Lancharro ("Spanish 2. General").

DURAN

See Allegra, Sullivan ("Spanish 2. General").

EGUILAZ

See Hernández Serna ("Spanish 2. General").

ESCOSURA

See Sullivan ("Spanish 2. General").

ESPRONCEDA

Bretz, Mary Lee. "Espronceda's *El diablo mundo* and Romantic Irony." *REH* 16 (1982): 252-74.

"Structuring his poem in interlocking cycles, Espronceda presents the eternal flux of illusion and disillusion that characterizes human history."

See also Pecellin Lancharro ("Spanish 2. General"); González and Ruiz-Fábrega ("Bécquer").

FERNAN CABALLERO

Valis, Noël M. "Eden and the Tree of Knowledge in Fernán Caballero's *Clemencia*." *KRQ* 29 (1982): 251-60.

Clemencia's (and Fernán Caballero's) fear of sexual passion and consequent rejection of the tree of good and evil and masculinity. Superbly argued.

See also Allegra ("Spanish 2. General").

GALLARDO

Bozal, Valeriano. "Gallardo, Miñano y Larra en el origen de la sátira crítico-burlesca." *CHA* 388 (Oct. 1982): 51-61.

All three authors offer a distorting perspective, involving different degrees of authorial and reader participation. A perceptive study.

See also Pecellin Lancharro ("Spanish 2. General").

GARCIA GUTIERREZ

See Sullivan ("Spanish 2. General").

GARCIA DE QUEVEDO

See Dowling and Sebold ("Zorrilla").

GIL Y CARRASCO

See Allegra ("Spanish 2. General").

HARTZENBUSCH

Hartzenbusch, Juan Eugenio. *Los amantes de Teruel*. Edición de Carmen Iranzo. Madrid: Ediciones Cátedra, 1981. Pp. 166.

LAFUENTE

See Moreno Alonso ("Spanish 2. General").

LARRA

Martín, Gregorio C. "La ascendencia catalana de Mariano José de Larra." *Crítica Hispánica* 3 (1981): 149-57.
    Documentary proof that Larra's maternal grandmother was of Catalan, and not Portuguese, origin.

Martín, Gregorio C. *Hacia una revision crítica de la biografía de Larra (Nuevos Documentos)*. (Série Estudos e ensaios.) Porto Alegre: Pontifícia Universidade Católica do Rio Grande do Sul and Editora Meridional Emma, 1975. Pp. 199.
    Exploding many of the myths propagated by Carmen de Burgos, Professor Martín discusses: the influence of Larra's father (an enlightened and dedicated doctor); Romantic traits (before 1823) and censorship (after 1823) of the theater (even Martínez de la Rosa's *La niña en casa* was banned); the protection Larra received from Fernández Varela and the Duque de Frías; the contradictions and mysteries of Larra's lifestyle; his relations with Ceruti and Carrero. Numerous documents; bibliography; index. A most useful study, combining careful scholarship, concision, and insight.

Martín, Gregorio C. "Larra, periodista uruguayo." *EIA* 2 (1976): 235-44.

Minor textual changes when Larra's "En este país" was published in *El Eco Oriental* in 1835.

See also Bozal ("Gallardo").

LISTA

See Martín, Moreno Alonso ("Spanish 2. General").

LLORENTE

See Moreno Alonso ("Spanish 2. General").

MADRAZO

Madrazo, Pedro de. *Córdoba*. Barcelona: Ediciones El Albir, 1980. Pp. 548; illus.

Facsimile edition. The first chapter was by Francisco Pi y Margall.

MARTINEZ DE LA ROSA

See Moreno Alonso ("Spanish 2. General").

MESONERO ROMANOS

Sebold, Russell P. "Comedia clásica y novela moderna en las *Escenas matritenses* de Mesonero Romanos." *BH* 83 (1981): 331-77.

Mesonero's satirical attitude toward Romanticism, balance, admiration for the eighteenth century, gift for detailed observation, appreciation of the everyday, influence on the realistic novel.

See also Soria ("Spanish 2. General").

MIÑANO

See Bozal ("Gallardo").

MORA

See Sullivan ("Spanish 2. General").

PI Y MARGALL

See Moreno Alonso ("Spanish 2. General"); Madrazo ("Madrazo").

PIFERRER

See Allegra ("Spanish 2. General").

QUINTANA

See Moreno Alonso ("Spanish 2. General").

RIVAS

See Sullivan ("Spanish 2. General").

ROCA DE TOGORES

See Hernández Serna ("Spanish 2. General").

ROS DE OLANO

Ros de Olano, Antonio. *Cuentos estrambóticos y otros relatos*. Prólogo, selección y notas de Enric Cassany. Barcelona: Editorial Laia, 1980. Pp. 283.

ZORRILLA

Dowling, John, and Russell P. Sebold. "Las singulares circunstancias de la publicación de la *María* de Zorrilla." *HR*
50 (1982): 449-72.

In *Recuerdos del tiempo viejo*, Zorrilla dramatized the
emotional crisis which he suffered at the death of his
father (1849), explaining in this way his failure to complete
María. In fact, García de Quevedo not only completed the
final two-thirds of the poem but in all probability wrote
part of the first third (as well as parts of *Un cuento de
amores* and *Ira de Dios*). The apparent "second edition" of
María merely reprints the dedicatory and title pages. A
well-researched article, full of interesting details on
the Grub Street of mid-nineteenth-century Spain.

Gies, David Thatcher. "José Zorrilla and the Betrayal of
Spanish Romanticism." *RJ* 31 (1980): 339-46.

Gies carefully distinguishes Don Juan from previous Romantic heroes. "Don Juan is not the messenger of revolutionary
zeal, frustration, egocentricity and pessimism. He is the
messenger of hope, the messenger of the Good Word. The play
that has long been regarded as the culmination of Spanish
Romantic drama is really nothing of the sort. What Zorrilla
wrote was a version of the traditional saint-and-sinner
plays of religious redemption in which he merely capitalized
on the current vogue for Romantic scandal."

See also Soria, Sullivan ("Spanish 2. General").

W